Robert R. Taylor and Tuskegee

ROBERT R. TAYLOR AND TUSKEGEE

An African American Architect Designs for Booker T. Washington

ELLEN WEISS

WITH A FOREWORD BY HENRY LOUIS GATES, JR.

NEWSOUTH BOOKS

Montgomery

Also by Ellen Weiss

North Kingstown, Rhode Island (1978)

*City in the Woods: The Life and Design of an
American Camp Meeting on Martha's Vineyard* (1987)

NewSouth Books
105 S. Court Street
Montgomery, AL 36104

Library of Congress Cataloging-in-Publication Data

Weiss, Ellen.
Robert R. Taylor and Tuskegee : an African American architect designs for Booker T.
Washington / Ellen Weiss.

p. cm.

Includes bibliographical references and index.

ISBN-13: 978-1-58838-248-1 (alk. paper)
ISBN-10: 1-58838-248-6 (alk. paper)

1. Tuskegee Institute—Buildings. 2. Taylor, Robert R. (Robert Robinson),
1868-1942—Criticism and interpretation. 3. Architecture—Alabama—Tuskegee—History—
19th century. 4. Architecture—Alabama—Tuskegee—History—20th century. 5. Tuskegee
(Ala.)—Buildings, structures, etc. 6. Architects—United States—Biography. 7. African
American architects—Biography. I. Taylor, Robert R. (Robert Robinson), 1868-1942. II. Title.
III. Title: African American architect designs for Booker T. Washington.
LC2851.T818T399 2011
378.761'49—dc23
[B]

2011039378

Design by Randall Williams
Printed in the United States of America

Overleaf: Robert R. Taylor, as photographed in 1906 by Frances Benjamin Johnston.
(Courtesy Library of Congress, Divisions of Prints and Photographs, photo LC J694-298.)

TO THE MEMORY OF

WALTER LITTLEFIELD CREESE

CONTENTS

"My experience is that there is something in human nature which always makes an individual recognize and reward merit, no matter under what colour of skin merit is found. I have found, too, that it is the visible, the tangible, that goes a long ways in softening prejudices. The actual sight of a first-class house that a Negro has built is ten times more potent than pages of discussion about a house that he ought to build, or perhaps could build."

— BOOKER T. WASHINGTON, in *Up From Slavery*

FOREWORD

HENRY LOUIS GATES, JR.

Robert Robinson Taylor (1868–1942), architect and educator, was the first African American graduate of the Massachusetts Institute of Technology, and the first professionally educated black architect in the United States. Between 1903 and 1932, he designed the major structures of Booker T. Washington's Tuskegee Institute and also Carnegie-funded libraries for two other black colleges in North Carolina and Texas. Born in Wilmington, North Carolina, a progressive city but also the scene in 1898 of the nation's first successful coup against a democratically elected government, Taylor learned construction from his father, Henry Taylor, a former slave whose white father (and master) had permitted him to pursue an independent trade, but without emancipating him.

Taylor heads an extraordinarily distinguished line of African Americans. His son, Robert Rochon Taylor, was a civic leader in Chicago and the first African American chairman of the Chicago Housing Authority. Chicago's Robert Taylor Homes, the nation's largest public housing project, was named for him, although his perspective would most likely have set him in opposition to the massive Chicago complex, which was demolished in 2007. Valerie Jarrett, a senior adviser to President Barack Obama, is the great-granddaughter of Robert Robinson Taylor and the granddaughter of Robert Rochon Taylor. Her mother, Barbara Taylor Bowman, is a distinguished early childhood development specialist and a founder of the Erikson Institute, and her father, Dr. James E. Bowman, is a pathologist and geneticist of international reputation. Ann Jordan, co-chair of the 1996 Clinton Inauguration and the wife of Democratic strategist and presidential adviser Vernon Jordan, is Taylor's granddaughter. The accomplishments of this family surely would have brought a knowing smile to the "Wizard of Tuskegee" who hired Robert R. Taylor.

Wilmington, North Carolina, even during the era of slavery, had allowed free and enslaved African Americans to work in the building trades, and by 1860 a quarter of the city's building and construction craftsmen were black. Indeed, after the Civil War and before 1898, Wilmington had gained a reputation as one of the most racially tolerant cities in the South. Not only did blacks succeed in the trades, but they occupied government offices and held lucrative jobs as restaurant owners, barbers, craftsmen, clerks, policemen, and justices of the peace. Even the collector of customs—a plum patronage position—of the Port of Wilmington was African American, and black voters actually outnumbered white voters.

Robert's father, Henry Taylor, who settled in Wilmington in the late 1850s, was an ambitious carpenter, merchant, and coastal trader, and his mother, Emily Still, was also the daughter of a tradesman; both were of mixed race. Robert's father built many important structures in Wilmington, including his own home, and by 1870 was the county's wealthiest black landowner. By the time Robert completed secondary school—ironically also making him one of W. E. B. Du Bois's "Talented Tenth"—he had mastered carpentry and had matured in a city with several self-trained black architects, many craftsmen, and even the white professional architect Henry Bacon, who designed the Lincoln Memorial in Washington, D.C. Perhaps it would have been a wonder if Robert R. Taylor had not grown up to be the nation's first professionally trained black architect.

In Taylor's time, MIT was home to many international students of a variety of hues—and even several women. Yet Taylor's enrollment in 1888 was unusual for a Southerner and extraordinarily rare for an African American. While some later black MIT graduates retain mixed feelings about their alma mater—angry over the isolation imposed on them by white fellow students—Taylor harbored no bitterness over his time there and always expressed his devotion to the school and its students. He excelled in Cambridge, remaining near the top of his class and even receiving a scholarship for his final two years of college.

HENRY LOUIS GATES JR. *is Alphonse Fletcher University Professor and the director of the W. E. B. Du Bois Institute for African and African American Research at Harvard University. A distinguished literary critic and historian, he is the author of fifteen books and has made eleven documentary films.*

In the summer of 1892, he worked as a "building mechanic" at a hotel in Oak Bluffs, the celebrated black enclave on Martha's Vineyard. From there, he corresponded with Booker T. Washington, who persuaded Taylor to come to Alabama's Tuskegee Institute upon his graduation. He began his long career there as an instructor in drawing and as the official architect to Washington's famed Institute. Taylor remained at Tuskegee for the bulk of his professional career, until the early 1930s. For a brief stint in 1929, Taylor traveled to Liberia to oversee the architecture and industrial training programs for the proposed Booker Washington Institute in Kakata. At Tuskegee, Taylor designed a vast array of buildings on the campus, including dormitories, the library, and the Chapel, which he considered his crowning achievement. As chief architect and director of the program in mechanical industries, Taylor could enact Washington's understanding that because modern industrial education was intellectually based, unlike the old craft practices, it would help blacks advance into higher berths in society.

As I wrote in my book, *In Search of Our Roots: How 19 Extraordinary African Americans Reclaimed Their Past* (2009), most of our ancestors are "anonymous, decent, overly hardworking people whose lives have yet to be chronicled. Until their stories are reconstructed and told, these ancestors of ours will not exist as human beings, as agents, as actors in the great human drama that is American history. . . ." Without history, without a sense of ourselves, we allow others to define, or forget, us. When I told the comedian Chris Rock about his illustrious ancestor, the Civil War soldier and South Carolina legislator Julius Caesar Tingman, he could not believe his ears. "It's messed up," he remarked in astonishment. "I was raised in a neighborhood where no one went to college or anything. . . . I assumed I would pick up things for white people for the rest of my life. Because that's what everyone did. . . . But if I'd have known this Julius, it might have taken away the inevitability that I was going to be nothing." We need books like Ellen Weiss's, and we especially need them for our children to let them know what we have been and what they can be. There is no higher calling.

Near the close of *Up From Slavery*, Booker T. Washington insisted that when African American boys and girls learned to cook, sew, grow crops, groom a horse, build a house, write a book, or practice medicine "as well or better than some one else, they will be rewarded regardless of race or colour. In the long run, the world is going to have the best, and any difference in race, religion, or previous history will not long keep the world from what it wants." Robert R. Taylor embodied the highest aspirations of Washingtonian principles, succeeding magnificently at his profession. But even he, as were nearly all other African Americans of his era, was limited by forces that defied the best efforts of even the most eloquent proponents of racial equality. I know you will share my enthusiasm for what Ellen Weiss has accomplished in telling this story, reconstructing this important life, and leading the way for others by showing us where our ancestors trod just a few short generations before.

CAMBRIDGE, MASSACHUSETTS
OCTOBER 2011

Sources of Photos and Illustrations

Page ii, Library of Congress, Divisions of Prints and Photographs, hereafter LC, J694-298.

Chapter 1: pages 6, 8, Josephine Cooper Collection, New Hanover County Public Library.

Chapter 2: 11, 13, 14, 15, 17, MIT Museum.

Chapter 3: 21, 22, M. F. Armstrong and Helen W. Ludlow, *Hampton and Its Students*; 23, 24, 33, 35, 36, Booker T. Washington, *The Story of My Life and Work, hereafter BTW, Story*; 38, 39, Frances Benjamin Johnston Collection at LC, hereafter FBJ/LC.

Chapter 4: 46, Tuskegee Archives, hereafter TA; 50, *Architects' and Builders' Magazine* May 1904; 54, LC ADE-UNIT 2580, no. 26; 60, BTW, *Story*; 61, FBJ/LC; 62, *Appleton's Popular Science Monthly* September 1899; 63, FBJ/LC; 64-71, Campus Maps, Michael P. Keller/Tulane City Center. 74, FBJ/LC.

Chapter 5: 76, TA; 81, Robert S. Brantley, hereafter Brantley; 86, FBJ/LC.

Chapter 6: 89, 93, FBJ/LC; 97, top, Brantley. 97, bottom, TA; 99, 101, FBJ/LC; 103, upper right, Ellen Weiss, hereafter Weiss; 103, bottom, FBJ/LC; 104, 106, Weiss; 107, drawings by Alissa Kingsley from Sanborn Insurance maps; 109, 110, FBJ/LC; 111, TA.

Chapter 7: 114, upper left, TA, lower left, Wesley Henderson; 115, TA; 120, *The Negro Rural School and Its Relation to the Community*, hereafter *The Negro Rural School*; 123, *Southern Workman*, May 1920, Hampton University; 124, *Opportunity*, May 1924. Wisconsin Historical Society, image WHi-75140; 126, *The Negro Rural School*; 128, *Negro Education: A Story of the Private and Higher Schools for Colored People in the United States*, 1917. Amistad Research Center, hereafter *Negro Education* (year).

Chapter 8: 132, Emmett J. Scott and Lyman Beecher Stowe, *Booker T. Washington, Builder of a Civilization*; 141, TA; 142, 143, M. Lewis Kennedy, Jr.

Chapter 9: 154, TA; 156, Tuskegee University, Physical Facilities Department.

Chapter 10: 162, MIT Museum; 164, New Hanover Public Library; 166, TA.

Catalog: Page 170, 172, 174, 177, FBJ/LC; 178, Detroit Publishing Co./LC-D4-19466; 179, 180, 182, 182, FBJ/LC; 185, 186, Weiss; 189, FBJ/LC; 190, Brantley; 192, 194, FBJ/LC; 195, Brantley; 197, FBJ/LC; 198, Brantley; 199, FBJ/LC; 200, Weiss; 203, 205, 206, FBJ/LC; 207, Weiss; 208, 209, 210, Brantley; 212, *Negro Education* (1916); 214, Weiss; 217, 219, LC; 220, TA; 222, 223, Brantley; 225, 226, FBJ/LC; 227, 228, 229, Weiss; 232, TA; 234, 235, Brantley; 236, FBJ/LC; 237, 238, Brantley; 240, 241, Weiss.

ACKNOWLEDGMENTS

Complex projects that take too long accumulate debts beyond memory's reckoning. But still I must try. Friends and colleagues have provided insight and information, valued connections, hospitality, kindly or stern encouragement as needed and, in some cases, the remarkable generosity of reading a draft. The short list would include Mardges Bacon, Jennifer O. Baughn, Robert A. Gonzales, Delos Hughes, Barbara Burlison Mooney, Mary Beth Norton, Jessie Poesch, Patricia Sullivan, Dell Upton, Hugh O. Williams, Mary N. Woods and four anonymous readers for two academic presses. Many more contributed critical information, insight, and editorial or technical support: Craig Barton, Joellen Pryce ElBashir, Deavereau Bemis, Michael Bieze, Betty Bird, Catherine W. Bishir, Brian Bockman, Charles Boney Jr., Alice Bowsher, Richard O. Card, Johni Cerny, Diane Cobb Cashman, Mary F. Daniels, Howard Davis, Allen R. Durough, Charles E. Dynes, Robert Gamble, Deborah S. Gardner, Henry Louis Gates, Jr., Wesley Henderson, Darian Hendricks, Linda Herman, Mary S. Hoffschwelle, Mark Jarzombek, Jeh V. Johnson, Karen Kingsley, Nina Lewallen, Kenny Marotta, Ellen Mertins, Betsy Panhorst, Jill Nelson, Susan G. Pearl, Thomas T. Potterfield, Jack Quinan, Kathy Reed, Keli Rylance, Tim Samuelson, Kenneth H. Thomas, Christopher Thomas, Jr., Enrique Vivioni, John E. Wells, John Whitfield, Alfred Willis, Tony P. Wrenn, Nordyca Woodfork, and Dreck S. Wilson who generously shared their expertise. Madeline Flagler and the Bellamy Mansion Museum in Wilmington brought me to Taylor's North Carolina home where Beverly Tetterton of the New Hanover County Public Library showed me Taylor's neighborhood and enriched my understanding, as she has from the beginning.

Members of Taylor's family have provided essential information and insight. I had the good fortune of talking to Helen Dibble Cannaday, Josephine Cooper, Ann Dibble Jordan, Dorothy Taylor, Edward V. Taylor, Sr., Edward V. Taylor Jr., Clarisse Dibble Walker, and Dr. Louise King Sindos. Gwen Persley Henderson, Edward L. Pryce, and Booker T. Washington's granddaughter Margaret Washington Clifford also gave of their Tuskegee memories.

Tuskegee University has its own cadre of talented historians and archivists. All Tuskegee architecture and planning studies are indebted to Richard K. Dozier's pioneering articles and dissertation. His early encouragement was essential. Archivists Daniel Williams, Cynthia Wilson, Sandra Peck, Cheryl Ferguson, and Dana Chandler helped as did librarians Linda Harvey and Vinson McKenzie. Tuskegee's holdings of its newspaper of record, the *Tuskegee Student*, do not include the decade of the 1890s, unfortunately. The widely available microfilm edition does not include that those years along with several others. I note this in the hope that libraries that have hard copies will keep them and that Tuskegeans will know that the papers cluttering their attics may be essential historical residue.

Also at Tuskegee, Clifford Wesson in the Physical Facilities Department granted me open access to the drawings and Dr. James McSwain of the History Department answered many queries. Johanna Hays gave generously of her own research while Dara Eskridge, a student who asked good questions and then proceeded to answer them, contributed too. Finally, Booker Conley, who cared for the buildings and preserved the drawings during his long career in the physical facilities department, shared his knowledge every step of the way. He, too, is a hero of Tuskegee's architecture.

Research librarians and archivists at all repositories are so practiced in their crafts that their gifts may be taken for granted. Patricia Windham and the interlibrary borrowing staff at Tulane University's Howard-Tilton Memorial Library located rare materials as did the staff at the West Tisbury Free Public Library in Massachusetts. Kimberly Alexander, Gary Van Zante and Laura Knott at the MIT Museum guided me through that essential repository and shared images as well as their own knowledge. This study originated as the publication for an MIT exhibition and, while that specific exhibit never materialized, the MIT Museum has since produced an elegantly designed traveling exhibition of Taylor and his Tuskegee career.

The staffs of many archives and libraries kindly answered my queries. I thank the Amistad Research Center at Tulane University, Livingstone College Library, the State University of New York at Buffalo, Trenton Public Library, Rockefeller Archives Center in Tarrytown, Moorland Spingarn Research Center at Howard University, Wisconsin Historical Society, New Hanover County Public Library in Wilmington, N.C., Macon (Georgia) Public Library, Columbia University Archives, Loeb and Widener libraries at Harvard University, the Phelps-Stokes Fund, Schomberg Center for Research in Black Culture, Meadville/Lombard Theological School, and Carnegie Corporation of New York. A summer stipend from the National Endowment for Humanities funded a pre-microfilming foray into the Booker T. Washington papers at the Library of Congress plus a pre-digital voyage through its Frances Benjamin Johnston photographs in the Prints and Photographs Division. C. Ford Peatross kindly showed me student drawings even before they were catalogued. The Graham Foundation for Studies in the Fine Arts supported Robert S. Brantley's photography.

Successive deans of the Tulane School of Architecture accepted unfathomable delays in completion. I thank Ronald C. Filson, Donna V. Robertson, Donald Gatzke, Reed Kroloff, Scott Bernhard, and Kenneth Schwartz for their patience. I am grateful to the Tulane University Provost's Fund for Faculty/Student Engagement and to Scott Bernhard, Michael P. Keller, and William J. Rosenthal of the Tulane City Center for the topographic maps. I thank Francine Stock, Keli Rylance, Cathy Ryan, David Armentor, and Alissa Kingsley for scanning, mapping, and other digital generosities. A three-year Favrot Professorship financed trips to Tuskegee and other research costs while a Tulane University Faculty Research Grant helped with editing and permissions. Finally, the dedicated team at NewSouth Books, led by editor-in-chief Randall Williams and publisher Suzanne La Rosa, and including Brian Seidman, Lisa Emerson, Lisa Harrison, Noelle Matteson, Sam Robards, Jeff Benton, and interns Chris Greene and Elizabeth McCord, took the manuscript to press with insight and excellent good sense.

INTRODUCTION

This is the story of an African American architect, Robert R. Taylor (1868–1942), who designed buildings for Booker T. Washington's Tuskegee Normal and Industrial Institute, where he also taught, directed the mechanical industries department, and managed the buildings, grounds, and infrastructure. Taylor grew up in racially progressive Wilmington, North Carolina, the son of a successful merchant and carpenter who, though nominally a slave, was virtually free. In 1888 the young man entered the architecture program at the Massachusetts Institute of Technology, becoming the Institute's first black graduate as well as the first academically trained African American architect.

This is also Tuskegee's story told in terms of campus development, industrial and architectural education, and the role of architectural design and building construction in Washington's agenda for progress, pride, and a place in the nation. Tuskegee was the largest and best-funded school for African Americans of its day. It modeled an interlocking system of progressive pedagogy and self-construction for a community—a city on a hill—to elevate a deeply impoverished, despised caste. Tuskegee graduates then fanned out across the depleted countryside to teach, farm, design and build, practice trades,

create wealth, and disprove racist predictions for failure. The philanthropically minded white visitors who financed most structures found the campus a near-utopia of attractive students, distinguished faculty, and a carefully crafted physical plant, a kind of institutional theater with permanent scenery and live-in actors. This is not to say that the production collapsed when the audience went away. The spectacle won most students too, mesmerizing them with productivity, cheer, and unaccustomed beauty. Tuskegee was a visually captivating assertion of Washington's scheme for racial success. Despite widespread pronouncements to the contrary, African Americans were moving quickly from slavery to high civilization and the Tuskegee campus showed it.

THE PLIGHT OF BLACK ARCHITECTS

During the hundred years following the end of slavery, this nation agreed to restrict African Americans to a limited existence that was so thoroughly separated from white people that the latter need never share theater seats, drinking fountains, or railway cars and waiting rooms. Nor should white people have to compete for jobs, housing or political power with an ethnic minority they chose to believe their inferior. Segregation limited black people to an undercapitalized economy with, at best, a few institutions such as churches, schools, and fraternal organizations with the resources to erect substantial buildings requiring an architect. While black communities could support black doctors, dentists, teachers, ministers, beauticians, and morticians, and black masons and carpenters could erect modest houses, shops, and churches without training, African Americans in cities could occupy technically advanced, aesthetically accomplished buildings that had been remaindered by whites who had moved on to newer turf. They did not need architects to design buildings appropriate to their needs.

Even so, some black designers did develop significant careers, a few crossing racial barriers to better or even luxuriously funded white patronage. Paul R. Williams (1894–1980) was among the most successful mid-century practitioners of any color, providing houses for the very rich and sometimes famous as well as substantial institutional and commercial buildings in Los Angeles and beyond. Clarence W. Wigington (1883–1967), the principal designer but never the chief of St. Paul's municipal architectural office, produced about ninety finely crafted, stylistically cohesive public structures—schools, fire stations, park buildings, and an airport terminal. Julian F. Abele (1881–1950), who stayed behind the scenes in Horace Trumbauer's Philadelphia office, is widely credited for such high-end work as Harvard University's Widener Library, Duke University, and the Duke family home in New York. Robert R. Taylor could be included in this group since wealthy whites financed most of his work. But these were philanthropists supporting a cause, not their own needs. Taylor's true client was Booker T. Washington. Taylor's modestly scaled, student-built structures are carefully tuned for visual amenity

through skills gleaned from his classical architectural studies at MIT. In addition to designing and supervising construction of most of Tuskegee erected between 1892 and 1932, Taylor taught mechanical and architectural drawing for industrial students, including those in the building trades, and he developed a pre-professional architecture program that helped black men enter mainstream design schools, get entry level office jobs, and launch independent careers. Teaching in and then administering the large boys industries department along with heading all aspects of campus development—buildings, grounds, and infrastructure—became his "day job," his separately compensated design labors relegated to his own time.

Buildings by black architects for African Americans are important because they sheltered precious institutions and because their presence signaled success by helping generate it. But black-built structures do not differ significantly from those by white architects for white clients. Bricks and mortar do not change with the makers' ethnicity. Programming is the same for black or white usage. Rooms and their arrangements fail to betray skin color even though race certainly conditioned the lives of those who built and inhabited them. Nor are inter-building relationships racially coded. Spaces between them and their closeness to roads are not racial affairs, although some serious analysts do disagree. Buildings have the same meaning for whites and blacks, this study suggests, although the greater difficulties in achieving the necessary wealth may make them more intensely felt. Therefore, it is the historian's task to find the human story behind each construction in order to understand how race affected their makers and users experience even if the stories do not impress the building's substance. This process demands scholarly exactitude since community values may be widely understood without explicit verbalization. Silence about intentions can be the safest repository when racist threats abound. Reticence in print, personal papers and family lore may also serve dignity, the refusal to acknowledge ill treatment helping minimize its sting. In the end, the literally constructive act of building is a silent assertion of a people's right to place if the institution has the power to protect itself. Tuskegee did.

Discrimination, however, did affect most black architects' practices if not the forms, as initial studies have shown.[1] Clarence W. Wigington, who learned by apprenticing with a white architect and then found job protection under civil service rules, appears to have dealt with his second-place status by exercising his leadership skills in the Urban League community service. Julian Abele may have stayed behind the scenes because of race or because he had a retiring nature. One egregious case does survive from the literature of segregation. William H. Moses (1901–1991) hid his race when competing for a high profile job for the Commonwealth of Virginia. Moses's submission won but he lost the commission after his color became known. Paul R. Williams stands out not only for his stellar cross-racial career but also for addressing race in print. Writing in 1937 in a mainstream magazine and again in a posthumously published memoir, Williams accepted the fact that he could not live in Los Angeles's best neighborhoods although he could well afford to and that he had to travel in Jim Crow railroad cars and stay in segregated hotels. But Williams also said that segregation was good because whites were a superior race, a position that fit his era but is repellent to ours. The race must acknowledge this fact, he wrote, and do so "without resentment" before it, too, could advance. Individual by individual, African Americans must "wake up"

to the opportunities before them. But white people too must "wake up" to black achievements and accept and celebrate them. This way, individual by individual, the black race would rise from "common savagery," as the white one had before. Williams came by these views by rejecting his youthful bitterness, accepting and then triumphing over the challenges discrimination imposed.[2]

Robert R. Taylor also thought deeply about race but he wrote little of it and even then privately. Taylor understood that slavery and its aftermath set back black advancement, and he dedicated his life to rectifying this situation. Although he was a public optimist in the Tuskegee mold, by the summer of 1919, after Washington had died and while white mobs were attacking black communities, he wrote privately that he could no longer assume that white people were fair-minded. Washington might well have said the same publicly if he were still living. But after that brief expression, Taylor returned to reticence in print and in letters that would be read by others. Traveling home from his 1929 African sojourn, Taylor worried about the difference between England, whose industry he admired and whose culture he loved, and Liberia, which discouraged him. But he excused the latter for its youth and distance from the mother country that had failed it. Taylor kept his own bad experiences to himself. We would be naive to assume that his encounters with prejudice and discrimination were not plentiful since he traveled often and worked with whites in many situations, developing in the process a reputation for interracial tact. Perhaps, because immediate tasks were foremost in his mind, or perhaps because Tuskegee's style was positive, he reserved public comments for good outcomes. With the exception of one impassioned letter that chastised a black YMCA administrator for failing to recommend black architects and builders to black institutions, Taylor focused on the immediate. If he was bitter about the limitations that race imposed upon his practice, his descendants did not know it. When he formally addressed students late in his career he did so in Washingtonian uplift: do what you can to do your best; be persistent; be hopeful. Saying otherwise would have been impolitic in an institutional culture that was not given to complaint.

ARCHITECTURAL CLASSICISM

If Taylor did not record unpleasant experiences, neither did he engage in architectural discourse. In this he was like most architects of any color—too busy to put on paper the theoretical or aesthetic issues to which he must have given thought. Taylor clearly believed that black-designed, financed, constructed, owned and occupied buildings were economic engines as well as monuments of achievement. They were "Negro buildings." Nor did he speculate as we might have wished about the possible interracial implications of particular forms. For example, we do not know what cultural messages, if any, were intended by monumental columnar porticos on Tuskegee's library, dormitory, and hospital. One might search for a reference—ironic or not—to "big house" colonnades such as those on the antebellum mansion a quarter mile away, or—without irony—to the slave talents that presumably crafted them. But a classical portico could also be best practice for any ambitious institution, never mind that this one sheltered those who could not ride in the white man's railway car, get justice in the courts, or vote in what should have been everyone's election. That the porticos did not stimulate racists into destroying the uppity enclave might be explained by Booker T. Washington's power and prestige or, more likely, by the limitations of architectural iconography in popular discourse. Most people are attuned to social behavior, not architectural.

Columnar porticos have long carried a loose association with Greek democracy—and slavery—but also with any authority. Several scholars have suggested that the South built columnar porticos at the turn of the turn of the twentieth century to recall, indeed rewrite, its antebellum past. Segregation and Jim Crow discrimination could visibly ride the columnar coattails that had been decreed as slavery's monument. But what does it mean, then, if these forms appear on "Negro buildings"? Is it important that the Carnegie Library's grand Ionic portico was built just when the new Alabama constitution was disfranchising most black citizens, when Jim Crow legislation and white on black violence were on the rise, when black secondary schools and colleges were abandoning courses in ancient languages or hiding them within industrial curricula, when Booker T. Washington used classical studies as a rhetorical whipping boy, and when "scientific" racism was "proving" innate inferiority. The author of an anti-Tuskegee screed who faulted the school for expecting a white man to doff his hat within its buildings and address a teacher as "Mister" did not get the message, if indeed one was intended, that a columnar portico might assert the equality he abhorred. This critic admired the campus for its order and beauty but failed to perceive a challenge to the racial hierarchy he was bent on enforcing. Tuskegee insiders might have been silent about architectural equality, but that does not mean that they did not understand their porticos as just that when safe among family and friends or in the quiet of their own thoughts.

TAYLOR'S BUILDINGS

We are left, then, with Robert R. Taylor's Tuskegee buildings. Their eloquence compels attention even without the knowledge that their designer was black. They are gently scaled, inventively triadic compositions with finely tuned proportions and discrete detailing. The rough textures and varied coloration of the student-made, student-laid bricks turn prosaic walls into mottled planes of considerable sensuousness. Taylor emphasized these hewn surfaces with sharp-cut windows and spare but strategically placed brick or wooden moldings. Windows vary in shape as well as size and they engage the viewer with their syncopated rhythms. Taylor adds the occasional irreverent touch such as a quoin-bordered large window that lights a stair landing poised above a tiny one that lights the residual space below. The device enlivens the rear walls of the four Emery dormitories but is featured front and center on the stair tower of Dorothy Hall. The second story of Tantum Hall has an irregular window scansion in the center, as if the architect had somehow missed a beat, that is echoed by another irregular scansion on the building's southern end. Two nearly identical large windows on the public side of the Office Building differ from each other because while one lights a room, the other, which has a wooden panel crossing the glazing to mark a landing, lights a staircase. Symmetrical facades may be varied in a variety of ways such as two entrances tucked into corners, as at Rockefeller Hall and Dorothy Hall. With shapes echoing the earthen ridges on which they sit, the buildings are generously spaced across green lawns that skim a pale red soil, keying into the nature that is all around them. The Tuskegee campus succeeds in evoking another era's gentility along with the heroic efforts for racial identity and interracial harmony that demanded their existence. Tuskegee's architecture and campus are not racially coded, but they grew out of racial conditions. The buildings that remain are monuments of creativity, devotion, and determination in the face of great odds.

Unfortunately, we can experience only a few of Taylor's interiors since most Tuskegee structures have been rebuilt within. The Office Building has some original interior fabric, the matchboard wainscoting and plaster walls with a picture rail that was standard as recorded in early classroom photographs. Logan Auditorium and the Chambliss Children's House are original as well. Logan needs renovation, but the Children's House, with its lovingly detailed original interiors, recently was beautifully intact. Chambliss, the most reusable historic structure, deserves careful reassignment as a monument of Taylor's talent and thoughtfulness. Plans and elevations that students of the 1920s traced from the now-lost original blueprints show normative internal arrangements for classroom and dormitory buildings. Frances Benjamin Johnston's photographs recorded Tuskegee pedagogy more than architectural character in 1902 and, in 1906, building exteriors more than interiors. She did not capture the special detailing or inventive solutions in stairs, common rooms, hallways, and the now-lost assembly rooms of Carnegie Library, Douglass Hall, the Huntington Memorial Academic Building, and Tompkins Dining Hall.

CAMPUS PLANNING

Campus planning issues are complex, as is to be expected from the erratic construction funding that spanned the five decades of this study. Planning in the sense of deciding what buildings would be erected in some near or more distant future and where they would go shows up in donor discussions such as those surrounding the Stokes sisters' six donations, the Tompkins Dining Hall, and the second agricultural campus of 1908 through the 1910s. The text will consider these and other issues in the following segments: "Building at the Beginning," "Growing the Campus Center," "The Chapel," "The 'Homemade' Plan," and "Growing the Western Campus" in Chapter 3; "More with the Stokes Sisters" in Chapter 4; "The Girls' Quadrangle," and the ineffective Warren H. Manning plan, in Chapter 5; and "The Agricultural Campus" in the Catalog. Catalog discussions also record other site or planning decisions such as the Emery dormitory locations or those of the greenhouses. Tuskegee's irregular topography would have any challenged attempt at the symmetrical or axial relationships among buildings that signaled "planning" at many culturally ambitious institutions. Even so, a 1916 report on African American education that recommended formalized strategies for upgrading modest institutions to the visual status of white colleges admired Tuskegee's accretive, "homemade" plan.

Tuskegee's campus is an accumulation of separately funded structures set on the crests and plateaus of steeply sided, irregularly shaped hills. Visual coherence comes from the richly textured institute brick and Taylor's sensitive scale and inventive massing. Buildings recall each other as the observer moves about, but they do so through material and scale rather than through formal duplication and organizing axes. The buildings weave their overall unity. The actual planning or siting decisions are hard to unravel because so many talents were involved. African Americans—Taylor, Booker T. Washington, his brother John H. Washington, landscape architect David A. Williston, other Tuskegee architects, and innumerable division or department heads—were probably the most important players, but white donors and trustees, and their design advisors also weighed in, or tried to. While opinionated whites sometimes inserted their well-financed oars, in the end they usually had less rather than more control. For example, New Yorkers Caroline and Olivia Egleston Phelps Stokes held definite views about their six buildings' locations. They visited Tuskegee often, argued for specific sites, and showed design urges of their own. But while they generally deferred to Washington in the end, the Principal, who spent at least half of his time raising money, would have had every reason to accommodate their wishes when they seemed right for his cause. For the four Emery dormitories, the donor's representative effectively dictated a new boys' housing zone without having seen the grounds because he feared fire. At the other pole, trustee Seth Low, who had developed Columbia University's Morningside Heights campus and was a physical as well as financial planning advocate, deferred to "those on the ground" after having his say for White Hall and the Agricultural Campus.

The complexities stemming from Tuskegee's caring contributors constitute one reason for a separate Catalog of essays on each Taylor building. Each entry is an independent narrative of funding, siting, design, construction, reception, and occupation. Each is written on the assumption that our understanding of this significant American place is most fully nurtured by probing the complexities accompanying the events. The author intends that these essays will elucidate some aspect of the Tuskegee achievement, as the evidence allows, to help us understand how the building program supported Washington's racial goals, how donors played their varied roles, how Taylor handled each construction while integrating it into a seamless theoretical web of pedagogy, institution-building, and racial progress. Taylor's wooden buildings must await future scholarship. They stood in the campus, in adjacent residential neighborhoods, in Tuskegee-led farm communities, and among the Tuskegee-produced rural schools that preceded the Rosenwald Fund's famous five thousand. Taylor's off-campus brick church of 1907 must be located so it can join Taylor's brick buildings elsewhere— in Selma and Birmingham, Alabama, plus those in Marshall, Texas, and Salisbury, North Carolina, a task that must be taken on by others. This study ends in Taylor's personal tracks. He retired to Wilmington in 1932 and abandoned the practice of architecture, but he worked for racial fairness for the ten years that remained to him. He died in the Tuskegee Chapel while on a visit, having just pronounced it his masterpiece.

Robert R. Taylor and Tuskegee

"You say you are a carpenter—house builder?"

"Yes, sir."

"You mean to say that you took contracts, planned and built houses?"

"Oh yes," replied the colored man.

"I never saw a colored architect. Say George!" to a man who had just entered, "here's a colored architect and house-builder from the South."

— DAVID BRYANT FULTON [pseud. Jack Thorne]

in *Hanover, or the Persecution of the Lowly* (1900) [1]

CHAPTER 1

WILMINGTON

It was sometimes possible, of course, for antebellum African Americans, free or slave, to work up into the economy and achieve considerable success. Booker T. Washington was explaining just this when he used the example of his Tuskegee Institute administrator and architect Robert Robinson Taylor: "Mr. Taylor's father was the son of a white man who was at the same time his master. Although he was nominally a slave, he was early given liberty to do about as he pleased." Henry Taylor (1823–1891), our subject's father, partnered with a white man who owned a sailing vessel in Wilmington, North Carolina. Taylor purchased naval stores and other merchandise that he turned over to this partner who transported and sold them. "In this way they made a considerable amount of money together so that after all the losses of the war, Mr. Taylor's father was able to send him from 1888 to 1892 through one of the best technical schools in the United States, the Boston Institute of Technology."[2] The school was, of course, the Massachusetts Institute of Technology, then in Boston.

We must take Washington's story seriously as the best explanation we have for Robert R. Taylor's breakthrough. Taylor believed himself to be and is now widely understood as MIT's first black graduate. He was also the first academically trained African American architect, although he never claimed this; perhaps he had too much respect for earlier black builder/architects he knew during his boyhood and the few black office-trained practitioners who preceded him. He was, like many productive and talented but less well-known designers, a quiet man.

ROBERT R. TAYLOR KNEW little about his white grandfather. In 1929, one Charles Taylor wrote from Glasgow, Scotland, to ask if Robert R. Taylor, who had just been in England and presumably attracted newspaper attention despite his retiring nature, could be a relative since he, the Scotsman, had a Jamaican ancestor. Robert Taylor replied that his father had said that his white father, Angus Taylor, had settled near Fayetteville, North Carolina. By the time of his death, Angus Taylor's property had "dissipated" so that no kin inherited, according to his grandson's reply to Scotland.[3] Angus Taylor (d. 1854) was born to a Scottish family that emigrated before the revolution to Bladen County, between Fayetteville and Wilmington. Most of the men left for the Bahamas after the war because they were loyalists who had lost their land. By 1840 Angus Taylor had moved back to Bladen County. In 1850 he owned $1,600 in property including seven slaves. Perhaps the seventeen-year-old Henry Taylor was one of them. Another might have been Henry's mother, whose name we do not know.[4] By the late 1850s, Henry Taylor had moved to Wilmington as a carpenter, coastal trader, and merchant. Robert R. Taylor's mother, Emily Still was also listed as a Fayetteville-born mulatto, her parents being carpenter Richard Still and Mariah Artis, both listed as mulatto in the 1880 census. Family tradition gives a foundling status for Emily—the child of an Irish sea captain and his wife who died in childbirth. The child was given to a black family to raise, a somewhat common occurrence according to the region's lore. Two of Taylor's siblings, John Edward and Sarah Louise, were able to pass as white and John's three sons actually did so during their adult years in Pennsylvania. The Caucasian-seeming Sarah Louise had "flaming" red hair but brother Robert, who was "clearly a Negro" even though he had light skin and "hypnotically" blue eyes, could not have passed even if he had wanted to.[5]

Carpentry ran in the Taylor family, at least by Henry Taylor's generation. Emily's younger brother Edward practiced the trade. Henry Taylor was one of the all-black construction crew of the Bellamy mansion, now Bellamy Mansion Museum, built between 1859 and 1861. After the Civil War Henry Taylor contracted the Hemenway School, a free school for whites given and staffed by New England women. Robert spent his boyhood learning carpentry and "the general details of building operations" under his father's supervision. By the time Robert R. Taylor finished secondary school, Henry had retired, handing over jobs to the teenager.[6] "Uneducated" by his son's standards but literate and clearly successful, Henry Taylor is also remembered as the county's wealthiest black landowner in 1870.[7] But perhaps his greatest achievement was that he sent his children (including, it seems, the girls) to distant institutions for study.

Henry Taylor's success was not unusual in Wilmington. As Tony P. Wrenn and Catherine W. Bishir have shown, African Americans, slave or free, had long been active in the North Carolina building trades. In 1827 Solomon Waddell Nash, a newly emancipated slave, launched a building career. Nash later became a slaveholder and trained "Negro orphans" in construction. Freedman Elvin Artis, contractor for the Bellamy House, gathered black carpenters, including Henry Taylor, and a notable plasterer, William Benjamin Gould, to form what the Bellamy family remembered as an all-black construction team. By the eve of the Civil War, a quarter of Wilmington's building craftsmen were free black or mulatto. Once, when a scaffold collapsed on a construction project, three white, two slave, and one free black carpenters who were working together fell to the ground. Carpenter James D. Sampson was liberated by his white father and became the wealthiest freedman in the city in 1860. Sampson sent his children North for schooling. Alfred Howe, who had purchased his freedom, came from a family of builders and probably worked on the Bellamy House. In 1871, he was supervising architect of St. Mark's Episcopal Church, building to drawings by the Boston firm of Emerson and Fehmer. In 1880, the black builder Lewis Hollingsworth, a member of St. Stephen's African Methodist Episcopal Church, drew plans for its Gothic Revival structure as well as built it. Alfred Howe's prolific construction career also included a large house that was designed by James F. Post, a New Jersey architect/builder who moved to Wilmington before the war and designed the Bellamy House. Post's own home was in the same block as the Taylor family but one street away.[9] The large house that Post designed in the late 1880s was for a Princeton-educated attorney who had married the sister of a Wilmington-raised architect then working in Boston, Henry Bacon. Bacon would go on to design the Lincoln Memorial in Washington,

D.C. The Taylor boy would have had many opportunities to learn that there is a profession called "architecture" that can be, and at the higher end is, separate from that of builder.[10]

Wilmington had long been a good place for black builders because there were opportunities in a tolerant, semi-integrated environment. Certainly there could be racial problems, as Frederick Law Olmsted recorded. In 1857 a hundred and fifty white workmen destroyed a house frame that black carpenters had erected and threatened more mischief in order to cut the competition. But there was a public outcry to protest the violence and a reward for information leading to an arrest.[8] As summarized by black novelist David Bryant Fulton, looking back on what seems to have been a golden age:

> "Up to but a few years ago, the best feeling among the races prevailed in Wilmington. The Negro and his white brother walked their beats together on the police force; and black aldermen, white mayor and black chief of police, white and black school committeemen sat together in council, white and black mechanic worked together on the same buildings, and at the same bench; white and black teachers taught in the same schools. Preachers, lawyers and physicians were cordial in their greetings one toward the other, and general good-feeling prevailed, Negroes worked, saved, bought lands and built houses . . . [T]he Negro has done his full share in making the now ill fated city blossom as a rose."[11]

But this remarkable peaceableness ended in November 1898 in a racist sweep during which the Democrats, who had just lost an election, drove away much of the black middle class and its elected representatives along with hundreds or thousands of poorer people. Because an elected city council was overthrown, the Wilmington "riot" constituted a coup d'etat. The number killed was probably in the low tens although some estimates have it that sixty died and fifteen hundred fled. Wilmington's enviable racial tone was gone, showing that a long tradition of racial neighborliness may be no match for orchestrated ethnic violence for political ends. The Wilmington insurrection introduced other "riots" over the next two decades that terrorized blacks into accepting discriminatory restrictions. But at first the losses seemed to be to the town itself. Employers in the factories and lumber mills found that newly hired whites had a poorer work ethic and expected higher pay than their black predecessors. Even the coup's leader, by then the mayor, remarked that Wilmington could not live without its usual stablemen, laundresses, and cooks.

After the insurrection, Robert R. Taylor, who had been far away at Tuskegee, told Booker T. Washington that Wilmington's experiences were "political murders" and forwarded to Washington a letter from his brother John with an on-the-scene report.[12] John E. Taylor was deputy customs collector for the port and therefore safe. The mob would not risk federal intervention by attacking a federal officer. John's family remembered that a carriage retrieved the children from school just before the eruption began. Guards, perhaps from the Customs House, were posted on the family's front porch. John Taylor himself went into the swamps to help those who were fleeing by foot.[13] Perhaps his brother's experiences reinforced Robert Taylor's natural inclination of saying little and remaining in the background, as he would do throughout his career.

ROBERT ROBINSON TAYLOR was born June 8, 1868, the youngest of Henry and Emily Taylor's

Figure 1.1. A c. 1905–07 photograph of the Taylor family home in Wilmington, with Robert R. Taylor and his two eldest children, Robert Rochon and Helen, in front. The white-haired man is his brother, John E. Taylor, and the women are members of John's family.

four children.[14] In the mid-1870s the family was living at 112 North Eighth Street, a now-lost house that Henry had built.[15] In 1884 Henry built another house [Figure 1.1], still standing, on the same lot for John's family.[16] The houses were in a racially mixed neighborhood of one- and two-story frame units inhabited by black, Irish-born white, and the occasional mulatto families. Close by lived a black or mulatto cooper, laundress, "lighterman," and dressmaker, and a white grocer, watchman, city employee, furniture dealer, and salesman. The roughly half-white block included the house where TV journalist David Brinkley grew up. The next block had the black Sadgwar family's "majestic" home. Frederick Sadgwar was described as an architect as well as a builder and financier. This house shared a garden wall with the MacRae mansion around the corner. Hugh MacRae, an insurrection leader, could have sallied forth just around the corner to deliver the insurrection's opening ultimatum to his black neighbor whom the insurrectionists had deemed the black Republicans' leader.[17]

The Taylor family's neighborhood included the Giblem Masonic Hall, which also abutted the Mac-Raes' garden wall. This three-story, stucco-covered brick building held a black Prince Hall lodge on the upper level, a city market on the ground floor, and, after 1926, a library financed by the black community because the city refused access to the public one. Built between 1871 and 1873 with Henry Taylor on the finance committee, the Hall remains a monument to black Wilmington's post-war independence and post-riot continuity. What has been described as the nation's first black agricultural and mechanical fair was set at the Masonic Hall in 1875. Surely the Taylor family shared in the festivities—the balls and orations, the baseball contests and costumed tournaments. Exhibits included carpentry achievements in finish woodwork, cabinetry, paneled doors, and winding stairs. Add the blacksmithing crafts, buggies and carriages, and masonry and one has a product range that anticipated the industries Taylor would direct at Tuskegee.[18] In another direction from the Taylor home, the family's religious center, the Chestnut Street Presbyterian Church, still stands. This is a distinctive little 1850s structure of vertical boards and battens with decorative verge boards and round-headed apertures.[19] Henry Taylor was on the committee that in 1867 purchased the building from a white congregation. Henry also helped organize an African American cemetery, Pine Forest, another arena of civic responsibility that stopped short of politics and office-holding.

The city's early prosperity was based in lumber and naval stores, but these products faded as the nearby pine forests dwindled. The economy shifted to transshipping cotton, with some manufacturing thrown in, since the port and several connecting railroads assured a speedy post-Civil War recovery. Established in the 1740s on a grid of square blocks, the town had expanded north and south on the armature of the same grid laid along a sometimes gently and sometimes steeply sloping ridge that paralleled the Cape Fear River. By mid nineteenth century, the sloping, gridded town had accumulated a distinguished collection of civic, religious, commercial, and domestic structures, several of them designed by architects from Philadelphia, New York, and Boston, port cities that had long supplied Wilmington's other commercial needs. The Bellamy mansion exemplifies Wilmington's trading ties with the New York origins of its stone paving and steps, louvered blinds, hardware, furniture, and the fourteen great columns for a home for Southerners.[20]

Robert Taylor attended the American Missionary Association (AMA) Gregory Normal Institute [Figure 1.2] about six blocks south of his home in another racially mixed area. The school's name honored a Massachusetts man who had given an orphanage and then a good deal more: a brick Congregational church, the institute's brick teachers' home, and the remodeled school itself, all set together in a single square.[21] David Bryant Fulton thought this church and school cluster "the most beautiful group of buildings in the city."[22] Gregory Normal Institute was one of many AMA foundations that spanned the South to provide elementary education to the children and grandchildren of former slaves while preparing older people for teaching. The academically talented could attend such AMA schools and colleges as Berea (Kentucky), Hampton (Virginia), Tougaloo (Mississippi), Straight (New Orleans),

Figure 1.2. Gregory Institute, Wilmington.

that education "spoiled" African Americans for work—meaning manual labor—Woodward recalled the boy who was "spoiled" from being an ordinary carpenter and was now "a very competent architect." "After graduating from the Massachusetts Institute of Technology, where he ranked with the very best among fifteen hundred young white men, he became for several years one of Booker T. Washington's most useful and productive helpers."[23] Woodward also noted that Gregory Institute had "spoiled" a dressmaker who became the principal of a large school, and also spoiled another young man who arrived at age twenty-two with almost no education but who quickly mastered Greek, Hebrew, and trigonometry and went on to Howard University where he graduated with honors. Woodward conveys the intensity that dedicated Northern educators brought to the enterprise.

Taylor's goal, set before his graduation, was for a liberal arts education at Lincoln University near Philadelphia.[24] Founded in 1854 as Ashmun Institute, Lincoln was the oldest college for African American men and the one with the highest tuition. It was also in the family. John E. Taylor married a girl who grew up near Lincoln, and Henry and Emily's second child, Anna Maria, married James Francis Shober, a Lincoln graduate who earned a medical degree at Howard University and then established a Wilmington practice.[25] Many years later, when Lincoln awarded Robert R. Taylor an honorary doctorate for his work in Liberia, he voiced his regret that he did not earn a Lincoln liberal arts degree before undertaking professional studies.[26] Instead, Taylor spent some time between his Gregory graduation and MIT at home working as "foreman of construction for some

Talladega (Alabama), Howard (Washington, D.C.), Morehouse (Atlanta), and Fisk (Nashville). Taylor was among many who benefited from the AMA's conviction that black children could meet the standards set by white New Englanders for their own offspring. One teacher, George A. Woodward of Weymouth, Massachusetts, arrived in the 1880s, during Taylor's last years, and wrote in 1902 about his experiences. Woodward remembered Taylor for an instructive anecdote. Responding to the canard

large concerns," one of them the Southern Cotton Seed Oil Company. It was in 1888 that he went to Boston armed with his father's support.[27]

There was precedence in white Wilmington for schooling at the Massachusetts Institute of Technology. William H. Chadbourn, son of a New Englander who had come south to operate a lumber company, graduated in engineering in 1886, two years before Taylor entered.[28] More tantalizing were the Bacon brothers, Francis and the younger Henry, whose New England engineer father had moved to Wilmington. Francis, a classical archaeologist, had studied architecture at MIT from 1874 to 1876. Henry enrolled in architecture at the University of Illinois for a short time and apprenticed in a Boston firm while Taylor was at MIT. Henry was two years older than Taylor. While no record of contact has surfaced, it is hardly impossible for them to have known one another as boys; adventurous children have always found ways to connect, and Wilmington was integrated in many ways. Taylor once wrote that he saw his first curve ball while playing in an alley with a white boy who then became a lifelong friend.[29] It is entirely possible that this white boy was Hugh MacRae, a slightly older child from the mansion around the corner who would, as an adult, help instigate the racist coup. MacRae graduated from MIT in engineering in 1885, coming home in time to advise a black childhood playmate about how to be an architect.[30] The Gregory Institute's New England teachers certainly could have pointed Robert to MIT for architecture, but the suggestion could have come from others, including white contemporaries.

CHAPTER 2

BOSTON

By his own account, Taylor was "the first or among the first colored graduates" of the Massachusetts Institute of Technology.[1] Class photographs and the occasional "c" or "colored" on transcripts suggest that there were earlier African American students, but Taylor was the first to earn a degree [Figure 2.1]. Race may have been less of an issue at MIT than elsewhere because of the many international students. One year near Taylor's class included young men from Brazil, Bulgaria, Canada, France, Guatemala, Hawaii, Japan, Mexico, Panama, Peru, Puerto Rico, Trinidad, and Turkey as well as several northern European nations. As a student in the colorful class of 1888 put it, failing to fine-tune categories to the absolutes that effective racism requires, "Sixty-seven percent were light-complexioned, thirty-three percent dark. Eleven percent wore eye glasses; one was color blind; and fifty percent thought they had mustaches."[2] Taylor would have been among the last fifty percent—putative mustaches—as well as the earlier thirty-three if this were his year under scrutiny. Taylor's coloring might have confused even serious classi-fiers; although he was clearly a tall, light-skinned African American, his eyes were blue-green.[3] While his architecture classmates were white men, mostly New Englanders, the program must have had an inclusionary spirit since its director, Francis Ward Chandler, encouraged women. He admitted them to a special two-year course and then transferred them to the program.[4] Sophia Hayden, the program's first woman graduate, earned the thesis prize in 1890; Lois Howe overlapped her and Taylor while taking the two-year course. Hayden then won the competition for the Women's Building at the World's Columbian Exposition in Chicago. Hattie T. Gallup and Marian Mahoney of the class of 1894 would have been two years behind Taylor.

Taylor's first year was spent in general studies with his full institute class, but during his initial semester he also took courses in freehand and mechanical drawing plus descriptive geometry, these being required deflections from the general curriculum for those students who planned to enter Course IV, the architecture program. His general freshman requirements were chemistry, military drill, French, geometry, algebra, and English. He also had to rectify his failed entrance examinations in history and geometry (he passed in arithmetic, algebra, geometry, French, and English). Five of these subjects were continued during the second semester with trigonometry and political history now added, and he corrected another failed entrance examination in the metric system.[5] William Robert Ware, who founded the MIT program in 1866, thereby beginning academic architectural education in the United States, wished for his students to be well grounded in the liberal arts before advancing to the design studio, a problem that most architecture schools still grapple with today.[6]

Taylor's education in the full Course IV began in earnest in his second year. During this and the two following years, Taylor proceeded with a heavy diet of about ten courses a semester. He would have studied mechanics, acoustics, structural geology, specifications, heating and ventilating, and sanitation, these technical subjects leavened with still more languages—German having been added—plus literature, political economy, five semesters of architectural history and, during every term, some form of drawing: freehand, stereometry, watercolor, working drawings, perspectives, the orders, shades and shadows, pen and ink (four required semesters), and watercolor (three required semesters). In addition to these subjects listed in his transcript and the published curriculum, Taylor would have studied architectural design by completing two monthly design challenges, a pedagogy derived from the Ecole des Beaux-Arts in Paris. They were a one-week sketch problem and a one-month building to be developed to finished drawings that adhered to a sketch or *parti* drawn during the first two days. MIT's four-year architecture degree was extended to five the year after Taylor graduated.

Taylor did well. He was at or near the top of his class, failing nothing and earning honors in trigonometry, architectural history, differential calculus, and applied mechanics. During his last two years he held the Loring Scholarship, which was based on need as well as achievement.[7] He did not study industrial education as some have assumed since he taught for and then administered the Tuskegee industrial program. MIT had a pioneer such program borrowed from Russian pedagogies, as Chapter 3 will discuss. But MIT's School of Mechanic Arts had dissolved by 1888.[8] MIT remembered its first black graduate, inviting him to join other distinguished graduates to speak at its fiftieth anniversary celebration in 1911. Taylor, for his part, recalled MIT with pride. When his widow informed the institute of her husband's death she said that he had wanted to attend his fiftieth class reunion. "He has always met his alumni obligations and loved his alma mater."[9]

MIT's academic program was demanding with classes seven hours daily. The most prestigious architecture program in the country if no longer the only one, MIT combined Ware's scheme of the Paris

Figure 2.1. Robert R. Taylor as MIT student.

Ecole des Beaux-Arts design education with liberal arts and technical classes, thus merging the format of discrete subjects purveyed in scheduled courses, a system familiar in American colleges and German polytechnics, with the French studio and competition arrangement. One assessment described MIT's program as sixty-five percent drawing and design, ten percent architectural theory, and twenty-five percent general studies. Director Chandler, an American who first worked in Ware's office and later studied at the Ecole, taught building technology and construction, while the Ecole-trained Frenchman Eugene Letang, aided by two MIT-trained assistants, Eleazer B. Homer and Frank A. Moore, directed Paris-style monthly design problems. Other faculty taught classes in ornament, life drawing, ink sketching, and watercolor. By modern standards, the curriculum demanded too many courses, but it produced well-informed professionals.

AS IN ALL ARCHITECTURE schools, students invented entertainments to counteract the stress. A yearbook caught the atmosphere: ascending the stairs to the room "consecrated to art and desecrated by the artists" one heard a humming which it would be "poetical but untrue" to ascribe to busy bees. On entering, the humming turned into a confused roar of voices from all nations, some working, some not, and a competition between a band of minstrels and another of whistlers, most of whom were performing as soloists. Floor-shaking rhythmic stamping punctuated the performances. In the Ecole tradition, the "infants"—Taylor would have been one that year—were helping their betters prepare competition entries, learning essential skills from the process. Electric lights helped dispel late-afternoon winter gloom. The anonymous Course IV wit then offered a redemptive take on the terrors of juried

reviews: "Whereas in all well-conducted abattoirs the custom is to slaughter before rendering, the process here is reversed and all work is rendered first and slaughtered afterwards."[10] Scheduled escapes helped, too. Each week the students were led past Henry Hobson Richardson's Trinity Church to the Museum of Fine Arts (then on Copley Square) to consult the plaster casts of figural sculpture and historic architectural ornament that the institute housed there. Consultation consisted of two hours of a "fine old time" playing hide-and-seek with the instructor among the statues, the students clearly "undaunted by the unsociability of the inhabitants."[11] This respite provided sufficient strength for another week of stamping, singing, and whistling.

Museum trips may have served as stolen recreation, but they were also important elements in a program that continually sought to cultivate "taste in color and form," to train the eye to visual values as attendants to "the scientific principles underlying sound construction" and "the mathematical and mechanical formulae."[12] MIT offered an art-based program as much as a scientific one. One observer thought Course IV should leave MIT because it failed to provide the support that was architecture's due. Course IV should join drawing and painting at the museum.[13]

Taylor's foray into architecture may have begun in the classically organized Rogers Building, a twin of the commercial structure that remains near Copley Square, or perhaps in the more industrially imaged New Building, later known as Walker Memorial. The New Building was under construction in June 1888.[14] A photograph of the Rogers Building's third- and fourth-year studios shows a four-room row with doors aligned in an enfilade that finishes in the library.[15] But the architectural drawing room may have been in the New Build-

Figure 2.2 MIT architecture class. Taylor is seated near the rear.

ing. This was a long chamber with exposed ceiling beams that were reinforced by metal tie-rods and a strut or inverted kingpost truss. Since the drawings and sculpture slathering the walls would have engendered aesthetic receptivity, students surely perceived the visual elegance of the beams and tie-rods as well as their expressiveness of purpose. The room's thick interior wall was encrusted with framed drawings, shelves holding plaster figure sculptures and architectural details, and storage cases. At one end, an arched opening through the brick wall led to the library, the arch a device that suggests the even larger arches through brick interior walls that Taylor would build for a Tuskegee industrial building.

The freehand drawing room on the Rogers Building's top floor, with its light wells and skylight, had also been furnished with plaster casts and, occasionally, live models. The second year class's studio had plaster orders placed centrally for close scrutiny plus particularly challenging casts of column bases, capitals, and entablatures at a scale so grand that two short segments of the column shafts brought the components to the ceiling. Classical schooling also came with the required purchase of some late version of the sixteenth-century classic by Giacomo Vignola, *Canon of the Five Orders of Architecture*. Also helping to lodge Doric, Ionic, and Corinthian indelibly into young minds were blackboard "memory drawings." Students had to make profiles of entablatures, capitals, and bases to an announced scale, dimensioning them by modules. They then stood before their handiwork to take the class's criticism, an exercise that surely trained the heart to the trauma of reviews as well as the eye to proportion and the mind to the facts of classicism. Students also did memory drawings of carpentry joints.

VISUAL EDUCATION ALSO CAME as it does to modern students. Eleazer B. Homer taught architectural history using two slide projectors so that students could "discriminate and analyze" paired buildings. And to make absolutely sure that no one suffered from visual deprivation, Ware's stunning collection of English and French architectural drawings was displayed in hallways, exhibition spaces, and studios. Someplace in the building students must have contemplated the virtuoso renderings of the ruins at Cori, Italy, that the student editors of *Technology Architectural Review* published in its first issue. The journal also published drawings of nudes from the Boston's Cowles Art School to make sure that

architects-in-training saw fine figure drawing.[16]

The student projects published in *Technology Architectural Review*, the monthly competition drawings, theses, and Arthur Rotch Traveling Scholarship entries and *envois*, exhibited a monumental classicism derived from the Ecole des Beaux-Arts, but mostly learned from the school's rationalist wing rather than the full-blown rhetorical mode. Eugene Letang wrote the competition programs until spring 1890, when C. Howard Walker, who had taught decoration, took over. Letang had been a student of Leon Vaudremer who was in turn trained by E. E. Viollet-le-Duc, making Taylor and his classmates architectural great-grandchildren of the font of Ecole structural rationalism. *Technology Architectural Review*'s published monthly problems, however, focused on the monumental classical rhetoric with dream-world schemes for a billiard hall by a lake or a monumental loggia. Weighted masonry, masterful proportions, and Hellenic colonnades often outspoke programmatic logic and reasonable scales, not to mention the possibilities inherent in new materials such as structural metal. Henry Bacon's "Art College in City Park," which the *Review* included in 1889, was among the grandest of such schemes although the designer was not a student. Bacon, a Wilmingtonian who could have counseled the young Taylor, was working in a Bos-

Figure 2.3. Taylor's thesis, a home for retired soldiers, elevation.

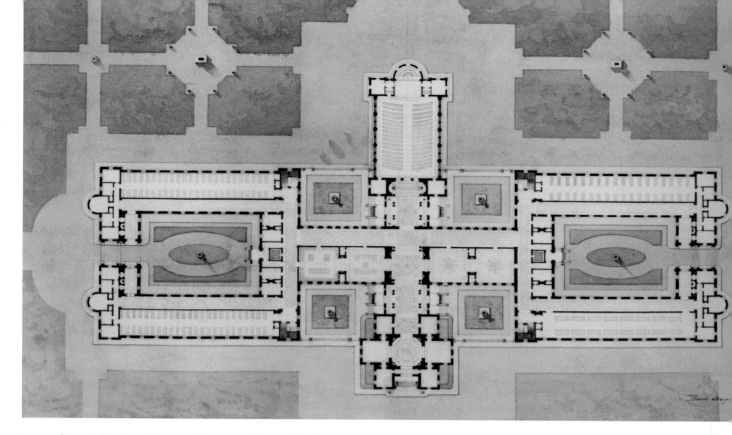

Figure 2.4. Taylor's thesis, plan.

ton office at the time he won the prestigious Rotch scholarship.

Technology Architectural Review also published some MIT final theses. They tended to be public buildings—courthouses, libraries, concert halls, aquariums, museums—programs that lent themselves to symmetrical schemes with courtyards, parallel projecting wings, and emphasized central blocks to dominate one or more axes. The thesis was the architecture student's final hurdle and was understood as a personal exemplar, an achievement to carry forward throughout a working life. Taylor's thesis, a home for two hundred aged Civil War soldiers, survives on two boards and in a brief handwritten description [Figures 2.3, 2.4]. The four-foot long elevation drawing is shaded with pale washes in blue and brown. The plan, with a few elements picked out in green, is on a smaller, three-foot board. The elevation's center is anchored by a domed, three-story block with a variety of arched or pedimented windows. This block, which contained officers' quarters, was flanked by one-story, arcaded hyphens that connect the courtyard wings to the central axis extending to the rear. The cross axis, parallel to the elevation, leads to four symmetrical, two-story ranges that contain between them two large courtyards. These ranges have slightly projecting end bays and a rhythmic disposition of windows, belt courses, and roundels. There are no large exterior columns. The names of Northern and Southern Civil War generals are inscribed in the frieze along the hyphens.

On "entering" the building through the drawing, one finds a hall that continues through the officer's block to the processional spine of a series of nearly square rooms that ends in the chapel. The middle room, with pilasters on the walls and four niches to hold statues, marks the intersection of a cross axis—the arcaded hyphens of the elevation—with more social rooms: parlors, a library, and a reading room. Taylor's description lingers on the right wing at the end of the cross axis, the hospital, that is identical in footprint and elevation to the opposite wing, the dormitory, the two kinds of care paralleled as two quadrangles with courtyard gardens. Taylor has fitted into the short sides service rooms that lack larger purposes such as wards or dining rooms, and put staircases in the corner bays that project on the exterior. There is care for interior-exterior correspondences. The watchman's stations at the end of each corridor are pulled out from the flanking service rooms into semicircular projections that aid surveillance of the grounds while adding light and the pleasure of a curved wall for the comfort of the watchmen within. Taylor's thesis shows something of the restraint, humane consideration, and dislike of bombast characteristic of his later buildings and of his writings.

Taylor's thesis demonstrated mastery of the principles of large-site, monumental classical planning, but this was not the only architectural lesson he would have learned at MIT. While "The Annex," which was modeled on a Russian factory that was erected at the Philadelphia Centennial, was taken down before Taylor arrived, other forays into industrial modes were soon available. The Walker Memorial Building declared its industrial content with ventilation chimneys used as an exterior formal motif. There was exposed wood, brick, and iron on the interiors and, as we have seen, exposed metal and wood ceiling structure even in an arts drawing room. But MIT then built a purpose-designed six-story Architectural Building—now known as Engineering B—that it occupied in fall 1892, just after Taylor left. This was the second monumental industrial construction near Henry Hobson Rich-ardson's Romanesque style Trinity Church and the Victorian Gothic, terra cotta-trimmed Museum of Fine Arts. Several blocks from the Rogers and Walker buildings, this early purpose-designed architecture school shared a party wall with Engineering A on the corner and, when the Pierce Building that shared the other party wall was built, formed a powerful, industrially toned but artistically detailed row.[17]

THE ARCHITECTURAL BUILDING—WHICH TAYLOR would have known while it was under construction and perhaps while under design—was an industrial loft block with brick exterior walls rendered on the front in a free mix of Classical and Romanesque motifs [Figure 2.5]. There were also exposed industrial vents to declare purpose and freshen the history. It may have been designed by Francis Ward Chandler. If true, it was probably integrated into Course IV's aesthetic attitude. MIT's Ecole-based architectural rendering style of idealized schemes washed in shaded tonal planes certainly trained the eye, but the abstraction implied in those planes could also encourage an aestheticized response to such fundamental facts of industrial or vernacular construction as unadorned walls. Vents or wood and metal structural parts or the lines of electrical wiring play roles similar to the named bits of Doric and Ionic orders or the skillful drawing that it takes to render them. The Architectural Building's drafting room with its iron posts supporting beams clearly assembled from layers of pine boarding bolted together, the bolts proudly visible, become expressive form. Delicate loops of electrical wiring suspended from the beams ended in transparent bulbs and horizontal reflectors floating above the drawing tables, the wiring adding a linear counterpoint and the bulbs a note of fragility to play against

Figure 2.5. *Architectural Building of 1892.*

the tough brick walls, metal posts, bolted beams, and matchboard ceiling.[18]

A photograph of an Architectural Building classroom shows blackboards for the memory drawing exercises that could be covered by wooden lattices that could fold down from the ceiling to display photographs of the Greek temples students studied during their first semester of architectural history.[19] Roman and Gothic architectures arrived in the second semester, the Renaissance in the third. Pull-down maps of Europe and a projection screen were fixed in front of the lattices while a tall cabinet stored the slide projectors or served as their pedestal when they were in use. The building's sixth floor was given to a freehand and figure drawing studio with a monumental generosity of space and light far beyond its Rogers predecessor. Wooden cases in alcoves for storing drawings or glazed cabinets of Italian ceramics edged or sometimes subdivided a broad open studio capped by rows of long skylights above parallel beams. Smaller studio areas could be isolated by curtains so that live models would not distract students assigned mere casts of the Parthenon frieze, the head of Michelangelo's David, or piles of geometrical solids. Daylight from above could be softened by window shades laid horizontally in the ceiling plane and diagonally against the skylight rows. There was also a photography room for recording drawings and making glass slides and, on the first floor, a darkroom. The third year architecture studio, with forty-four desks, was on the third floor, and the fourth year studio was on the fourth floor, along with the library. Second year had fifty desks on the fifth floor, where there was also a women's rest room.[20]

The Architectural Building's below-grade basement was activated for teaching too. With a ceiling height of seventeen and a half feet, the basement was illuminated from its upper walls by the ground-level windows that were visible from the exterior. The building's exposed furnace and fans, materials testing equipment, and experimental plumbing stacks mixed real use and technological explorations. Nearby, students shaped plaster into historic ornament. Glass cases with models of construction details and plumbing devices lined a basement exhibition gallery even though that room's main task was to display the monthly competition drawings after the juries had posted their findings. Interior photographs of the older Rogers and Walker buildings also show an abundance of challenging machinery for metallurgy, mechanical engineering, or manufacturing electricity. One might imagine each designing generation trying to understand how mere architecture could contain such tigers.[21] The Architectural Building did so by incorporating machinery into exhibit space, implying aesthetic continuity. Taylor would not follow the industrial references of the Walker and Architectural Building exteriors at Tuskegee. His Boys' Trades Building, built six years later, had a horizontal spread suitable to the rural setting and a two-story veranda under a classical pediment in front. It has a genteel flavor to go with the Chapel

next door. But frank industrial messages emerge in the rear: plain wings, large openings, and long roof monitors to suggest serious machinery and modern production processes within.

Lessons from the Architectural Building exterior may also have informed other aspects of Taylor's Tuskegee work. The Chapel contrasts brick and rough-cut stone details. Taylor designed it three years after he left MIT. The Boston structure's subtle brick facade displayed differences among several types of window heads—arched, flat, and segmental—and a rhythmic banding of vertical windows stacked under arches and between the rounded corners of the piers that carried into Tuskegee work. There were slight projections of the wall surfaces framing the arched entrance, ventilation grilles at the top, careful emphases made by bands of projecting brick at the upper levels and/or rough-cut stone lintels and continuous sills on the two lower ones and a smooth stone frieze serving as a base for the piers of the three middle stories. Wit, a well-trained eye, and a range of mutually reinforcing sensibilities went into this. Taylor's detailing would recall these lessons.

TAYLOR'S MIT SUMMERS WERE also filled during these years. He worked as a "building operator" with the Southern Cotton Seed Oil Company in Wilmington at least once and spent two or three more doing construction and repairs of a hotel on Martha's Vineyard.[22] This was in Cottage City, now Oak Bluffs. These earnings must have been important even though Henry Taylor's descendants considered it a measure of their ancestor's success that he could send his children to distant schools. It would be important to Robert Taylor that he could send his five children, girls and boys, through college.

While at MIT, Taylor also worked as a salesman for a firm selling artist's materials, or so one memoir says, to help make ends meet. There is an unconfirmed tale that he lived in the basement of a mathematics professor's house, serving as houseboy and babysitter.[23] School records place him on Beacon Hill his first year and then at 367 Northhampton Street in the South End, a brick row house that was owned by one Sarah Floyd in 1888.[24] This was a racially mixed neighborhood and something of a student ghetto with a Chickering piano factory nearby as well as a railroad. Chester Square, which was considered elite, was close at hand, as well as the new home of the Ebenezer Baptist Church, which had come from Beacon Hill to accompany its black parishioners who were also moving up. It was a dynamic and probably very interesting neighborhood for a young man from a small Southern city.

ACCORDING TO TAYLOR'S OWN account, upon his MIT graduation five schools offered him "the direction or organization of the industrial work, and after some hesitancy I responded to the call to the Tuskegee Normal and Industrial Institute, at Tuskegee, Alabama to serve as its architect and instructor in architectural drawing."[25] But he also said that he started practicing architecture immediately after graduation, designing several private and public buildings. These probably were in Cleveland but would seem to constitute an improbably fast start were it not for the fact that Taylor was fastidious in his claims. His correspondence shows great care for accuracy and his natural dignity would have kept him from exaggerating. F. D. Patterson, Tuskegee's third principal, wrote that Booker T. Washington discovered Taylor as young draftsman in a white design firm in Cleveland and was struck by his presence and his educational background. His daughter-in-law also understood that the Tuskegee

connection was made in Cleveland, a favored Northern destination for black Carolinians from the Wilmington and Fayetteville areas and likely to have the connections to welcome him.[26] Taylor did have one Course IV classmate from Cleveland, George W. Andrews.

But Taylor also left hints that he could have met Washington in Boston, where the latter visited in 1890 and 1891.[27] According to an undated press release by Taylor but written in the third person, "Immediately after his graduation, he was offered a number of positions in schools and with business organizations." Washington approached him several times to urge him to come to Tuskegee as teacher, builder, and architect. "He declined this offer several times having no intention of teaching, but rather of going into business for himself. He promised, however, to visit the school, which he did shortly after. This visit resulted in his becoming interested in he building program of the school..."[28] In August 1892 Taylor, still in Massachusetts, appeared to have at most a distant contact with Washington. Earlier that summer Taylor had written to him from Cottage City (now Oak Bluffs) on Martha's Vineyard to apologize for his late reply to Washington's letter, which had just arrived accompanied by a Tuskegee catalog. In early August Taylor apologized again because an accident had prevented their planned meeting. Replying in kind, Taylor included two MIT catalogs with a note that the one for the Architecture Department was a student publication.[29] Washington and Taylor may have met when Taylor was still a student, as some believe, or they may have first been face-to-face in Cleveland, as Patterson had it. It the end it did not matter.

CHAPTER 3

TUSKEGEE BEFORE TAYLOR

EARLY BUILDINGS AND ENDURING PRINCIPLES

Booker T. Washington founded the Tuskegee State Normal School for Colored Teachers in 1881 on an edge of the Alabama "Black Belt"—black for its soil and for its people too, as he would later put it.[1] Washington modeled his school on Hampton Normal and Agricultural Institute in tidewater Virginia where he studied in the mid 1870s and taught from 1879 to 1881. Washington shifted the state-founded Tuskegee to a private school with some state funding because Hampton Normal and Agricultural Institute (as it was known until 1929) had taught him that private schools were freer to perform. He also took from Hampton the melding of academic studies with agricultural and industrial curricula, character building as a rationale for drudgery, brick manufacture as a student industry, night schooling for the poorest students so they could work by day, marching, inspections, co-education, Sunday night inspirational talks, fundraising from concerned Yankees, and the savvy interlocking at every level of both image and reality of architecture and building. The critical difference is that while Hampton's founder, teachers, and architect were white, Washington would build on black talent alone. Tuskegee's all-black staffing would show its students that the children of slaves could find their place in the world. Adding evidence of its graduates' success, Tuskegee would show the watching white world what African Americans could do on their own. As with John Winthrop's Massachusetts Bay colony, Washington's city upon a hill was an experiment that many were watching.[2]

Soon after arriving, Washington wrote back to Hampton about the "beautiful little town" of Tuskegee. "Its quiet shady streets and tasteful and rich dwellings remind one of a New England village," a trope he may have known more from his mentor, Hampton founder Samuel Chapman Armstrong than from a summer job in a Connecticut hotel.[3] Tuskegee, the Macon County seat and at one time a prosperous residential and trading center, was "high and healthy" and luxuriantly green with, indeed, many of the charms of the Northeastern archetype. Thirty years later the town would also strike a traveling Englishman as proof of a favorite British town-planning theorem. It was "a beautiful garden city . . . unconsciously planned long before the notion of garden cities had been a matter of deliberate intention."[4] For Washington, the New England village would continue to be a frequent desideratum, trotted out for the school's suburb, Greenwood Village, or for campus tree-planting campaigns. Even Frederick Douglass himself might have applauded the New England tinge of Washington's vision. Douglass's admiration for New Bedford's houses and gardens reminds us that the region's abolitionism made it a special place in African American history. Douglass also understood that black people living in orderly, well-tended homes would win acceptance.[5] Black Southerners could be housed in freedom's image along with its solid worth. Those Northerners who came to see—and their numbers were legion—would find themselves in a familiar-seeming community even though they had to travel though a dreary and dilapidated land in order to get there.

Washington would have learned about growing a campus by watching Hampton's expansion. In 1869, within a year of its founding in a remaindered army depot, Armstrong had commissioned its first purpose-built structure, the brick-over-wood-frame Academic Hall [Figure 3.1] that faced the busy Hampton River estuary.[6] Academic Hall's designer was an architect who would soon achieve great stature. Richard Morris Hunt was the first American to study at the Ecole des Beaux-Arts in Paris and was leading the professionalization of architecture as well as designing for the financial and social elite. Hunt's Academic Hall at Hampton was three stories high with a cruciform plan and it looked as if it alone could insure the school's future through the tenacity of its presence. Paul Baker, Hunt's biographer, credits its quality not only to the designer's abilities but also to Armstrong's conviction that an attractive physical environment shapes its inhabitants' character. Good design was an educational tool, counting for far

more than mere respectability or prestige.[7]

Academic Hall was completed about the time that Washington arrived. Merely seeing it rewarded the boy for the hardships he endured while getting there. "It seemed to me to be the largest and most beautiful building I had ever seen. The sight of it seemed to give me new life. I felt that a new kind of existence had now begun—that life would now have a new meaning." He had reached the promised land and he "resolved to let no obstacle prevent me from putting forth the highest effort to fit myself to accomplish the most good in the world."[8] Written two decades later, Washington wanted readers of *Up From Slavery* to give buildings to inspire Tuskegee's students.

Washington would have seen next Richard Morris Hunt's Virginia Hall [Figure 3.2] go up, its

Figure 3.1. Hampton's Academic Hall with boys' tents.

construction timed to stimulate donations from Hampton commencement visitors. Because he would have seen the actual construction this time, Washington might have seen the architect supervising it from drawings or even enjoyed his personality while on site visits. Ralph Waldo Emerson found the architect to be spirited, inspired, vivacious, enthusiastic, "loaded with matter," and yet folksy and unpretentious. Washington would eventually share many of these characteristics along with the ability to charm.

Hampton offered other opportunities to understand the building trades: courses in freehand and mechanical drawing and work in brickmaking, sawmilling, and woodworking on campus buildings and off-campus jobs. Washington would have

heard in dedication speeches and probably other occasions as well that a carpentry education meant not only the ability to erect good houses but, more importantly, "intelligence, self-mastery, skill" and a full understanding of the intellectual and moral significance of manual labor.[9] All careful, intelligent work led to personal growth.

Washington earned a Hampton secondary school diploma, tried other professions, and returned to teach by the time the third Richard Morris Hunt building, a replacement for the fire-destroyed Academic Hall, was underway.[10] By now he surely understood that architecture—that is, purposeful design with conscious aesthetic attributes—articulates an institution's identity. It not only impresses visitors, it can empower its occupants, too. Washington would see to it that building photographs laced the articles and books he generated

Figure 3.2. Hampton's Virginia Hall.

to publicize Tuskegee because buildings exemplified permanence, power, and the school's highest ideals. As Richard Dozier has put it, self-respect or "race-pride," the goal that underlay Tuskegee's every endeavor, is best expressed in its buildings.[11] Therefore, Washington knew that he needed an architect, just as he knew that the race needed many black architects to make a place in the world. No wonder he wanted to gather Robert R. Taylor, the only academically trained black designer, into his fold.

BUILDING THE BEGINNING

By November 1892, when Taylor arrived at what had just been renamed the Tuskegee Normal and Industrial Institute, there was a substantial plant of a dozen or more brick and frame structures, many of them cottages or cabins that were used for shops, classrooms, and faculty and student housing. They occupied an abandoned plantation a mile from the center of the town. Even before classes began on Independence Day, 1881, in a church and a shanty closer to the town center, Washington had arranged the purchase of the hundred-acre Bowen farm. He needed the land to expand the basic secondary school program he had been hired to direct to what he wanted: agricultural and industrial programs to support an expanded school and to help students support themselves and to serve as a practicum for advancement. As teachers, they could pass these skills on to youngsters in rural backwaters. Washington and assistant principal Olivia A. Davidson gathered donations to purchase land, organizing entertainments, borrowing the down payment from a Hampton administrator, and traipsing through

Figure 3.3. Porter Hall.

New England the following summer for further contributions. At the first year's closing ceremonies, blacks and whites marched together from the town center to the Bowen farm to set a cornerstone on the foundations of the destroyed house. They named the new building for Alfred Haynes Porter, a Brooklyn minister who gave what he could.[12]

Porter Hall [Figure 3.3] was soon under way. Lumber that had been purchased on credit was on the grounds before the cornerstone ceremony. Lewis Adams, the influential black merchant and mechanic to whom the school owes its foundation, was in charge of the construction crew, volunteer and hired. Washington once observed a black master carpenter supervising a white volunteer who had been a slaveholder, surely a promise of the better times to come.[13] The Phelps Dodge Company gave a tin roof. Washington invited country people to come and explore the finished structure, which they did with trepidation, "treading lightly and cautiously, as if they were afraid they would hurt the floors." They touched doorknobs, blackboards, plaster walls and furniture, amazed that "all this would have been brought into existence for the benefit of Negroes."[14] Porter Hall would house academic and administrative components but not the farming or industrial operations.[15] Boys' industries and girls' mattress making would develop east of Porter, and cooking, sewing, dressmaking, millinery in several small structures, two of them the "dear cabins" left from plantation days. Students then dug a hillside basement under Porter for a brick dining hall, kitchen, and laundry. Porter's first floor contained offices, a library, reading room, some of the six classrooms and a guest bedroom. The chapel and more classrooms occupied the second level. A boys' dormitory was initially planned for the third floor, but this was reassigned to girls before the building

was finished.[16] Boys had to sleep in cold discomfort in off-site cabins where they earned starring roles in tales of the school's perilous beginnings. Porter also had a small printing office that signaled intentions.

Porter Hall was razed in 1905, its administrative functions having moved to a new generation of brick structures: its offices to Robert R. Taylor's Office Building; its classrooms to his Huntington Memorial Academic Building; its library first to Alabama Hall, then to the Principal's 1890 frame house, and, finally, to Taylor's Carnegie Library; its chapel to the Pavilion and then to Taylor's Chapel; and its girls' dormitory to Alabama Hall then a host of later buildings—Taylor's Huntington, Douglass, Tantum, and White halls among them. One visiting graduate regretted Porter's destruction since it was the seed of all that was now standing.[17]

Other buildings then accumulated in a line running east and west from Porter Hall along the northern edge of a narrow plateau, the buildings facing south across campus road and then across some flat land between the school's road and the

Figure 3.4. Drawing for Alabama Hall.

parallel public road [See 1897 Campus Plan]. The brick Alabama Hall girls' dormitory appeared west of Porter in 1884, and a little behind and below it, the name evoking Hampton's Virginia Hall. Alabama Hall [Figure 3.4] was planned in summer 1883 for a hundred boys but by the following February it too was given over to the girls, the boys now gaining Porter's third floor. Two framed drawings for Alabama Hall plus one for the Principal's cottage were exhibited in 1884 in New Orleans at the World's Cotton Exposition, shown with other student achievements in clothes, canned food, a bedstead, an essay on teaching, diagrammed sentences, mathematics and natural philosophy exams, and "inventional and geometric drawings."[18] Students helped make Alabama's door and window frames in the Slater Carpentry Shop under the direction of Raymond Thweatt.[19] Alabama Hall would acquire low wings by 1893 and a professional-seeming three-story addition with brick window hoods by 1896. In 1884 a water tower arrived just east of Porter. Then came, still further east, the brick Armstrong Hall boys' dormitory (1888), which was renamed in 1892 for the deceased Olivia Davidson and which also had classrooms and a larger printing shop.[20] Armstrong Hall was built by students under the direction of carpentry instructor William C. Brown "who also planned the building." Hampton graduate Warren Logan, who arrived in 1883 and spent his career at Tuskegee, remembered that Armstrong was the first building "for which the plans were made by the teacher of architectural drawing."[21] The *Southern Letter* credited Brown with a wood-frame lower annex of Alabama Hall, a barn, cottages, and a "rude pavilion" roofed with mulberry branches that held many more than Porter Hall's chapel. Buildings were now coming from drawings by black men, but not to the quality Washington would have known from Hampton. The *Southern Letter*, a monthly Tuskegee paper modeled on Hampton's *Southern Workman* and similarly aimed at Northern philanthropists, celebrated student and graduate successes as well as continuing construction. More donations were always needed because the school was not growing fast enough to supply all the requests for teachers. Further, there were more young people wanting entry than it could accommodate.

While Porter, Alabama, and Armstrong were underway, the school was also erecting a sawmill, foundry, blacksmith shop, and wooden structures for other trades in an industrial zone at the eastern end of the campus road with the entrance nearby. An 1883 grant from the newly founded John F. Slater Fund for the Education of Freedmen supplied the carpentry shop and water tower already mentioned, plus a sewing machine, mules, a wagon, and nine months of a farm manager's salary.[22] Black and white townspeople would come to this entrance to buy goods—brooms, bricks, mattresses, wagons—plus services: getting their horses shod and handbills printed. The foundry and machine shops repaired agricultural machinery for the region as well as the Tuskegee farm, there being reportedly no other such help within thirty miles.[23] Washington once termed Tuskegee an "industrial village" that, he claimed, stood on the ground where slaves were once bought and sold.[24] Slave sales are otherwise unknown in this particular spot, but "industrial village" nods to well-known New England examples with a reputation for benign paternalism and social progress.

Tuskegee's growing industries quickly replicated the range of technical services that slaves had provided on the larger plantations. Founder Lewis Adams had learned shoemaking, harness making and tinsmithing as a slave and after Emancipation built a solid business in town, gaining widespread respect and some political power. Washington was referring to Adams when he wrote that "a Negro mechanic manufactures the best tinware, the best harness, the best boots and shoes, and it is common to see his store crowded with white customers from all over the country. His word or note goes as far as that of the whitest man."[25] Adams, who would head the Tuskegee tinsmithing division, remembered the region's range of slave skills. Macon County had twenty-five carpenters, eleven blacksmiths, three painters, two wheelwrights, three tinsmiths, two tanners, and fourteen shoemakers, and they lived better than their brethren, sometimes independently. Even though owners might contract their services, Adams wrote, it was the artisans who knew their crafts' particulars and who carried out the work.[26] W. E. B. Du Bois noted the phenomenon in a 1902 report, *The Negro Artisan*. Slave carpenters, blacksmiths and machinists did specialized work in the plantation economy and for the nascent industrial one as well. Slave mechanics took the places of white ones in flourmills, sawmills, and railroad shops. Slave ironworkers manufactured weapons for Confederate soldiers while slave engineers ran the railroads that hauled the soldiers to the front. A black Chicago engineer who corresponded with Du Bois wondered why poor white boys would fight to maintain a system that had kept them from such good jobs.[27] Washington argued that tolerance and respect would grow as whites benefited from blacks who acquired the modern versions of traditional skills, but in reality black mechanics now had to compete directly with white ones. Washington's challenge was enormous.

BRICKS

Washington began Tuskegee's brick industry after deciding that cotton, his first notion for a cash crop, would do poorly in the school's hilly grounds with depleted soils. There were no brickmakers in the neighborhood so students could conjure up the stuff of their own shelter and sell it to others. The poetic resonance of self-construction out of the people's very earth appealed to donors and suggested the recipients' worth. From the institute's point of view, bricks memorialized foundational struggles. *Up From Slavery* details the repeated kiln failures and attendant despair upon trying to start brick manufacture. Washington joined the students, standing in knee-deep mud to help with the nastiest part of the labor and, reportedly, pawned his only precious possession, a watch, to finance the eventually successful burning. Challenges can lead to failure, Washington told students in Sunday night chapel talks, but perseverance eventually wins the day.

Brickmaking also emerges from others' accounts.[28] J. F. B. Marshall, the Hampton administrator who loaned Washington the farm's down payment, wrote that Tuskegee's hills had excellent clay along with a woodlot for fuel and that he knew that the young men were impatient to begin their new building. The only impediment was the two hundred dollars needed to hire a foreman. The Slater Fund soon met the salary of H. Clay Ferguson, a Hampton-trained farm manager with brickmaking experience. As then-student William Gregory remembered it, the first bricks were made in the deep valley west of Alabama Hall between Robert R. Taylor's Tantum and Douglass halls. "The bricks were carried to the place of building in wheelbarrows, in our arms, in sacks, and any old way. This was more like fun for us than like work. We worked day and night."[29] Town merchant and neighbor Edward Varner, who had donated equipment from his own abandoned brick business, purchased most of the first kiln. Perhaps the molds that Varner had given the school had made bricks for the pre-war colonnaded Varner mansion, Grey Columns.

Brick buildings continued after Alabama Hall. By the end of 1892 there were the brick foundations of the wooden barn, the three-story brick Armstrong Hall boys' dormitory, a Forge and Blacksmith Shop (1889) that remains as Tuskegee's oldest standing building, as well as the three-story Cassedy Industrial Building and the Steam Laundry, discussed below. By 1893 Taylor's brick buildings were beginning. Tuskegee's bricks would also be used for buildings across Macon County and in the adjacent counties. In 1900 a Tuskegee graduate, A. J. Wilborn, purchased 100,000 Tuskegee bricks to build a store on the courthouse square.[30] William Gregory would lead the brickmaking division until 1919, when he retired. The institute tried to continue its manufacture for a few years but in the end closed the division.

Brick buildings at a nascent black institution would have signaled permanence and ambition as did brick buildings at young white schools. For a black school, however, the meaning would have greater intensity—the implied permanence visibly challenging attacks or threats thereof that white schools did not face. Washington understood that brick buildings for African Americans had special powers because they denied justifications for discrimination. "My friends, there is an unexplainable influence about a black man's living in a brick house that you cannot understand," Washington said to a teachers' convention. A row of brick houses in Birmingham occupied by Germans told the world that these were not a lazy or shiftless people.[31] Brick would say the same about African Americans. On another occasion he addressed the same point with "a two-story brick house that has been paid for."[32] Or on still another, "A white man knows the Negro that lives in a two-story brick house whether he wants to or not. When a black man is the largest taxpayer in a community, his neighbors will not object very long to his voting and having his vote honestly counted," an optimistic forecast indeed considering the perils of jealousy and the civil rights battles that lay ahead.[33] Washington once recalled hearing poor whites discuss driving "that nigger school teacher"(himself)from town. He could not impress these people with Latin, geometry, or physics, but brick Alabama Hall turned the tide. "The building brought them and they became our best friends." Friction, Washington's word, would surely vanish when the prejudiced white man saw that the black man that he despised owned a brick house.[34] Washington always assumed the best from the white world around him, or at least he did when in print or before an audience.

Brickmaking and brick masonry continued to model the virtues of simplicity, humility, thoroughness, and cooperation that would inevitably lead to racial success, at least in Washingtonian rhetoric. "We can succeed in putting up good buildings only in proportion as every one performs well his part in the erection of each building. We can succeed only in proportion as the student who makes the mortar, who lays the bricks, puts his whole conscience into that work, and does it just as thoroughly as it is possible for him to do it." The student who is mixing mortar to the best of his abilities must do it still better the following day. The student who is laying bricks must do so even better the following week.[35] The Principal then charged students with protecting the buildings that kindly white friends had given them and that their predecessors had erected. He was proud when he heard an older student reprimand a younger one for graffiti. "'Don't do that. That is our building. I helped put it up.'" [36]

In the end, Tuskegee's brick industry lent the campus much of its visual as well as moral character. Varied colors coming from different firings spatter the walls of its historic structures—ochres, siennas, deep reds, russets, and shiny purples. Robert R. Taylor wrote that the colors—"light cherry" to "dark brown" and "dark purple," depending on the burning—mixed in the eye to make a "harmonious and characteristic color" for each wall's "strong and rough surface." [37] The mottling and pitting that holds the hues brings tactility to flat wall planes that set off the engaging textures that remind the viewer of the Tuskegee ideal of self-construction. Taylor celebrated the homemade bricks' richness with careful proportioning of the wall surfaces, their sharp-cut openings and corners, and modest or even restrained detailing. The smooth-surfaced, evenly colored purchased bricks that were used sporadically in the 1920s and systematically from the 1930s continued to unify the scene, the reds intensifying the surrounding soil's pink cast in contrast to the flat greens of grass and trees. Bricks unified the campus visually and attached themselves to the school's history. At the fiftieth anniversary, in 1931, the former head of the academic department, by then a college president elsewhere, remembered that Tuskegee's rolling hills were once stripped to red sand and clay. But patient, persistent effort spurred by a craving for beauty had transformed this dismal scene into "vistas of verdant loveliness that delight the eye and rest the spirit. Willing hands, still in the training, have reared these buildings from the soil on which they stood, laying the foundations of character

and competence on which a race must rise." [38] The rhetoric still served. Washington on his own and then armed with Taylor had succeeded in bonding unskilled student labor, design proficiency, and high purpose into visual charm, or even "beauty," as a route to a higher civilization.

DESCRIBING THE DREAM

Brick would continue to serve as visual identity, substituting for the formal planning that might have performed the same role at a school with flat grounds. Grand planning with centralizing axes that control relationships among buildings were the era's preferred way of pulling an ad hoc assemblage into an image of collective purpose. But Tuskegee's structures had to be placed wherever they could fit on a series of irregularly shaped, steep sided plateaus. Even so, visitors, even those from the earliest days, admired the physical plant for more than tidiness and evident prosperity that so differed from the decrepit countryside around it. Northern travelers found it truly lovely. As early as 1885 the *New York Evening Post* contrasted the school's "beauty" to the town's dilapidation. [39] A decade later, one could read that the institute's new buildings dwarfed nearby plantation houses, "monuments to a past once thought glorious." Tuskegee was "modern" and clearly the better for it. [40] The Arts and Crafts entrepreneur Elbert Hubbard overdid his enthusiasm: It was an "ecstasy in brick and mortar" as Athens was an "ecstasy in marble." [41] The more moderate *Outlook* noted "a group of buildings which for architectural beauty and for efficiency of design would be a credit to any college in the land." [42] Only one, a traveling Englishman, missed the "orderly" layout of unnamed Northern institutions. "Buildings are dotted here and there over the somewhat rugged site, with small eye to picturesqueness or dignity of general effect." But he found the students' "little cubicles," their rooms, "simple, neat, clean, fairly comfortable, but entirely devoid of luxury or upholstery," presumably a virtue, and he admired Taylor's Carnegie Library and the Chapel for, respectively, "architectural ambition" and "real originality of design." "Everywhere one sees the evidence of a great organizing capacity, a great inspiring force, a tireless, indomitable singleness of purpose—in short, a true magnanimity."[43]

As for the black press, the Tuskegee campus earned plaudits even when the Northern paper was opposed to the Washington's approach to racial remedy. The *Voice of the Negro* admired the "magnificently disciplined" students and "the vast sweep of the plant" even though it deemed the buildings "poor and crude for the most part." But even crude buildings served as advertising, it noted, because the students had built them.[44] The article then faulted Tuskegee's dependence on industrial capitalism and deplored the concentration of power in one man. Editor J. Max Barber supported the oppositional Niagara movement then challenging Washington's leadership. Barber's views would eventually cost him his profession as Washington hounded the apostate beyond any job that would give him a platform.[45]

There are other accounts to show the effectiveness of Washington's carefully orchestrated spectacle, particularly for those who were uninvolved in intraracial politics. Julia Ward Howe, whose recollections give us the *dramatis personae* and the Tuskegee script even though they are short on the settings, evokes the situation. In 1894 the seventy-five-year-old reformer from Connecticut performed the "unwelcome but imperative duty" of traveling from Atlanta to see what needed to be seen. Howe and six other women arrived in the dark after a discouraging trip through a desolate coun-

tryside. "What had we found? 'What went ye out in the wilderness for to see?' We found order, thrift, industry, good English, good manners, and good taste. . . Here was a spot taken out of the wilderness, redeemed from barrenness by intelligent labor." The guests were given the full treatment—dinner with Mr. and Mrs. Washington that had been prepared by a cooking class and then evening chapel with "thousands" of cheerful students and teachers, a flattering invitation to speak, the Chautauqua salute, spirituals. The following morning the visitors reviewed the day's schedules, toured farms, classes, and shops, and enjoyed the aura of contented human activity with happy, attractive, uniformed students performing their assigned tasks. "Truly, in leaving Tuskegee and going into the ordinary world I did not feel that I stepped up from a lower level but rather down from a height of serious endeavor and purpose."[46]

Students' memories do not differ that greatly from visitors even though they had far more opportunity for disillusion to set in. William H. Holtzclaw published an account of the privations in which he was raised and, then, the dazzling splendor before him as he arrived at the fabled place. "There was Armstrong Hall, the most imposing structure I had ever seen. Then came Alabama Hall, where the girls lived. How wonderful! I could hardly believe that I was not dreaming, and I was almost afraid I should awake."[47] Elizabeth Wright, another early arrival, was more analytical. "I was very young and coming from the country where I had never seen a comfortable dwelling, the sight of the large brick and wooden buildings made a lasting impression upon my mind. It was a hard thing for me to understand how a man of my race could have acquired so much and I did not comprehend it clearly until I was out of school."[48] Wright decided to become the kind of woman that Washington was as a man and, like Holtzclaw, founded a "little Tuskegee" after trials and violence that Washington himself did not have to endure. Wright's school was Voorhees Industrial Institute, begun in 1897 in Denmark, South Carolina. Holzclaw's Utica Normal and Industrial Institute, founded in 1903, is now part of Mississippi's junior college system. John W. Robinson, who came in the mid 1890s, remembered "how little and insignificant I felt when I entered the school-grounds and was told that all those buildings and all those acres of grounds were a part of the Tuskegee Institute." The reality behind the rumor was "almost overpowering."[49] A photograph of Robinson and his collection of African textiles, a byproduct of his "little Tuskegee" in Togo, is in Chapter 6. In 1988 the novelist V. S. Naipaul interviewed an elderly man who had arrived in 1913. "When I came here and saw all these buildings, and the dining hall and the tablecloths, fourteen students to a table, girls on one side, boys on the other, it was like Heaven—I'd never seen anything like it."[50] This epiphany would have happened in Tompkins Dining Hall with its vast high-ceilinged space that a country child could hardly have imagined before seeing it. Mealtime rituals with timing, tablecloths, sitting together and conversing, would have been a remarkable sight for any back-country child, even without the architectural grandeur.

Tuskegee could also impress the city-bred and, as well, those from distant lands. In 1895, Lewis Smith took a train from Chicago to the Atlanta Exposition, cashed in his return ticket, and traveled on to Alabama, falling in love with the countryside as he went. "Tuskegee was a surprise to me; it surpassed my fondest hope. The majestic buildings, the monuments to the fidelity and building skill of past classes, the well-designed landscape architecture, made me

feel that I had at last found the place where I could be prepared for real life."[51] Smith became a butter maker at an Illinois dairy plant. Rash Behari Day, a Bengali Hindu, came around 1908 to the "very beautifully planned" Tuskegee because it offered better opportunities in electrical engineering than Hampton did. Years later, Day commented on the good roads, attractive buildings, and well-kept lawns, gardens, and trees in this distant outpost.[52] As late as the 1930s, Cleveland Eneas, a Bahamian who had been sent to learn the printer's trade, found himself in "acres of sheer beauty." The rolling lawns, flowering shrubbery, paved roads, sidewalks, and "correctly spaced and majestic buildings" made an "oasis in the desert," a "magnificent spectacle." Decades later, when he was writing, Eneas could see the school as a paramilitary establishment, but he remained permanently attached to "the sweet, sweet spirituality abiding in that place." Despite the annoying controls, "Here was where the starch was placed in our backbones."[53] Another student of that era wrote that the grounds were inspirational for teachers, students, and visitors. They were "classrooms" for nature study: botany, home flower gardening, lawn care, and professional landscaping. Graduates' home gardens showed the Tuskegee-instilled aesthetic as a way of life.[54] The institute's second principal, Robert Russa Moton, thought Tuskegee more beautiful in 1931 than in the Washington era. The "transformation of red sand hills to a garden of beauty," he thought, was "the Negro's artistic contribution to civilization."[55] Even in 1988, Tuskegee impressed the well-traveled V. S. Naipaul. The ensemble was "an achievement on the American scale: scores and scores of Georgian dark-red brick buildings set about the landscaped hilly grounds."[56] Naipaul thought he was seeing the school through the eyes of its first arrivals because he knew the joy his parents would have felt if their people, the Indian minority of Trinidad, had such a place. For those who had little of the world's goods and less hope of achieving them, Naipaul reminds us, Tuskegee would have appeared "dreamlike" indeed.

WOOD

By 1883, when carpenter Raymond Thweatt arrived, Tuskegee was equipping itself for wood construction as well as brick. As brickmaker William Gregory recalled, during the early years "We could do almost everything in our own way but build a house. Whenever we wanted a house, we had to get someone from the outside."[57] In 1884 students were helping Thweatt make window and door casings for Alabama Hall.[58] Soon, a number of small structures, including a cottage for Washington and his family, joined Porter Hall and the three repaired outbuildings that had come with the land. Boston donors provided a steam-powered sawmill in 1886 so the school could turn its own trees into lumber.[59] Two years later the *Southern Letter* was asking for a mortising machine so it could make doors. Students were already making flooring, ceilings, and all parts of a house except for doors and window sash.[60] Students then built Hamilton Cottage, a two-story frame girls' dormitory near Alabama Hall, the name honoring a Hampton and Tuskegee musician who organized traveling quartets. Hamilton's facade would fix the building line along the west side of the girls' quadrangle that eventually emerged in 1910. Hampton carpentry graduate John W. Carter and his students built a two-story frame house for Washington in early 1890. Washington's second wife, Olivia Davidson, their newborn son, and two older children barely escaped with their lives when their cottage burned. The 1890 Principal's House was the second building south

of the internal campus road after the brick forge. It faced north towards Alabama Hall, internalizing the campus from the public road, and provided a view towards the campus and distant barn.[61] After 1899, when Taylor finished The Oaks, Washington's brick house on his own land across the public road, the library that had moved from Porter to Alabama Hall would occupy the Carter-built house until the Carnegie Library was finished.

Just as the offices, chapel, classrooms, and dormitory that had once fit into Porter Hall were dispersing into industrial, residential, and academic zones, farming also moved to the northwest corner of the first land purchase. This was on the far side of a deep valley west of Alabama Hall and Hamilton Cottage, the nascent girls area. In 1889 the school built a frame barn on a brick foundation at the valley's upper end, a site that could be seen in the distance from Washington's 1890 house. Connecticut donor Moses Pierce, who also helped with early land purchases, must have funded it because he chided Washington for asking for a brick barn. "Wood serves in our climate, why not in yours?"[62] No one mentioned the possibility of arson if indeed that was on Washington's mind. A cupola provided broad views in all directions for students willing to climb to the top.[63] In 1895 the wooden barn burned with significant loss of animal life, as Catalog 21 discusses. Pierce may have funded the farming area windmill and water tank but probably not the brick dairy, recently destroyed, that was erected ten years later. There milk was turned into cheese and butter using the advanced equipment in a laboratory-like environment.[64] Washington always sought modern technologies because he wanted students to see that scientific agriculture offered opportunities that the pre-industrial drudgery they had always known lacked. Brick barns came only after Taylor calculated the savings on maintenance.

Tuskegee also acquired a collection of plain or ornamented wooden buildings that lent domestic scale and intimacy since they were scattered, eventually, among the more imposing brick ones. During the 1890s there was a primary school in the valley near Alabama Hall that was replaced in 1901 by a larger and more progressive model in an adjacent residential area, and, discussed below, a bible school that was designed by architecture faculty from Columbia University. There was a substantial house for senior girls, Parker Cottage. As early as 1883 there was a barracks for boys' housing like ones for girls at Hampton. A second was built by 1900.[65] There were also on-campus teachers' cottages, the Taylor-designed Pinehurst Hospital, and a nearby house for the physician. But frame buildings, which are hard to maintain through tough times, have all been lost.

One wooden structure to which Washington attached particular significance is the four-room Practice Cottage (1895), a "model" farmer's home set close to the public road to inspire passersby. Small groups of senior girls rotated through, living on their own with a housekeeping budget. Since the brick Agricultural Building was soon built on its west and the brick Carnegie Library on its east, the Practice Cottage ended up "in the shadow of the massive brick buildings which surround it" according to Washington's fond understanding. It had "accidentally strayed in from a country road," complete with a "trim and well-kept air such as all country homes can have, no matter how poor and simple they may be."[66] Washington always urged interior decor that farm wives could make from found materials so that children would be raised with cheer and stimulation. George Washington Carver expanded on this directive by developing

Tuskegee clay-based paints that he displayed as color-coordinated samples so graduates could live in style on a tight budget. Guests were invited to take a meal the girls had prepared with their future families in mind and to purchase for their summer homes the cretonne-covered barrel chairs the girls had made.

Growing the Campus Core

The Tuskegee plant had been developing along an east-west axis, actually southeast to northwest, along an internal road with an entrance and the industries in the east. Moving west one found then Armstrong Hall boys' dormitory, Porter and a wind-powered water tank in the middle, and Alabama Hall girls' dormitory and by 1890 Washington's frame home in the west. A now-lost plan of the school grounds was shown at the Montgomery state fair in November 1886.[67] The campus road connecting the eastern entrance, with nearby industrial buildings and boys housing, to the Principal's house and the girls' housing in the west ran parallel to the public road and served daily life and special occasions. Students marched this route to and from meals, classes, and evening chapel. On grand occasions such as graduations or parades to welcome the distinguished, they marched it again. For one late night arrival a "thousand" students and teachers stood aside the road waving flaming pine knots to welcome a guest's carriage at the eastern end. They then fell in behind the vehicle to accompany him to the Principal's house in the west. The visitor was the ailing Hampton Principal Samuel Chapman Armstrong, immobilized by a stroke.[68] American presidents came, too. For William McKinley's appearance in December 1898, when many were angry that he did not send federal troops to quell the Wilmington riot a few weeks before, a reviewing

Top, Figure 3.5. A Tuskegee parade for President McKinley, 1898: waiting for the parade in front of Principal's 1890 house with McKinley in center of porch. Bottom, Figure 3.6. Disbanding the McKinley parade, eastern campus, 1898. Drawing students' float left center.

stand stood in front of Washington's house. [Figures 3.5, 3.6] On that great day, students marched in lines, west to east, carrying sugar canes topped by cotton bolls, mistletoe, and palms. They also rode on floats that illustrated trades, one of them being architectural drawing. A few showed the poorer production methods in use before Tuskegee's better methods took hold.[69] Thanking students for their contributions, Washington noted that they had built well considering that they had never seen floats. In 1905, when Theodore Roosevelt stopped by, sixty-one floats passed by, students demonstrating their newly won skills on moving wagons.[70]

During the succeeding decades more buildings would accumulate along Tuskegee's internal road. The frame Phelps Hall Bible Training School, designed by Columbia University professors William Robert Ware and A. D. F. Hamlin as the first of the Phelps Stokes sisters' six donations, was constructed from 1890 to 1892. Ware had founded the architecture course at MIT that trained Taylor and then went on to found another at Columbia. Phelps Hall would stand until the 1980s after it was moved in 1933 to a spot next to Rockefeller Hall. Taylor's brick Science Hall, later Thrasher, was dedicated in 1893 even though it remained unfinished for years. In 1901 his Carnegie Library with a projecting columnar portico appeared next to Washington's frame house and, subsequently, the Office Building east of Washington's frame house, Huntington Memorial Academic Building on the north or older side of the road, and, by 1909, the short ends of White Hall girls' dormitory and the monumental domed Tompkins Dining Hall. The entire row, excepting Phelps Hall and the Principal's House, were brick. All brick buildings but one, Huntington Memorial Academic Building, survive. Building sites on each side of the road were stag-

gered so that the south-facing structures address the gaps between the north-facing buildings and the north-facing buildings address the gaps between the south-facing ones [1897 Campus Plan, page 64]. There was a rhythm, like giant footsteps marching in alternation—left and right, north and south of the roadbed—that enlarges the act of walking. The strategy differs from the more usual symmetry that sets buildings so they face each other but that also makes the route more static. Too many buildings are missing today to experience this, but some sense remains of the road as processional route as well as a historic core.

THE PAVILION AND NEGRO CONFERENCE

One early structure that was not in either line along the campus road but, rather, on leased land across the public road, deserves attention even though it does not survive. The Pavilion was a "rude temporary shed" with backless bench seating spiked onto posts fixed in the earth. Carpenter William C. Brown assembled it in the mid 1880s. The walls were of rough boards draped with bunting, Spanish moss, and palmetto leaves on special occasions. The Pavilion held many for graduations and, after 1891, the annual Negro Conference—Washington's outreach effort, and one not borrowed from Hampton—to any farmer who could get there.[71] Tuskegee offered dinner. The white Tuskegee publicist Max Bennett Thrasher described the scene that mesmerized him and many later visitors. Late arrivals crowded the doors and windows "like bees about the mouth of a hive," shutting out the dusky light within. Attendees had come by oxen, steer, bull, mule and horse in "as strange a collection of beasts and vehicles, I am sure, as was ever brought together." Women wore homespun dresses and "ludicrous" headgear. Men in overalls and collarless shirts emphasized their remarks from the floor by pounding ox-goads on the ground. The many elderly "aunties" and "uncles" could speak as they saw fit as long as they did not complain about matters that could not be changed.[72] Thrasher's terms might seem demeaning if they did not also reflect Washington's affection. The Principal admired the generation formed in slavery and encouraged it to work towards owning land. Like a camp meeting but without the hellfire and damnation, Washington exhorted his audience to effort and new hopes by interspersing practical instructions with success stories taken from those standing in front of him. On other occasions observers charged the Principal as "incorrigible" in his "unscientific open-handedness" with those whose best days were behind them. He cheerfully allowed himself to be conned regularly by an elderly man who claimed he was fattening a turkey for the Principal's Thanksgiving dinner.[73] Washington is often charged with regularizing behavior, as if behavior under his

complete control was all that he wanted. One needs to revisit his openheartedness. The Pavilion would remain after the Negro Conferences moved to the Chapel. An 1899 bird's-eye view shows an intention to rebuild it with clapboard walls, framed sash windows, and a monitor roof even though by then the Chapel could be used for large meetings. The Pavilion burned in 1918 but was not rebuilt.

JOHN H. WASHINGTON BUILDS

Several structures from the pre-Taylor era, such as the wooden boys' hospital and Willow Cottage or the brick Cassedy Industrial Hall (1891) and Steam Laundry (1892) were designed and built by John H. Washington, the Principal's older brother.[74] John H. had also attended Hampton but later than his sibling. He graduated in 1879 and spent five years with a federal engineering unit where he presum-

Figure 3.7. Cassedy Industrial Hall.

Figure 3.8. Steam Laundry, third floor added.

Laundry's very name is redolent of Washington's exhortation to "put brains and skill into the common occupations of life" so African Americans could compete. White men with steam laundries were displacing the "old Negro woman and her washtub." Black men who once monopolized barbering were losing out to white "tonsorial artists" just as black yard men were falling to white "landscape gardeners," black whitewashers to white "house decorators," and black "mammies" to white "nurses." The Steam Laundry was making its claim to the race's future through modernization of traditional tasks.[75]

ably enlarged his construction skills. John H. first served Tuskegee as business manager and then as Director of Industries, organizing the boys' trades programs. Photographs of Cassedy Industrial Hall and the Steam Laundry show sturdy brick boxes with apparent chimneys or ventilators extending wall buttresses above the building line and organizing facades into a grid that extends to punctuate the skyline. Cassedy had an irregular bay scansion that is inexplicable from the exterior, therefore intriguing, since it implies varied processes within. The drawing rooms on the third floor were behind the arched windows. The Steam Laundry was built at two stories with the twin buttressing strips between the windows that were capped with chimney-like pinnacles that read against the sky. The building soon gained a third story, the twin buttressing continuing vertically. But all but a few of the pinnacles were lost in the expansion (Fig. 3.9). The Steam

Washington must have realized soon that it took more than a Hampton-trained builder, even his brother, to produce a distinguished campus. A plan for a tool building drawn by John H. Washington lacks wall thickness, apertures, and the sense of materiality that a professional would bring even to a simple project.[76] John H. also lacked essential interpersonal skills. Rockham Holt, a biographer of the Tuskegee agriculturalist George Washington Carver, said that John H. tried to persuade his brother to fire Carver. John H. had "little understanding of the man of science, nor did he wish to get understanding. Being antipathetic to the Carver type of mind, he could not admit there was any good in it."[77] Taylor would also be on the receiving end of this personality. John H. would pepper him with memos—tirades they often seemed—about things done or undone. A visiting staff person's assessment was most direct. "I am very sorry for Mr. J. H. and in spite of his temper I like him and supposed I was on the best footing with him. In his highly nervous condition I do not believe him capable of self control and his responsibility is too heavy for him."[78] As children, John H. had protected his brother, breaking in his rough-woven shirts to save him the pain.[79] John H. worked as a miner, sending money to his brother to help him at Hampton. Booker T. Washington, in turn, protected his brother, crediting him with record keeping, the boys' drill, the band, apiculture, the poultry division, and fruit canning as well as many timely construction achievements. But the Principal must have known that he needed an architect, like Richard Morris Hunt, with native talent and the best training and who could work with others if he was to have a distinctive campus.

INDUSTRIAL EDUCATION

Washington needed an architect but he also needed a drawing instructor to elevate trades education to the national standards. Washington fixed his ambitions in industrial education early, seeing to it that a description of the brickyard, sawmill, and carpentry shop appeared in a national survey of the subject published in 1887 by the Commonwealth of Pennsylvania as it prepared to start its own schools. Industrial programs of the 1880s were rooted in those of the Imperial Technical School in Moscow as shown at exhibitions in Vienna (1873) and Philadelphia (1876).[80] Pioneering American programs at the University of Illinois and the St. Louis Manual Training School stemmed from Vienna. MIT's decade-long endeavor that closed before Taylor came, stemmed from Philadelphia.

The crucial idea underlying the Russian strategy was the revision of apprenticeship training by separating fundamental procedures from product manufacturing. This was done through a sequence of graded skills that were likened to the finger ex-ercises with which pianists gain dexterity. Skill sets were taught in a classroom setting rather than a shop and could be independent from specific craft applications. "Instruction rather than construction" would produce flexible, intellectually involved mechanics prepared for the coming technological changes in the industrial era. These newly inventive artisans could analyze complicated problems, devise solutions, and supervise others—becoming a technologically savvy management class geared to factory production.

The Moscow program specified conditions for instruction. Each trade must have its own classroom and shop and each shop must have tools and a workstation for every student. The course curriculum and daily study plans must be posted on shop walls for all to see. And drawing was each trade's foundation. Students drew plans and elevations of their projects before making models of them that, in turn, guided production. Drawing, then, functioned as a conceptual or, one might say, theoretical stage of making. The daughter of a Hampton industrial arts teacher, John Henry Jinks, remembered watching students draw furniture joints in her father's classroom. Students then made models, workbenches being substituted for drawing tables. Only then did they cross the hall to the carpentry shop to build actual joints under the carpentry teacher's direction. Jinks (1865–1930) was a family-trained English cabinetmaker who later studied industrial education at Pratt Institute and then, in 1896, came to Hampton.[81]

The practicum aspect of Tuskegee's industrial education, whether it be making tinware for the dining room or erecting buildings, has its own roots in "learning and labor" of many American schools of the nineteenth century. At Oberlin College, a bootstrap foundation of the 1830s, all students worked

Figure 3.9. Problem in Arithmetic. Normal students calculate number of bricks in Office Building walls, 1902.

four hours a day in the Manual Labor Department even if they were well off. The practice repeated in spirit a century later at another self-supporting school-community, Frank Lloyd Wright's Taliesin Fellowship. At Oberlin, women did the housekeeping while men skinned logs and erected buildings. But everyone farmed and everyone incorporated their experiences into their literary studies by writing about them.[82] Oberlin, a pioneer interracial as well as coeducational college, would send black graduates to teach at Tuskegee but usually in the academic department, not boys' industries.

Oberlin's writing-about-farming anticipates Washington's insistence that students "correlate" or "dove-tail" studies by writing about their trade assignments in English classes. Dovetailing could mean merging drawing as well as writing throughout the curriculum. One traveler watched night students in an arithmetic class calculate the cubic yards of earth needing to be removed for the Carnegie Library foundations. They figured the area from stakes in the ground and then studied Taylor's drawings to get other dimensions. Each student then explained the excavation in a "neat scale drawing from which a particular builder could have worked."[83] They may also have written the lesson in an English class, integrating several systems of representation while learning some construction basics because, as future teachers, they might have to build their own schools. And, as teachers-to-be, they were learning abstract processes through direct experience and, therefore, how to bring such understanding to others.

No wonder teachers in the Academic Department could be found roaming the shops at day's end to find subjects for the next day's lessons.[84]

Frances Benjamin Johnston photographed twin dovetailing assignments in 1902. Teachers-to-be measured walls of the Office Building while it was under construction, perhaps sketching them as well, so they could figure the brick numbers. Johnston also recorded the classroom equivalent. Here, younger students were solving an arithmetic problem about bricks that was written on the blackboard. A stack of wooden blocks provided visualization. The most common dovetailing exercise was that of describing a new trades technique for an English class or, at year's end, to a commencement audience. Writing, talking, drawing, and measurement assured replicable comprehension even if it also diverted English classes from the literature that the college-educated teachers were yearning to teach. The academic faculty complained that dovetailing tilted Tuskegee towards narrow vocational education, but Washington insisted on its worth. Washington thought that boys should write about the design and construction of a model house and girls about its decoration and furniture. No one need write about bravery, crime in the cities, or the landing of the Pilgrims.

Tuskegee's pedagogy was in some part simply

Figure 3.10. Problem in Brickmasonry: arithmetic with blocks as aids, 1902.

progressive education. Washington would have known such phrases as "learning by doing," "from the concrete to the general," and "head, hand, and heart" from Hampton and, as well, from his colleague and wife, Olivia A. Davidson, who had studied at a Massachusetts teachers' college. Donald Generals has argued that Washington was a devotee of the early nineteenth century educators Johann Heinrich Pestalozzi and Friedrich Froebel, applying their reforms before John Dewey did. And Bettina Berch has suggested that Frances Benjamin Johnston's Hampton photographs of 1899 underscored the school's progressive pedagogy rather than the training in drudgery that some have charged. Berch argues that the photographs that the Museum of Modern Art published in 1966 were selected to support this widespread misinterpretation.[85] Perhaps W. E. B. Du Bois and his intellectual heirs gained polemical clarity by reading Washington's disinterest in classical studies as a cynical bargain with whites to keep blacks in agricultural and industrial serfdom. But Washington followed Hampton's lead and put that icon of progressivism, a kindergarten, in Tuskegee's practice school. This was the third Alabama kindergarten and it turned institute children into avid adventurers in learning, according to Warren Logan, a long-time Tuskegee administrator. Tuskegee children did not have "the indifference and even repugnance to textbooks we hear of as common in white schools."[86] Washington, for his part, routinely fed his enthusiasm: while it took the white race "two or three thousand years" to get to the present level of civilization, black children, who had "the advantage of all the mistakes the white race has been so long learning" and who were "born into this thing," were on the right path at the start.[87] Washington had cleverly subverted the widespread racist assumption that the black race would forever trail the white one because of a late start in climbing some imagined ladder of civilization.

Educational reformer Johann Heinrich Pestalozzi had first promoted manual training as early industrial education to help poor children gain marketable skills. But he soon came to view it as appropriate for the well-to-do because handwork, he found, clarified thought. Interlocking "head and hand" created an independent, thinking citizenry well prepared for democracy. In the American racial context, manual training for younger children and industrial education for the older were sufficiently ambiguous in their implications to suggest what the auditor wanted to hear, as August Meier has shown. When the pedagogy was applied to black people, the overtly racist could hear discipline for caste-bound agricultural and industrial workers or "Schooling for the New Slavery," as the title of Donald Spivey's critique puts it.[88] The merely paternalistic might understand industrial education as a route to economic independence for the downtrodden. As Raymond Wolters has observed, immigrants in the Northern cities welcomed industrial education as an upward propulsion to better wages—no offense meant, none taken.[89] Finally, racial liberals or even integrationists could see industrial education as right for all—black and white, rich and poor.[90] An early history of the American Missionary Association's educational efforts claimed that even prestigious Northern colleges deemed industrial education essential to any liberal arts curriculum.[91]

Washington's commitment to industrial education was also pragmatic financially. The John F. Slater Fund for the Education of Freedmen, which had supported Tuskegee during its critical first years, promoted trades learning with increasing vigor. The Slater Fund would provide Taylor's salary when he came and, about the same time, its directors decided to concentrate support on a few black schools rather than many. Washington intended that Tuskegee be among the select. The Slater Fund has been accused of pushing industrial work for caste-defining purposes while lessening support for black collegiate work, as if industrial training were a lesser nurture for a supposedly lesser people. But the Slater Fund was also proud that African Americans were achieving at higher levels. In 1893 the fund reported that there were two and a quarter million literate African Americans of which two hundred and forty seven were studying in European universities. There were already seven black colleges, two hundred fifty lawyers, and seven hundred forty doctors—proof of black ability.[92]

Washington has long been faulted for low educational standards in his industrial as well as academic programs and for using his prestige to divert funding from collegiate studies at other institutions, exacerbating the racial divide.[93] But one could also argue that he had to deal with virulent racism all around him to get any kind of education that would help the destitute to a better life. Many whites believed that the barest schooling "ruined" black workers by encouraging expectations beyond their abilities and opportunities. In addition, public money was thought wasteful for black children because they were supposedly incapable of abstract thought or the independent judgment citizenship required. These views were increasingly enforced by violence or the threat thereof as well as by neglect. The prejudice was so strong that historian Raymond Wolters was surprised that any education, even the industrial, could survive at all.[94] A fuller accounting might find Tuskegee's achievements outweighing its institutional flaws or even its theoretical limitations. This is the situation that Booker T. Washington would navigate and in which Robert R. Taylor would participate as architect, buildings and grounds director and, especially, as industrial teacher and administrator. He was part of a success where, perhaps, none should have been.

ARCHITECTURAL, MECHANICAL DRAWING

In November 1891 Washington announced plans to add architecture, surveying, and "other higher branches" to the technical side of the industrial programs.[95] Perhaps he had already heard of the MIT student that could bring this ambition to fruition. Washington actually hired two drawing teachers in 1892, Taylor for architectural drawing and "principles of woodworking" and William Eugene Hutt from the St. Louis Manual Training School for mechanical drawing and "principles of metal work." The St. Louis school's director C. M. Woodward recommended Hutt in response to Washington's solicitation for African American talent.[96] A Woodward-written article found among Washington's papers says that his new type of industrial teacher was "almost an artist" yet "somewhat of a scientist," a man as able with words as with tools and drawing pens but whose shop had the discipline of a scientific laboratory. Industrial education was an independent endeavor, Woodward wrote, with its own moral and aesthetic values that fed students' spirits. "The consciousness of growing power, both mental and manual, gives a satisfaction which throws a charm over every department of school work," a point of view that Washington and Taylor would heartily share.[97] Hutt did not work out, but his hiring illuminates Washington's vision.

Tuskegee practiced some level of architectural drawing from the start. Carpenters and masons had to be able to read drawings even if they could not make them. Tuskegee's Hampton-trained carpentry teachers of the 1880s must have known something of drawing because, as we have seen, three student drawings for buildings under construction plus "inventional and geometric drawings" were exhibited in New Orleans as early as 1884.[98] Four years later, the Hampton-trained William C. Brown, carpentry foreman and architectural drawing teacher, was showing students how to dig foundations, plan and frame a house, and make out bills of lumber—these computations based on drawings.[99] Carpenter John W. Carter, the Hampton graduate who built Washington's 1890 frame house, taught drawing. His 1891 annual report said that students drew "simple objects," floor plans, sections, levels, and miters.[100] Drawing classes before 1891 (when Cassedy Hall was finished) took place in a converted henhouse left from the Bowen plantation that was at other times a girls' industrial building.[101] Architectural drawing was present before the architect arrived.

Drawing became a talisman of Washington's pedagogy since he saw it as the intellectual or executive part of making, as we have seen. "That drawing certainly did make a big fuss here," William Gregory recalled. "Why Mr. Washington even got so that there could be no cooking without drawing . . . We had to have drawings and blueprints of bricks, and everything. Some one was always coming in asking how to do these things, so these drawings and blueprints helped to show them just what we did."[102] Even John H. Washington advocated it. "When a student was able to make a detailed drawing of the article to be made, he has accomplished one-half of the work."[103] As Richard Dozier has put it in his analysis of Tuskegee's architectural education, drawing is an intellectual means of organizing and developing mechanical processes.[104] That drawing was essential to understanding, thus planning, had a special resonance for African Americans. Many, including Taylor, believed that slave artisans worked under white direction alone and therefore did not plan their own work, thereby not having the chance to develop the executive and business skills to parlay their crafts to prosperity. On a more immediate level, builders needed scaled drawings to estimate materials and costs, as John W. Carter had already shown.

TEACHERS BUILDING

Drawing as pedagogy quickly turned into drawing as a tool when Tuskegee graduates went to work. Tuskegee, the normal school, sent new teachers into the remote countryside to make schools where none had been before or to extend existing three-month sessions that were held in cabins and churches into more permanent institutions. Southern states provided slender salaries for black teachers for two or three months, but not the buildings because, the reasoning went, taxes collected from black people were insufficient. Recent scholarship has shown that taxes collected from black people were substantial but were diverted to white schools.[105]

Tuskegee-trained teachers, then, might have to erect schools or their own homes, both of which, Washington insisted, should be intelligently organized and attractively finished frame structures so they could be agents of uplift in bedraggled log and board hamlets. But short school terms meant that teachers should be able to draw and build as additional means of support. Preachers from Tuskegee's Phelps Bible Training School should also be carpentry-abled so they could fix up their crude churches or build them from scratch. They also might supplement meager incomes with Tuskegee-honed skills while simultaneously raising standards in farming and construction. Washington was clear. The ability to draw a house was as essential a life skill as building one, and building a house was as essential as growing one's own food. The Tuskegee graduate must do it all to be more than a "smart" man, one who parades useless knowledge but actually depends on others.[106] In 1908 Tuskegee held a school-wide competition for drawings for a four-room house to cost $600 or less. Entries were to include plans, specifications, and estimates. The entire student body was invited to enter but an architectural drawing student won it.

Teacherly construction achievements from the 1880s on are impressive because efforts under extraordinary circumstances resonate even if the level of architectural sophistication does not. Most of these were reported in the *Southern Letter*, Tuskegee's missive to future Northern patronage. In 1887, a graduate wrote that he could fix up his shambles of a schoolhouse because Tuskegee had skilled him to do that.[107] A "model Tuskegee graduate" of the class of 1891, C.A. Powell in Thompson, Alabama, skinned the logs from trees he had felled to erect his building.[108] N. E. Henry of the class of 1893 erected the first school in Ramer, Alabama.[109] Other teacher-built triumphs in Alabama during the 1890s were those by J. R. White in Clintonville, J. J. Smith in Crenshaw County, Ellen McCullough in Mason Grove, J. R. Wingfield in Jefferson, and C. E. Frederick in Orrville. Patrick Foster built and then taught in nearby Columbus, Georgia. Examples from further afield came from John T. Hollis, class of 1885, in Richland, Georgia; Lewis Ivey of the class of 1886 in Macon, Mississippi; John R. Pierce in High Point, North Carolina; and "SRM" in Paschal, Georgia. The *Southern Letter* often gave its front page to photographs such as the two-story turreted school in La Pine, Alabama, that had been drawn and erected by S. D. Rhoden. This energetic man, like many students, was unable to stay the full Tuskegee course, but he learned carpentry and architectural drawing, agriculture, and other pursuits before going out as a teacher. Ellen Mc-Cullough of Mason Grove, Alabama, whose letter appeared in July 1898, may not have been the only woman who built a schoolhouse. In November 1889 a "trained girl teacher" showed the neighborhood men how to do it and the following year a young lady in Lowndes County, Alabama, wrote that she too planned to build.[110] Washington rendered the image of a tool-wielding woman builder at mythic scale. "View the picture of a black woman teacher from the Tuskegee Institute teaching a school for weeks under an oak tree, then with hatchet and saw leading the way in the building of a school-house." Washington pitched her heroism as prelude to the fact that she would be paid a pittance and would have to close school when she and the older children planted cotton so that they might be able to afford a seven-month session the following year.[111] Schools were emblems of racial self-help, as G. W. McRae, of Pinkard, Alabama, made clear. "I want to build a school house that will be a monument to this county."[112] Taylor would be entering an established Tuskegee tradition when he and others designed small schools for the most deprived of American children.

Tuskegee graduates also extended the architectural and constructional message when they became industrial teachers. James A. McCarty, a plumbing graduate of 1890, performed his specialty at the West Virginia Colored Institute and then drew plans for the trades building where he would teach architectural and mechanical drawing.[113] Another account has McCarty and students building a water tank atop a seventy-seven-foot high steel frame for which he had also made the drawings.[114] Carpenter John H. Michael of the class of 1892, who began as an industrial teacher at Mt. Meigs, Alabama, designed and built for the Slater Industrial and State Normal School at Winston-Salem, North Carolina, using student workers so they could gain experience. Michael later taught carpentry and mechanical drawing at Knoxville College in Tennessee and supervised construction of the Negro Building at the Appalachian Exposition of 1910.[115] William J. Edwards, who arrived at Tuskegee in 1889, built the first structure for Snow Hill Normal and Industrial Institute in 1894 in Wilcox County, Alabama. And a Tuskegee graduate drew plans for Booker T. Washington Hall at the Robert Hungerford Institute in Eatonville, Florida. This was founded by Russell C. Calhoun and Mary Clinton Calhoun of the class of 1888.[116]

This pattern would continue after Taylor took charge, bringing the Tuskegee-honed point of view throughout the South. Gabriel B. Miller, who graduated in 1900 with a normal diploma, a certificate in carpentry, and "a fair knowledge of architectural as well as of mechanical drawing," established a carpentry division at the Fort Valley High and Industrial School in Georgia. He organized a shop, built the benches, and then set up a drawing room so that the students could work out projects in advance. Miller would soon submit plans and specifications for a two-and-a-half story girls' dormitory, an elementary school, and a large brick building, all of which he built.[117] Percy Dorman of the class of 1897 drew plans for and then built a hundred houses in Forth Smith, Arkansas. Dorman was also teaching, his students working with him on Saturdays and vacations.[118] In 1914 Tuskegee graduate R. A. Daly designed and built the "imposing and majestic" Bedford-Collins Memorial Hall at Snow Hill, Alabama. The three-story brick building, the largest in the county, reflected Taylor's Tuskegee classicism but in a naïve fashion.[119] Some would build without

also being teachers. John L. Webb, a 1912 carpentry graduate, became a Hot Springs, Arkansas, contractor who erected a large bathhouse. And James E. Wright of the class of 1908 was an architect and contractor in Brunswick, Georgia.[120]

And then there was Jailous Perdue, a man whose place in Tuskegee lore became a Washingtonian morality tale. Carpenter Perdue left Tuskegee in 1891 a "failure" because he could not do the academic work no matter how hard he tried. His academically successful older brother, Augustus C. Perdue, became a contractor in Muskogee, Oklahoma, but some six years later returned to work in the Tuskegee repair shop while earning a certificate in architectural and mechanical drawing. Augustus C. Perdue's drawings are in the Library of Congress. Jailous, the "failure," worked in Montgomery as a construction foreman and designed his own home, hiring Tuskegee men to build it. Jailous then became assistant foreman on Taylor's Chapel and The Oaks and then head foreman for the Carnegie Library, Rockefeller Hall, and Huntington Memorial Academic Building. He worked on White Hall and Tompkins Dining Hall and had "entire charge" of Milbank Agricultural Building. By 1916 Jailous Perdue would be teaching carpentry at the institute. "Thus it was that the man who failed succeeded and returned to the scene of his failure a success."[121] In true Tuskegee mode, further effort trumps "failure" and skills beyond the academic count in the end.

CHAPTER 4

TAYLOR AT TUSKEGEE

THE 1890S

Robert R. Taylor arrived at the recently re-named Tuskegee Normal and Industrial Institute in November 1892 as the only academically trained African American architect. Tuskegee offered a beginning architect unusual opportunities to design and erect buildings, but with heavy teaching responsibilities attached. Booker T. Washington must have emphasized the design part when recruiting Taylor, since the latter noted later that he had never wanted to teach and had rejected five such offers. (At Tuskegee, he stopped teaching as soon as he decently could). Designing and building Washington's expanding school, however, must have been so compelling to Taylor that he was willing to move to the deepest South.

During his first Tuskegee decade he showed signs that he could be what he eventually became, an effective and valued academic administrator. In fact, it was Taylor's educational agenda that first engaged his new community's awareness. The *Southern Letter* reported that "we are making an especial effort to raise the grade of our industrial work by supplementing and reinforcing it with mechanical drawing and teaching the students not only how to do the work, but the principles embodied in their respective lines . . . Under Mr. Taylor our students are not only taught how to do carpentry work, but how to draw the plans of simple buildings,

estimate their costs and make out bills of lumber, and are to taught to work out general problems in construction." [1]

The following month, the *Southern Letter* noted student enthusiasm for drawing cottage plans and estimating costs. Soon thirty-five older boys in the building trades were working in groups of eight around jerry-rigged tables—boards on sawhorses—on the top floor of Cassedy Hall. The program proved its worth within two months by furnishing plans for a flight of iron-supported stairs that could be built in the different divisions involved by working from blueprints. Pieces no longer had to be carried from shop to shop since the drawings sufficed. Students from the wheelwrighting, blacksmithing, and printing divisions also enrolled in drawing so they could make furniture, wagons, and other products from standardized, interchangeable parts. [2] By 1895 the Cassedy Hall drawing room was a well-lighted, 27x39-foot area with twenty-one proper tables, blueprinting equipment, a storage case, and a set of instruments and drawing board for each student, as Russian pedagogy required. [3] By the end of the decade the division would move into an even larger room with forty-seven tables and instruments for thirty-six in the Taylor-designed Slater-Armstrong Memorial Trades Building. [4] And by 1901 there were 320 young men and women from many if not all

Figure 4.1. Taylor (standing at far right) and Drawing Class.

trades enrolled in the drawing classes.[5]

Taylor's own accounts enlarge these events to the sweep of human progress with drawing as the foundation of making. Before his arrival, Taylor later wrote, "The mechanical work was largely in the hands of men trained in the old way, who did their work usually without definite plans or drawings. Introducing plans, blue-prints, and specifications as part of every mechanical job, however small, and instructing the students in making and using drawings, led to changes which inevitably follow newer and better ways of doing things."[6] Normally fair in his claims, Taylor failed to acknowledge such predecessors as Raymond Thweatt, William C. Brown,

John W. Carter, and John H. Washington, who also worked from drawings that they probably made. But these artisans did not know enough about design to meet Booker T. Washington's expectations and make architecture. And by the time that Taylor arrived all but Washington's brother were gone. Washington presumably told Taylor only about the past's inadequacies since he was being hired to cure them.

Taylor developed his architecture program in increments. With William Eugene Hutt from the St. Louis Manual Training School initially teaching mechanical drawing, the Principal's report to the Slater Fund for 1893 noted that Tuskegee now had both mechanical and architectural drawing. But Hutt would soon leave for failing to meet expectations. The 1893–94 catalog listed Taylor as an architectural and mechanical drawing teacher, while the 1894–95 catalog suggests that the school now had mechanical drawing alone. The missing "architectural and" could be a printer's error or perhaps was simply unnecessary at the level the students were actually working. A photograph captioned "Class in Mechanical Drawing" that was published in 1895 in *Harper's Weekly* shows twenty-two students clutching T-squares and boards posed outside Cassedy Hall. Taylor, looking younger than some of his charges, stands proudly to one side. The image appears again in the 1895–96 catalog as "Class in Drawing" and is now joined by comparable shots of shoemakers (eight students), printers (twenty-two), brick masons (twelve), blacksmiths (thirteen), and students of the "science of cooking" (twelve).[7] The last alone might have been excused from drawing.

DRAWING FOR ARCHITECTS

As the program evolved, the catalogs became more specific. Plane and solid geometrical drawing were to be taken during the students' first two years, according to the 1895–96 edition. Beginning in the junior year, students in most trades took mechanical and "class-room drawing," the latter probably the specialized trades work taught in the classrooms attached to each shop, as in the Russian system. Classrooms appeared in shops in the Boys' Trades Building that was built at the end of the decade. Juniors would also learn foreshortening, perspective, geometrical drawings, sketching, historical ornament, and figure and "constructive" drawing. Two "Middle Classes" added clay modeling, instruments, and shades and shadows. Then came options. One was mechanical drawing with "scale drawing," a track that would lead to "working drawings, estimates of material, design, isometric

drawings." The senior class in this track did still more working drawings, construction, advanced design and shop work, and they studied curved and twisted shapes, "lengths and bevels of pieces at different angles," and "the development of surfaces."[8] Three years of freehand drawing were also available in the normal or academic program.

The 1894–95 catalog also listed a three-year carpentry course with basic woodworking during the first year. Structural framing, setting windows and doors, sizing studs and joists, and shingling, weatherboarding, and flashing came during the second. Stair building and cabinet and furniture making arrived in the first term of the third year. Sketching and drawing eaves brackets from "original and selected designs" appears along with furniture, machinery work, estimates and "sixteen problems in carpentry" in that year's third term. The fourth term was spent on "original and experimental work." In 1894 Taylor asked by way of the *Southern Letter* that the school's Northern friends donate books. He wanted Palliser's *American Architecture* as well as *Model Dwellings*, *The Building Budget*, and *Suburban and Country Homes*.[9]

Organizational disparities between the 1895–96 catalog and that of the previous year make comparisons difficult, but it seems that it was in 1895–96, if not the year before, that a few seniors could learn about construction, strength of materials, history of architecture, estimating, specifications and contracts, and design. In 1897, students could supervise on- and off-campus construction and, the catalog promised, enter competitions for upcoming buildings.[10] An architecture course was jelling. Now architectural drawing, so specified, began in the students' second year with wood and brick construction, working drawings, "detail," and design. Students were also to make estimates and

write specifications, undertake a "brief review" of
the history of architecture, and continue freehand
drawing, eventually completing three years of it. As
Tuskegee explained much later, freehand drawing
trained the eye to correct proportions and grew the
skill of rapid notation that the architect would need
for design as well as communicating with clients.[11]
By 1901–02, the third-year freehand drawing class
would be under the Academic Department, where
architecture students could also gain "artistic training." Huntington Memorial Academic Building
would have a large drawing room lit from three
sides.

From 1896 and on, then, architectural drawing was reaching beyond the teacher/builder, the
preacher/builder and even the carpenter/builder to
approach that of the designer. Architects of the late
nineteenth and early twentieth centuries increasingly designed buildings without erecting them,
serving instead as the client's on-site representative
in enforcing the contract drawings and specifications. Washington wanted this modernity as well.
"We must not only have carpenters but architects"
among the race. "We must have not only persons
who can do the work with the hand, but persons
at the same time who can plan the work with the
brain."[12] These words came a few years later, but
Washington would have understood from his
Hampton days that architects design fine buildings
without necessarily building them and that such
works can bring pride and identity to their users.

Washington also wanted black architects for
pragmatic reasons, to help the race recapture its
share of the building trades, which had expanded
under slavery. He argued this with an anecdote
about a slavery-trained contractor whose thriving
business died when he did because there were no
black men to carry it on: there were plenty of youths

who excelled in languages and literature, but not in
design and construction.[13]

Washington also would have known that black
architects could direct construction jobs to black
builders. In 1902, W. E. B. Du Bois, then an Atlanta
University sociologist, organized a survey of and
then a conference on "The Negro Artisan." The report includes Washington's opening address, quoted
above, along with the survey results. Carpentry,
masonry, plastering, printing, barbering, tailoring,
blacksmithing, and dressmaking garnered the most
responses among the thirty trades Du Bois queried
by mail. Two respondents called for architectural
education. Henry N. Lee wanted one or more black
architects in Memphis because black builders were
not allowed in white architectural offices to see the
plans up for bid. Alexander Hamilton Jr., on the
other hand, a successful Atlanta contractor, wanted
to build to individual client needs. Most of his firm's
work came from stock plans, he wrote, because
"unless a person wants an original or an elaborate
design in a house, he doesn't care to employ an
architect." But Hamilton had a thirst to design. "I
only attempt pencil floor plans and once in a while
a crude elevation; but my desire is to take a course
in architectural drawing, which there seems small
hope of gratifying."[14] A decade later Du Bois would
conduct a second survey, this one titled "The Negro
American Artisan."[15] One contractor responded
that one percent of Atlanta's architectural offices
were open to black builders. Matters were not
improving.

OTHER PROGRAMS

If architecture courses were unavailable to Alexander Hamilton in Atlanta, the rudiments could be
found elsewhere. In the 1902 survey, Du Bois queried black industrial schools. From the ninety-four

that responded, he could summarize thirty-three curricula. Six schools sent full course listings and, of these, four had at least one course in "architecture." They were Lincoln Institute in Jefferson City, Missouri; the Agricultural and Mechanical College for the Colored Race in Greensboro, North Carolina; Shaw University in Raleigh; and Claflin University in Orangeburg, South Carolina. The Greensboro program scheduled a year of architecture, however it was defined, for second-year industrial students and a second term during the fourth year. Claflin University, however, listed a two-year program within its college division that appears to have a proper shape.

Claflin's pioneer architecture curriculum dates from 1890, well before Tuskegee's, and bears the distinction that its teacher, a Claflin-educated carpentry instructor, published his lectures. Robert Charles Bates's *Elementary Principles of Architecture and Building* (1892) has long been known to architectural bibliographers but without the awareness that its author was black. The book escaped Du Bois's bibliographies of African American authors, but it was displayed in the Negro Pavilion at the 1907 Jamestown Exposition. One recent reader has found Bates's compendium overly reliant on James Fergusson's *A History of Architecture* but good on construction issues.[16] Bates wrote the president of the Slater Fund, Rutherford B. Hayes, that Claflin's assets included a collection of drawings and photographs of European and American buildings, a library, and a cabinet of stone and wood samples.[17]

Bates and Claflin did produce progeny. In 1893, graduate William Wilson Cooke began designing and teaching at what is now Savannah State College. Cooke then came back to Claflin in 1897 to replace Bates and designed and developed what he described in 1900 as a "Preparatory Course in Architecture." The program faded after 1907, when Cooke entered the U.S. Treasury Department's Office of the Supervising Architect in Washington. Cooke eventually moved to Ohio, where he designed post offices. Claflin never offered the real-world construction opportunities of the ever-expanding Tuskegee nor a cadre of school-based talent.[18] Richard Dozier has identified still another early program at the Negro State Normal School in Montgomery, Alabama, that began in 1895–96 and was directed by Henry Talbot, who trained in an industrial school in England and practiced there for fifteen years.[19]

By the mid-1890s then, Claflin, Tuskegee, and probably the Montgomery school could offer a starter architectural curriculum to African Americans. Hampton's contribution to building is important but was not as ambitious as Tuskegee's towards design. In the 1870s Hampton had architectural, freehand, and mechanical drawing so that Hampton-educated carpenters could bring the basics to Tuskegee. In 1896 Hampton opened its Armstrong-Slater Memorial Trade School, where one presumably found carpentry, bricklaying, plastering, frame construction, and house painting along with the drawing that John Henry Jinks came that year to teach, as Chapter 3 detailed. Hampton inaugurated a formal construction department in 1923 but did not acquire an architect until 1934, when William H. Moses arrived with a professional degree from Pennsylvania State University.[20]

THE TUSKEGEE CERTIFICATE

The architectural drawing course outline in the Tuskegee catalog for 1895–96 was presumably what William Sidney Pittman completed in 1897 when he earned the first certificate in architectural drawing. The certificate shaved a year off his subsequent

50

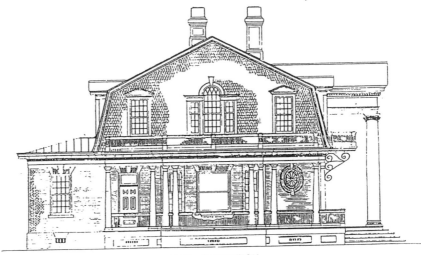

END ELEVATION

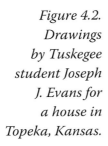

Figure 4.2. Drawings by Tuskegee student Joseph J. Evans for a house in Topeka, Kansas.

FRONT ELEVATION

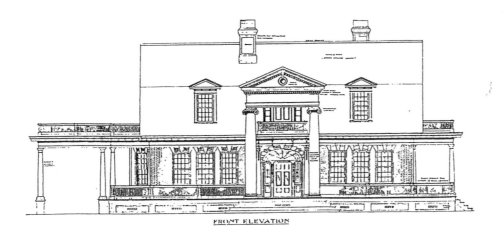

FIRST FLOOR PLAN

four-year architecture degree at Drexel Institute in Philadelphia. Pittman was the son of a Montgomery washerwoman and, he believed, a white architect. He came to Tuskegee in 1892 at age seventeen, earned his normal diploma with wheelwrighting as his trade, but then continued as a "post-graduate" for the certificate. William Gregory remembered him among the enthusiasts who took up architectural drawing when Taylor began teaching it. He was "the brightest one here. Others tried it but soon got tired and left it off."[21] Pittman would come back to Tuskegee to teach and to irritate many. His character derailed his talent and stellar connections, as Chapter 5 will explain. [22]

Meanwhile, with new energies from the returned Pittman but also from the Pratt-trained Wallace A. Rayfield, who came in 1899, the architecture curriculum expanded once again. The 1901–02 catalog repeated Taylor's 1895–96 program but with further requirements: attending lectures in the heating, electrical lighting, and plumbing divisions and visiting these shops regularly with or without the drawing instructor's guidance. Certificate aspirants must also assist the architects in the drawing room, help supervise construction, and undergo an examination.

With the new century, Tuskegee now began promoting the certificate by publishing an enthusiastic article in the national black press. According to its author, Washington's secretary Emmett J. Scott, since Tuskegee's strengths in industrial education were now comparable to those in medicine and law at other institutions, it was worth the family sacrifice to earn architectural qualifications. This was a nervy assertion since Tuskegee did not have the professional program comparable to medicine or law and it was only a secondary school with opportunities wedged into an extra year, not a university.[23]

The argument could have come from Taylor, from Washington, or from the ambitious and frequently exaggerating Pittman himself. Soon thereafter, in 1904, Washington summarized the entire drawing curriculum in *Working with the Hands*.[24] All industrial students, including those in the night school, took elementary and freehand drawing during their first year and mechanical drawing during their second year of trade work. At the end of the third year they learned to make "blue, solar, and black prints." During fourth year, building trades students wrote essays about class excursions to other shops, the brickyard, and construction sites. In a parallel track in architectural drawing, the students assisted in the design office and on the construction site, visited other shops, and took classes in heating, lighting, and plumbing as the 1901–02 catalog prescribed. "Many of the most satisfactory and imposing buildings of the school were designed in our architectural department," Washington concluded, implying that his increasingly impressive campus was the product of his pedagogy and proof of its excellence.

Pittman not only agreed with the publicizing administrators, he provided some proof of the certificate's merits by sending student drawings to the mainstream journal, *Architects and Builders Magazine*. "Mr. Pittman does not claim that he is graduating 'architects,'" its editor wrote in 1904. Tuskegee was preparing men to work in architectural offices while they completed degrees at advanced institutions. The editor regretted that he could show only two of the drawings Pittman had furnished, but he thought that every example showed work of the quality expected in the leading architecture schools.[25] The fluidly organized plan and elevation for a Colonial Revival house that the magazine did publish was a significant undergraduate achievement by any standard [Figure 4.2]. The house was by Joseph J. Evans of the class of 1904 and intended for Mrs. H. I. Miller of Topeka, Kansas. Tuskegee's architectural programs remained as an academic route into the profession, but in 1919 one teacher, the office-trained William A. Hazel, left to inaugurate a degree program at Howard University, the first in a black university. Small numbers of African American architects would continue to graduate from MIT, Drexel, Carnegie Institute (now Carnegie-Mellon University), University of Illinois, Cornell, University of Southern California and elsewhere, and they would continue to learn in offices, the old-fashioned way. Tuskegee was never the only route in.

Some Tuskegee-Educated Architects

Who, then, were the Tuskegee-educated architects that Taylor, Pittman, Rayfield and others prepared early in the twentieth century? Dozier estimates that fifteen men had earned architectural drawing certificates by 1913, and that eight of them worked as design professionals while the others became teachers or builders (these numbers will shift as the evidence does). In 1912, Tuskegee sociologist Monroe N. Work thought that there had been five architecture certificates plus eighteen in building and contracting.[26] At least three products of this era took their certificates to mainstream institutions and then careers. William S. Pittman, the first, followed his Drexel Institute degree with five years of teaching before moving to Washington, D.C., and then to Dallas to practice. Vertner W. Tandy earned a normal diploma in 1904, an architectural drawing certificate in 1905, and a Cornell architecture degree in 1908. Tandy's career included high-profile commissions for wealthy African Americans in and around New York City. His Hudson River valley home for Madam C. J. Walker, the hair products mil-

lionaire, is well-known.[27] John Brent was inspired by his office-trained, Washington, D.C., father, Calvin T. S. Brent, to attend Tuskegee. John Brent studied carpentry for two years and architectural drawing for one, finishing in 1907. He worked as a carpenter and then in Tandy's office before earning a Drexel degree in 1912. Brent's best-known building was a Buffalo YMCA built during the 1920s.[28]

Tuskegee also produced architects who practiced without further schooling. Richard Dozier has reconstructed the academic career of Charles Sumner Bowman who arrived in 1892 as a night student. He worked full time, banking his salary with the institute and taking evening courses before becoming a day student in 1895. Bowman earned his normal diploma with a carpentry certificate in 1898 and then moved west. Picking up the story in Kansas City, others have learned that Bowman directed an industrial program, designed and built a large building, and from 1902 practiced on his own.[29]

John A. Lankford, generally accepted as the race's first successful independent practitioner, is often credited to Tuskegee, which might be true for inspiration but not for education. Lankford was there for a year after six or seven in scientific and industrial studies at Lincoln University in Missouri. His 1896 Tuskegee certificate was in steamfitting with some extra credits in physics and chemistry. It was the following year that he studied architecture with the International Correspondence School, a distance-learning program of such substance that William Robert Ware wanted Columbia University to accept its credits.[30] After several more moves, building completions, and still more degrees, Lankford established himself in Washington, D.C., where, in 1902, he designed the True Reformer Building, an African American "capitol," or so it seemed, not far from the federal one. A multistory fraternal lodge with offices, shops, hotel rooms, and entertainment spaces, it remains as a monument of the era's endeavors. Lankford's churches have a wide geographic range since he was supervising architect for the African Methodist Episcopal Church.[31]

The International Correspondence School, based in Scranton, Pennsylvania, helped other Tuskegeans to professionalism along with an uncounted number of other African American architects. L. W. Driver, a grandson of Tuskegee founder Lewis Adams, earned his normal diploma plus a certificate in cabinetmaking, took the Scranton courses and, reportedly, became a registered architect.[32] The Hampton-trained Charles T. Russell headed the Tuskegee carpentry division for several years and then designed and built for black Richmond. In one biographer's opinion, he effectively served an architectural apprenticeship at Tuskegee and therefore can be counted as Tuskegee-educated.[33] Those schooled elsewhere who learned by teaching and working in the in-house design office were Walter T. Bailey, Wallace A. Rayfield, James A. Melby, and William A. Hazel. Bailey, Melby, and Rayfield came from mainstream institutions (Illinois and Pratt). Hazel, who may have known Taylor from a North Carolina boyhood, was office-trained.

Finally, one must note the Caribbean students when estimating the school's architectural reach. Puerto Rican Isidoro Colon, who earned a certificate in 1909, was teaching in Ponce by 1914. Antonio Escabi, who studied at the "Tuskegee Industrial College" from 1908 to 1912 according to his Puerto Rican registration, became an independent architect and contractor in Mayaguez. Three more earned normal diplomas in 1912 and architecture certificates the following year: Angel Whatts-Echavarria, Alphonso Reverson, and Jose Lino Falu-Zarzuela.[34]

The first two worked in Wallace Rayfield's Birmingham office before returning home. Edward E. Davila, who finished in 1909, worked in Boston. Reverson became a building inspector in Yabucoa.[35] Whatts-Echavarria's Puerto Rican registration notes that his Tuskegee years (1909–13) included finishing high school. This draftsman worked for Falu-Zarauela from 1913–15 and taught mechanical drawing. Whatts-Echavarria, Escabi, and Falu-Zarzuela were registered as architects in 1928 when Puerto Rico required it for practice.[36] Tuskegee also trained Cubans. Miguel Marin came in 1895, Julian Valdes in 1897, and Delphin Valdes and Celestin Ramirez in 1899.[37] Luis D. Valdes (the relationship of the three Valdes boys is not known) was considered one of the brightest of his era, winning the senior-year, all-school drawing competition in 1908 and, a few months later, a much more important competition for a Havana leprosy hospital.[38]

A COLLECTION OF DRAWINGS

A collection of thirty-six drawings, once bound in an album that was shown at the Paris exposition of 1900, provides a closer look into Tuskegee's drawing program.[39] Some drawings date from fall 1899, when Taylor was no longer teaching, but many are from Taylor's years and all from his program. Nine by girls are elementary mechanicals—elevations, axonometrics, and perspectives of geometric solids. There are a few complicated still-life piles of hollowed cubes and pentagons. There are also freehand still-life studies by girls, including two particularly fine ones by Dora M. Lawrence. Annie F. Gale from Massachusetts was teaching freehand drawing as well as physical culture in 1895–96.[40]

The drawings signed by boys were all directed to trades. There are patterns for men's clothes, an elevation of a miter elbow, a pattern for a bathtub,

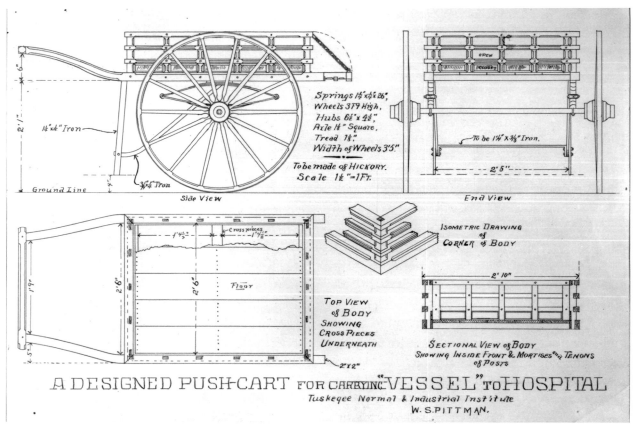

Figure 4.3. William S. Pittman's drawing of a hospital cart.

several buildings, and many wagons and carriages. Some of the last are stunning, the student having artfully fitted seven or eight plans and elevations onto the paper in the manner of an Ecole des Beaux-Arts *analytique*. William S. Pittman executed five wagon studies and a cottage plan. Pittman's cottage is a version of a common Alabama type with a central hall, an even disposition of four nearly square rooms on either side, a veranda wrapping the front, and a U-plan gallery behind the block that connects a projecting kitchen on one side with a projecting bathroom on the other.[41] Another building, drawn by Augustus C. Perdue, is for a substantial asym-

metrical Victorian house with a veranda on two sides. The three other architectural drawings, all by S. C. Harris, show elevations and a partial section of a two-story house with a veranda, brackets, tall chimneys, and a steeply pitched main roof behind a bevy of subsidiary ones capping projecting bays and pavilions. All suggest that a substantial practice was intended for Tuskegee graduates—large houses for the urban bourgeoisie as well as farmers' cottages.

TWO REPORTS

Two departmental and divisional reports, one by John H. Washington on the larger industrial department and the one by Robert R. Taylor on his drawing division, provide a view into Tuskegee construction, both on campus and off for, respectively, 1896–97 and 1897–98. We learn, for example, that Arthur Ulysses Craig, a physics and electricity specialist trained at the University of Kansas, assisted Taylor in the drawing room. Craig had installed Macon County's first electrical lighting when he wired the Chapel to Tuskegee's own generator. By 1901, when he left, Craig had built a campus telephone system.[42] In 1897–98 the architectural and mechanical drawing division had eighty-nine day-school students from the industrial department, seven special pupils, and ten journeymen, graduates, or teachers enrolled in evening courses. The division functioned in part as an office that bid for work on-campus and off and paid professionals and students for individual efforts.[43] Off-campus ventures could be at some distance. During 1896–97, students drafted plans for a dormitory at the Christiansburg Industrial Institute in Virginia and blueprints for a second new structure at Mt. Meigs Colored Industrial Institute, near Montgomery.[44] "Our architect, Mr. Taylor," designed for this school an assembly room seating five hundred with classrooms on the second floor. If completed, which is not clear, this would be Taylor's second Mt. Meigs structure (the first discussed below).[45] Christiansburg Industrial Institute, founded in 1868 by the Society of Friends in Cambria, Virginia, turned a plantation "big house" into a schoolhouse, an awesome reversal of meaning in the eyes of many beholders. Booker T. Washington became a Christiansburg trustee the year the dormitory was built (1896), and maintained the relationship until his death in 1915. Tuskegee would contract a second Christiansburg building in 1910.[46]

The drawing division's main tasks in 1896–97, according to John H.'s report, were at home: the Chapel, the Slater-Armstrong Memorial or Boys'

Trades Building, and a house for business manager Warren Logan. The division also drew furniture for the carpentry shop, carriages for the blacksmithing and wheelwrighting divisions, and blueprints for the tinsmithing division's 98 coffee- and teapots, 198 water pitchers, 136 dishpans that were intended for Tuskegee use or, perhaps, for sale. The tinsmithing division also used drawings to make gutters and tin roofing for campus buildings and a livery stable in town.

John H. Washington's report also summarized other trades divisions. The carpentry division made school furniture, did roof framing, and made partitions for Science (Thrasher) Hall, woodwork for the Chapel and the Boys' Trades Building, and small projects and repairs both on- and off-campus. This division had nineteen full-time student workers who did their academic work at night, twenty part-time or day-student workers, and four outside journeymen. The masonry and plastering division laid bricks for Science Hall and the Chapel, built two chimneys for rented houses, did additions to teachers' cottages, and the concrete work, probably flooring, at the Chapel and the Slater-Armstrong Memorial Agricultural Building. The house and carriage painting division had applied its skill to Porter Hall, to Parker Cottage for Senior girls, to the carpentry division's furniture, the tin roofing of five buildings, several interiors, and townspeople's buggies. It had seven full-time or night school workers and twelve part-time or day school workers. The report then requested an additional water tank to permit brick industry to expand to market demands since the division now supplied three counties.

John H. Washington's report did not, of course, bring up interpersonal tensions. These appear in the correspondence. Writing to his brother about the Warren Logan house, John H. said "Mr. Taylor is very elaborate in his plans as he does not wish to build a house that will not be a credit to him as an architect." But the Logan drawings were incomplete, he complained, so that he could not make estimates. Furthermore, surreptitious additions to the Parker Cottage such as double flooring on the second story were costing too much.[47] In 1896 Taylor and Lewis Adams, the Tuskegee founder who now led the tinsmithing division, were both making $600 a year to John H. Washington's $500. The average salary of the sixteen other industrial teachers was $370.[48]

Robert R. Taylor's characteristically brief 1897–98 division report numbers 177 students from twelve divisions in drawing courses.[49] These included brickmaking, shoemaking, harness making, and machine molding among the less predictable drawing-based divisions. Seventy-nine took drawing classes during the day and ninety at night. The day students drew their trade division projects—furniture, wagons, tinware, men's suits—before going to division shops to make them. Taylor's division also did construction drawings for the Chapel and Science Building, preliminary designs for the Boys' Trades Building, and additions to Hamilton Cottage, the 1889 frame dormitory for girls. Taylor estimated the work's value at $76,000 and charged the institute a five percent fee of $3,800 for his architectural services. Five percent was the American Institute of Architects's prescribed fee. Taylor also requested more support for the following year: a full-time assistant instructor instead of the two part-timers who were also working elsewhere, longer class meetings, a textbook, more drawing instruments, better blueprinting equipment, and drawing tables with a drawer for each student. Six months later the staffing issue would surface again. He could not continue to teach while also designing Huntington Hall girls' dormitory,

as Washington had expected.[50]

TAYLOR'S EARLY BUILDINGS

Taylor's first Alabama building was an industrial structure at Mt. Meigs, the Tuskegee offshoot near Montgomery. Cornelia Bowen, who established Mt. Meigs at a ruined resort, was born in a cabin that later held classes on the farm that would become Tuskegee. Bowen graduated with the first class in 1885 and then set about doing exactly as Washington instructed. She succeeded at farming. Olivia A. Davidson, Tuskegee's co-founder and Washington's second wife, was Bowen's other inspiration, she later recalled.

Tuskegee carpentry and wheelwrighting students built Taylor's Mt. Meigs building with the Tuskegee-trained industrial arts teacher, J. H. Michael, and his boys. A *Southern Letter* photograph shows the building to have two triangular gables marking two entrances, the gables inscribed into the same plane and below the larger gable of the building volume so that one slanting side of each small triangle coincided with the sides of the great one, the triangles ascending in size to suggest a level of abstraction.[51] It is tempting to assume that one of J. H. Michael's boys on the construction team might have been Samuel M. Plato, a family-trained carpenter who had abandoned his ambitions to be a lawyer while at Mt. Meigs and decided on architecture. Plato later took International Correspondence School courses and designed for prosperous white patrons in Marion, Indiana. Perhaps working with Taylor recruited him to the profession.

Taylor's first identifiable Tuskegee structure is the brick Science Hall, better known by the 1903 renaming that memorialized the devoted Tuskegee observer, Max Bennett Thrasher. (See Catalog 1) Most of the exterior remains. Science Hall had laboratories and classrooms on the lower two floors and a boys' dormitory on the third. Construction started in early 1893 but lagged four or more years, perhaps because there was no hovering donor to please. Since there were 500,000 bricks already on hand more than a year after construction began, the *Southern Letter* suggested that friends might give money for lime and hardware.[52] Thrasher Hall's tripartite massing is emphasized by three stories of columnar verandas on the central segment that are flanked by simpler secondary brick elements.

In 1893 Taylor also remodeled Armstrong Hall, by then renamed for the deceased Olivia Davidson Washington, and he built a five-room cottage for the school's first physician, Dr. Hallie Tanner Dillon, a sister of the artist Henry O. Tanner. By summer 1894 Taylor would have produced a brick boys' bathhouse with toilets, three teachers' cottages, an expanded blacksmith shop, and completed plans for a "large brick classroom building," presumably Science Hall. He also filled Washington's 1891 wish list for a teacher of surveying by laying out a "residential village," probably lots bordering the campus on the south or west, that Washington was developing as his "model" suburb Greenwood.[53] And Taylor must have been satisfying Washington's wish for affordable cottages for sharecroppers, tenant farmers, and even landowners. By February 1893 Taylor would have devised the "picture and working plans" for two- and three-room cottages, copies of which were given to those attending the annual Negro Conference.[54] Teachers and ministers were expected to distribute them throughout the countryside or build them for their own occupancy in the remote outposts where they were posted. The buildings were models for rural aspiration. Washington also exhibited cottage plans at the Colored Teacher's Association in Montgomery and, the following year, conference attendees again received "pictures of comfortable homes with directions for building." A few years later, a white carpenter wrote for a copy so that he too could build better housing.[55] In 1914, when Washington established the Baldwin Farms community of forty-acre parcels, purchasers could have a Tuskegee-built, expandable house for $300.[56]

Taylor was an immediate success with his demanding employer. Washington wrote in April 1893 that he had given excellent satisfaction and was wanted for the following year—with a raise. Perhaps the architect did not reply, because in mid-August the Principal wrote again, directing the letter to brother John E. Taylor's Wilmington address and offering $60 per month plus board. Robert R. should reply if this was not satisfactory.[57] By early September, Taylor was back and responding to memos in the spare but purposeful manner that characterized twenty-two years of Washington correspondence.

During the summer of 1894, while supervising Science Hall and the boys' bathhouse, Taylor also lectured at Tuskegee's "colored Chautauqua," a one-time experiment in Alabama reading circles to increase adult literacy. Olivia Egleston Phelps Stokes, donor of the Phelps Hall Bible Training School and, with her sister, the Chapel, funded it. Taylor also spent time in Boston "getting information along his special line."[58] Taylor was a man of initiative, as Washington put it when he was chastising the other drawing teacher, William Eugene Hutt, for lack of same. Even though the mechanical drawing instructor had the same education as Taylor, Washington said, it was the latter who was "constantly leading in his work, working in season and out of season. Instead of having someone to lead him he is constantly making suggestions as to what should be done." Hutt should learn from his example. Nine months earlier Hutt had politely but firmly protested Washington's criticisms and offered his resignation. He thought he was teaching well even though his shop time was limited by added night school assignments.[59] Hutt became a band and orchestra instructor, a clerk in the treasurer's office and, by 1896, had left the scene entirely.

THE ATLANTA EXPOSITION

The fall of 1895 found Taylor at the Cotton States and International Exposition in Atlanta, oversee-ing the Alabama exhibit in the Negro Building. He must have heard Booker T. Washington's address on opening day, the speech that "electrified the audi-ence, and the response was as if it had come from the throat of a whirlwind," as one observer heard it.[60] In this famous if mis-characterized "Atlanta Compromise," as W. E. B. Du Bois later termed it, Washington promised a productive pool of black labor if Southerners would only cast down their buckets among their traditional helpers rather than importing foreigners who had no loyalty and would probably unionize. African Americans wanted eco-nomic opportunity but not social or political equal-ity, he assured the nation. They too would cast down their buckets, remaining in the rural South rather than fleeing to safety and opportunity in Northern cities. Washington saw the race's best chance in independent farming on its own land. "The soil, sunshine and rain draw no color line . . . The stream and the river, the trees and the birds, the animals, the grass and all the rest, draw no color line." Cities only yield frustration.[61] But Washington also wanted black people to move beyond poverty and help-lessness as tenants and sharecroppers to become self-employed, scientific farmers who owned their land and enjoyed a well-furnished house filled with

books, newspapers, and the other accoutrements of a cultured life. Tuskegee taught that, too. The "Atlanta Compromise" appeared to some to signal that a cooperative Booker T. Washington would render African Americans into compliant low-wage workers who accepted disfranchisement in return for an economic foothold. But another aspect of Washington's message—and Washington's most persistent theme for the future—was that African Americans were already making rapid economic and cultural progress, accoutrements and all. By challenging the popular assumption that the people were degenerating without slavery's armature, fail-ing in productivity and character, Washington was being assertive indeed.[62] Soon Washington would be even more forceful, declaring that the "bluest blood in Massachusetts" would be degraded and Christian civilization a failure if members of the white race oppressed the dark one.[63] He would also demand equal treatment before the law. "Accom-modationism," Du Bois's charge, is too narrow a term for Washington's strategy.

The Atlanta Exposition was the first to follow the World's Columbian Exposition of 1893 in Chicago, where fair organizers had denied African Ameri-cans a collective display in an independent build-ing despite well-organized efforts to get just that. Frederick Douglass and Ida B. Wells wrote bitterly about this turn of events and meant to publish their pamphlet in three European languages to alert for-eign visitors to the true state of race relations. It was humiliating, they said, to have black achievements shown only in the Haitian and Liberian pavilions, in needlework in the Woman's Pavilion, a few school displays, unedifying Midway sideshows, or the sight of African Americans doing menial work.[64] If the Atlanta Exposition's Negro Building and Washing-ton's speech were giant steps forward,[65] its Midway was not. It had Chinese and other "native" exhibits, including a "Dahomey" village with purported cannibals that evoked the rage of the African Methodist Episcopal Bishop Henry M. Turner. Turner charged the proprietor with hiring "lazy, good-for-nothing negroes from New York" to jump around and act the ape. "Stop your lying about the negro!" Turner demanded. West Africans were far more peaceable than some of the whites who were staring at them. As for the idea that the "progress" on exhibit proved that there was a "new negro," Turner had plenty to say about that. The excellent products on display were made by "the same old negro" who did everything under slavery. These were the people who built the mansions, the carriages, and the fine furniture. They made elegant clothes and cooked famous meals. The only novelty that Turner could detect was the black man's freedom to choose his vocation and the "new white man" who was actually learning something.[66]

The exposition Midway also had an "Old Plantation" concession with minstrel entertainers. But despite this and other insulting displays such as "whites only" signs on pavilions and the occasional rudeness, Frederick Douglass's son saw well-dressed black visitors enjoying themselves and treated with respect.[67] Alice M. Bacon, a white Hampton teacher, thought that African Americans were treated well and that their attractive selves constituted proof of the progress claimed. Their visible prosperity would not be lost on an Atlanta business community ever seeking new customers, she thought. But a black Atlanta editor disputed such warm assessments. African Americans should not come unless they wanted to be gouged and insulted, he responded.[68]

Just as the traveling African Americans constituted their own exhibition, so did the Negro Building and its staff. This too was a "surprise and an education on the race question" to whites and to black country-people alike, Bacon thought. It was a "revelation" for one elderly black woman who cried as she viewed the displays. Young people found "a new incentive to industry, a new hope for the future, and a new reason for bearing patiently present disadvantages."[69] Bad experiences were only temporary and their effects could be overcome, a truly Washingtonian point of view.

The Negro Building itself was a 25,000 square-foot structure with flag-topped pavilions and a classical pediment over the entrance. Sculptures within the pediment showed a log cabin and plain wooden church on one side and a large house and stone church on the other—the literal progress, reading left to right, of a people as seen in their buildings. Black artisans under the black contractors J. P. King of LaGrange and J. W. Smith of Atlanta built it. Although Washington believed an African American designed the building, recent scholarship has named a white man.[70] Inside, one could contemplate the produce of home and farm, patents and manufactures, paintings by Henry O. Tanner, sculpture by Edmonia Lewis, and "native" or "uncivilized" crafts that Bishop Turner had brought back from Liberia. Turner wanted reparations for slavery and thought that African Americans should colonize Africa for their own sakes. They would escape prejudice while playing their part in the divine plan to bring Christianity and skilled trades to that continent's good but benighted people. One wonders how Taylor would remember the Liberian crafts and Turner's contentions when, three decades later, he traveled there to inaugurate the industrial education segment of that prescription.

Hampton and Tuskegee both showed student work at Atlanta as did the Armstrong Manual Training School in Washington, D.C., these three leading the school displays. Hampton showed plans and measurements of student-built houses. Tuskegee showed trades and agricultural achievements: a carriage, a buggy, a phaeton, a farm wagon, plus a foundry cupola and a one-and-a-half horsepower steam engine that the iron-working division had cast. One observer judged the workmanship as professional as that by any commercial manufacturer.[71] Taylor, who installed and supervised the Tuskegee exhibit, must have built the "beautiful arch" that attracted the eye. He also installed exhibits for the Alabama State Normal and Industrial School (now Alabama State University) and at least one other black industrial school. Taylor gave Tuskegee $25 because a fire had destroyed the barn and dairy herd, but Washington had to promise anonym-

ity.[72] Now twenty-seven years old, Taylor would have been one of the "intelligent, well-dressed, well mannered young men and women, graduates or teachers of the schools they represented," who were even more educational than the exhibits they were explaining.[73]

THE CHAPEL

While in Atlanta explaining Tuskegee to strangers, Taylor was also revising plans for a new Institute chapel, working in his room when not on fair duty. He was drawing in mid-October, "putting all strength on the plans" two weeks later, and sending the results to Washington in early November.[74] Olivia Egleston Phelps Stokes, who had given the Phelps Hall Bible Training School, announced the gift of a badly needed chapel in May 1895. Heirs of the Phelps and Dodge fortunes and of abolitionist and philanthropic traditions, Olivia Phelps Stokes and her sister Caroline were the first of Tuskegee's many women donors of buildings.[75] Washington had sent Taylor's first chapel designs that summer, to which they requested more "simplicity," as the history of the building's site, form, and reception that Catalog 2 will detail. These revisions were Taylor's other Atlanta task. The sisters were active in siting decisions that amounted to planning, eventually agreeing to open land on the west rather than a smaller plot near Phelps Hall [see 1897 Campus Plan]. They wanted to nest their donations together. The Chapel, as they named it, was built over the course of two years of student-made bricks, as expected, but it also had student-

Figure 4.4. Chapel Exterior.

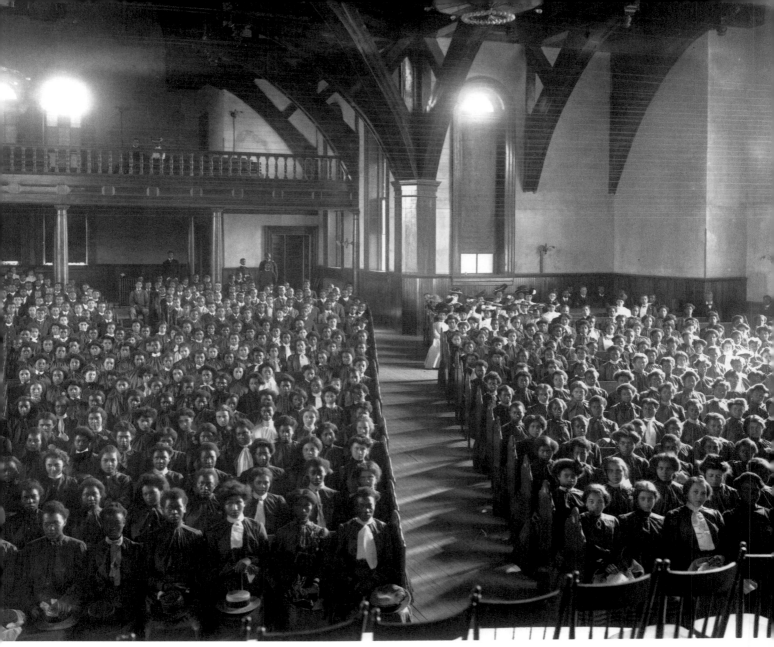

Figure 4.5. Chapel Interior, girls' side.

designed pews and cornices. [Figure 4.4]

The Chapel quickly became central to Tuskegee life. It held Sunday services plus daily evening devotions that supplied guidance from the Principal, if in town, and from any visitors who were willing to share their wisdom. A Bengali student said that the Chapel was the school's "common room," like a family parlor. Decades later he remembered the nightly music and the Principal's warm humor, his "fatherly simplicity."[76] Washington sometimes asked students to sing for the assembly songs from their distant homes, folding in the homesick while collecting "plantation melodies" for preservation. He might have to repeat the request several times before a soft solo voice would begin a song remembered from some backwoods church or cabin. The white

Figure 4.6. Farmers' Conference assembly in the Chapel.

journalist and Tuskegee publicist Max Bennett Thrasher wrote of such an occasion: "The quaint, high-pitched melody rises and falls—a voice alone—until a dozen quick ears catch the theme and a dozen voices are humming an accompaniment. The second time the refrain is reached a few voices join in boldly, a hundred follow and then thousands, sending up into the arches of the roof such a volume of sound as one is rarely permitted to hear."[77]

Another vespers was recalled by the white civil rights advocate Mary White Ovington in 1905. First,

the organ and the band "rolled out the sound." Then Washington led that day's visitor to the rostrum and a pageant was underway. Columns of uniformed boys and girls marched to stirring music two by two from their separate entrances down the aisles, past the rostrum, and then up to their seats. "The procession was unhalting, seemingly endless."[78] At the service's end, first the girls then the boys marched out two by two, again to music, down an inner aisle to the platform where they were examined for posture and dress. They then crossed along the platform edge to a side aisle and left through their separate exits.[79]

SPECIAL OCCASIONS

The Chapel was dedicated to religious services in accordance with the sisters' wishes. But because Tuskegee had no auditorium other than the leaky Pavilion, they graciously allowed it to be used for concerts, graduations, the annual Negro Conference. It would be another decade before an auditorium below Tompkins Dining Hall was opened and three until Taylor's even larger Logan Hall auditorium appeared.

For the February Negro Conferences, which had occupied the jerry-built Pavilion, the Chapel now sheltered the picturesquely garbed farmers and farm wives instead of uniformed students who marched in and out to tempos of communal joy or mechanized control, depending on the interpretation. Sharecroppers and tenant farmers sat beneath electric chandeliers to hear how modern, scientific farming, as George Washington Carver was leading it, meant profits, land ownership, cottages, and security.[80] Crowded further by fascinated journalists and Northern philanthropists, the Negro Conference must have been among the Chapel's finest hours, for it sheltered those who may never have seen such a structure, much less been invited to enter it and call it their own. Washington was clear: the building belonged to the race, not just the institution.

The Chapel also held the annual theater that was Commencement but garbed here as an agricultural fair. Again, the region's farmers were invited. They gathered long before daylight, their animals and wagons lining the roads for miles and swamping the institute's valley and fields. Food was plentiful and free, and visitors could picnic on the lawns. Whites were invited too and some came. Inside, students strutted their skills across the Chapel stage, timing demonstrations so the drama had shape. A young man in overalls walked onto the platform and started a small steam engine that then blew a whistle. Thereupon, boys and girls hurried in from all directions. A carpenter completed a model house frame, a mason laid a segment of brick wall, a farmer milked a cow, a blacksmith shoed a horse, a tailor

assembled a suit, and a girl fitted a dress on another. Sometimes girls washed and ironed to Tuskegee's labor-saving methods, explaining as they went how they cooked, canned, or made hats. In 1901 Washington's daughter Portia told the audience how to make a dress. Guests remembered the heartfelt songs, the engines and lathes, the veterinary student who cleaned a horse's teeth, and the "plain talk" instructions for building a carriage, managing a steam pump, or restoring worn-out soils. It was a "first class agricultural fair" except for the probability that the students had carefully rehearsed each "plain" talk in "dovetailing" English classes.[81]

ONE FRAME AND FIVE BRICK STRUCTURES

The second half of the 1890s provided other design assignments for Taylor and the architectural

Figure 4.7. Parker Cottage for senior girls.

TUSKEGEE INSTITUTE 1897

BUILDING KEY

1   Porter Hall
2   Alabama Hall (girls)
3   Armstrong/Davidson (boys)
4   Forge (now Band Building)
5   Cassedy Industrial Building
6   Science Thrasher Hall
7   Phelps Bible Training School
8   Principal's 1890 House
9   Slater-Armstrong Memorial
    Agricultural Building
10 Steam Laundry
11 Hamilton Cottage (girls)
12 Parker Cottage (girls)
13 Practice Cottage
14 The Chapel
15 Barracks
16 Cemetary
17 Creamery
18 Site of 1889–1895 barn
19 Pavilion

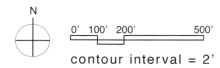

contour interval = 2'

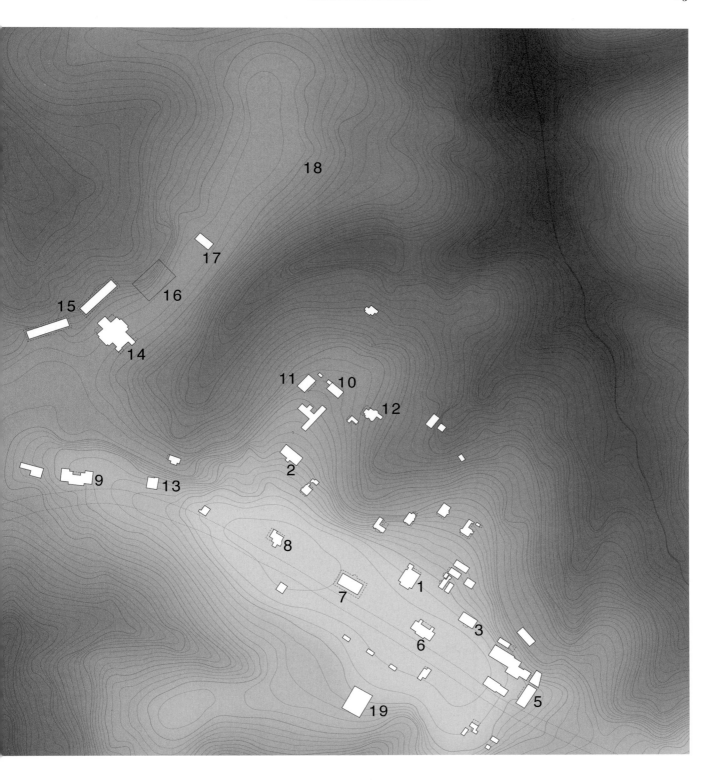

Tuskegee Institute 1903

Building Key

1   Office Building
2   The Oaks
3   Carnegie Library
4   Huntington Academic
5   Rockefeller Hall (boys)
6   Boys' Bathhouse
7   Power Plant
8   Parker Cottage (girls)
9   Huntington Hall (girls)
10   Douglass Hall (girls)
11   Girls' Bathhouse
12   Creamery
13   Cow Barn
14   Horse and Mule Barn
15   Pinehurst Hospital
16   Dorothy Hall
17   Lincoln Gates
18   Boys' Trades Building
19   Emery I (boys)
20   Children's House

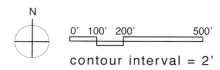

N

0' 100' 200'   500'

contour interval = 2'

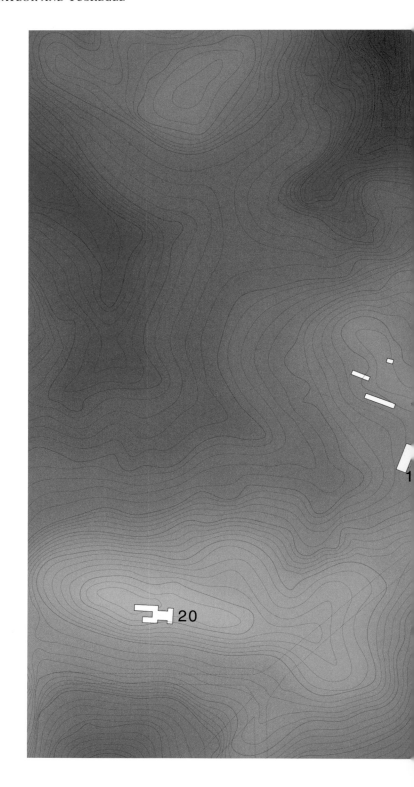

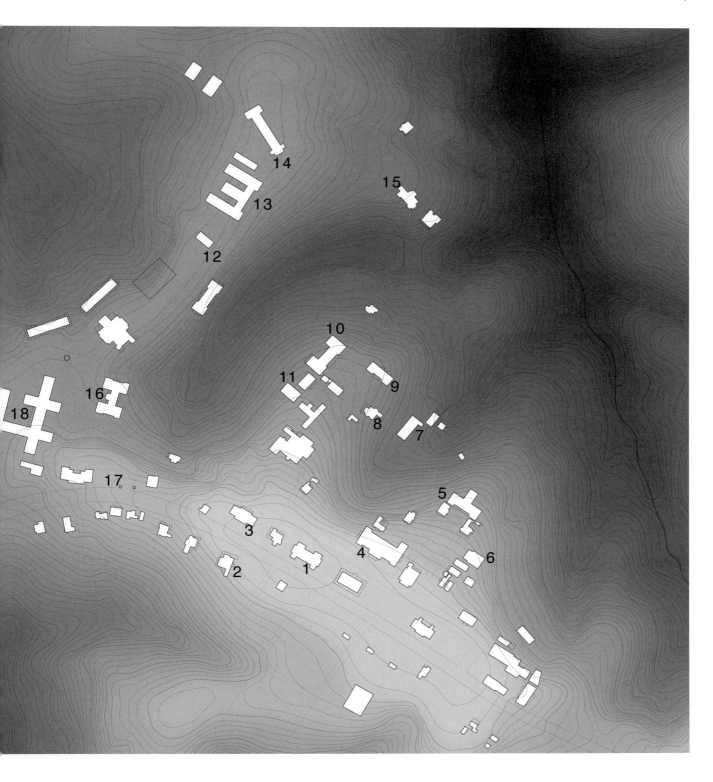

TUSKEGEE INSTITUTE 1911

BUILDING KEY

1   White Hall
2   Girls' Quadrangle
3   Tompkins Dining Hall
4   Tantum Hall (girls)
5   Andrew Hospital
6   Four Emerys (boys)
7   Milbank Agricultural Building

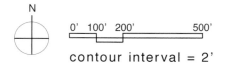

N

0' 100' 200' 500'

contour interval = 2'

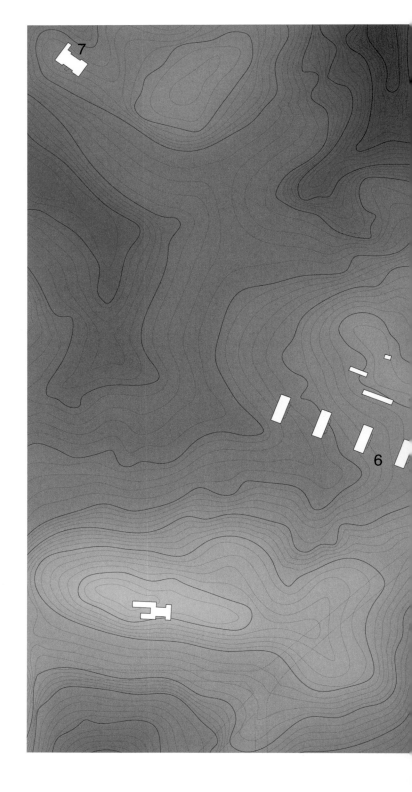

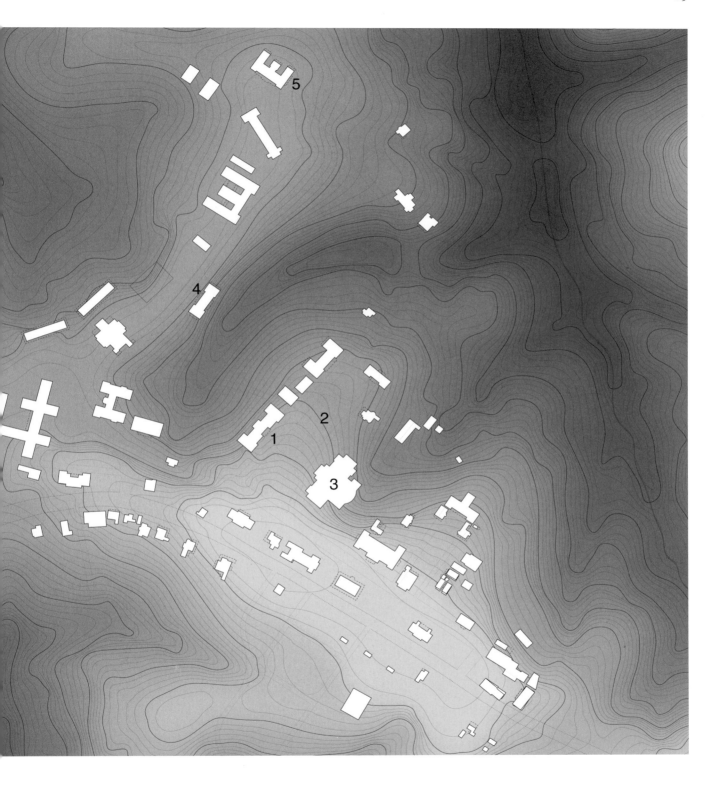

TUSKEGEE INSTITUTE 1932

BUILDING KEY

1	Second Power Plant
2	Frissell Library
3	Armstrong Science Building
4	Logan Hall Auditorium and Gym
5	Sage Hall (men)
6	James Hall (women)
7	New Laundry (now Visitors' Center)
8	Gregory Apartments
9	Pinehurst Apartments
10	Willcox Trades Building
11	Chambliss Children's House
12	Horse and Mule Barn
13	Veterinary Hospital
14	Cow Barn

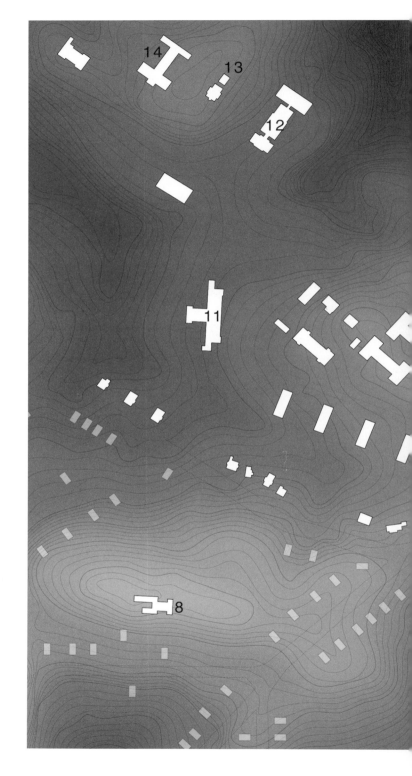

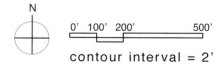

contour interval = 2'

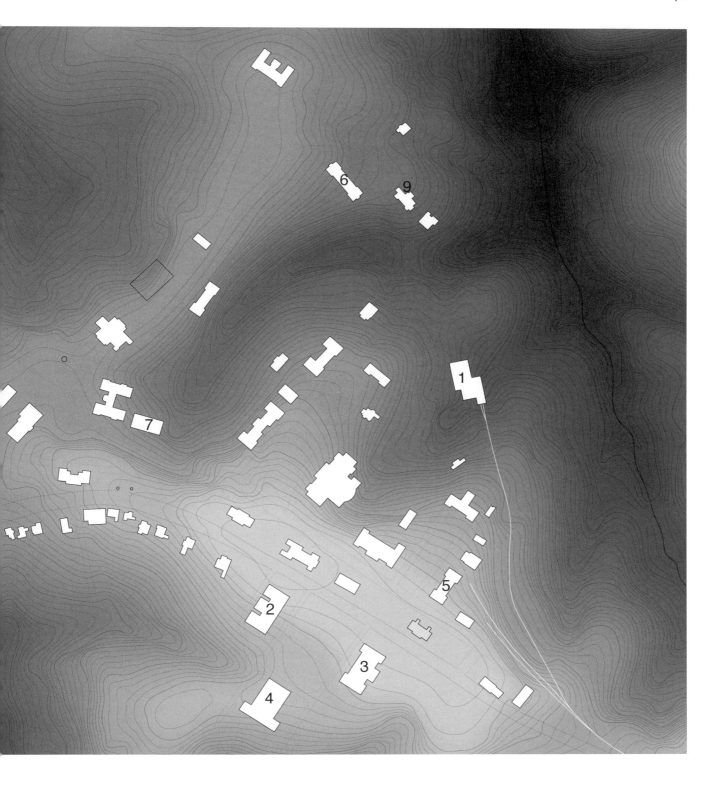

drawing room, Taylor doing preliminary drawings at home and then supervising the student draftsmen. The Parker Cottage, a substantial house used as a senior girls' dormitory, had full housekeeping and entertaining facilities, including a guest room, so the students could practice home management at a substantial level.

In 1894, Brooklyn attorney A. W. Parker gave a thousand dollars for a "model poor man's cottage." Washington had sent a sketch, presumably Taylor's. By January 1895 Parker's little abode had expanded into the two-and-a-half-story frame house that the donor first learned about when he saw the revised drawings. Parker thought this version would promote unrealistic expectations, frustrating graduates when they could not achieve such grandeur on their own. But Washington said that Tuskegeans really could aspire to large houses because they often achieved them. On another occasion he published photos of still larger ones owned by black businessmen and professionals throughout the South and beyond. Parker gave in gracefully and paid the bills, but he remained concerned that the school was making a mistake.[82] Parker Cottage was larger than Washington's 1890 house, but not as grand as The Oaks, the brick house Washington would soon build for private ownership. Robert Russa Moton, Tuskegee's principal after Washington's death, would remodel Parker Cottage for his campus residence. It was demolished in 1962.

Tuskegee must have seemed a permanent construction site during the late 1890s, with several buildings underway at any one time. An 1896 *Southern Letter* described the academic year's improvements: neatly fenced grounds, widened walks, grass lawns and flower beds, new machinery in all shops, a cupola on the foundry, an enlarged printing office, a better bake oven, new brickmaking equipment,

and the campus telephone system. The Chapel was still under construction, it noted. A Taylor-designed frame hospital and nurse-training school had appeared, but Science Hall remained unfinished, its third floor just begun. Taylor did not design the Slater-Armstrong Memorial Agricultural Building, although he soon designed the frontal additions and the connecting veranda. Intended to lure the black agricultural scientist George Washington Carver from Iowa, Slater-Armstrong was initially named to honor radical abolitionists who helped finance John Brown, as Catalog 21 considers. It was dedicated in 1898 after one of Tuskegee's nighttime spectacles with lamps in every window and fireworks above, this one honoring the U.S. Secretary of Agriculture. "The whole campus was as light as day."[83] Carver would be the first black director of a federal agricultural experiment station, a coup for Tuskegee since he was the only black agriculturalist who met federal qualifications. Soil restoration experiments, potato studies, and cotton hybridization took place inside this building until 1908 when another was erected elsewhere. This building then went to Home Economics and was, still later, rededicated to honor Margaret Murray Washington, a Tuskegee administrator and the Principal's third wife.

Another celebration worth worth remembering even though it took place years later marked the arrival of a British colonial administrator in Africa, Sir Harry H. Johnston, whose procession passed under a gate of greenery arched over the campus road. There were British and American music and flags and addresses from Washington and a South Asian student. Johnston was a "moderate but outspoken white supremacist" in Louis R. Harlan's estimation, but he still stayed ten days at The Oaks, presumably in the ground-floor guest room with bath. Johnston thought Mr. and Mrs. Washington exceptional, even exotic, like Italians.[84]

Built in 1899, the fifteen-room Queen Anne style house with a guest room and bath on the ground floor for the likes of Johnston or John D. Rockefeller Jr. was a gift of private ownership on Washington's own lot so that his family would have a home if he died or was incapacitated. Here Washington could entertain distinguished visitors but also have more privacy than provided by the 1890 house or even Parker Cottage. Washington's study was on the second floor, overlooking his backyard farm with its chickens, pigs, and vegetable gardens.[85] Washington found gardening and animal husbandry relaxing, and he used his grounds to demonstrate the crop rotation and other stewardship skills that he urged on poorer farmers. Photographs of Washington tending his livestock showed that he had not risen above those he served or, in another reading, that his pleasure in such part-time productivity bound him to the gentleman-farmer class of the philanthropists he was courting.[86] Huntington Hall Girls' Dormitory, also of this era, is discussed in Catalog 5. It was the first of Taylor's many brick dormitories and the structure that Taylor was working on when he complained that he could not also do all the teaching.

GROWING THE WESTERN CAMPUS

In December 1898, shortly before construction of The Oaks began, Washington and Taylor met to select a site west of the main campus and on a lower plateau for the Slater-Armstrong Memorial Trades Building—better known as Boys' Trades—to replace the hodgepodge of shops in and around Cassedy Hall. Washington and Taylor also intended to choose a nearby location for a comparable girls' industrial building, but because this was to be the Stokes sisters' third gift, its location and therefore its

construction was postponed by months of discussion with these thoughtful women who had design ideas of their own. The northern rim of "the valley" (later "White Hall valley") was long given to wooden barns. (See Catalog 21.) Tuskegee would also build two brick dairies along this rim, the first in 1889 and the second, which stood until recently, ten years later. The southern part of the rim was relatively flat although it was lower than the main campus center. Starting with the Chapel next to the established cemetery, and on through the Boys' Trades Building, this area worked well for structures with larger footprints than the early campus could handle. [See 1897 and 1903 Campus Plans, pages 64–65] There were also, west of the Chapel, two wooden army barracks that housed boys similar to those that had housed girls at Hampton.[87] [Figure 4.8]

Taylor consolidated the industries that were in the jumbled eastern zone into an organized spread of wings and courtyards for the Slater-Armstrong Memorial (Boys') Trades Building [Catalog 4]. Two stories high in the front, it was entered through a two-story veranda that is redolent of noble purpose and domestic ease. The façade's genteel qualities struck a tone the Phelps Stokes sisters would have approved as a neighbor to their Chapel. Boys' Trades burned in 1918 and was replaced by the present five separated Willcox Trades Buildings designed by Tuskegee teacher William A. Hazel and his Washington, D.C., partner Albert I. Cassell, a Cornell graduate. With the eventual construction of the Girls' Industrial Building, Dorothy Hall, close to the Chapel and Boys' Trades, then the four Emery boys' dormitories, and the Booker T. Washington Monument as a pivot, this spacious zone would coalesce into a comfortably arranged center to which the main entrance to the school has moved.

By century's end, Tuskegee's and Taylor's

achievements were substantial. Building upon Washington's goal of progressive industrial education with drawing as an essential component, Taylor developed a broad design and construction program to serve farmers and teachers, provide basic skills for all industrial divisions as well as the building trades, and be a starter education for professional architects. Almost as an aside, he designed and erected distinguished buildings that staked out a gently paced, spatially relaxed, attractive campus that would nurture students and provide institutional identity into the twenty-first century and, one hopes, beyond. Taylor's buildings alone, even without his teaching and administration, would have been an achievement for a twenty-something architect of any color.

Figure 4.8. Western Campus. Slater-Armstrong Memorial Trades Building in center. Left foreground, 1890s practice school, Slater-Armstrong Agricultural Building behind it, first Emery dormitory, Boys' Trades Building, Dorothy Hall from rear.

CHAPTER 5

CLEVELAND AND ALABAMA, AN INTERLUDE

The turning century found Robert R. Taylor in a shifted career in a different Northern city and with a family and new responsibilities. He had married Tuskegee English teacher Beatrice Rochon in a Roman Catholic ceremony in St. Martinsville, Louisiana, in May 1898. The following April his son Robert Rochon Taylor was born. Robert Rochon Taylor, or Robert R. Taylor Jr., as he was sometimes styled, would become the Chicago public housing administrator for whom the notorious high-rise projects were named.[1] In a celebratory mood, or perhaps emboldened by responsibility, the new father marked the very day of the boy's birth by asking Washington for permission to publish in a professional journal the Chapel, the Boys' Trades Building, and some other structures he had designed. He would not discuss costs beyond what had already been published.[2] The idea languished, it seems, but a month or so later, in late spring 1899, Taylor left Tuskegee for Cleveland, much to everyone's surprise. Washington first heard of the defection in May while on a ship bound for Europe.

Taylor finally explained himself that August. He had wanted for some time to learn newer building technologies and he now felt free to do so because the drawing courses were firmly established. He could leave "with justice to the school and honor to myself."[3] Arthur U. Craig, who was in charge of

the electric plant but was also a mechanical drawing assistant, could have taught with the help of James B. Nesbitt, a recent graduate, but it is more likely that Wallace A. Rayfield had already been hired as a badly needed second drawing instructor. Washington had met with Rayfield in New York. A November 1902 photograph taken by Frances Benjamin Johnston shows Rayfield with a drawing class of about twenty and an unidentified assistant.[4] Taylor's break, however, would be more geographical than professional. Even in Cleveland, Taylor wrote, he kept thinking about courses and arranging student projects in harness making, shoe making, and tailoring. He could not stop planning the students' day because it had become his habit.[5] Most important, however, is that throughout his three Cleveland years Taylor remained Tuskegee's architect, sending down the drawings for ten or more brick buildings along with a handful of wooden ones and supervising the construction of some in trips down or after he returned.

MORE WITH THE STOKES SISTERS

Taylor's Cleveland period serves the historian because, as with the Chapel discussions from Atlanta, correspondence had to substitute for face-to-face meetings. The first Cleveland design was for Caroline Phelps Stokes: the Girls' Trades Building, or Dorothy Hall as it was dedicated. Letters between

Figure 5.1. Wallace A. Rayfield and Drawing Class, November 1902.

Caroline Phelps Stokes and Washington and between Washington and Taylor remain although not between Taylor and Stokes even though they must have known each other from the Chapel adventure. The sisters may never have realized that the architect was not in Tuskegee, but they were pleased with his work nevertheless, giving him a June 1901 vacation trip to Chautauqua and Buffalo. Taylor could have seen photographs of his Tuskegee buildings that were also at the Paris exposition of 1900 because the panels reappeared at the Buffalo Pan American Exposition. Taylor thanked Washington for news of the sisters' gift, showing that for special rewards as well as for design, communication between the sisters and the architect went through the Principal.[6] In 1901 Caroline Stokes was also building "The Tuskegee" in New York City, a model apartment building for African Americans. As a child whose mother had instructed her about the living conditions of the black poor, Caroline had written that tenement housing was as bad as prisons. But "The Tuskegee" was designed by Caroline's nephew Isaac Newton Phelps Stokes, a housing expert and architect. Isaac Stokes had studied social housing at the Ecole des Beaux-Arts in Paris and, by 1901, had co-authored New York's tenement reform laws.[7] While in Cleveland, Taylor would also design the boys' and girls' bathhouses for Tuskegee, working with activist donor Caroline Phelps Stokes, as Catalog 8 details, plus buildings given by others: the Carnegie Library, Rockefeller Hall, the Office Building, Huntington Memorial Academic Building, a girls dormitory named to honor Frederick Douglass, and extensions to the Boys' Trades Building.

CLEVELAND

Taylor's Cleveland career beyond his Tuskegee work remains to be explored. According to his own account of this period, he first worked for another architect and then on his own. The architect was Charles W. Hopkinson (1865–1950), a Cornell graduate who had designed a John D. Rockefeller-funded settlement house. Those drawings would have been finished before Taylor arrived, but a Hopkinson-designed lodge for a Rockefeller estate would have been on the boards while Taylor was present. Hopkinson may have had a particular sympathy for African Americans since he designed houses in Oberlin, an abolitionist town with the college that pioneered multiracial education.[8] Taylor's first Cleveland address was 9 Blu (or Bloe) Court, but by October 1899 he was at 28 Myrtle Court, a two-story frame house on a bluff that overlooked railroad yards. The neighborhood was erased around 1910 for a railway expansion, but before then it had been ethnically mixed, with a synagogue a few blocks from Taylor's home. His immediate neighbors were white—a policeman, cabinet manufacturer, blacksmith, dry goods clerk, railroad motorman, and teacher. The 1900 census listed Taylor as an architect, but a more recent study

of Cleveland's African Americans considered him a "Negro in the engineering field" as well as the architect who had designed and erected all of Tuskegee's buildings.[9] The "engineer" designation along with that of "builder," as he is sometimes characterized, reflects competence in three arenas but not the fact that he was not a registered architect, as some have assumed. Neither Alabama or Ohio required registration until 1931.

Taylor soon regretted the move. By July 1900 he was telling Washington that "It is not an easy matter to leave off suddenly the effect of seven years continuous work in any line and I find myself even now, after more than a year's interval, almost unconsciously planning students' work and making changes in the course of study in spite of the fact that I keep very busy in other lines." If there were work at Tuskegee that he could do successfully "and in a manner to be of some service to humanity," he would consider returning.[10] That October, when his daughter Helen was born, Taylor wrote again that he was thinking about returning and would respond soon to Washington's last letter. He then switched the subject to Washington's recent speech on imperialism and the rights of the governed, as the press had reported it. He also expressed pleasure that the Girls' Industrial Building and Huntington Hall construction were advancing.[11] Taylor then reminded Washington about an overdue bill for The Oaks and he suggested changes on the Slater-Armstrong Agriculture Building, presumably the facade extensions shown in the November 1902 photographs. A year later, George Washington Carver would complain that Taylor was late in sending the drawings, leaving himself and William S. Pittman "working in the dark" on laboratory fittings.[12] In early 1900 Washington also instructed Taylor, Carver, and John H. Washington to make changes on the poultry house, the cow barn, and the dairy. William Henry Baldwin, chairman of the board, had liked Taylor's barn plans, Washington said.[13] Still without a decision, the architect continued his Tuskegee interests beyond architecture, suggesting, for example, that if Huntington Hall were to be emptied for commencement guests, bellhops should be on duty all night in case of emergencies.[14] During the summer of 1901 matters remained unresolved. He was thinking about Washington's idea for a new title, "Assistant Director of Industries," and wanted to hear more. He was busy, he wrote, because there was more work than ever in Cleveland's history.[15]

THE DIRECTOR OF INDUSTRIES

Taylor negotiated well. By February 1902 he was signing letters as Director of Industries, his title for the rest of his career. John H. Washington used the same handle at the same time but then became Supervisor of Industries, a post from which he could oversee the girls' trades and agricultural departments as well as Taylor's bailiwick. Both had moved up. By then Taylor had been traveling between Ohio and Alabama. In October 1901 he was in Cleveland "looking into methods of applying power to widely different points from one central source," that is, a central power plant—Tuskegee would build one ten years later.[16] That December he was on campus after several weeks' absence.[17] The following February he was managing the topographic survey for the consulting landscape architect Warren S. Manning's campus plan (which Chapter 6 will consider), and dealing with problems in the printing shop.[18] The Manning survey was incomplete in early March so new buildings could not be sited or the roads laid out. That July, Taylor asked Washington if the school could resume surveying the village area behind the Children's House. They had stopped when Manning

came but must resume since more cottages were needed. In April, Taylor, in Cleveland, was drawing the Office Building, the boys' bathhouse, Rockefeller Hall, Douglass Hall, Huntington Memorial Academic Building, and extensions to the Boys' Trades Building. That May he quaintly asked Washington to excuse his absence because his wife would soon be ill (she was was pregnant), but John H. Washington wanted him to come back immediately to manage lagging construction sites. "It is quite noticeable that the school is not getting the best results from the men, as many of the instructors—in my judgment—are taking advantage of your absence and not paying as much attention to the work as they should . . . The school is paying out an immense amount of money each week for hired labor, and unless the instructors can be made to push these men to the greatest extent, the school suffers."[19] Besides, brick production was slow, and someone must order the iron for the Office Building. Two days later, Taylor wrote his friend Emmett J. Scott to explain his wife's illness: the "gentleman expected three weeks before" had finally arrived. This was Edward, his third child.[20] One might take Taylor's indirection in informing Washington about his wife's condition as a sign of the Principal's prudery, but it could also be that Washington counterbalanced his rapport with crowds with formal relations to those close at hand. A Bengali student's description is worth recalling on this point. The boy, invited to dine with the family, found that the Principal "seemed to be the most serious man on earth, and his wife and sons, it had appeared, had the same kind of fear of him as the students had. After leaving the dining table he sat in an easy chair in the drawing-room, opened the Bible, and began to look at his favorite passages. This was his regular after-dinner work." The student then concluded that Washington's strength lay in a "full faith in divine justice" and the ultimate triumph of right. Therefore, his soul held "only love and not a bit of hatred," observations that might reflect Washington's Sunday evening chapel talks better than the boy's dinnertime observations.[21]

Taylor did not move his family to Alabama before September. He was in Tuskegee in July when he sent a construction report on four Cleveland-designed buildings to Washington's summer home in Massachusetts. He was, he wrote, searching nearby Montgomery and Opelika for builders to supplement the local supply, and he asked Washington if he could resume surveying lots behind the Children's House. More cottages were needed in Greenwood Village.[22] In September he went north to settle "unfinished matters" and pack up three small children and an ill wife. He wrote then that he needed a month to finish the Academic Building plans.[23] That November 1902 Frances Benjamin Johnston photographed the Cleveland buildings in their various stages of completion. Dorothy Hall and the Carnegie Library were finished, Rockefeller and the girls' bathhouse closed in and glazed, the Office Building roofed but unglazed, Douglass Hall's walls rising, and the Huntington Memorial Academic Building foundations begun. The calm photographs do not reveal what memos make clear, the confusing simultaneity of several ongoing construction sites for which labor and materials had to be juggled. Keeping track of staff, day and night students, and hired skilled and unskilled workers, getting materials to each site on time, and integrating it all into the curriculum would be Taylor's job from here on out.

TURF WARS

Wallace A. Rayfield, who taught Taylor's courses after fall 1899, with the assistance of recent graduate James Bernard Nesbitt, was the first Taylor

replacement in the drawing room after Taylor went to Cleveland.[24] Sometime in mid 1900, at the start of Taylor's second Ohio year, William S. Pittman returned to teach and to manage blueprinting process for all trades students, his official assignment. Taylor would send drawings to Alabama for review by Washington, the board, and sometimes John H. Washington or others, and then make the changes after the drawings were returned. In summer 1902 Taylor was revising the Huntington Memorial Academic Building plans in Cleveland, sending them down, and asking Washington to tell Pittman to take them to the Executive Council for approval.[25] But Pittman apparently did not see matters that way since he claimed full design credit for that structure later in his career and he demanded full responsibility for others. Within months of his return from Drexel, Pittman asked to be put in charge of all architectural drawing done on the grounds. He also wanted to determine—or at least to suggest—what should be built and to design the buildings and draft construction documents. He would be pleased to teach upper-level drawing classes only and to be assisted by Miss Kelley in freehand drawing. And he required photographs, drawings, and pictures for the drawing room walls to make them more "self suggestive."[26] Perhaps Taylor feared losing Tuskegee commissions to the aggressor, but it is more likely that he was frustrated that his talented former student was self-destructive. Taylor seems to have helped Pittman get work at Voorhees Normal and Industrial Institute in Denmark, South Carolina, which Taylor had visited in November 1902. Pittman appears have designed at least two buildings for that "little Tuskegee."[27]

Rayfield must have felt pushed, too, since Pittman was also trying to carve into his classroom bailiwick. In 1901 Pittman invited Washington to the drawing room to view student work he had assembled for a Charleston exposition. Booker T. Washington Jr.'s drawings would be displayed to special advantage, he noted. Pittman also prepared a prospectus for a special course in architectural and mechanical drawing that only he would teach. There seems to be something both flamboyant and churlish about a beginning professional who would send Washington two small cottage designs for "some conference purposes" with a note scribbled onto his cover letter saying that he was "under orders from Mr. Taylor" to send the drawings so that the Principal could offer criticism, suggestions, or approval "as the case may be."[28] It is hard to imagine Taylor taking this tone when he was drawing small cottages for the Negro Conference a decade before.

Both Rayfield and Pittman would have significant careers after Tuskegee. Rayfield's work would extend across the South from his base in Birmingham.[29] Pittman moved to Washington, D.C., in 1905 and a few years later to Dallas. A talented designer and—after 1907—Booker T. Washington's son-in-law, Pittman had the ambition, training, and connections for a stellar career. He would achieve large buildings in Washington, Dallas, and Houston and enjoy a significant reputation.[30] Paul Revere Williams (1894–1980), the first fully successful independent black practitioner, had heard of Pittman when he was a teenager in Los Angeles. Williams's teachers had said that the black community could not support an architect, but the courageous young Williams reasoned that if there was one black architect there might as well be two.[31] Pittman's ambitions were eventually betrayed by his difficult personality. In 1911 the head of a Kentucky school told Washington that his son-in-law was the first architect under consideration for a large building because he had made a favorable early impression. But he received poor

endorsements from his referees and he examined the site only cursorily. The favored candidate then became Tuskegee and Cornell graduate Vertner W. Tandy.[32] Separated from Washington's daughter Portia in 1928, Pittman abandoned architecture to publish an inflammatory newspaper. He spent two years in a federal prison for sending obscene material through the mail and, long after his release, died a pauper.

CLASSICISM

If Washington and Taylor failed to give Rayfield or Pittman brick buildings to design, perhaps this was because the Principal realized that it was the Director of Industries who had a profound grasp of architectural classicism. Columnar systems, whether at small scales (verandas) or large ones (porticos), must not only be executed correctly—grammar and diction in place—they must also articulate a larger rhythm that governs the whole. This is a subtle art that can best be learned by studying long-loved historical examples along with those buildings' most admired recent progeny. Most of Taylor's Tuskegee buildings have one- to three-story verandas at the entrance with wooden columns that could be turned on institute lathes. Taylor's columns are Roman Doric with torus moldings at capital and base. In photographs, they appear to have been made with entasis, the slight inward curvature of the shaft as the column rises. Along with the entablatures above them and, usually, balustrades above the entablatures, they are executed with a mastery that betrays Taylor's thorough classical education—all those MIT blackboard memory drawings. The historic black and white photographs show them to have been painted in a tone similar to or slightly darker than the brick behind them, emphasizing that they are of the building, not picked out to stand forth from it. Columns could be found on several small porch entries to the Chapel [Figure Cat. 2], the two-story veranda on the rear of Dorothy Hall as seen in a photograph [Figure Cat. 13] of the Lincoln Gates; the entrance into the Boys' Trades Building [Figure Cat. 4]; the veranda at Rockefeller Hall [Figure Cat. 9]; and the three-story veranda on Thrasher Hall [Figure Cat. 1]. At both levels of the Douglass Hall veranda the columns were clustered in threes at the ends, a device from Palladio that strengthens the corners visually. But at Douglass Hall there were also paired columns bracketing the central entrance and single columns between those and the outer three. The rhythm reads, left to right: 3, 1, 2 (entrance) 2, 1, 3. At Douglass Hall [Figure Cat. 12], at Huntington Hall [Figure Cat. 5], and at Huntington Memorial Academic [Figure Cat. 11], the veranda on the first or entry floor has columns set on the porch floor with a balustrade behind them

to protect the unwary from falling.

But on the upper floors of Douglass and Huntington halls' two-level verandas and on the side entrances to Huntington Academic, the columns rest on piers, not on the veranda floors. The piers are the height of encircling balustrades and continuous with them, together bounding the upper porch, a standard Renaissance motif. To maintain proportions, the shorter columns at this upper level must have correspondingly thinner shafts than those on the first floor, and this shift of column weight lends lightness to the upper porches of Douglass and Huntington halls that corresponds to the full-arched second-story windows that lend a lift-off to the building not found in the flatter segmental-arched windows of the first floor. There is a careful

Figure 5.2. A recent photograph of Carnegie Library.

visual calculation and a resulting expansiveness that proves Taylor's talent and the worth of his classically honed precision.

The subtle use of such modestly scaled classical detailing, which also serves as a proportional template for the whole, is almost unnoticeable in the reticence in which it stands. These small-columned verandas, painted in tones like that of the brick, do not prepare the viewer for the sudden appearance on the front of the Carnegie Library in 1901 of full-volume classicism with projecting two-story Ionic columns supporting a pediment. These white columns, painted to stand out from their brick background, would have been too large to be turned on institute lathes. While Carnegie libraries for white communities—and for black ones as well following Tuskegee's first—usually had large columns, Tuskegee's architectural assertion begs consideration in its racial context. Arguing for industrial education so the poor could gain an economic foothold, Washington derided classical high schools with their "Latin and Greek" because they taught silly adornments for those of little worth—people who could not make things that others needed. *Up From Slavery* is peppered with such rhetoric as are other examples of Washington's prose. He once characterized "Greek and Latin" as culture "bottled up and sealed in abstract language" that made it inaccessible to others. A culture must come from the people's own history, not a foreigner's.[33] Washington hated poverty because it denied the basic decencies. The notion of a naked boy living in squalor but studying French grammar upset him because French would not help the boy's material condition. This is just the trope with which W. E. B. Du Bois would take issue. "One wonders what Socrates and St. Francis of Assisi would say to this," referring the boy's wish to grow intellectually

despite his condition.[34] But perhaps Du Bois and his intellectual heirs have read Washington too literally. The rival leaders thought they benefited from their joint effort to use the other as a rhetorical whipping boy. Washington was not denying higher education to his people, as the Du Bois faction would charge. Even *Up From Slavery* makes that clear. "When a Negro girl learns to sew, cook, wash dishes, *write a book . . .*" or "When a Negro boy learns to groom horses, grow sweet potatoes, build a house, *practice medicine . . .*" as well or better than anyone else, each would be rewarded regardless of race. (Emphasis added.)[35] Du Bois's "Talented Tenth," his professional leadership class, could spring from Tuskegee soil as well, albeit with further schooling.

What might seem then a contradiction between Taylor's architectural "Latin and Greek," his confident classicism at dual scales, and Washington's rejection of classical high school curricula, fades under a fuller consideration of Washington's values. Washington was an aesthetic activist who insisted on the validity of simple things: nature, flower gardens, an orderly home, direct prose. A Sunday evening chapel talk lectured students on John D. Rockefeller's "no tom-foolery" because he used no Latin or Greek quotes. "He speaks and writes in a plain manner, with one syllable, not two, or two, not three. His is the power of simplicity, without showing off, and he may be the richest man in the world."[36] Washington's own prose is measured, clear, and often humorous—analogous perhaps to Taylor's carefully proportioned but minimally adorned Rockefeller dormitory or his subtle ventures in wit on other buildings. Taylor's work, even at its barest, is persuasive because of its clear expression, integral detailing, sharp-cut walls, triadic massing, and abiding sense of proportion. The discretion implied by modest verandas on subtly shaped volumes has allowed some to view them as "factory-like," a fitting judgment if one interprets Washington's grand effort as a cynical bargain to provide the New South with docile serfs for factory and field.[37] But Rockefeller Hall's elegance is as pronounced as its austerity, its arresting quality suggesting instead "the power of simplicity without showing off," certainly a broadly humane virtue. Along with the four Emery dormitories the only Taylor building history that suggests endless parings of visual amenity by a thrift-minded donor, the projecting bricks at eaves-level still delineate the carefully honed architrave, frieze, and cornice, all in brick, of a ghosted classical entablature. Even at their most austere, Taylor's buildings align with a positive assessment of Washington's determination to build the broad economic base from which a middle class might grow. Taylor's Tuskegee models a humanely scaled, visually rich world where impecunious and neglected youth might feel at one with themselves and perhaps with the larger world. The campus would help nurture black people into a higher and happier state of being and, not incidentally, force white outsiders to accept its parity with their own.

The suggestion of architectural parity raises the question of how such assertive classicism as the Carnegie Library's large columns was viewed by whites. Alabama's racial divisions had been more fluid than elsewhere in the South around the turn of the twentieth century, but the lines were hardening, according to historian Sheldon Hackney. In 1900, Montgomery segregated streetcars despite a protesting boycott. In 1902 Montgomery divided railroad station waiting rooms and, in 1905, disbanded the city's last black militia.[38] Tuskegee's executive council sited the Carnegie Library on January 1, 1901, the year during which Alabama would ratify a constitution that effectively disfranchised most African Americans. In 1901 Booker T. Washington was excoriated throughout the South for taking a meal with Theodore Roosevelt in the White House. He only worsened matters a few days later by marching with Roosevelt as they were awarded honorary degrees at Yale. Washington dined that day with the university president and others, including Roosevelt's headstrong daughter Alice, who purposefully sat near the black man. The white South now *knew* that Washington had abandoned the promise implied in the Atlanta speech of 1895 that he would not seek social or political equality for his people. Four years later, when he lunched with financier John Wanamaker and his daughter in a Saratoga Springs hotel, the white South was so consumed with rage that Washington had reason to make special provisions for his safety on the return trip home.[39]

Surely then, whites must have viewed Tuskegee's large columns as another societal challenge. But as yet there is no evidence of whites bridling at buildings emblazoned with western architecture's supreme emblems. Columnar porticos on white institutions of the turn of the century have been interpreted as evoking an antebellum golden age to accompany discrimination and segregation. As both Catherine Bishir and Richard Guy Wilson have shown, the grand columnar houses and courthouses of the early twentieth century reified racist triumphalism.[40] One wonders, then, why this discussion does not surface at Tuskegee. One anti-institute screed faulted the institute for other behaviors but not for architectural hubris. Stanton Becker Von Grabill, a German musician living in town, printed his pamphlet under the pseudonym "Rupert Fehnstroke." Von Grabill protested that he, a white man, was expected to doff his hat inside a Tuskegee building and address a teacher as "mister."

He accused Washington of preaching equality and the school of being a hotbed of sexual impropriety. But he also found the "small city" enchanting, its fundamental evils admirably masked by order, polish, cleanliness, and culture.[41] Nor do we read complaints from the other end of the spectrum—blacks or more liberal whites who opposed Washington because of his apparent compromises. No one protested the portico as a wasteful expense or accused Washington of toadying to white elites by mimicking their forms. Nor do we have complaints that more spare structures such as Rockefeller Hall or the Emery dormitories were too plain, unworthy as expressions of the race's ambitions and achievements. Neither opinion—too grand if columnar, too deprived if not—has yet to surface.

Architectural language, then, may be freer of specific meanings than we sometimes suppose. Building forms are too ambiguous to convey them unless intentions are spelled out between designer and client or in dedication rhetoric. Even if specific associations are called up, messages work best when several levels are thrown into play, the multiple allusions absorbing the observer's attention and intensifying the experience. Verbally articulated meanings also become lost over time, changing with shifting building usage or cultural context. Absent the founders' intentions, the Carnegie Library portico might best be viewed as race-neutral. An architect has taken the opportunity to work to the highest professional standards, signaling through the process the school's significance, the builders' capability, and the occupants' deservingness. Washington's secretary Emmett J. Scott suggested just that when he wrote that the library's "classic outline—a noble structure of artistic symmetry and beauty" would appeal to anyone who appreciates architecture. According to Scott, "pride of race, though not so written in the courses of study, is as much a part of Tuskegee's work as agriculture, brick-making, millinery, or any other trade, and quite as important." Like Tuskegee's faculty, with its high culture, correct behavior, and undeniable ability—modeling "pride and respect for colored men and women who deserve it because of their character, education, and achievements"—the buildings insisted that only the best would do. Continuing with Scott's bold explication, Tuskegee rejected the popular assumption that "anything is good enough for a Negro school."[42]

THERE IS ONE FURTHER possibility to bring to the Carnegie portico and its columned successors Tantum and White halls [Figures Cat. 15 and Cat. 18], the Tompkins Dining Hall [Figure Cat. 16], and Andrew Hospital [Figure Cat. 19], an interpretation that suggests that large orders might be not only race-neutral but also race-positive, albeit in silent, private ways. African Americans knew that skilled slaves built antebellum plantations. Tuskegee was a quarter mile from the Varners' Grey Columns, with its three sides of double-height projecting columns that were impressive in scale but unlearned in their parts. Grey Columns would not have survived an MIT blackboard critique. The Varner family supported Tuskegee, and Grey Columns was a compelling presence at the last turn of the road when traveling from town to the institute. But Tuskegee was also less than a hundred miles from a monumental and correct Doric portico with a particularly moving racial history. Talladega College, an 1867 American Missionary Association foundation, was housed in a Greek Revival boys' academy built in 1858. According to the historian Augustus Field Beard, the white founders of the black Talladega College set the school in this building to honor the race whose labors had reared it. Beard named slave carpenter Ambrose Headen, who had been "sorrowing most of all" because his own children could not attend the school he had helped build.[43] But then they did. "I rub my eyes and try to wake myself. When my boys and girls come home from school with their algebra, Greek and Latin books . . ." Headen said, ". . . I say to myself are these my children that were slaves a few years ago, counted no more than cattle?"[44] Washington admired Talladega, sending it academically talented Tuskegee graduates, including his son Davidson. He tried to get Rhodes scholarships for its top graduates. Perhaps these great columns reverberated in Tuskegee minds, their heroic profiles weighted with pride. But if so, the institute's culture of brevity and discretion has muffled those discussions to our ears.

WASHINGTON, AESTHETIC ACTIVIST

Discussion of Tuskegee's architectural language, its visual character, style, or even design in terms of construction or interior planning, is rare. Pittman assessed design subtleties on the Huntington Hall facade but Taylor, Scott, Logan, and Washington marked building completions in terms of the number of students who learned their trades on each construction. Washington's voluminous prose, as well as that by his assistants, publicists, and supporters, interweaves every aspect of the Tuskegee endeavor into a web of mutually reinforcing practices that interlocked pedagogy, production, economic progress, and interracial tolerance. Even though Washington never voiced an overarching style-and-race theory or indicated how a "Negro building" might differ from "white" ones in terms of plan or elevation, he frequently criticized individual projects. He once told Taylor that the new boiler plant (designed by Walter T. Bailey) did not harmonize with the other buildings

and that its landscaping looked "patchwork." He then complained that since so much money had been spent on a ground-level water tank or "reservoir," it should have been more ornamental.[45] But both constructions were hidden deep in the valley behind Rockefeller Hall and the other old-campus structures. Sitting on a high plateau, Rockefeller and a half dozen other structures put their backs to the offenders. It would have cost a visitor some determination to find them. On another occasion, Washington insisted that a farmyard plan must consider the "prominence as well as convenience of the hog lot so that people could see the small pigs and the larger ones when either walking or driving past."[46] Even the humble had to perform.

Washington knew John Ruskin, as Michael Bieze has shown, his language often echoing that of the British art critic whom black as well as white Americans had taken up as guide.[47] To Washington, beauty was as essential as morality and work. All together would lead the race to a higher civilization. Like Ruskin, Washington admired arts sourced from non-classical traditions. Traveling in Denmark in 1911, Washington praised the cultural empowerment that a Danish agricultural school offered young men and women because it taught pre-industrial "old Norse" crafts rather than Renaissance or ancient Greek arts. That which is "distant, foreign and mysterious" is not better than that which is familiar and close at hand, Washington wrote. Studying one's own people rather than distant others inspires "faith in one's self, in one's race, and in mankind."[48] While he did not propose an American American architectural folk source—those might be the wretched, dirt-floored cabins from which he wanted everyone to flee—he did promote the musical equivalent of "plantation melodies," collecting them from arriving students from remote places. He valued the songs

Figure 5.3. Booker T. Washington.

for their expression of feeling.

Nature was another wellspring of Washington's aesthetic attitude. Nature brought renewal, as photographs of him and his children on a Sunday woodland ramble proclaim. Nature did not discriminate. Washington lavished attention on flowers and trees, urging their planting at farms and rural schools everywhere as sources of joy as well as signs of success. He put Tuskegee's second greenhouse near the town entrance so visitors could enjoy flowers in every season. Washington initiated and then judged flower-arranging competitions in the students' dining hall. Every table had to have a centerpiece of field flowers, moss, or greenery and he was happy to revise student efforts in order to teach taste.[49] The dining hall held special significance for Washington because it was where he inculcated the habit of regular meals as he would have known them from childhood service in a white household but not in his slave mother's cookhouse. Students were unlikely to have known the ritual either. One recalled that had never seen a knife and fork before coming to Tuskegee and had to learn their usage by watching others.[50]

Washington's devotion to design detail was so complete that one might imagine him wishing that he could do it himself. A manufacturer who wanted to place his steel stacks in the Carnegie Library shifted his attentions from Taylor to the Principal when he realized who would actually decide.[51] Washington had a well-honed sense of the fitness of objects to their purpose. He asked Taylor to design a dining hall coffeepot because the one in use looked like an ordinary water pitcher.[52] Even Washington's memorial volume chided him for ignoring pressing matters for weeks on end in favor of "mysterious" conferences over plans for a four-room cottage for his night watchman. The result was a gardened showplace and still another demonstration of right housing for those of modest means.[53] Washington laced his talks to country people with directives to paint and whitewash their houses and fences, plant flowers where they could be seen from the road, and make decorations from found materials so cabin interiors would be homey. Margaret Murray Washington helped by distributing pictures cut from magazines to countrywomen in her Saturday classes. The images would stimulate their children's senses and curiosity.[54] Washington once criticized plans for a son's house, the drawings promising an uncomfortable, impractical structure that Taylor's forthcoming redesign would surely improve. It had a direct entry into the sitting room, an overlarge dining room, and a dearth of blank walls against which one could put furniture. Washington thought it "best to stick closely to Southern models when building in the South. These complicated cut-up houses sometimes built in the North do not answer the purposes of the South."[55] And a plain, simple, dignified building would be far more satisfactory in the long run, he concluded. He used photographs that he had commissioned of the institute to publicize it in the mainstream press: *Scribner's Magazine, Survey, Colliers, Saturday Evening Post, Outlook,* and *Harper's Weekly.* And he published the substantial houses of his black associates, ministers, businessmen, and doctors from Topeka to Atlanta and north to Cambridge to show that prosperity and its solid investment were also part of the race's traditions.[56] From pragmatic planning to imagery, Washington understood that better housing and fine community buildings—churches, lodges, schools, offices—proved racial progress and nurtured interracial harmony. Splendid buildings contradicted the widespread notion that black people were doomed without slavery's armature. They were, rather, a rock-hard assertion of worth, a fist against the sky.

CHAPTER 6

THE DIRECTOR OF INDUSTRIES I

COALESCING THE VISION

Taylor returned from Cleveland in 1902 to a life of intensified labors with far broader administrative responsibilities. Nevertheless, by working evenings and weekends at home, he continued to design. The oeuvre at the time would have included the 1890s' buildings Science Hall (soon to be renamed for the deceased Max Bennett Thrasher), the Boys' Trades Building, the Chapel, and Huntington Hall. Finished or underway from designs done while he was in Cleveland were the Carnegie Library, Office Building, Dorothy Hall, the boys' and girls' bathhouses, Rockefeller Hall, Douglass Hall, and Huntington Memorial Academic Building. The frame buildings would have included Parker Cottage, the Practice Cottage, Pinehurst Hospital, the Children's House, barns, silos, and other agricultural buildings, and many cottages.

Brick production had improved while he was away. The July 1902 *Tuskegee Student* contrasted the poorer handmade bricks of the Cassedy Hall era with the machine-made "Indian red" ones in Douglass Hall. With the new steam machinery, students could make thirty thousand bricks a day, compared to the earlier period's nine hundred. Brickmaking had become a popular trade because of Tuskegee machinery and the promise of prosperity. Frances Benjamin Johnston photographed the main campus

road looking west probably from the water tower [Figure 6.1]. A corner of Phelps Hall intrudes into the left, blocking part of Washington's brick house, The Oaks, in the distance. Next on the row facing the campus road comes the Office Building, windows not yet in, and then a white sliver of Washington's 1890 frame house, then a gap, and then the Carnegie Library. A teacher's cottage at the bend of the road partially blocks the rear of Dorothy Hall in the far distance. The roof of the Boys' Trades Building is visible to the left, behind Dorothy, and the Chapel with its tower is to the right. Entering the picture from the right is the front of Alabama Hall and then, in front, a frame cottage. The foundations of the coming Huntington Memorial are in the immediate foreground. Fixing the scene in arrow-like purpose is the straight road, terraced to clear it from the lower land to the right, or north. There are sidewalks on each side and regularly spaced young trees with whitewashed trunks punctuating the route like drumbeats in a march.

As Director of Mechanical Industries, Taylor continued to report to John H. Washington, now the General Superintendent of Industries. John H. was overseeing Agriculture, Girls' Industries, the nascent nurse-training program, and Boys' Trades. But he continued to nag his junior about construction mishaps, worker misbehavior, and messy construction sites. "Some weeks ago I gave you an order," he complained. "Maybe you don't see my notes. Many orders I give are not carried out."[1] The memo track makes it clear that Taylor was actually reporting directly to Booker T. Washington. John H.'s complaints eventually subsided, perhaps because the Principal had intervened with his brother. He would not want to lose Taylor a second time. Linda O. McMurry, whose biography of George Washington Carver reveals so much about the school's inner workings, charges Washington with being too demanding of his faculty and staff, over-assigning them and expecting perfection in every task.[2] But unlike the charismatic Carver, Taylor was a good administrator, a team player and background person who was happy outside the limelight. Taylor could handle simultaneous problems in different tracks

that would have overwhelmed others. Washington, who understood those with whom he worked, would have valued these abilities.

Taylor's Department of Mechanical Industries was the school's largest and, perhaps, the most complex in its applications. In 1906, it had twenty-two divisions, each with its own faculty, assistants, shops, and classrooms. In comparison, there were sixteen divisions in the Agricultural Department,

Figure 6.1. View to the west over campus road, November 1902. Left to right: Phelps Hall, The Oaks in the distance, Office Building, Carnegie Library, Boys' Trades in far distance, Dorothy Hall rear behind a frame teachers' cottage, The Chapel, Alabama Hall, unidentified teachers' cottage, and foundations of Huntington Memorial Academic Building.

ten in Girls' Industries, and ten in the Academic Department. A random selection of Taylor's divisions includes printing, wheelwrighting, tailoring, harness making, tinsmithing, electrical engineering, steamfitting, sawmilling, plumbing, carpentry, brickmaking, and mechanical and/or architectural drawing—a range of pre-industrial and modern trades. Taylor would have overseen the budgets and staffing of each division's shop, office, and classroom. He would have coordinated each division's curriculum with other divisions and the academic department. And he would have organized each division's practicum, the work students did on alternate school days. This last was essential for building and maintaining buildings, grounds, and infrastructure, also his responsibility. And it all had to be done "as much as possible" as self-construction for economy and for instruction, using Tuskegee's own talent and labor.

HIGH IDEALS

Tuskegee had around seventy-two "Negro buildings" in 1905, said to be the largest such assemblage in the nation. John A. Lankford, who had earned a steamfitting certificate and was then practicing architecture in Washington, D.C., praised Tuskegee students for sawing their own lumber, burning their own brick, molding their own hardware, milling their own trim, and "building independent, manly character, which will bring forth fruit as long as time."[3] Lankford, with a science and technology background from elsewhere, must have become aware of architecture during his Tuskegee year because he later studied it through the International Correspondence School. He could see that Booker T. Washington's attractive and seemingly self-constructed "city" was acquiring a utopian tone. It was an island of order, polish, and good cheer in the discouraging South.

To hear Washington tell it, Tuskegee divisions choreographed themselves into a performance when a building went up.[4] The sequence began when Tuskegee-built wagons pulled by Tuskegee-bred horses hauled the dirt from a student-dug excavation. Student wheelwrights, blacksmiths, and harnessmakers had already honed their skills by making the wagons and harnessing the mules. Then came the brickmakers. These boys learned their true worth as they saw their products assembled into walls. They had learned brickmasonry and plastering "theory" in one hundred and eighteen classroom lessons, from reading trade journals, and from their architectural drawing classes, but the real diplomas were embedded in Tuskegee's walls. That is how one found out if he has "learned to be a brick-mason, or whether he has merely learned things about brickmasonry."[5] Students in the sawmill division planed the lumber after having studied trees, felled them, drawn, scaled, and graded the lumber they had cut, designed and molded the templates, and maintained the machinery that had modernized their exploits. Carpentry students did the interior trim and tinsmithing students the gutters and roofing. Plumbing and steamfitting classes installed radiators, sinks, and toilets while the machinery division kept it all running with the machine parts the foundry division had cast. Machinery students worked with eleven steam engines, seven steam pumps, twelve boilers, water-works, and the attendant piping, valves, gauges, and recording apparatus to prepare for their careers. The electrical engineering division installed telephones and arc or incandescent lighting. The mechanical drawing division taught every trades student essential skills while those in advanced architectural drawing did the building's presentation and production drawings. When Taylor told the tale he wound the narrative back to the Tuskegee-sewn worker overalls.[6] He could have mentioned but did not the Agricultural Department's meat and produce that the girls cooked and served to fuel the entire effort. Washington's account of the grand production continued: "these object lessons of their own handiwork," the buildings, "stand clustered over many acres, a city in itself built by young coloured men."[7] Or, on another occasion, "It will be seen that the school is a community unto itself, in which buildings can be erected, finished, and furnished, the table supplied the year round, and economic independence achieved in a large measure."[8] Washington bent his vision towards the popular romance of the self-sufficient community but he veered away just before arrival, as he must. No industrial school can be fully self-sufficient, he cautioned, since students are starter artisans who work slowly, make mistakes, and waste material. When they finally master their trades, they leave for the wider world. Education must preempt production because the institute's true products were the attractive, cultivated people who would fan out into the world, rise economically, serve others, and end racial discrimination through sheer ability.

AND LESSER REALITIES

The Tuskegee ideal, however, was readily compromised, as happens in any human institution. While the *Tuskegee Student* might celebrate building dedications by declaring the numbers that learned their trades on the job, internal studies charged frequent failure to instruct because of the pressure of production. Too many left each construction site as low-skilled "hired hands" according to Joseph Citro, who has collected the problems and thought about his findings.[9] Washington commissioned some evaluations for his own guidance while others came from sympathetic outside observers. By 1900, Citro

charges, Tuskegee's solid teacher-training program had become subservient to the industrial departments. Teaching was no longer the only diploma, merely one possible vocation or "trade" that the student could choose. In 1903, Roscoe Conkling Bruce, the Harvard-educated director of the Academic Department, complained about deficiencies in teacher preparation, particularly in English and geography. Worse, Bruce continued, future machinists did not have enough physics, farmers enough chemistry, or carpenters enough mathematics. The weakening academic program, as he saw it, also impacted the industrial work.[10] Problems surfaced throughout the institute. A landscape gardening student told Washington that during his ten months' residency he had worked hard planting trees but was never told their names, why they were chosen, or how to care for them. The Principal instructed George Washington Carver to "take hold of the matter" and do better by this boy.[11] Production pressures in the laundry division meant that the washing machines could not be stopped so that a machinery division instructor could show students how they worked. The dressmaking "theory" classes were, at best, basic drafting, but even that was done by a few students, the others watching.[12] Another visitor did praise Girls' Industries. W. B. T. Williams, a black Harvard-educated Hampton teacher who visited in 1906 on behalf of the General Education Board, thought that Margaret Murray Washington was accomplishing some of the institute's best work.[13]

Taylor's building trades divisions did not escape criticism. W. B. T. Williams thought that students were sacrificed "to some extent" to donors' expectations of seeing their gifts materialize quickly. Speed distorted what should have been a student-paced process, leaving them as "hired hands" under temporary journeymen who, if they instructed at all, did so by rule-of-thumb methods rather than by systematic class and shop procedures.[14] In 1903, the white New York auditor who oversaw institute finances on the board's behalf complained to trustee chairman William H. Baldwin that, even though the institute had known for four years that a building boom was on the way, there were only a dozen competent student joiners and fifteen bricklayers. He charged that since skilled students were unavailable in sufficient quantity, the number doing low-level labor was rising as were those receiving no training at all.[15] E. T. Attwell, a respected Tuskegee teacher whom Washington had asked to look into the problems, described a class in brick masonry in which the teacher was stymied by the classic problem of calculating the number of bricks needed for a wall. The students' hour was wasted.[16] Attwell also found wanting an architectural drawing class. The teacher dictated instructions for the students to transcribe, a tedious process that could have been eliminated with textbooks and a library. Class time could then be given to discussion, the students thinking rather than copying.[17] The following year Lloyd G. Wheeler complained that poorly taught students were throwing bricks on and off the wagons, causing breakage and waste. Wheeler then faulted the repair division for hasty work that would have to be done again—and paid for as another job.[18]

Still another set of pedagogical problems came with a 1903 curriculum change that alternated academic and industrial work on full-day cycles, rather than the previous period's half-day rhythm. A carpentry student might begin a project on his shop day but lose it to someone else the next day because of production pressures. The second student did not fully understand the first's intentions and the first lost the "spiritual mastery" that comes with completing a task.[19] A science teacher thought

the alternating day schedule was also to blame for Academic Department ills. "I cannot believe that our students are not interested," he wrote, "or that the work is too heavy for them. Nor am I prepared to admit that the average native ability of our students is below that of similar bodies gathered in other similar schools." In the end, he found Tuskegee's graduates less able than Hampton's.[20] Criticism extended to the students' personal habits, another aspect of Washington's grand design. The head of the Boarding Department complained that the Principal did not realize how bad the students' table manners were because they behaved well when Washington was in residence. The director was concerned about embarrassing the school at the coming anniversary celebrations.[21] Since Washington spent at least half his time away fundraising and politicking, his morning campus horseback rides, a stenographer trailing, caught only the most visible problems. He depended on others for a fuller assessment.

Gaps between the ideal and the real in boys' industries would have been squarely among Taylor's responsibilities.[22] While his systematic thinking, as revealed in succinct, point-numbered memos, must have grappled ceaselessly with the issues, his notes do not address them directly. The institute-wide, alternate-day scheduling would have been discussed during meetings of the Executive Council, on which Taylor sat. Taylor worked closely with division heads to develop curricula, shops, and staffing and to maintain inter-divisional coordination for construction, but reality must have stood someplace between Washington's ennobling vision and situations that may not have been as dire as Citro's assemblage implies. Linda O. McMurry's two deeply researched Tuskegee biographies offer a warmer assessment of the school's educational achievements. Whatever views emerge, it is clear

Figure 6.2. *Boys' Trades Building with window frames for Tompkins Hall on left and Tantum Hall on right.*

that Taylor was straddling, as if standing on separating ice floes, the ever-competing demands of a complex human institution.

The concerns that actually emerge from the Taylor-Washington correspondence fall far from issues of race pride and character building that Lankford admired from a distance, the sweeping optimism of Washington's integrated vision, or the educational weaknesses as Citro has shown them. Most memos dealt with pragmatic issues such as recommendations for hiring and promoting or responses to Washington's directives transcribed from his daily horseback rides. Messages for a few days in 1903 serve as a sample. In a rare case of Washington's wit surfacing internally, as opposed to his public utterances where it flourished, the Principal said the wheelwrighting division was in a rut—it must make more wagons because a town merchant wanted to buy them. He then told Taylor to check

that the wells were in good condition and send the final costs for Rockefeller Hall. Taylor next sent a list of needed electrical equipment—a foundry blower, a generator, and milking machines—because the Westinghouse Corporation would make a donation. He then asked the Principal to decide whether to cut a new door into a classroom. The request had come from a division head to John H. Washington, who passed it to the Director of Industries with the instruction that the latter must ask the Principal, a sequence that illustrates Washington's well-known micromanagement as well as the ritualized route to access his attention. Then came matters of a shelf in one teacher's office and a picture hanging in another's—each request going up separately. Later that day Taylor told Washington that the girls' bathroom, which had just been cleaned of graffiti, was ready for inspection.[23] A few days later Washington asked Taylor to organize the grounds staff so it could quickly fill in gullies after a rainstorm had washed them out. Taylor asked Emmett J. Scott, Washington's private secretary, to persuade the Principal to put David A. Williston, the newly hired Cornell-trained teacher of horticulture and landscape gardening, in charge of the grounds. Washington did so immediately.[24] Even Beatrice Taylor found herself swept into the fray, reporting as a committee chair about roads, sidewalks, and tree plantings in residential Greenwood.[25] The correspondence is fuller when Washington was traveling, revealing more of the enterprise's true scale. For example, during the summer of 1904 Taylor's letters summarize plans for a sewerage system (not executed then), barns and other farm buildings, and construction stages on an Emery dormitory, Tompkins Dining Hall, and the Huntington Memorial Academic Building. Each of these would be complex challenges in themselves, stars of Taylor's quiet juggling act.

GREENWOOD

The "Village of Greenwood," Beatrice Taylor's civic endeavor, was the summary name for off-campus housing to the south and west after 1892. In early 1893 Taylor and students had platted more lots in the "progressive village" or "model suburb" that Washington saw in terms of the New England archetype and the period's imitations. Churches were to meant to border a central park that was maintained by residential taxes. In 1902 a Village Improvement Association was overseeing the two thousand or so residents through an elected Board of Control. The board maintained "moral, physical, and spiritual repair" or, more specifically, moder-

ate entertainments, proper lawn care, and Sunday shop closures. Washington presided at Association meetings when he could. In 1901 Tuskegee had replaced its on-campus practice school with the larger Children's House in Greenwood and in 1904 the Hampton-based Southern Improvement Company, a for-profit black development enterprise, platted a gridded extension that echoed the block size, shape and Vitruvian orientation of the Tuskegee town grid. Just as the ancient Roman architect said they should, diagonals of the squares addressed the cardinal directions. The orientation works on the town's topography but not in Greenwood, or at least not in the same way.[26]

FIRE, WATER, ELECTRICITY, SEWERAGE

Taylor may have gained help from David Williston when it came to rain-washed gullies and other assignments, but he continued to manage campus infrastructure, as we can see in his 1904 report. Ever searching opportunities for publicity, Emmett J. Scott had asked Taylor for a copy of this internal document so that he could write an article about "The Negro's Attempt at Community Life" for publication.[27] The report summarized the mix of old and new systems in use. About fifteen buildings had steam heat, the rest being warmed by stoves and fireplaces. Some water was pumped to a few fire hydrants, but safety continued to depend on strategically located water buckets, an inadequate solution to a continuing threat since the school periodically lost buildings to fires. Fires took Washington's first cottage (1889), the dairy herd and barn (1895), the boys' barracks with the possessions of seventy-five students (1911), a cow and mule barn (1914), the Pavilion (1918), the Boys' Trades Building (1918), the Chapel (1957), and as recently as the 1990s the Huntington Memorial Academic

Building and the brick Dairy Barn. Warren Logan said privately that the 1895 fire could have been arson because the dogs had barked in the night, suggesting that strangers were present.[28] The 1957 Chapel fire started when lightning ignited the roof, coincidentally in the month following the successful conclusion of the Montgomery bus boycott. Black churches and homes in Montgomery—just forty miles away—were being dynamited or burned by white racists in reaction to the bus boycott court decision, but this was not that.[29] Nonetheless, arson at African American schools was always a threat even if an under-recorded one. Washington addressed the problem with guards, but there may have been other attempts and even successes. Tuskegee could have failed to acknowledge a suspected arson because silence maintained dignity and denied the perpetrators the satisfaction of knowing that their message had been received.

Taylor's 1904 report also deals with other aspects of the infrastructure. The institute had been well supplied with electricity thanks to the now-departed Arthur U. Craig, the Kansas engineer who had electrified the Chapel. By 1898 Tuskegee was selling power to the white town, starting with a politician's house and continuing on to a church, a shop, and the railroad station. Electricity may have achieved the tolerance that Washington believed productivity would bring. In 1904 the school owned a General Electric dynamo and a Brush arc machine that had been adapted for incandescent lighting and it had just purchased another dynamo and was negotiating servicing more of the town. Craig had also installed an institute telephone that reached the Marshall farm four miles away.[30]

Sewerage, water supply, and sanitation were the most critical infrastructure elements since the school suffered periodic if unpublicized bouts of typhoid, malaria, and smallpox. According to the coming-to-Tuskegee memoir of Thomas Monroe Campbell, the smallpox quarantine line in 1899 was near Grey Columns, the antebellum mansion a quarter mile east. Campbell concluded his harrowing four-month journey to the mythic Tuskegee by crossing that line. Fifty sick students were in a temporary hospital in Parker Cottage and no one died, but soon afterwards typhoid and malaria killed five boys, including Campbell's brother.[31] Since the school's buildings crested the high grounds, those with indoor toilets simply piped refuse over the hillsides where the outhouses stood and where storm-water runoff joined the effluvia. This was an improvement over what the institutional management expert Alice J. Kaine had seen in 1895, when the slop deposits and attendant odors were only a few feet from the girls' dormitories. Girls were expected to carry refuse buckets up and down fence stiles to reach a more distant location but failed to do so, for which they must not be faulted, she said. The expert recommended a gate.[32] By 1904 there were sewerage plans made by a Mr. Tufts of Atlanta, but the project languished for years because of cost.[33]

As for water, Taylor's report informs us that it came from wells, from a single pipeline from the town's spring-fed system, and from other springs a mile away. Water was piped to the above-ground circular tanks called "reservoirs," which Washington had faulted for their appearance. From there it was pumped to the high metal tank near Porter and Huntington Academic. Hot water was available in the kitchens and laundry. Agricultural water was a separate system taken from a creek to a brick reservoir and a second raised tank near the barns. Using his experience overseeing Tuskegee's water systems, Taylor designed and supervised the water supply at the Calhoun Industrial School in Lowndes County,

Alabama, that was installed by a New York construction firm.[34] Calhoun was an independent endeavor founded and staffed by Northern white women who were allied with Hampton and Tuskegee.

In 1903, the year before Taylor's report, the newly arrived institute doctor John Andrew Kenney made a comprehensive study of the institute's sanitation problems. Kenney spared no sensibilities in describing the sights and smells near the slaughterhouse as well as the toilets, outhouses and empty fields that students used when nothing else was at hand. Kenney proposed such interim strategies as mixing night soil with earth to make fertilizer until a proper sewerage system could be built. The latter, he admitted, would require a princely donation. Kenney's list of nauseous areas makes one wonder that visitors seemed not to have noticed. "Every-body, every day sees the bright side, the pretty flowers, trimmed grass, clean walks & well-kept lawns" as if visual charm neutralized all other senses.[35] John H. Washington directed Taylor to assign the problems Kenney had outlined to Williston.[36] Kenney continued to advocate for basic health measures throughout the Washington era, suggesting at one point that the old "closets" or outhouses were preferable to flush toilets because they used cleansing lime. Indoor plumbing was still sending raw waste into the ravines where it could fester. While Kenney's descriptions of outfalls that compromised wells are appalling, Joseph Citro has suggested that Tuskegee's sanitary conditions were no worse than those in most Southern towns of the period.[37] Whatever the reality, visitors could still view the grounds as an idyll, a model for the students' future and for a black nation beyond. Taylor continued to supervise campus infrastructure for the rest of his career. In 1930 he announced that new wells and piping for natural gas would be ready for the coming fiftieth anniversary celebration.[38] And he wrote during his retirement that his work with water, lighting, heating, sewerage, roads, and walkways was as important as systematizing the industrial courses or designing buildings.[39]

TOMPKINS DINING HALL

These less-visible campus tasks and the resulting workload may account for the fact that Taylor was not the primary designer of the largest building of the Washington era, Tompkins Dining Hall. James W. Golucke, a white Atlanta architect with extensive courthouse experience, including that for Macon County in Tuskegee, was that building's author.[40] [Figures 6.2, 6.3] We do not know why this self-trained Georgian was awarded the lucrative commission when Tuskegee was a showcase of black talent and when several academically experienced black architects were now on hand. It may be that none, including Taylor, had the experience with steel and concrete the building's size required. But Taylor was construction supervisor even before October 1907, when Golucke died. As Catalog 16 recounts, Taylor made many other contributions to its realization, from programming and structural design to persuading the board to agree to the behemoth.

Tompkins's blocky mass and imperial scale, along with such historically loaded architectural elements as a dome and three grand entrances bounded by very large columns, suggest a different and more domineering sensibility than Taylor's. Many interpretations might "explain" the shift but no persuasive ones have surfaced in Tuskegee prose. A domed structure with giant orders is a forceful counter-argument to cultural racism—weighted grandeur facing down white disdain. Few Southerners had any experience with grand institutions. County courthouses might be emblems of a white power

Above, Figure 6.3. Tompkins Dining Hall. Below, Figure 6.4. Tompkins Dining Hall interior. The hall now has ten paired supports and a visible beam structure reinforcing the span.

structure but they were usually smaller than this building. Macon County's courthouse was small, and it was the locus of a racist political challenge in 1904. If Tompkins strikes the observer as imperial in tone, perhaps it could be understood as an African American capitol or even as an emblem of Washington's Pan African reach. *Up From Slavery* was now translated into non-European languages and Tuskegee would host an international conference in 1912. Perhaps it responded to Hampton's domed library, meeting the mother-institute's imagined challenge. Arabella Huntington, who gave the relatively modest Huntington Memorial Academic Building in 1902, funded Hampton's grandiloquent exercise in Beaux-Arts classicism two years later. One critic has interpreted Tompkins as a training ground for an emerging black professional and managerial elite.[41] Or perhaps its grandeur merely reflects the overarching importance that Washington assigned to the act of dining together. He particularly wanted the hall to have a clear span, without intermediary posts, so students could feel their unity. Washington thought that regular meals taken together would take the race even farther from slavery's familial privations.

WORSENING RACISM

During the first part of the twentieth century discrimination and enforcing violence towards African Americans escalated in every aspect of public life. If Washington's formula for racial harmony were working, it should have been different. Macon County had been relatively safe because of Washington's political skills and the school's contribution to the local economy. But as Robert J. Norrell has told it, Alabama congressman J. Thomas Heflin's October 1904 courthouse speech attacking both Washington and Theodore Roosevelt was applauded a scant mile from the rising Dining Hall.[42] Heflin had been appointed to fill the term of Charles Thompson, Washington's recently deceased congressional ally and electricity consumer. Still another crisis came from the deceased congressman's renegade nephew who, as state representative, tried to tax Tuskegee farmland at commercial rather than educational rates. The bill was defeated but only after costly efforts.[43] Matters were worsening far beyond Macon County, of course. D. W. Griffith's dramatic film version of Thomas Dixon's scrofulous *The Clansman* would soon play to enthusiastic whites across the nation. Dixon, meanwhile, claiming only sympathy, had argued in "Some Dangerous Aspects of the Work of Tuskegee" that education for economic independence might be laudable in principle but was actually setting up black people to be murdered by whites wherever the separate but necessarily competing societies clashed. The only solution, he wrote, was mass emigration to Africa.[44]

Then, in a reprise of the flap over the dinner at the White House of four years earlier, Washington was again spotted socializing with a powerful white Northerner, merchant John Wanamaker and his daughter, at a Saratoga Springs hotel.[45] Southern newspapers openly called for Washington's assassination and the institute's destruction, as he told Francis Jackson Garrison in a rare letter admitting discouragement. But black education was in for hard times on all fronts, he continued, steering the subject away from Tuskegee and his own person. Spreading disfranchisement argued against any schooling since literacy would be unnecessary for those who could not vote. Primary education was eroding, especially in the countryside where "matters are going backward," and industrial education was faring no better. Black masons, carpenters, and architects, unlike the black ministers and teachers who served only their own, competed with whites for work. Garrison, a descendant of abolitionists, replied that he had long feared that a sudden whirlwind of passion might sweep across the South and destroy Tuskegee in the process.[46] This is far from the racial peace that Washington said would come when masses of attractive, productive, and culturally aware graduates provided whites with needed goods and services.

As the Wilmington insurrection had already shown, middle-class wealth and manners might stimulate white-on-black violence rather than prevent it, a reality that would be reiterated with escalating frequency—Atlanta in 1906; Springfield (Illinois) in 1908; and East St. Louis (Illinois), Elaine (Arkansas), Tulsa, Chicago, New Orleans, Washington, D.C., and Omaha during the following years. In four September days of 1906, marauding gangs

pulled blacks from Atlanta streetcars for beatings. Whites swept middle-class black neighborhoods, targeting "uppity" homes and lives—exactly the people who should have been safest if Washington was correct. Around thirty were killed, hundreds injured, and thousands more driven from their homes and businesses.[47] Still, even with race relations worsening, Tuskegee remained a safe zone. The Pinkerton detectives that Washington hired to estimate the potential for trouble during Theodore Roosevelt's 1905 visit found no credible threats. In 1912 the parents of Rosa Parks would move to Tuskegee because of its reputation for racial harmony, schools, and work for Parks's carpenter/builder father.[48] As Norrell has described it, the

Figure 6.5. Replica early buildings next to the Chapel at 1906 anniversary.

white town and the black suburb nurtured a peaceful if unsymmetrical détente, the whites enjoying a sense of superiority to those not in a "model community" like theirs. White Tuskegee thought of itself as more cosmopolitan, refined, and benevolent than other Southern towns.[49]

Racial discrimination and segregation increased throughout the first half of the new century, hardening from customs and laws that were enforced by violence. Responding to increasingly ugly conditions, W. E. B. Du Bois, Monroe Trotter, Ida B. Wells-Barnett, and others pursued a civil rights agenda from the greater safety of the North, challenging Washington's national leadership by casting him as compliant. Washington seemed overly beholden to powerful whites for his personal success and the school's continued existence. The "Tuskegee Machine," as Du Bois termed Washington's political network, had long been allied with a Republican White House. Washington could deliver Northern black votes in return for patronage that he could wield as purposefully as any other politician. While the "Tuskegee Idea" was widely understood as the sum of Washington's gradualism with industrial education and economic development as non-political means to civic security, the Principal was also secretly funding legal challenges to Jim Crow and fighting as best he could the 1901 Alabama constitution that disfranchised most African Americans.[50] As Robert J. Norrell has argued, by 1910 Washington had openly protested railroad discrimination, lynching, unfair voting qualifications, under-funded education, segregated housing, and discriminatory labor unions—a civil rights agenda that the National Association for the Advancement of Colored People would later pursue.[51] Meanwhile, nasty stereotyping in the popular press was caricaturing African Americans as ugly and foolish, while others were writing that the race was not only innately inferior to the white one but, without slavery's armature, rapidly degenerating into incompetence and criminality. Indeed, black people would disappear altogether because, as Native Americans had supposedly proved, the price of inferiority must be extinction.

Norrell's point is that Washington's continuing insistence that African Americans were actually doing the opposite—achieving independence, wealth, and high culture—undermined discrimination's rationale. Michael Bieze has considered Washington's use of fashionable white photographers who portrayed him as a cultured Victorian *pater familias* in order to contradict racism. Moreover, Bieze suggests, in the twentieth century Washington would use more black photographers and dynamic, modernist compositions of, for example, Washington haranguing railroad station crowds. This visual approach suggests less dependence on middle-class white acceptance and an increasing activism.[52] In a similar vein, an unpublished biography by Marquis James argued that Washington's benign mood in *Up From Slavery* has overshadowed his earlier *Future of the American Negro*, a collection of anti-lynching letters that he had managed to publish in white newspapers across the South.[53] Washington's early civil rights assertions are not news, but they have been insufficiently appreciated.

THE TWENTY-FIFTH ANNIVERSARY

Norrell's reevaluation of Washington's strategy offers a multilayered context for Tuskegee's twenty-fifth anniversary celebration. The grand pageant of April 1906 was designed to cheer on the students and staff, bind the school to its traditional donors, return to it the limelight increasingly taken by others, and defy steadily worsening conditions by displaying education's efficacy and black people's worth. The handsome campus, the dignified, college-educated faculty, and the enthusiastic students with their attractive uniforms and demonstrable achievements were proof of a progress that defied popular prejudice. This race was on no trek to oblivion. Eminent whites traveled South to do honor, trailing journalists behind them. Andrew Carnegie made his only institute appearance, as did Harvard president Charles W. Eliot and Secretary of War and future president William Howard Taft. William Lloyd Garrison Jr. and Oswald Garrison Villard were among those with abolitionist ancestry.[54] Black and white worthies filled the Chapel platform, taking in Tuskegee's aura of sweetness, pragmatism, and solid

Figure 6.6. John Robinson (right) with African crafts, at 1906 anniversary.

success. The *Tuskegee Student* noted a sprinkling of white faces throughout the audience as well. Most of Frances Benjamin Johnston's photographs of students in shops, fields, and classrooms were taken during her November 1902 visit, but she returned for an anniversary session to record exhibits, buildings, and institute officers and their families. Four pictures are of Robert and Beatrice Taylor and their four children. Johnston also shot a reconstructed version of the modest wooden church across town in which the enterprise began [Figure 6.5]. Statistical charts inside the building showed that Tuskegee's progress paralleled that of African Americans across the nation. The replica building also held exhibits from six "little Tuskegees" founded by graduates in towns from Topeka, Kansas, to Eatonville, Florida. Still other charts showed African American literacy as higher than that of peasants in eastern Europe,

an observation that the hostile could take as proof that Tuskegee was teaching black superiority.

Architecture was active in Washington's argument. The primeval wooden church had Taylor's brick Chapel on its northern flank to illustrate the race's rise from simplicity to grandeur as well as to remember Tuskegee's raw beginnings. Another reconstruction, the henhouse that once sheltered drawing classes and girls' industries, stood on the wooden church's southern flank.[55] The mock henhouse was just north of the Boys' Trades Building, with the drawing room in the nearest wing, and it faced Dorothy Hall, another weighty improvement. Historical exhibits, which were in the Carnegie Library, included photographs of the McKinley and Roosevelt visits, the first student-made wagon, essays, the first student-made desk—borrowed from Washington's office—and West African fabrics and carvings belonging to Tuskegee graduate John W. Robinson. Robinson had spent six years directing cotton cultivation in the German colony of Togo. He had founded an agriculture school on the Tuskegee model but was falling afoul of investors bent on using African workers in ways that did not meet Tuskegee standards nor lead to self-sufficiency and independence. Thus Robinson's colonial career was foundering on principle even before he drowned in 1909.[56] The *Tuskegee Student* commented on the crafts' fine quality, noting that European tastes had not yet made their destructive inroads on native sensibilities. The comment is of considerable boldness considering the larger racist context [Figure 6.6].

One anniversary description lingers. William Clarence Matthews, an 1893 graduate who had gone on to Andover and Harvard, said that the grounds were "neat and orderly like a New England town" but regretted that Porter Hall had been razed. It was to Tuskegee as Faneuil Hall was to Boston or Hollis to Harvard. True to his academic leanings, Matthews measured progress by counting faculty from northeastern universities. In 1893 Tuskegee could only boast Taylor, but by 1906 there was another from MIT, three from Columbia, three from Harvard, two from Cornell, and one from Brown joining those from the more expected Fisk, Atlanta, and Oberlin.[57] Academic credentials certainly measured one kind of progress, but not the one that would impress the most people. Buildings performed that task better.

Tantum Portico and Valley Behind

Tantum Hall girls' dormitory was the anniversary celebration's demonstration construction. Work was just beginning, but visitors were invited to the shops to see windows being framed [Figure 6.2] or to the clay pits, the brickyard, and the site to see every step from raw material to rising wall. Tantum has Tuskegee's second monumental Ionic portico but it is on the building's east side [Figure 6.7], or rear, not its entrance side, overlooking the valley to the backs of brick Douglass and frame Hamilton girls dormitories plus the girls' bathhouse. Tantum's west-facing entrance has syncopated windows along its horizontal sweep that defers to the nearby Chapel's vertical thrust. [See Catalog 15] In spring 1906 the valley behind and below Tantum was subdivided into a grid of fenced pens with animal and fowl sheds in a row. Visitors could survey the livestock while walking the rim. Romantic landscaping, with informal trees in pasture-like lawns, first appeared on a 1911 topographic map, well after Tantum had been completed. So the stunning interaction of the high Ionic portico and the softly greened lawn with trees swirling through it may be later artistry rather than a coordinated vision.[58] The revised valley style with curving paths is best known from parks and estates by Frederick Law Olmsted, to whom Washington had once applied for professional guidance.[59] Tuskegee's own landscape architect, David A. Williston, would have also known the style since he trained at Cornell under Liberty Hyde Bailey, a master of the mode.[60] The scene's luxuriant beauty invites reverie and it invites interpretation. One could read the scene as a didactic meditation on the value of farming to African Americans—the lawns an image of rural independence, as Kenrick Ian Grandison has proposed.[61] Farmers attending the annual Negro Conferences sometimes parked their vehicles in the valley's southern end. For them, Tantum's Ionic portico could signal, capitol-like, the ennoblement of all black-worked ground within the conference's sphere of influence. Or perhaps the context made Tantum a plantation "big house" that sheltered poor farmers' daughters rather than those of the planter class. Perhaps the portico honors the quarter-century-old brickmaking trials that took

Top, Figure 6.7. A recent photograph of the Eastern face of Tantum Hall. Bottom, Figure 6.8. Valley in 1906 with animal pens, looking southeast from Tantum construction. Douglass Hall in center, Huntington Hall behind it on left, Huntington Memorial Academic Building roof on horizon.

Figure 6.9. Recent view of valley looking north towards rear of James Hall.

place just below it. Meaning for Tantum's colonnade and the valley below also remain unassigned in modern times. Margaret Washington Clifford (1921–2009), a Booker T. Washington grandchild who was schooled on campus from kindergarten through her first master's degree, said she never noticed the columnar portico even though she lived in White Hall, which overlooked it. When asked about the valley's use, Mrs. Clifford said that she did not remember any, although it would have been good for parties.[62] The landscape architect Edward Pryce (1914–2007) thought that a road had been intended through the valley's depth for the portico to face. Taylor's granddaughter Ann Dibble Jordan, a civil rights activist who grew up in the doctor's house at the valley's northern end, thought the portico was simply Tuskegee "outdoing the South."[63] Compelling visual richness supports a range of attendant ideas, like a free radical ready to attach to that which is brought to it.

GROWING THE GIRLS' QUADRANGLE

Tuskegee's spatial heartland by 1910 and, to a lesser degree, today, is the long lawn bordered by girls' dormitories that spill down the hill from the Carnegie Library portico at its high point. The 600-foot long swath is 125 feet wide, broad enough for meaningful use but not too wide to dilute the power of the northward sweep. With its irregular tree canopy and its edge of red brick buildings with white trim, it is a classic space and memorably executed. [Figure 6.9] Older photographs show trees regularly placed along the paved walkways or lanes bordering the long sides. While the area was first known as a "court" and then as the "White Hall Lawn," this study terms it a "quadrangle" to secure it among the others of its scholastic type. Historian Kenneth Severens, who found it "breathtakingly beautiful," chose Thomas Jefferson's erudite exemplar at the University of Virginia for comparison. Tuskegee's loose, "organic" character fit the agricultural institution while Virginia's uniformity and precision suited its academic mission.[64] On Sunday afternoons, the only time boys were allowed to come in, boys and girls could relax and mix while listening to a band playing from the rustic stand that David A. Williston had designed.[65]

The girls' quadrangle, so familiar and memorable as an archetype, evolved over a ten-year period without leaving evidence that an overall concept had guided the series of separate decisions that formed it. These had to include the demolition of the historic Alabama Hall, a building that was central in Tuskegee lore as the first fruit of brickmaking. The resulting space would not be a naïve accident since there was no shortage of the architecturally informed. Quadrangles would have been fundamental to both Taylor's and Williston's Beaux-Arts educations. Taylor sat on the Executive Committee that made some critical decisions. Booker T. Washington would have seen academic quadrangles as would any number of donors and board members, not to mention their design advisors. One of the latter, whom George Foster Peabody brought in, was the Boston planner and landscape architect Warren H. Manning. As a February 1902 *Tuskegee Student* put its hopes from Manning's visit, "The essential unity of the buildings will be better preserved in the future than heretofore and the grounds will be laid off and kept hereafter with regard to their permanency and beauty." But Man-

ning's later sketch for the area shows Alabama Hall still standing and the area behind it filled with new buildings stepping down the hill. Manning's 1908 "plan"—really a graphic exercise—is without scale, topography, or clear representation or labeling of existing or proposed structures. It is hard to take it seriously.[66]

There were still other design mavens cruising the scene. The planning-activist trustee Seth Low, the former president of Columbia University, had developed that school's rigorously organized Morningside Heights campus where a library portico addressed a centralizing open space. Low became chairman of the Tuskegee board in 1907, when the quadrangle's outlines began to emerge. While Taylor could well have envisaged the great space in January 1901, when the Executive Council sited the library, there are reasons to doubt that scenario. A bird's-eye lithograph that had been published some six months earlier serves as a planning document of the period. It is a wish list of new buildings put in their places as well as a record of those already on the ground and it proposed a completely rebuilt, symmetrical Alabama Hall on its existing site. If erected, the new Alabama Hall would have been the largest structure on the campus. It would have ended forever a library-headed quad. The same Executive Council meeting that sited the library also decided to pipe Alabama for steam heat. The "old, ill-formed, and unsymmetrical" building, Tuskegee's triumph in brickmaking perseverance, seems to have been meant to stay.

The eventual quadrangle's open ground first emerged at the lowest end. In 1904 an expansive frame annex behind Alabama Hall was razed, clearing a "girls playground" bordered by Huntington Hall on the lowest side, Parker Cottage on the east, and Douglass Hall on the west.[67] [Figure 6.11]The

Figure 6.10. Recent photograph of quadrangle looking South to Carnegie Library.

first building on the western edge had been the frame Hamilton Cottage (1889) that set the building line for the girls' bathhouse to its south (uphill) and Douglass Hall to its north (downhill). Huntington Hall defined the short northern, lower side while Parker Cottage and then Tompkins Dining Hall edged it on the east. A January 12, 1907, sketch-plan puts a monument to William Henry Baldwin Jr., Tuskegee's deceased board chair, where Alabama still stood.[68] J. A. Melby, a drawing room instructor, signed it. Melby's drawing turned John H. Washington's Steam Laundry, which was then functioning as a commissary since a more modern laundry was in Dorothy Hall, into a dormitory, blocking the last hundred feet of the eventual quad.

It was not until July 1907 that Taylor wrote to Washington that "Our plan is to remove the Commissary, Alabama Hall and the other buildings, making this into a large court." Those then in New York—Seth Low and Washington—wanted to keep Alabama and put the Baldwin monument in front of it, but Taylor pointed out that if Alabama were eventually razed, leaving the monument alone in front, it would not be on the court's centerline. Taylor wanted an uninterrupted "long vista" towards the distant Pinehurst Hospital, below and beyond the hillside quad. Low and Taylor met that August, Low praising the idea of "shifting" Alabama Hall "to the other side of the road," this road being the paved walk or lane on the court's west side. The previous month, Low, Washington, and Brooklyn housing philanthropist Alfred T. White had negotiated the shifted Alabama into the large White Memorial Hall girls' dormitory that was built on the quadrangle's west side. Low and the Baldwin monument's sculp-

GIRLS' QUADRANGLE
1903

BUILDING KEY

1 Alabama Hall
2 Girls' Dormitory
3 Steam Laundry/
  Commissary
4 Huntingdon Hall
5 Parker Cottage
6 Tompkins Dining Hall
  (begun)
7 Carnegie Library
8 Girls' Bathhouse
9 Hamilton Hall
10 Douglass Hall

GIRLS' QUADRANGLE
1910

BUILDING KEY

4 Huntingdon Hall
5 Parker Cottage
6 Tompkins Dining Hall
7 Carnegie Library
8 Girls' Bath House
9 Hamilton Hall
10 Douglass Hall
11 White Hall
12 Girls' Quadrangle

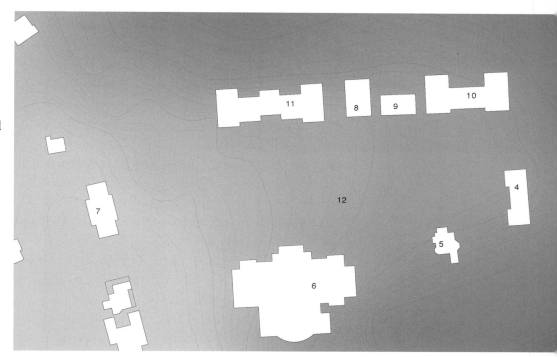

Figure 6.11. Girls' Quadrangle area 1903, top, and 1910, bottom.

tor, Karl Bitter, then wanted to put the monument at the head of the quadrangle, not in it, but on a small terrace at the road level, the Carnegie Library serving as backdrop. This was done and is where the Baldwin Monument stood until 1922, when it was moved to where Taylor had wanted it all along, the void between the Carnegie Library and the Office Building, where it stands today.[69] Taylor may have envisaged the quadrangle in January 1901 and even prorated the cost of heating Alabama until his idea could be enacted. Experienced with the complications that donors and advisors brought to planning decisions and with the puzzles that attend simultaneous construction and occupation, Taylor could have bided his time, allowing the quadrangle that now seems so inevitable to emerge through an indirect process with persistent prodding from a patient man.

EXECUTIVE TRAVELS

Unlike his first Tuskegee years, when the Phelps Stokes correspondence showed design discussions going through Washington, the older and more proven Taylor would deal directly with white men and women in distant places. In January 1905 he went to New York to present sewerage plans to the trustees and defend the dining hall plans.[70] Even though the trustees rejected the sewerage, Washington must have admired Taylor's presentation because he raised his salary to $130 a month and told him to choose a site and draw a house that the institute would build for him.[71] The house was a two-story, vertically proportioned frame house, now destroyed, on the Montgomery Road facing the campus. Taylor's son Edward remembered his father doing architecture evenings and weekends within.[72] The following year, Langston University in Oklahoma offered Taylor its presidency. Taylor

turned it down after a $400 raise. It would be a "far-reaching calamity" to lose this man, Washington wrote.[73] Taylor was not, however, the perfect colleague for everyone. Business Manager Warren Logan once cautioned Washington that Taylor and William H. Carter, an accountant, would not work together. If anyone tried to force the situation, Tuskegee might lose both. Taylor served as acting principal for a week when Washington and Logan, the usual second-in-command, were away. He was also acting General Superintendent of Industries that week for John H. Washington.[74] And he often had other oversight responsibilities such as special committees for sensitive staff or academic problems. On one occasion he evaluated classes in the Academic Department, reporting to Washington that student work was incomplete and lacked detail. The school needed to be "rigid" about detail.[75]

Taylor made several more New York trips in 1907, staying at the Brooklyn YMCA. In March he met with the widow of deceased board chairman William H. Baldwin to discuss her husband's monument with that project's instigator, *New York Evening Post* editor Oswald Garrison Villard, with sculptor Karl Bitter, and with architect William Welles Bosworth.[76] He was serving as the monument's producer, assembling the support and talent. Taylor would have been a freshman during Bosworth's senior year at MIT and he could have met him again at the Buffalo Pan American Exhibition, where Bosworth was a planner. Taylor also examined kitchen equipment for the dining hall, laundry machinery, and fixtures for the poultry yards.[77] There was another Northern trip in June to inspect girls' industrial schools for the Dorothy Hall expansion.[78] In July he was there again, this time for as long as a month. He consulted with Villard and met with board chairman Seth Low in his city home to strategize the presentation of the White Hall dormitories to the donors. Low gave Taylor a card of introduction in case he could not be present.[79] Low was a progressive reformer with a record of working for racial equality. He opened public schools to African Americans when he was mayor of New York and brought students of varied ethnic, religious and economic backgrounds to Columbia University when he was its president.[80] He would be active in Tuskegee management and planning, working with but not overruling Washington and other Tuskegeans. Low worried about the steep hillside on which White Hall was being sited, but he made it clear that he would defer to Taylor's judgment because he admired his abilities. During the planning of the second agricultural campus, Low deferred to Washington often because of his wish for Tuskegee's independence.

Despite increasing responsibilities away as well as on campus, Taylor's name seldom appeared in the *Tuskegee Student* with those of other faculty and administrators. There were brief mentions of a vacation in Wilmington and, in 1905, talks in Memphis and Richmond, the latter city hosting a meeting of agricultural and industrial colleges.[81] In early 1906 the *Tuskegee Student* noted that he was improving the campus for the upcoming anniversary and building a railroad spur for visitors' private cars. Even with habitual inattention to this quiet man's labors, the sparse coverage given his tragedy—the loss of his wife—surprises. Beatrice Rochon Taylor's death shocks, even, for the brevity of its representation as well as its fact [Figure 6.12]. On August 11 she had been ill but was improving after what her descendants believe was a miscarriage. On September 8 there was a bare note in the social column that her sister and his brother John E. Taylor attended the funeral. A September 1 letter

from Taylor to Washington, thanking him for his sympathy, suggests that the service was to be that day, meaning that she must have died during the week that Taylor was acting principal and acting Supervisor of Industries.[82] Funerals and obituaries usually earned considerable attention, so these laconic snippets suggest a man not only willing to remain in the background but actively bent on doing so.

Beatrice's death left Taylor with four children, Robert Rochon, Helen, Edward, and Beatrice [Figure 6.13]. Although his wife's sister came to live with the bereaved family, his son Edward remembered that their father assumed the responsibilities of two parents.[83] Even so, Taylor was back at his desk within

Figure 6.12. Beatrice Rochon Taylor, April 1906.

Figure 6.13. Robert Rochon, Beatrice, Helen and Edward Taylor, April 1906.

the week. Work continued throughout the sorrow, judging from the flow of memos. Directives for campus construction hardly missed a beat even though their author must have been sorely distressed. Taylor proposed that the anniversary's replica wooden chapel be moved to Greenwood to serve the suburb's Baptist congregation.[84] Construction of the Negro Building for the Alabama state agricultural fair in Montgomery, which was designed by the recently arrived architectural drawing teacher Walter T. Bailey, was underway and taking much of Taylor's time with the complexities of coordinating materials and labor some distance away.[85] On August 22, before Beatrice's death, Taylor had asked Emmett J. Scott to intervene on his behalf for the prestigious job of

designing the Negro Pavilion for the coming exposition in Jamestown, Virginia. In October, Taylor thanked Scott for the letter of recommendation and said that he would soon send his drawings to Giles B. Jackson, the fair's organizer.[86] The *Tuskegee Student* noted that Bailey and Wallace A. Rayfield had also entered and that Rayfield was a finalist as was the Tuskegee former steam-fitting student John A. Lankford. William S. Pittman won. Pittman had left in May 1905 and, after winning, would marry Booker T. Washington's daughter Portia.[87]

FIVE OTHER TUSKEGEE ARCHITECTS

Since Taylor no longer taught after becoming Director of Industries, the school needed other architects to teach drawing. But Taylor never relinquished his design responsibilities to incoming architects, as he said he had planned to do with William S. Pittman. In a letter to Washington in which he detailed Pittman's poor work habits, he said that full design assignments were to fall to him in stages. But the young architect was doing poorly in many ways. He did not remain in the drawing room after five as did others. He did not check the students' work. He did not learn surveying even though Taylor had offered to teach him. And he did not help with classes when needed. He was a good draftsman but had made too many mistakes on the Huntington Memorial Academic Building and other drawings. Taylor thought he was being lenient, accepting his "peculiarities and constant dissatisfaction." But he could not tell if Pittman's letter to Washington, to which he was responding, was a resignation or a request for a salary increase. Washington was also losing patience with "this curious and troublesome individual."[88] Soon Taylor would suggest a raise for Wallace A. Rayfield, the Pratt-trained mechanical drawing teacher, because he was "a painstaking man" who spent his money on books.[89] Although Taylor asked that Tuskegee continue both Rayfield's and Pittman's positions, the latter chose to leave. Rayfield, who seems to have been relegated to teaching without any design assignments even after Pittman was out of the way, left two years later.[90] Taylor and Washington may have preferred the talents of a new hire, surely a galling situation for Rayfield, who had come in 1899 and would have wanted the design work that he achieved after he left.

Pittman's vacated slot went to Walter T. Bailey, who came in September 1905, a year after his architecture degree from the University of Illinois. He had applied in 1904, when he graduated, and spent the year in offices in Champaign and Kewanee, Illinois.[91] Bailey was soon directing the architectural drawing division and would continue to do so until around 1915, when he left for Memphis. His 1911 division report noting that the best of his thirteen drawing students could teach a special course for advanced carpentry and brickmasonry students, shows initiative in broadening student opportunities that Taylor would have appreciated.[92] In 1906 Frances Benjamin Johnston photographed Bailey instructing six young men posing with the Architectural Drawing exhibit for the twenty-fifth anniversary celebration [Figure 6.14]. An array of work is pinned to the wall: shades and shadows exercises, wood framing details, molding and cornice profiles, classical niches and doorways, and what may have been a shaded perspective of the Tompkins

Figure 6.14. Walter T. Bailey and Architectural Drawing Exhibit, 1906.

Dining Hall, then under construction. Most of the drawings are more sophisticated than the exhibition itself, with its crudely painted background of the five classical capitals on five identical columns. The capitals should have had differently sized and proportioned shafts. But Washington criticized the exhibit for other reasons. The drawings showed too many buildings that Tuskegee students would never be called upon to design rather than the cottages, barns, and rural schools that were needed.[93] Stylistic shifts suggest that Bailey did some designing. Another hand than Taylor's is visible on the windows and parapets of White Hall [Figure Cat. 18]. According to the *Tuskegee Student*, Bailey drew the cold storage facilities, dining hall furniture, cottages, and changes to the coming horse and cow barns [Figure Cat. 21]. Bailey, like Pittman and Rayfield, used Tuskegee as a launching pad. In 1910 he won a competition for remodeling St. John's African Methodist Episcopal Church in Montgomery and, shortly thereafter, remodeled the Old Ship African Methodist Church in the same city. His largest achievement was the 1925–1930 Knights of Pythias Temple, in Chicago.[94]

Still another drawing room denizen in the early twentieth century was James A. Melby, who made the sketch that removed Alabama Hall for the girls's quadrangle. Melby was the rare draftsman in this particular hothouse who claimed no buildings. Born in Toronto in 1878, Melby had studied civil and architectural engineering at the University of Illinois for three and a half years. Leaving without a degree, he worked as a draftsman for Engineering News Co. and came to Tuskegee from Atlanta in August 1906. Melby soon merited a raise because he was an "energetic and wide awake man"—Taylor's phrasing. Melby later told Taylor that he wanted to leave for Hampton for better pay and was gone by 1909. He resurfaces in 1921 in the Louisville office of the black architect Samuel M. Plato and, by 1925 was in Washington, D.C., where he practiced for almost two decades, in 1940 as a "junior architect" in federal employ.[95]

William Augustus Hazel was the final Tuskegee teaching architect of the Washington era. Taylor had asked the Principal to hire the fifty-five-year-old in 1909.[96] Hazel was from the same Wilmington free black community as Taylor but his family left before the Civil War, ending up in Cambridge, Massachusetts. According to a descendant, he was apprenticed to stained-glass artist John LaFarge in 1875 and became a glass dealer in St. Paul where, in 1887, he successfully sued a hotel for civil rights violations. Along the line he apprenticed as an architect. When he arrived in July as drawing room head he was assisted by Andrew N. Grant but six months later Hazel was the assistant—to Bailey.[97] Hazel taught mechanical drawing, billed the school for plans for a shed at the Montgomery Fair, lectured about poet Paul Laurence Dunbar at institute clubs, designed rural schools that were built many times, advised on the dining hall's interior coloring, designed exhibits, and in 1915 arranged the flowers for Booker T. Washington's funeral. As head of the Architectural Drawing Division he signed blueprints for Building B of the New (later, Willcox) Trades Buildings that replaced Taylor's Boys' Trades after it had burned. Hazel designed the replacements in partnership with Albert I. Cassell (1895–1969) a Cornell graduate, Howard University teacher, and another distinguished black practitioner. In summer 1919 Hazel left for Howard to help begin the first professional degree program for black architects.[98] Louis H. Persley, a teacher and architect who became Taylor's design partner, appears in Chapter 8 because his era followed Booker T. Washington's.

CHAPTER 7

THE DIRECTOR OF INDUSTRIES II

WASHINGTON'S LAST YEARS

At the end of the new century's first decade Taylor was receiving honors and working directly with donors rather than through Washington. Three new buildings—White Hall (designed with Walter T. Bailey), Milbank Agricultural Building (designed by William S. Pittman), and the Tompkins Dining Hall (designed largely by James W. Golucke)—were dedicated in three ceremonies during the February 1910 board meeting at Tuskegee. Guests gathered in the auditorium that had been slipped under the Dining Hall and Seth Low led Taylor to the stage. As with Christopher Wren at St. Paul's, Low said, Taylor's monument was all around him.[1] In April Tuskegee gave a dinner to honor Taylor and John H. Washington. Tables for 200 arranged as a "W" and a "T" stood on the lawn and H. E. Thomas, the Steam Engineering Division head, read a history of the institute's buildings.[2] Taylor's own remarks typically skipped the rhetorical staples of his personal feelings and long Tuskegee memories to detail the new buildings' material origins. The clay and the timber, the harnesses and shoes for the mules, some of the iron work, and even the workmen's overalls were dug, cut, forged, shaped or sewn by Tuskegee students from matter sprung from the school's own soil.[3] In reality, sources for the Dining Hall's materials spread from Birming-

ham to Savannah for the steel, iron, concrete, terra cotta, lime, cement, wood, plate glass, and metal roofing. But Tuskegee's soil still yielded the most visible matter, bricks, and Tuskegeans contributed their skills. Taylor reminded his audience that this last was what counted.

Taylor's dignity and his humility on this as on all occasions must have been reliable since he had to behave to Southern expectations when it was essential. Later that year Taylor went to Montgomery in the exceptional position of Tuskegee executive/MIT graduate acting the role of common tailor to measure a state schools superintendent for a suit. It was an institute gift that the official would wear when traveling around Alabama. Not only did Taylor know how to measure a man for a suit, a skilled operation, but he must have been chosen for purposes of some mysterious diplomacy.[4] In 1914, the discreet administrator traveled to New York to settle a matter of such potential embarrassment to the institute that his correspondence with Washington never hints what the issue might be. He met for several hours with Seth Low and then went to Philadelphia to talk to the Lord Construction Company's attorney. The party, Taylor wrote, "made a clean breast of the whole thing." While in Philadelphia he also studied a veterinary hospital

Top, Figure 7.1. Carnegie Library, Wiley University. Bottom, Figure 7.2. Recent view of the building, now used for administration.

at the University of Pennsylvania in preparation for Tuskegee's coming one.[5]

Taylor's design reputation was beginning to expand geographically as well his travels. As early as 1903, *Cassier's Magazine* of engineering termed him "the best equipped in training and experience of any Negro architect in the United States."[6] In 1907 a Mobile newspaper summarized his achievements. He had designed and built most of the big buildings at Tuskegee, a large brick church in town, and two unnamed libraries in other states. He laid out the "landscape features" of several schools and public institutions, sites that scholars have not yet identified. The paper noted his MIT degree and said that since he was the son of a prominent North Carolina contractor he was also a "practical builder," a compliment in Tuskegee circles and in Taylor's self-estimation as well.[7] The Mobile article was occasioned by the city's planned thirty-acre National Negro Fair, a bold attempt to compensate neglectful representation at earlier expositions but one that never came to fruition.[8] The two unnamed libraries were Carnegie donations at Wiley University in Marshall, Texas [Figures 7.1, 7.2] and Livingstone College in Salisbury, North Carolina [Figure 7.3]. Washington eventually helped arrange for Carnegie libraries at twenty-nine black schools, but only three of them are by Taylor.[9] As for one possible international project, in 1908 he sent books and unspecified blueprints to C.A. Correa in Mexico City.[10]

Taylor's reputation was also growing beyond the Northeastern reformers who had given buildings and served on the board. A 1910 letter from Darwin D. Martin, an executive of the Larkin Company in Buffalo, to Frank Lloyd Wright, Martin's architect and friend, instructs him to write to Booker T. Washington for Tuskegee work. Martin would pay Wright's fees as a way of helping him recover from professional setbacks stemming from his scandalous life. "Their latest architecture there," Martin wrote Wright, by "a Boston Tech graduate of color, the teacher of architecture at Tuskegee, is a good deal more in sympathy with your work than is that of some of your avowed imitators, because it is more decent and consistent."[11] Martin's assessment is perceptive because it ignores stylistic categories to suggest that both designers' strengths lay in their artistic integrity.

Martin was one of the "hundreds of influential people who visit Tuskegee annually" (his phrase) and was thus directly acquainted with the buildings. Martin had been corresponding with Washington for almost a decade and had dined at The Oaks in April 1909. He must have studied the recently finished Palmer Cottage, because his company later asked for its plan for furnishing it or—the request is ambiguous—the company's own "Larkin cottage" that might be a model or exhibition house for its mail-order goods. Or the company may have meant to furnish still another Tuskegee building.[12] Wright failed to act on Martin's suggestion, perhaps because it came with reprimands about his personal behavior or perhaps because Wright's sense of self meant that he should not have to pursue small commissions in out-of-the-way places.

Wright probably knew about Tuskegee, if not its architect, through his uncle, the prominent Unitarian minister, Jenkin Lloyd Jones, whose Tuskegee support dates at least to 1887 when Wright was also a parishioner. Jones addressed the National

Figure 7.3. Carnegie Library, Livingstone College.

Negro Conference in New York in 1909 with the assertion that the current "scientific" racism was "a recrudescence of the ethnology of slavery under the guise of a superficial science," a point of view we accept today.[13] In 1928, with the patient Martin's financial backing, Wright would design a Rosenwald school near Hampton Institute that has been widely published but never built.[14] One has to regret that Wright did not do as Martin advised, that Wright and Taylor did not interact, and that Tuskegee does not have a Frank Lloyd Wright building.

An Unpleasant Episode

Racism surrounded Tuskegee as it did any African American community, but Washington's policy of a dignified optimism meant that immediate disputes may have remained unacknowledged. One exception has been found among Taylor's papers. In February 1911 the trustees asked Taylor to hire Walter Franz, a white heating engineer from Cincinnati who was installing the power plant, to make a topographic map of the grounds. The map, the first that showed the valley's romantic landscaping, would help engineers lay steam piping from the power plant to the buildings as well as helping plan sewerage and water systems then under discussion.[15]

But the Tuskegee steamfitter H. E. Thomas complained that Franz was one of "these high salaried white 'grafters'" who were criticizing Tuskegee workmanship but whose own work had serious deficiencies. "It is purely the old story of sizing up a good teacher's work from the "'Color' stand point," a habit that was "very discouraging to the competent colored instructors who by hard work, night and day at poor pay, made Tuskegee's present high grade industrial standards possible . . . 'Our chickens are already coming home to roost' as a result of our recent weak policy in having these so called white men coming among us to do work." Thomas quoted Franz as saying that he did not "believe in a 'd . . n . .' doing this kind of work," (ellipses Thomas's) after Thomas had explained why something had been done a certain way.[16]

Franz had written to Washington charging black incompetence and Thomas was responding to that letter. Taylor had earlier told Washington that Thomas was the plant's chief engineer, but he then sent the Principal a six-page conciliatory missive citing misunderstandings, explaining conditions, recording an occasion when Franz praised Tuskegee's construction, admitting some problems and, finally, suggesting that whatever "crudeness" in construction Franz might have observed, it was more than offset by Tuskegee's mission to advance the students' education.[17] One wonders how many more such episodes marred this publicly sunny bastion of interracial harmony.

Tasks, Travels, and a Marriage

Taylor's skills in interracial tact increasingly sent him traveling. Now he was working directly with board members and donors. In April 1911 he met with Seth Low in New York City to discuss a proposed refrigeration plant and to study such installations at Columbia and Low's own farm.[18] Low had offered to send his and Columbia's refrigeration engineer for an on-site consultation, outlining the idea's wisdom but also making it clear that he would fully understand if the institute found such help embarrassing. Washington should feel free to decline the offer.[19] In May, Taylor met with Low at his Bedford estate and then with housing philanthropist A. T. White at his city home.[20] He was back in Tuskegee in early June, available to serve as an outside critic for an Illinois dormitory designed by someone else. The traveling Washington had mailed the plans for comments. Taylor's few notes, all directed to such practical matters as wider stairways for fire safety, came with a polite and even apologetic tone.[21] Later that month he was back in New York to meet with the trustees about the water supply.[22]

In July 1911, Taylor was writing from Boston, where he had been studying hospitals and discussing Tuskegee's coming one with potential donors. This meeting required a design response that he provided the following month with eight blueprints of plans, elevations, and sections of the future Andrew Hospital that he drew while in New York. Taylor was also arranging a laboratory for George Washington Carver, remodeling the dairy or creamery, adapting a carriage house to a dormitory, changing Milbank Agricultural Hall, and designing cottages and faculty houses. He wanted Washington to approve drawings for two houses and check their already-staked locations. Washington's involvement was still expected every step of the way.[23]

Taylor was also concerned with private affairs, seeking to sell to the institute two houses he owned in Greenwood Village.[24] All along he had non-institute interests, a sawmill, real estate, business investments, that needed to be tracked. In 1911 Tuskegee gave him a $240 raise, bringing his salary to the level of J. R. E. Lee, the head of the Academic Department.[25] He was now one of Tuskegee's top four earners excepting Washington, whose salary was unpublished. This must have been a needed correction since Taylor was running the largest institute department plus supervising buildings and grounds. Except for the Cleveland hiatus, he had been on staff since 1892 while Lee came in 1906. That July Washington asked Taylor to design a house for Lee, a "plain dignified brick structure" in the colonial style.[26]

There were to be still other tasks and rewards for 1911. MIT invited Taylor to Boston in April to speak at its fiftieth anniversary celebration, as discussed below. And he remarried. In the fall of 1910 Taylor had joined Washington's North Carolina tour when it arrived in Wilmington for the Principal's first visit since the 1898 coup. Three thousand people reportedly met the train. The white-owned main auditorium and its standing room were equally divided between the races for Washington's address. "For forty years, the Negro has been the subject of discussion," Washington told the crowd. "In fact, it was hard to understand how the Negro had lived through so much discussion." But black people were here to stay and education would make co-existence better for all. The speech was deemed a rousing success with whites offering the use of their autos and carriages and a leader of the 1898 riots saying

that he was now a convert to Negro education.[27] Perhaps this trip provided the forty-three-year old widower with an introduction to or re-acquaintance with Nellie Green Chestnut, a thirty-five-year old schoolteacher whom he married the following year. Her family was living in the house Henry Taylor had built for his eldest son John.[28] Tuskegee welcomed the new Mrs. Taylor with a series of festive receptions and provided her with a ready-made family to which she eventually responded with a fifth and final Taylor offspring, Henry Chestnut Taylor.[29]

THE MIT ANNIVERSARY SPEECH

Taylor was among fifty invited alumni and faculty at the Boston conference honoring MIT's fiftieth anniversary. His short paper, "The Scientific Development of the Negro," is in the conference publication. Taylor's talk contains valuable biographical information and offers a rare glimpse into some of his views.

Since slaves were directed by white masters who supervised their work "according to plans and methods definitely laid out," he argued, they could not develop managerial skills as whites did. Slaves may have been experienced builders of houses, boats, bridges, and buggies and knowledgeable farmers, too, but "whatever skill of hand that may have been developed, the Negroes were an unlettered people, and therefore lacked the mental training to back up the skill of the hand."[30] This is not how W. E. B. Du Bois viewed history when he wrote that slave artisans directed their own work even though a white owner might contract them out.[31] Virtually free urban artisans (such as Taylor's father, a literate but unschooled mechanic and merchant) were even more likely to contract their own work and keep the profits. But either the son seemed not to have his father in mind or he may have understood that his own intensive higher education gave him executive skills beyond Henry Taylor's. The son could handle simultaneous projects, direct others, and plan complex future operations. "Executive ability or the chance to develop it by taking charge of work, of a business, laying out the plans, gathering the workmen and material, keeping everybody busy, looking ahead to avoid delays, these things which seem so natural to those with different surroundings and which are a part of their inheritance, had no part in the colored man's life."[32] Even after forty years of freedom, Taylor continued, one rarely met black engineers, chemists, and architects in the South. The young could not be aware of these professions as they could of medicine and the law so the disparity was perpetuated. Taylor expressed some modest pride that he had been able to apply methods he had learned at MIT, "if not the plans in full, certainly the spirit." But key to any success, he concluded, was "the love of doing things correctly, of putting logical ways of thinking into the humblest task, of studying surrounding conditions, of soil, of climate, of materials and of using them to the best advantage in contributing to build up the immediate community in which the persons live, and in this way increasing the power and grandeur of the nation."[33] Taylor was no orator, but he was one with Booker T. Washington's vision.

TAYLOR GETS ANGRY

There is one other window into Taylor's principles in a 1915 letter to Jesse E. Moorland, the head of the Colored Men's Department of the Washington, D.C., YMCA. A rare but welcome change from his usual discretion, Taylor wrote pointedly in this private communication.[34] Taylor had asked Moorland to promote black architects for all black YMCA buildings across the country, but Moorland had replied that he would not do so because, as the head of a single unit, he did not have authority elsewhere and because he disliked the black-designed YMCA building in which he worked. Taylor agreed that YMCA chapters were sovereign but argued that Moorland could still be influential. He was familiar with the District of Columbia building because he had visited it often, making a point of asking around to gauge its success because he was interested in its architect. He heard little negative criticism. The architect was William S. Pittman, his former student and problematic colleague. But even if Moorland disliked the building, Taylor continued, surely this opinion should be outweighed by the encouragement it offered to young men who wanted to be architects. Generous white men who financed black YMCAs would surely want to make this additional contribution. Further, Moorland was seriously misinformed in thinking that a YMCA was too complex a building type—tougher, say, than a church or school—for the supposedly less experienced black architect. Any competent designer, Taylor pointed out, begins by studying other examples and "getting the atmosphere" because all new buildings improve upon their predecessors. "There has never yet been the 'last word spoken' in any kind of construction because people do not stand still but are continuing to improve." Progress would soon antiquate the newest, most expensive New York office building. Taylor could recommend several colored architects and contractors that Moorland could pass along to YMCA leaders. The contractors Windham Brothers of Birmingham and Farrow of Atlanta had the capital and experience to undertake large jobs, he noted.

Parts of Taylor's letter are worth quoting in full for the energy that undergirds his calm concision when deep convictions were on the line:

I am writing to you this rather lengthy letter and I hope you will pardon my freedom in writing you, but as an architect and as one who has done a great deal of work, both for the colored and for white, I feel very keenly the implied charge which you make of incompetency . . . There are not a great many colored architects and engineers in the country—comparatively few—but the number is increasing and I am glad to say that because of their work they have gradually gained the confidence of the public. I realize that in any movement which borders on that of the pioneer, that it takes some courage and some determination, but I believe that any risk which we may take in any operation, in any business or in any occupation, we will be fully repaid when we see that more and more avenues are being opened up for colored young men and colored young women, and the best lesson that we can give them is to let them see with their own eyes the things which have been actually accomplished by colored men and by colored women. I believe this would be among the greatest contributions that we can make towards racial progress.

This is a Booker T. Washington position, of course, but it is delivered in Taylor's firm if less practiced voice.

RURAL SCHOOLS PROGRAMS

Washington had determined from the beginning to bring elementary schools to every black child in every rural hamlet, an ambition that he first activated by teaching architectural drawing and carpentry to teachers-in-training. As we have seen, graduate teachers were grateful for whatever construction skills they had as they built from scratch or repaired facilities in remote locations. Tuskegee's school efforts stepped up to a new level

in 1895 when Fisk graduate Clinton J. Calloway joined the Extension Department and turned a one-teacher shanty at Kowaliga plantation into a three-building, eleven-teacher plant that was in session eight-months of the year. Calloway then returned to Tuskegee to apply himself to primary schools for Macon County.[35]

Around 1904 Washington lured the Standard Oil executive Henry Huddleston Rogers and the Philadelphia heiress Anna T. Jeanes into the endeavor. In 1907 the Jeanes estate launched a million-dollar program for industrial education using traveling supervisory teachers, a program that would expand across the South and even into Africa. She also financed some school construction. Rogers gave more school buildings, perhaps as many as forty-two in Macon and adjoining counties, according to Horace Mann Bond. Washington reported that "nearly fifty" new buildings for eight- or nine-month sessions were completed between 1905 and 1911. By 1912 Tuskegee's Carnegie Library was circulating among Macon County's fifty-five schools fourteen book collections for children and adults plus agricultural and other technical texts.[36] The one H. H. Rogers school that we can identify, Solomon's Chapel, about five miles from the institute, was painted and had a blackboard and a flower garden, these three elements serving as emblems of Tuskegee influence.[37] Washington always urged flower gardening for aesthetic enrichment. A small school at Chehaw, the village at Tuskegee's mainline railroad stop, was especially targeted for flowers.[38] Washington continued to push for better school design. In 1907, he asked Taylor to send him school sketches that would avoid "the usual stiff formal appearance."[39]

In summer 1911 Washington asked Taylor to draw plans for one-, two-, and three-room schools, copies of which would go to the countryside to

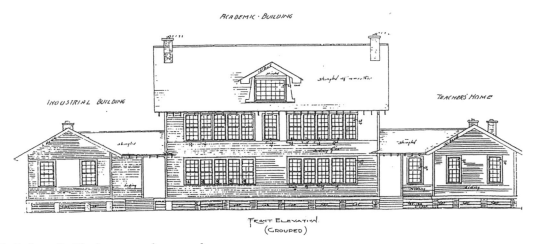

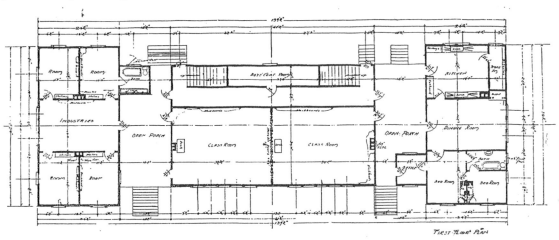

*Figure 7.3. Robert R. Taylor, two plans and
elevation for a county training school.*

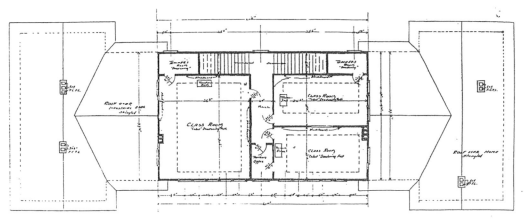

guide carpenters. The Jeanes Fund or an unnamed "someone else" would pay.[40] Even though some state money was now being assigned to black school construction, he wrote, "for the lack of a plan the school houses do not look well and are not conveniently arranged." Taylor replied that he was adding blackboards and desks that a country carpenter could make, and he reminded Washington that Dr. Dillard had recently made the same request.[41]

James Hardy Dillard directed the Anna T. Jeanes Foundation and, after 1910, the John F. Slater Fund, which he immediately led into founding privately funded but publicly owned "county training schools." Begun in Louisiana and Mississippi in 1910 and 1911 with Slater funding that went directly to state educational offices, these middle schools were to become agricultural and industrial high schools as their students matured. County training schools also depended on black community donations, usually land and labor that constituted a second tax since the people were paying taxes that generally went into the white system. The strategy of using private philanthropy to get public schools to those denied them would have a future.

THE COTTAGE SCHOOL

While several school types appeared under Tuskegee auspices, although not just then the country training school, Washington singled out what he called the "cottage school" for special attention. The much-publicized Rising Star cottage school near Tuskegee had replaced a rough board shack that stood next to a dilapidated church that Washington liked to claim was the worst-looking building he had ever seen. The cottage school was a square-plan, hipped-roof, clapboarded house that was raised higher above the ground than the usual tenant cabin. With a veranda across the front, glazed windows, a kitchen wing extending behind, and gardens and outbuildings situated across several acres, it looked like a successful white farmer's home as well as a model to which Tuskegee graduates could aspire. A graduate teacher-couple lived and taught within. Academic subjects were tackled in the sitting room or veranda, cooking in the kitchen, and farming in the fields and barns. After hours, the hard-working couple opened their home as a community center so that adults too could learn scientific farming and home management.[42] Washington published *Rising Star in My Larger Education* in 1911 and in the social science journal *Survey* in 1913, suggesting that he still considered it the best even though Tuskegee was then developing other models.

JULIUS ROSENWALD JOINS IN

Washington met Julius Rosenwald, president of Sears Roebuck and Company and experienced donor of black YMCAs in Chicago, in the spring of 1911. Rosenwald visited Tuskegee that October, spending time at Rising Star and the Children's House kindergarten in Greenwood. A year later Washington asked Taylor for a schoolhouse design to be built for $600.[43] Taylor fired off a rare memo of exasperation asking the Principal to tell business manager Warren Logan that he must fund the drawings so that Tuskegee could meet Rosenwald's expectations. Sears experts would use the drawings to estimate the manufacturing cost. If they could be prefabricated for less than what a country carpenter and donated labor would cost, a new means of production would be in place. The cost of making drawings was minimal, Taylor insisted, while Tuskegee's entire history showed that what was truly expensive were the problems that came from immature plans. Besides, without plans how could one estimate for fundraising purposes? "We would be moving around in a circle."[44] Taylor noted that he had returned the state's proffered schoolhouse plans because they would be too costly to build.[45] Taylor was dealing with a similar issue at the same time for the new hospital—trying to stall drawing the perspective to be used for fundraising until after the plans were complete.

According to Mary S. Hoffschwelle's exacting analysis, Washington was nurturing Rosenwald's interest gently throughout this period because the Principal wanted the philanthropist to think through every issue for himself.[46] In September 1912, the month Washington asked for the $600 design, Rosenwald decided to fund partial costs for six experimental schools in three adjacent Alabama counties. They were built. In 1914 he escalated the offer to a hundred Alabama schools under the management of Clinton J. Calloway and the Tuskegee Extension Department. Between October 1914 and July 1915 Calloway managed the fundraising for and construction of twenty-one schools in six counties. Rosenwald's contribution was a third of each school's cost, the other two parts coming from the state and the community. By 1920, 638 schools in ten states had been built under Calloway's management. But that year Rosenwald moved the program to Nashville, severing it from its Tuskegee roots and ending the racial intimacy of black professionals working with black communities in part because a white schools expert hired to study the results found compromised construction in some communities.[47] The Rosenwald Fund construction program continued until 1932, erecting overall 5,000 schools and a few hundred ancillary buildings spread throughout the South.

Of the experimental six begun in 1912, the first (completed May 1913) was at Loachapoka in Lee County. This community collected the match the quickest. The Loachapoka building was of country church form with an entrance in the narrow end, under the gable, and five windows spaced down each long side. It had no signifying belfry or cupola. Then came Notasulga in Macon County, which in one photo looked like a modest tenant cabin with the entrance set in the long side parallel to the roof ridge. Notasulga was the result of a nine-year crusade by a determined woman, reminding us that black communities had struggled on their own to get schools ever since Emancipation. The Loachapoka and Notasulga buildings do not show a designer's presence. One of the six was erected by fourteen-year-old Robert Rochon Taylor during his summer vacation. A Tuskegee student of carpentry and brickmaking, Taylor's son first built a shack to house ten workers and then the three-room building. He made a $400 profit because George Washington Carver gave him the paint. His father helped with the financing and periodically drove the fifteen miles in a horse and buggy to encourage him.[48]

The other members of the experimental six varied in their architectural competence. The form of the Brownsville school in Macon County, finished in the spring of 1914, is unknown as is that of Little Zion in Montgomery County.[49] Big Zion in Montgomery County was a tightly organized, gable-roofed building with a raised porch sheltering the entrance.[50] The asymmetrical facade had single, double, and triple windows—the three configurations implying differing internal uses such as a cloakroom, industrial room, and classroom, hallmarks of a progressive one-teacher institution.

MADISON PARK

Still another of the experimental six, one that Hoffschwelle has identified as Madison Park in Montgomery County, steps far from the vernacular church and cabin typologies that characterize many rural schools and far from the Rising Star cottage model to suggest an architectural future: schools rendered as civic rather than domestic or religious presences.[51] Madison Park has two banks or groups of five double-hung windows with, above them, a broad gable projecting from the main roof to centralize the long side. The long side reads as a façade, the gable implying a classical pediment that ennobles the two classrooms below. When a folding wall between classrooms was open for assemblies or community meetings, the pediment gained a fuller civic meaning. Smaller volumes that are roofed at the same pitch as the main block, and set only slightly back from the main building line, bracket the classroom unit. These rhyming elements, at least one of which has an entrance porch incised into the minor volume at the corner, clasp the long block between them or, differently read, extend the classrooms into the landscape. The bracketing ends turn the triadic facade into a five-part composition—the pediment in the center, the ending of the window banks on each side, and the little entry units. These are classical organizing strategies that stem from the sixteenth century's Andrea di Pietro, familiarly "Palladio." Cloakrooms were probably in the entries and the industrial room was in a rear projection behind the classroom block.

Perhaps Madison Park was one of the schools that Taylor or the drawing division was designing in August 1911 or preparing in October 1912 for the Sears estimators. Two unlabeled photographs are in the frontispiece of *The Negro Rural School*, a 1915 Tuskegee plan book, but the plans are not included. A montage of four modest church- or cabin-like schools surrounding a centrally placed Madison Park, as if to illustrate design progress, is in *Negro Education*, the 1916 federal study discussed

below.[52] The *Southern Workman* published Madison Park [Figure 7.4] and a smaller version of the type, a one-teacher unit [not pictured here] with a bank of seven windows and the two incised corner entries under the building's single hipped roof.[53]

Banked or grouped windows as at Madison Park signaled advanced education for pragmatic reasons as well as for the glassy civic expression that differed so dramatically from the country vernacular. Banked windows provide a more even light than separated single windows as at Notasulga or Loachapoka or, for that matter, Tuskegee's own practice schools—the one in the valley from the early 1890s and even the programmatically and architecturally progressive Children's House of 1901. Banked windows became emblems of modernity to those who read Fletcher B. Dresslar, a school hygiene and facilities expert at the George Peabody College for Teachers in Nashville and the author of the report that persuaded Rosenwald to sever his program from Tuskegee and plant

Figure 7.4. Madison Park Rosenwald school, 1912.

Figure 7.5. Community gathering at the Eastern Shore Industrial School (a county training school), Baldwin County, Alabama. W. A. Hazel's classroom building is in the background with distant administration building.

it in Nashville. According to Dresslar, windows must be double-hung and operable from top and bottom to maximize air circulation. Interior transoms would ventilate further. More importantly, classrooms must be illuminated from one side only, the students' left, so that their writing right arms would not cast shadows on their papers (lefties were out of luck). Windows must face either east or west because some direct sunlight was wanted but only for part of the day. A southern exposure would provide too much and a northern one none at all.

It follows, then, that if a school such as Madison Park had east- or west-facing classroom windows parallel to a road that ran north and south, the building's long façade with its emblematic windows and pseudo pediment would present a different image from that for churches and houses. But if a Madison Park-type school was on a road that ran east and west so that the short end faced the street because the window banks looked east or west, the end piece with the corner porch and column would be a volumetrically complex, asymmetrical face to the road. This too would be pointedly different from doors flat-cut into the center of a country church's gabled end. Dresslar did not want schools to look like churches because, like Washington, he thought denominationalism divided communities.[54] As an educator, he would have looked for rural school typologies that did not depend on churches or houses. The Madison Park solution worked for any roadway orientation, the corner porch's shadowed void reading from long-side or short-side views.

The signature forms of the Madison Park type—a corner post with incised veranda to mark an entrance and banked or grouped windows on the long wall—would reappear and work their way across the land in 1921 and after in designs by others in the Rosenwald Fund's own plan books. But Madison Park's "pediment" would not follow. It was an attractive and meaningful visual element, but the fold into the main roof would have been difficult for a country carpenter and risked leakage while offering no interior amenity to justify the extra expense. The later Rosenwald books would also rearrange other Madison Park motifs so that two different designs for each size of school (one teacher, two teachers, three teachers, etc.) would offer more options for managing east- and west-facing windows against various road alignments. Madison Park's visual sophistication suggests a classically trained mind such as Taylor's, but the forms could also have come from other streams of school building history.

TUSKEGEE'S SCHOOLS BOOK

Independently of the evolving Rosenwald system, in 1915 the Tuskegee Extension Department published a 130-page plan book, *The Negro Rural School and Its Relation to the Community*. This is the one with the frontispiece privileging Madison Park and, perhaps, the other experimental Rosenwalds, but there are no drawings for these examples within. The schools that *The Negro Rural School* promoted were different.

Southern states were now hiring white agents as supervisors of black public education. These agents arranged philanthropic support for county training schools in a funding format similar to that which Washington and Rosenwald were evolving. The Rockefeller-funded General Education Board paid the agents' salaries, so no public money was involved. From around 1912 to 1918 James Longstreet Sibley, who came from a distinguished Georgia family complete with its own Confederate general, was Alabama's agent. Sibley opened the first Alabama county training school for black high school students of agriculture, industries, and teacher preparation in Coosa County in 1913.[55] The Slater Fund was particularly active in the county training school

movement, serving as its principal philanthropy as Rosenwald was for the primary schools.

The Negro Rural School was directed towards several initiatives including county training schools as well as Rosenwald's or anyone else's schools for smaller children. The architectural drawings reflect this spread, the text inviting readers to order Tuskegee's free blueprints for any building depicted. The book also purveyed ideas for fundraising, blackboards, grounds layout, and heating and sanitation that assumed the barest of community means. A rural artisan could, for example, use its drawings to make a stove with an under-floor air intake plus a vented exhaust, and there were plans for outhouses and for a sheet-metal urinal. The text recommended the liberal use of lime and purchased toilet paper. At the other end of the skills scale, *The Negro Rural School* published an Alabama Polytechnic Institute (now Auburn University) engineer's device to bring well water to a drinking fountain that would require purchased parts and a plumber to assemble them.

Beyond heating and sanitation, *The Negro Rural School* introduced ten school types ranging from one-teacher units through two-story central schools for older primary students, to a county training school. Perspectives of a one-teacher school, a four-teacher school, a two-story central school [Figure 7.6], and a teacher's home to go with the county training school were executed in a sketchy hand and signed with initials of William A. Hazel, the office-trained designer who was then teaching at Tuskegee. Hazel's buildings were in an unadorned arts-and-crafts vein with bands of double-hung windows and visible rafter ends under the projecting eaves. Even Hazel's one-teacher model had a multi-windowed classroom, a second room for industrial work, a kitchen, library, and two cloakrooms, the progressive spatial hierarchy signaled

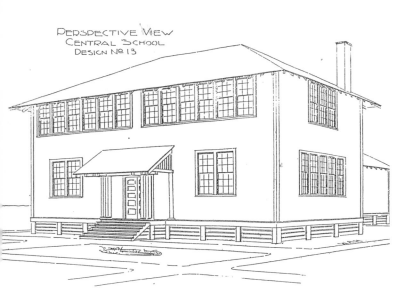

Figure 7.6. Central school plans by W. A. Hazel that were widely used for county training schools.

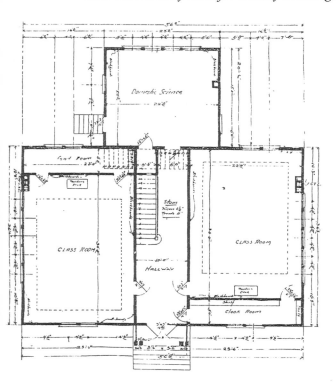

by window size. A built version was photographed in Davenport, Alabama, next to a simple industrial building shown in four drawings in *The Negro Rural School* that are in Taylor's hand.[56] Drawings for a two-story county training school with two symmetrical single-story wings are unsigned but also in Taylor's hand. A teacher's home, with a bathroom, was in one wing and an industries shop, with a toilet in a small room, was on the other. Built examples of Taylor's county training school are unknown. Taylor's hand also shows in a cottage-school plan of the Rising Star type. Sibley, Alabama's agent for Negro schools, directed Taylor in the particulars of this house.[57] A third but less-informed hand made an elevation and plan for a three-room teacher's cottage that could be expanded. Blueprints were also available for buildings that were not illustrated such as a combination girls' dormitory and girls industries building and an academic structure meant to expand a county training school. *The Negro Rural School* also included ideas for the grounds. George Washington Carver drew layouts of ornamental and edible plants for use on small sites. The larger, six-acre sites had a baseball diamond, a garden edged by fruit trees, an orchard, and berry patch interwoven with a poultry yard, shops, and barns, a teacher's house, and an industrial building for blacksmithing and carpentry.

Hazel's drawings of central schools for older primary students and photographs of built county training schools show that his building, rather than Taylor's, was widely adopted for this new educational venture. A federal study of black colleges in 1916, *Negro Education* (discussed below), published photographs of a two-story county training school built to Hazel's central school design in Lowndes County.[58] Jackson Davis, Virginia's former state agent for Negro schools who was traveling around

1918 to study black rural schools on behalf of the General Education Board, photographed the Hazel-designed county training schools at Carrollton in Pickens County, Charity in Lowndes County, and in Tuscaloosa County.[59] All were two stories high and have odd elevations that freshened classical standards by suggesting that the programming within overrode the old rules. Their eccentricities, such as a lengthy band of windows on the second floor with isolated pairs flanking the door on the first floor, are worth analysis.

Assuming that these buildings faced south, an almost continuous window band on the second floor, actually two bands of six windows each, lit two classrooms behind it. The partition between the rooms could be folded away for assemblies or a community meeting. That the eaves might project far enough to shadow the windows in winter as well as summer is suggested in a photograph of the Tangipahoa Parish County Training School in Louisiana, built to Hazel's design in 1920. The shadow line reaches almost to the sills of the upper floor while the background trees are bare.[60] Hazel's plans put a library and an office behind the two classrooms on the second story.

Classrooms are differently oriented on the ground floor, however, their long dimension running perpendicular to the façade to accommodate a central hallway, rather than parallel as on the second floor. The hall ran from the entrance to stairs in the building's rear. Therefore, the banked or grouped windows that illuminate the students' left side are on the side elevations, not on the front. But the teacher's desk then had to switch ends so the windows could be on the students' left. Assuming, again, a south-facing entrance, the teacher's desk would be in the front or south side if the ground floor classroom were on the building's east side and in the

rear or north, near the stairs, if the classroom were on the building's west side. The paired windows on the right side of the door (as the observer faces it) light the cloakroom behind the teacher's desk in the eastern classroom. The paired windows on the left side of the door (as the observer faces it) light the backs of students in the west classroom. The plan's visible residue in the odd elevations of the three sun-hit sides can serve as an emblem of racial idealism or segregation, depending on the viewpoint. But it clearly conveys an appealingly frank visual sensibility.[61] In 1924 the Urban League's *Opportunity* published a Hazel county training school, a two-story "potential Tuskegee" near Mobile [Figure 7.7]. Cheer and encouragement would seep into the community from its gardens, fruit groves, county fairs, and conferences, *Opportunity* promised.[62] By 1931 there would be 390 Slater Fund-financed county training schools in fifteen states. More Hazel schools may surface among them, and perhaps the Taylor county training school as well.[63]

When Rosenwald moved his program to Nashville in 1920 he hired the white Samuel L. Smith as its administrator, replacing Tuskegee's Clinton J. Calloway. Smith had been a student of Peabody College for Teachers' Fletcher B. Dresslar, the schoolhouse expert. Smith was also the state's agent for black education in Tennessee. Smith and Dresslar acted, perhaps to a limited degree, as architectural designers or, at the least, as demanding clients for *Community School Plans*, a Rosenwald-funded plan book that spread aspects of Tuskegee's *The Negro Rural School* across the South and into the future.[64] But *Community School Plans* had less instruction in heating and sanitation and many more buildings, all of them drawn in the professional hand of one E. M. Tisdale. *Community School Plans* was widely influential with both races and it offered more de-

Figure 7.7. Tuskegee's Western Campus, 1916. Chapel left, White Hall right, Tantum in middle, wooden barns in distance.

signs for large schools, some in brick. Several look like Madison Park. As Hoffschwelle has shown, the banks of windows, the flanking end volumes with rhyming roof pitches, and incised porches with a corner column can be found on 1920s' Rosenwald schools throughout the South.[65] If Madison Park turns out to be Taylor's design, it could be his most influential work.

Negro Education, the Colonial Revival, and the "Homemade Plan"

Two years after Washington's death in late 1915, the Phelps-Stokes Fund and the federal Bureau of Education published an institutional study of black vocational schools and colleges. The Welsh sociologist Thomas Jesse Jones wrote it with the assistance of white students who, as Phelps-Stokes Fellows, were learning to apply social science research to race issues. Most of the book *Negro Education: A Study of the Private and Higher Schools for Colored People in the United States* deals with financial,

curricular, staffing, and management issues, the findings rendered in statistics and charts, but unlike most such analyses, it also delved into architectural and physical planning.[66] This part was written by the Fund's president, architect Isaac Newton Phelps Stokes, the Ecole-educated nephew of Olivia and Caroline Phelps Stokes and expert on tenement housing. Assisting Stokes on the chapter "Buildings and Grounds" were two travelers, architect A. H. Albertson of the Howells and Stokes architectural office and Albertson's educator wife.

Negro Education weighed in on architectural language, as few education analyses did, promoting the "American Colonial" as best for its perceived truth to materials, intimacy with nature, domestic scale, rural associations, and beauty, utility and "severe simplicity."[67] American Colonial rooms had lower ceiling heights and fewer stories than the preceding "mansard" or "academy" style. Staircases had shorter runs for quick evacuation in case of fire, and when no emergency was underway the inhabitants enjoyed an intimate relationship to nature because they were closer to it. Stokes and Albertson praised Hampton for its colonial style buildings but singled out Tuskegee by awarding it four full-page photographs. The subjects were Andrew Hospital, Tompkins Dining Hall, the New Laundry [Catalog 20], and a bird's-eye view of the western campus showing Tantum Hall and White Hall as well as the Chapel. [Figure 7.7]

The popular Colonial Revival of the early twentieth century suggested an Anglo-Saxon identity for everyone, including eastern European and Mediterranean immigrants, even though it could also render a sense of entitlement and an implied British ancestry for those who expected such acknowledgement. It was used on a museum of Jewish history and also for working class housing because it was, somehow, "democratic." It was a "style for all classes." [68]

The most interesting segment of the visual argument that the Albertsons and Stokes brought to *Negro Education* was their observations about how black schools could upgrade their incrementally developed, ad hoc campuses into deliberately symmetrical, centralizing plans that would be like those at leading white institutions by inserting axial corridors into pre-existing "haphazard" arrangements. An earlier Olmsted firm scheme intended to reorganize the accretive Harvard University campus into a symmetrical whole could have served as inspiration. [69] *Negro Education* published before-and-after plans for Claflin University in South Carolina, Livingstone College in North Carolina, and Hampton Institute in Virginia. Drawings indicated the buildings that should be retained—or duplicated for a symmetry—and those that should be moved or demolished to achieve an organizing axis and community-defining central green. But the Albertsons, who visited Tuskegee, did not propose such interventions there. Tuskegee "just grew," they wrote, "and is still growing with such direction as immediate development suggests." It was among the six schools they saw that showed "attention

to a general plan," albeit a "homemade" one. The Albertsons did see "evidence of great care" in the school's planning and upkeep. [70] They also praised it for assigning individual departments to separate buildings, as did Claflin, Voorhees, and Virginia Union University. They offered no reorganization proposals because they must have seen that the hills made it impossible. Tuskegee's fingerlike ridges, none parallel to another, its irregularly shaped plateaus, and steeply sided ravines meant that the resulting "disorder," as it might appear on paper, would constitute its own form.

Negro Education's proposals for cohesive campus development at Claflin, Livingstone, and Hampton fail to support later critics' contention that the Phelps-Stokes Fund and the Bureau of Education promoted industrial education as a lesser learning for a supposedly lesser people, as in a caste system. The Stokes and Albertson renovation schemes imply that African American youth should have as stalwart a sense of institutional identity and collective purpose that privileged white students enjoyed. Historians Eric Anderson and Alfred A. Moss Jr. have charged W. E. B. Du Bois and his intellectual progeny James D. Anderson and Donald Spivey with misreading *Negro Education* for polemical purposes. [71] Anderson and Moss find that *Negro Education* recommended for black schools the progressive reforms that were normative in white ones: modern languages rather than Latin and Greek, the social as well as the physical sciences, and American as well as European history. Thomas Jesse Jones and the Phelps-Stokes Fund were dedicated to black advancement and, with help from Isaac Newton Phelps Stokes and Mr. and Mrs. Albertson, understood that buildings and campus layout could further the cause. [72]

SOME PLANNING EPISODES

Tuskegee did receive occasional expert landscaping and planning advice even after an unsuccessful attempt to bring in Frederick Law Olmsted, the profession's head. In 1894 Washington met with Olmsted in Massachusetts and offered to pay his expenses from Asheville, North Carolina, where he was working, if he would donate a plan. An influential Tuskegee advisor, J. L. M. Curry, praised the idea. "It is impossible to estimate what an educatory influence in morals and aesthetics such an object lesson has."[73] This was just when Olmsted was retiring because of illness. Then there was the Warren H. Manning episode of 1902, whose report was supposed to lead to an "essential unity" that promoted "permanency and beauty." A useless graphic emerged some years later but not much else, as Chapter 6 discussed. More realistic suggestions came in early 1911 from the city planner John Nolen, who gave a slide lecture and wrote a report.[74] Nolen spent his Tuskegee day with Taylor, John H. Washington, and David A. Williston.[75] Nolen recommended a topographic survey, changes in the path from the private-car railroad siding, another location for the drill grounds, narrowing some campus roads, moving the band stand, relocating the heating plant, informal rather than gridded platting of Greenwood Village, and a forestry division in the Agriculture Department. He praised those who had developed the school to date, a compliment to his companions of the day and to Washington. Low agreed to the topographic map and said that Nolen's report should go to the trustees. The heating plant did change locations, a decision that may have antedated Nolen's visit.

Despite minimal results from visiting professional planners, the Tuskegee campus was a public success, admired by those who wrote about it as we saw in Chapter 3, "Describing a Dream." It was a tapestry of loosely woven zones that shifted shape, meaning, and even location under pressure from various necessities but also under the continuing guidance of Booker T. Washington (for thirty-five years—until late 1915) and Robert R. Taylor (for forty—until 1932). The campus is the cumulative result and the visible record of a multitude of individual siting and design decisions, as the Catalog shows for each Taylor building. The tapestry was woven by complexities in fundraising, construction management, the institute's educational goals, simultaneous occupation and construction, and the expectations of individual donors who might have their own ideas of how things ought to be. Overriding it all was an hypothesis to prove—that the "Negro race" was rapidly progressing. Finally, and with a sensitivity that was their own, Washington and Taylor continually engaged Tuskegee's most powerful actor of all, the rugged topography that they wrestled with daily and must have loved. In the end, what mattered were the intimately scaled, inventively modeled, homemade brick buildings, the charming gardens, the well-tended lawns, disciplined and cheerful students, and the hills and valleys that surprised visitors even as they shaped a special place for a people. Tuskegee was built to place and process more than to plan, but it made magic anyway.

CHAPTER 8

THE DIRECTOR OF INDUSTRIES III

THE MOTON YEARS

Booker T. Washington died from the effects of a stroke in November 1915.[1] He was fifty-nine, in poor health for a long time from several causes, including high blood pressure, that were exacerbated by his inability to slow down or take the time to get proper medical help. He left a hole in the national firmament along with the substantial institution he had built from scratch. In 1915 Tuskegee's faculty of 197 taught 38 trades and professions to 1,537 students with the support of an endowment of two million dollars. The simple funeral in the Tuskegee Chapel was attended by multitudes—rich and poor, black and white. Robert R. Taylor, representing the Executive Council, was an honorary pallbearer. Adella Hunt Logan, Warren Logan's wife and a suffragist who had been hospitalized for depression, leapt to her death from Huntington Memorial Academic Hall. Memorial services were held around the country.

Two photographs published in a memorial volume represent Tuskegee Institute as Washington had liked to see it. One shows the beasts and buggies that had brought farmers to the February Negro Conference parked in the valley's southern end. The background is White Hall and Tompkins Dining Hall visually fused into a block of institutional power. [Figure 8.1] The caption for the second photograph reports that Washington staged it. He wanted to feature part of the dairy herd grazing in the foreground. [Figure 8.2] The Tompkins Dining Hall dome and White Hall cupola rise above the tree line, suggesting capitol-like urbanity or even an Emerald City.[2] [Figures 8.1, 8.2] Both photographs foreground agriculture, the cows in the second shot and in the first the farmers that Tuskegee served if we read the vehicles as their representatives. Both apply architecture to convey the institution's significance.

Tuskegee now needed a Principal. After considering Acting Principal and long-time Business Manager Warren Logan along with Washington's personal secretary and political assistant Emmett J. Scott, the board selected Robert Russa Moton, a Hampton Institute administrator. Moton also headed Washington's National Negro Business League and he had the confidence of Margaret Murray Washington, Seth Low, the Tuskegee board, and the officers of such collegial actors as the Phelps-Stokes Fund and the General Education Board. Taylor supported him too. Moton would continue Washington's strategy of racial progress, a public face accepting of Jim Crow restrictions, and hidden activities of another persuasion. Moton's dark complexion and reputedly pure African ancestry was a

Top, Figure 8.1. Southern end of the valley with farmers' buggies, c. 1910–12. White Hall girls' dormitory with cupola and Tompkins Dining Hall with dome. Bottom, Figure 8.2. Washington-directed photo, c.1910–12, of part of the dairy herd.

matter of pride and a silent rebuttal to those who claimed that Washington owed his abilities to his white father. Moton too could appear subservient when needed, believing as he did that the moral force of honorable behavior would prevail in the end. Over six feet tall and sturdily built, Moton could enforce honor's image. A deft politician hid within.

Taylor's responsibilities during the Moton era were initially unchanged: directing the largest department; designing, erecting and maintaining buildings; coping with grounds and infrastructure; and acting behind the scene as needed on various tasks, sometimes of a sensitive nature. Correspondence from 1919 suggests the distance he continued to travel since the Stokes sisters' work some twenty years before by working directly with donors. Writing from New York in July, Taylor reported progress on the Booker T. Washington monument with the board. Taylor recommended Charles Keck as sculptor "provided no competent colored person is found."[3] Keck would not enter a competition but he would visit Tuskegee, provide any number of sketches, and work with any architect including the school's own. But Taylor was also recommending William Welles Bosworth, the MIT-trained architect of the Baldwin Monument, for the setting of Keck's figures.

Taylor was also looking for a brickmaking instructor on this Northeastern swing since William Gregory was due to retire. He searched for a head of the new automobile mechanics division and he had the privilege of writing to William A. Hazel in Tuskegee that the trustees decided on Hazel's design to replace the Boys' Trades Building, the fire-destroyed one that Taylor had designed twenty years before. Hazel and architect Albert I. Cassell of Washington, D.C., were then revising the drawings.

It was more than a year later when Taylor and Keck discussed the inscriptions for Washington's monument as board chairman William Willcox had conveyed them. Taylor objected to one quotation, unfortunately unrecorded, because it could be read as supporting discrimination. "There is a veiled suggestion that we may not be ready for certain privileges of the law, but as soon as we are ready, these privileges will be granted."[4] In his usual systematic fashion, Taylor outlined this view's two errors. One was that African Americans were not ready for full citizenship and the second was that whites would freely grant it at some later date. If Taylor was unusually outspoken on the inscription issue, perhaps it was because he was writing in private but also because white mobs had been attacking black neighborhoods across the country. As Moton later put the conundrum, whites could hardly expect blacks to "stay in their place" when they, the whites, were clearly not staying in theirs.[5] Taylor did tell Keck that he liked another proposal: "I will let no man drag me down so far as to make me hate him." This was the clearest expression of Booker T. Washington's life, Taylor wrote, "love to all mankind, a sentiment close to the nobility and grandeur of 'Love Thine Enemies' . . . Hate is in the world; has been, and will be for a long time to come. The thought expressed, therefore, of doing good for evil; of going twain when you are compelled to go one mile, is a sentiment which should not be inter-racial alone, but should apply to humanity."[6] [Taylor's punctuation.] Another proposal under discussion was executed as the central panel: "We shall prosper in proportion as we learn to dignify and glorify labor and put brains and skill into the common occupations of life." Flanking inscriptions are, on one side, "There is no defense or security for any of us except in the highest intelligence and development of all" and on the other the one Taylor admired "I will let no man drag me down so far as to make me hate him." Keck's two figures are a man rising from his seat on an anvil and plough while clutching a book and a compass. Washington, behind him, raises a veil. Labor is clearly the point, but technology and knowledge lead the ascent from the pre-industrial basics. The monument was dedicated in May 1922.

A MODEL COMMUNITY AND THE VETERANS HOSPITAL CONTROVERSY

Relations between Tuskegee Institute and the town of Tuskegee, the seat of Macon County, had been so smooth after the consolidation of white power in 1901 that its leaders could congratulate themselves on having a "model community." The white-governed town understood that it was more cultured, cosmopolitan, and refined than other Southern communities, as Robert J. Norrell has analyzed the paternalism.[7] Perhaps the town even included the institute's college-educated faculty in its self-assessment. In any case, white-owned businesses certainly valued prosperous patrons even if they were black. In August 1922, with Moton traveling and Taylor serving as Acting Principal, an incident took place that could have destroyed this fragile peace. A black boy from the town killed a white minister's son in a scuffle. The news spread quickly and whites were coming in from the countryside, presumably for a lynching. Instead, the sheriff arrested the black boy and two others and jailed them in the next county to get them away. W. W. Campbell, town banker and institute trustee, asked Taylor to keep matters quiet at the school, which he did, working late into the night with black and white community leaders to see that there was no further violence. The tension lifted

the following day.[8] But soon, a more threatening disruption arrived to mar what should have been the entire region's economic uplift, the staffing of the only federal Veterans Administration Hospital for African Americans.

W. E. B. Du Bois and his scholarly heirs have misjudged Booker T. Washington's apparent compliance with Southern ways, in Norrell's estimation, undervaluing his assertion of racial progress and ignoring his open demands for civil rights that predated those of the NAACP.[9] Robert Russa Moton also appeared to accept racist strictures to the detriment of his reputation among Northerners who brought a more radical stance to the table. In 1922, with a struggle erupting over the staffing of the nearby Veterans Administration Hospital, Moton seemed so compromising that he even confused his friends, as Raymond Wolters has put it. But Moton's apparent docility was tactical.[10]

The hospital for six hundred black American men wounded during World War I was to stand next to the institute, in part on institute land. Five months before the contract was signed, Taylor went to Washington to meet with the Treasury Department's supervising architect to lay a railroad spur into the grounds.[11] But it was the hospital's administration and staffing that would cause the rift. Two different federal agencies had promised the black institute and the white town medical and administrative professionals of their own race.[12] The town wanted white staffing badly enough to circumvent an Alabama law that made it illegal for a white woman to nurse a black man. White nurses would supervise low-wage black "nurse-maids" for hands-on care even though the institute was now graduating fully qualified black professionals. The hospital could have drawn both black and white physicians from across the country, but the compromise—hiring both—violated the state's segregation laws. The battle was national because the hospital was and because Moton inherited Washington's presidential access. Unlike his predecessor, however, Moton could work with the NAACP, and that body brought the decisive pressure to bear. The heated battle lasted a year and a half before Moton, the institute, and the NAACP finally won black staffing. But first there was a Ku Klux Klan parade and a possible crossburning at an institute doctor's home.[13]

In an early July evening of 1923 the resurgent Klan staged a parade of twenty or so Klansmen draped in purloined hospital sheets. Whites claimed that Moton, then in New York for a trustees meeting, had left Tuskegee early because he was afraid for his life. Indeed, a knock-on-the-door committee that reportedly included W. W. Campbell, the institute trustee who had helped contain the previous year's racial crisis, threatened him and the school. Margaret Murray Washington was at her summer home on Long Island and Moton's family was at theirs in Virginia. Andrew Hospital medical director John A. Kenney had already sent his family north and he also left after a white patient said the Klan planned to kill him. But the parade was peaceful because, as oral tradition has it, armed graduates joined the uniformed Tuskegee Cadet Corps in a line along the campus edge. Or perhaps it was peaceful because it was planned that way, "like a Masonic or Pythian event."[14] The institute could have chosen this second interpretation to minimize the crisis and ease eventual reconciliation or to defang the Klan by failing to acknowledge its power. In either reading, the school had to refrain from reacting to the implied insult, which it did. A scheduled dance took place and Acting Principal Robert R. Taylor stood on his veranda, face to the public road, to watch the parade pass by. A tall man, he would

have projected an air of calm detachment. Three days later Taylor wrote to a Mobile newspaper to correct its account, copying the letter to NAACP secretary Walter White. A Mobile reporter had interviewed Taylor and had made, Taylor was sure, an unintentional error. Moton had left Tuskegee well before the board meeting because of scheduled fundraising, not out of fear. And he, Taylor, had not said that threats had not been made against any incoming black hospital workers, only that threats had not been made against institute personnel.[15] The careful distinction implies that Taylor wanted the world to understand that while white on black violence was certainly possible, Tuskegee could handle the situation. Soon after, Moton appointed Taylor to the newly created position of Vice Principal, strengthening his authority to act in emergencies.[16] But the Vice Principal never relinquished his regular duties as Director of Industries and head of buildings and grounds.

THE DEPARTMENT OF MECHANICAL INDUSTRIES

It was during this period that Taylor published one of his rare essays. Offering views into his main task, "Tuskegee's Mechanical Department" appeared in 1921 in Hampton's, Southern Workman.[17] The department now had 778 students studying 25 trades. Some of them—wheelwrighting, carriage trimming, and blacksmithing—are redolent of the pre-industrial world from which the school sprang. Others were clearly modern—linotype, auto mechanics, photography. Programs varied from one to three years in duration with most taking the longest time. They varied in popularity. There were sixteen students in sheet metal and seventy-eight in auto mechanics. Automobiles are seductive for all youth but they promised even more to African Americans as a way around Jim Crow railroad and streetcar humiliations. Taylor noted that shoemaking and tailoring were especially favored because one could start a business with a modest capital investment. Because Tuskegee's goal was independent graduates, Taylor added accounting and bookkeeping divisions to the department to give industrial students a leg up on business matters. The Mechanical Department's thoroughness earned praise two years later for its "unsurpassed" Tuskegee-trained troops that served in France. They had learned wireless and telephonic communication as well as "the technical lines of artillery" in Taylor's bailiwick.[18] The Tuskegee Airmen of World War II had precedence in earlier wartime preparations.

Drawing remained central to Tuskegee's industrial education. All students took a short course in projective and geometrical drawing before embarking on a trade. Students had to draw, dimension, and name every part of each object before they made it, although Taylor admitted this was not always carried out in practice. Students had to work from others' freehand sketches even if they were unable to draw themselves. Each shop still had a classroom for the trade's academic or "theoretical" studies. For example, before learning to make a table, students would gather in the furniture classroom to learn about tree biology, wood types, drying methods, and the specific joints suited to special purposes. Trades courses were arranged in "definite form" and in a "sequence of operations" so that skills developed logically from the simpler to the more complex—the Russian pedagogy formulated so long before. But unlike the Russians, Tuskegee students also continued to learn from practical application. Students in the building trades still worked on campus construction. Taylor noted that their attitude changed when they were working on real buildings rather than drawings or models. "There is an interest, a personal touch, a devotion in the job which is to remain as a part of the school and which he [the student] constantly sees in his work which is hard to arouse in any other way."[19] Although Taylor used the masculine pronoun, he also noted that girls were welcome in any division. Girls had learned printing, men's as well as ladies' tailoring, shoemaking, accounting, Linotype, carpentry, and harness making.

Taylor's essay also describes how the bookkeeping division was integrated into the industrial program. Every job in every division had a number, and each student filed a time card with that number so they and others could calculate their contributions' value. Students had to requisition materials and, at the end of the project, compare their estimated with their actual costs. They gained experience in estimating, a task that Taylor himself did well and that endeared the institute to building donors. Advanced students in the building trades served as construction foremen, submitting work plans, ordering materials and tools, and formally requesting labor or building components from other divisions. Taylor illustrated this process with an engine installation for an electrical plant. Machine Division students planned each step from offloading the engine from the railway car, ordering concrete foundations from the masonry division, and belting the engine to the dynamo. The students estimated each cost and then purchased the labor or supplies from another division. Other exercises with no money changing hands also taught business practice for solo tradespeople. A student who declared the intention of owning his or her own shoemaking shop, for example, might partition off a space in the school shop, "pay" rent and taxes, "purchase" supplies, insurance, and a license, "solicit" business, "hire" other students, keep books, and be evaluated on the calculated financial results. The system had been developed in the shoemaking division but by 1921 was applied beyond it.

Taylor folded other opportunities into the industrial programs. Advanced students could work as teaching assistants. Boys could study more than one trade through interdivisional group courses so they could teach in smaller industrial schools. Group Course B, for example, pulled together machine shop, steam engineering, applied electricity, plumbing, and auto mechanics. Another group combined wheelwrighting, blacksmithing, painting, and carriage trimming. Divisions also operated commercially, as a former student remembered. Harold Webb, who had studied plumbing and heating at Tuskegee before earning a University of Illinois heating and engineering degree, returned for a Tuskegee career. Under Taylor's direction, Webb's division served as plumber for white residences, the clients furnishing the transportation.[20]

Taylor also oversaw still more educational enrichment. Every division had a student club that was responsible for guest lectures, instructional films lent by manufacturers, social events, and committees to oversee the shop, repair broken fixtures, and prevent fires. There were summer programs for elementary school teachers who did not have the benefits of a Tuskegee education with required trades supplementing the normal school. They could learn and then teach woodworking to the level of making blackboards, washboards, flower boxes, or picture frames. The department also offered special courses in basic carpentry, concrete laying, leatherwork, blacksmithing, and painting to agricultural field agents so they could show farmers how to improve their facilities and maintain equipment.

Devising these programs and managing them was Taylor's day job. He did architecture at home evenings and weekends, according to his son Edward.[21] No wonder he took on a design partner in 1920, the architectural drawing division head Louis H. Persley. Steel and concrete construction for large buildings may have had short shrift in Taylor's education, but big buildings were becoming the order of the day and the younger man, trained at Carnegie Institute of Technology later than Taylor was at MIT, probably contributed a needed technological and structural education.

PERSONAL AND OTHER MATTERS

Taylor had still other professional and business concerns during the Moton period. According to his daughter-in-law, he designed and built his own sawmill in Macon County, as she remembered it, or in Opelika in neighboring Lee County according to another family member. His son Robert Rochon managed it at one point.[22] Taylor invested in his brother's Wilmington shoe store and a barbershop, and, later, in the black-owned Birmingham construction company, T. C. Windham & Son. This firm would build the five Willcox Trades Buildings as well as large Taylor and Persley buildings at Tuskegee, Selma, and Birmingham.[23] He also prospered from the black-owned New York-based Oakley Chemical Company.[24]

Robert Rochon Taylor, the boy who built a Rosenwald school when he was fourteen, had graduated in architecture and construction. In 1922, he was working with his father as a contractor. Robert Rochon began architectural studies at Howard University but then changed direction, earning a business degree at the University of Illinois. By 1926 the young man was an assistant to the president of the black-owned Liberty Life Insurance Company of Chicago, a firm for which Taylor and Persley may have designed an expansion.[25] Robert Rochon used banking, insurance, and mortgage lending as tools for helping African Americans purchase homes. By 1928 he reportedly built forty houses on his own and then planned and managed Julius Rosenwald's Michigan Boulevard Garden Apartments for Negroes. This complex of 420 units on six acres with gardens and courtyards, a nursery school, social services, and rooftop promenades forms an instructive contrast to the twenty-eight buildings in the notorious Robert Taylor Homes, the sixteen-story slabs named posthumously to honor Robert Rochon Taylor's service to the Chicago Housing Authority. In 1938 he was its first black board member, an appointment that the NAACP and Urban League deemed a triumph. Twelve years later he resigned the chairmanship during the political firestorm caused by his proposal to house the poor in scatter-site, small-scale buildings, a solution now considered optimal for dealing with spatial segregation. Robert Rochon's great-granddaughter credited him with public housing for 50,000 persons, plus help towards ownership for another 7,000. She has characterized him as "arguably the most powerful nonelected African American inside the most politically powerful Democratic 'machine' in the country."[26] But all this was yet to come.

One of Robert Rochon Taylor's siblings was also finding her way in the mid-1920s. Sister Helen had graduated in music from Fisk University and was a YWCA social worker in Denver. She returned to Tuskegee in 1926 to marry Dr. Eugene H. Dibble, the hospital director. The Tuskegee press made much of the nuptials.[27]

It was during this period Taylor wrote a third-person autobiographical press release that lists events and associations that do not appear elsewhere, including designs for a Mosaic Templar building in Montgomery and an Elks' Rest in Birmingham. Taylor was a Mason, a Mystic Shriner, and an Elk. He was a member of the Alabama State Teachers Association, the National Negro Teachers Association, the National Negro Business League, the American Specification Society of Chicago, and a board member of the Liberty Life Insurance Company of Chicago. Clubs included the Society of Institute Architects of Boston, Alpha Beta Sigma fraternity, the Appomattox Club of Chicago, the Musolit Club of Washington, D.C., and the Allied Technical Arts Club of Tuskegee. But his greatest satisfaction, the press release concluded, came from his work as Director of Industries—preparing artisans, mechanics, and industrial leaders. "Into this work he has put his best thought and energy."[28]

In 1925 Taylor attended a National Negro Builders Association conference at Hampton that he had helped organize. A group photograph shows fifty-five gentlemen, all but seven appearing to be black. Two MIT professors addressed the assembly, one of them discussing testing of structural materials. The other speaker was the now elderly C. Howard Walker with whom Taylor had studied. Charles T. Russell, who had taught carpentry at Tuskegee and was now a Richmond architect and builder, was there, as was Calvin McKissack of the Nashville design and construction firm. Hilyard Robinson, who would become a distinguished modernist, attended.[29] Two years later, with Moton on a four-month trip around the world, Taylor led the institute. Ceremonial duties included hosting distinguished visitors, giving Chapel talks, and receiving the cadet corps' traditional New Year's greetings. An observer wrote that the Acting Principal was deeply moved.[30]

THE MISSISSIPPI RIVER FLOOD

The year 1927 also included a significant non-architectural task. Secretary of Commerce Herbert Hoover appointed Taylor to the Colored Advisory Commission that was charged with monitoring refugee camps for African Americans displaced by the Mississippi River flood. The Tuskegee press now characterized Taylor as a civil engineer.[31] Moton, who chaired the commission, put his personal secretary Albon Holsey and Taylor on the south Louisiana investigative team.

The commission's task had political dimensions because Hoover's presidential hopes rode on the Northern black press's positive review of the Red Cross's care of black flood victims. Northern papers were reporting levels of control and brutality verging on slavery. African Americans, they charged, were forced to remain in their camps when whites were allowed to leave theirs because landowners feared that their low-wage labor would flee North. But there were other reasons for the commission to approve Secretary Hoover's disaster management. As John Barry has explained, Moton's support was to be rewarded with a massive land redistribution scheme when Hoover became president.[32] Hoover would use Rockefeller money to buy large plantations to be subdivided for purchase by black farmers, cutting out the bondage elements of tenancy and sharecropping. According to Hoover biographer David Burner, the scheme fell victim to philanthropic cold feet on the part of Julius Rosenwald (in this telling} as well as to the Great Depression.[33] The loading of such consequences onto the commission's plate, consequences that went far beyond the flood's immediate tragedy, called for judicious staffing.

Holsey and Taylor joined New Orleans bishop Robert E. Jones to inspect fifteen southern Louisiana camps. Their travels would have been the same as those of Tuskegee graduates Jesse O. Thomas, a field secretary of the National Urban League who wrote for *Opportunity*, and Claude A. Barnett of the Associated Negro Press who joined Holsey's group at Lafayette. Holsey published in the widely circulated *Tuskegee Messenger* vivid glimpses of people in distress. The committee had traveled by train on tracks that had been elevated above the rushing waters because hundreds of men standing in water to their waists had worked around the clock to raise them. The frightened faces of the displaced people they met reminded Holsey of the stranded deer who had to jump from the tracks as the train approached. Many flood victims had never seen a railroad or electricity, which only worsened their terror. The team found conditions at the Baton Rouge camp good but those at Opelousas wretched. Holsey talked with a cold, hungry woman who was standing in mud and water. She wanted to leave but was not allowed to because, she was told, her home would be destroyed, the well poisoned, and the land awash with dead animals and their stench. "What I care about stink," she protested. "I always live in stink. I rather be in stink than up here where we are treated like dogs."[34] *Opportunity*'s editor thought the investigators stood in the uncomfortable position between "the questioning eyes and poised pens" of a Northern press that was well aware of the peonage and brutality that was the black Southerners lot and its own understanding of the white South's repugnance to federal intervention. It was to the committee's credit, *Opportunity* wrote, that it inspected the camps "with polite but open eyes."[35]

Taylor did not record his responses other than in an address to a Wilmington audience shortly after he returned.[36] He skipped the harrowing hardships upon which most flood narratives dwell to say that the camps in which the African Americans shared in the management were the successful ones, an opinion also voiced in the official reports. Those run by white-on-black directives were less successful. He was reassuring in his tone but he quickly switched to proposals for managing the river so that such a flood could not happen again, thereby staying well within the Moton-Hoover agreement. Privately, however, the Louisiana team expressed concern over the victims' mental health. They were grateful for the Red Cross's and others' kindness but they were overcome by worry about their homes and livestock and despondent about the future. There were fewer recreational opportunities in the black camps than in the white ones to help maintain hopefulness, a need that Taylor would express more fiercely after he retired and the subject was black recreation in Wilmington.[37] The southern Louisiana team asked for better facilities at six camps along with screened dining structures at three others, tableware, closing one camp because it was marshy, more cots for all, black social workers and nurses to teach health and home economics, black visitors with the freedom to observe, and the elimination of armed white guards within the compound.[38] Presumably guards would still be outside.

THE TAYLOR & PERSLEY PARTNERSHIP

Louis Hudison Persley (1890–1932), who taught drawing at Tuskegee from 1915 to 1916, returned from army service in September 1920 as head of the Architectural Drawing Division. Persley was from Macon, Georgia, but had studied at the prestigious Lincoln University near Philadelphia, where Taylor had once considered going, and graduated in architecture from the Carnegie Institute of Technology. In 1916 he designed a church in Athens, Georgia, that has been described as a reduced version of

Taylor's Chapel but that was also a popular type of the period.[39] It is not known if he went abroad during the war.

In July 1920, Taylor wrote to the Macon veteran to ask him to return. He would find a larger and better-lit drawing room in the Willcox Trades Building A than in the Slater-Armstrong building.[40] Taylor and Persley soon entered into a design partnership that produced large buildings at the institute and elsewhere over the next decade. Their Taylor & Persley, Architects letterhead named specializations in lodge buildings, houses, and schools of various sizes and it promised sketches, working drawings, and construction supervision. Persley died in 1932 at age forty-two of kidney failure and Taylor, by then ill himself, retired shortly thereafter.[41]

Taylor & Persley's design language moved a step away from the triadic massing, sensitive scale, studied proportions, and astutely placed spare detailing that characterized the buildings that were Taylor's alone. Ellen Curtis James Hall, a nursing student dormitory near the hospital finished in 1921 [Catalog 22], and Sage Hall, a 1922–1926 boys dormitory [Catalog 23], are similar in plan to the earlier Douglass, Huntington, and Tantum halls but differ in visual character. They have dormers to light attic bedrooms plus bedrooms in the basements or ground floors for a total of four usable stories, changing the scale—the apparent size—even as it fits more rooms in the footprint. Uniform windows increase the institutional flavor but projecting eaves and rafter ends, paired brackets, patterned brick surfaces in several colors, and other design devices in an Arts and Crafts vein do meet the need for effective enrichment. The Chambliss Children's House of 1931 is more in tune with earlier Taylor five-part classicism but it too abandons the varied window shapes and syncopated rhythms of the earlier practice if only because the manufactured steel windows meant straight lintels [Catalog 24]. The partnership did change the number of windows in the classroom banks or groups to ease the façade into a varied rhythm. The Chambliss auditorium has exposed metal trusses, a structural material that Taylor had avoided. For even larger buildings with complex programming and big spaces, such as Logan Hall [Catalog 25] or the Colored Masonic Temple in Birmingham, the partnership built in concrete and steel. The partnership also allowed solo practice. In 1922 Persley alone designed the Chambliss Hotel, or "The Block," [Catalog 24] and, in 1928, a two-story brick and stone funeral home in Macon.[42]

SELMA, BIRMINGHAM, AND SNOW HILL

Taylor & Persley began immediately with substantial steel and concrete buildings erected by the Windham Brothers Construction Company,

the black-owned Birmingham firm with which Taylor was directly associated. From August to December 1921, the team erected the Dinkins Memorial Hall at Selma University.[43] [Figure 8.3] An academic building for a Baptist school with a chapel or auditorium on the third floor, it replaced the destroyed Dinkins Memorial Chapel of 1903. C. S. Dinkins, the school's president from 1892 to 1901, focused on literary and theological studies, limiting industrial training. The long north-facing façade has more than fifty large windows, most with straight lintels grouped within a grid of horizontal bands and vertical quoins or, for the central bays, thicker wall buttresses that strengthen the walls where the chapel's roof frame touches down. It replays Taylor's defense of the Tuskegee Chapel wall buttresses some two decades earlier. The short sides

Figure 8.3. Dinkins Memorial Chapel Building, Selma University.

Figure 8.4. Colored Masonic Temple auditorium.

with fewer openings are enlivened by contrasting patterns in colored bricks. There are three tones of ochre or cream and three different reds in fields made entirely of stretchers or of headers that are edged by frames in a contrasting color and, with the largest fields, striped in a closely related hue. The patterns are visually involving, helping maintain scale by enriching the higher wall levels to keep us looking upward.

Taylor considered the Birmingham Colored Masonic Temple, or the Most Worshipful Prince Hall Grand Lodge, as the partnership's most important non-Tuskegee work. Built from 1922–1924 for $657,704, it is eight stories tall and remains in excellent historical condition. There were lodge rooms on upper floors, a drug store with a soda fountain on the ground floor, sixty or so professional offices,

and a balconied auditorium or ballroom that could entertain two thousand. [Figure 8.4] Throughout the age of segregation, the Masonic Temple was the center of black Birmingham's social life with its concerts and cotillions, social and fraternal events, and towards the end, civil rights meetings.

The Colored Masonic Temple exterior shows Taylor's struggle with the problems stemming from the horizontal classical ordering system when it is applied to an office building's vertical mass, a problem with which most architects of the period had to grapple. [Figure 8.5] Four Corinthian columns standing on a rusticated stone base bind the next three floors to encompass a total of four. Taylor extended them to greater height than the order's proportional rules allow by including segments of the implied entablature's architrave and frieze, thereby allowing three stories with the same window dimensions. Above the extended columns there is a continuous dentil cornice, the one that correctly caps the entablature segments extending the columns. This wraps the two sides of the building that are bounded by streets and supports the pediment over the four full columns below. The entablature appears somewhat awkward from the distance because it is close to the total building's mid-section, but the gridding of the upper levels with pilasters and a continuing entablature two stories further up helps. The Corinthian columns, the entablature sections above them, the well articulated cornice, and the richly sculpted pediment suggest imperial Rome as MIT architects would have taught it and, as well, Italian Renaissance revisions of that language for modern purposes. Again, Taylor would have learned this sculptural classicism at MIT but did not use it in its proper materials, cut stone, until now. The temple front also alludes to an earlier white Masonic temple in Birmingham. But since the white lodge did not include the expanded program of offices, shops, and entertainment spaces as did the black building, its classicism only had to handle a three-story volume in a rectangular mass that had the rough proportions of a classical temple. For Taylor himself, the Colored Masonic Temple's true significance was its all-black authorship and ownership, from financing to construction and occupation. "This building is a notable achievement in demonstrating the fact that colored men are capable of handling large enterprises."[44]

Taylor & Persley's third non-Tuskegee structure is Wallace Buttrick Hall, a one-story, public county training school that was built about 1930 in brick and steel at the private Snow Hill Institute in Wilcox County, Alabama. A Tuskegee graduate inaugurated this "little Tuskegee" in a log shanty in 1893. For some years the Colored Literary and Industrial School at Snow Hill, later Snow Hill Normal and Industrial Institute, was among the most successful Tuskegee offshoots. In 1918 it had twenty-four buildings; one of them, designed and built by another Tuskegee graduate, was reportedly the largest structure in the county. Snow Hill had thirty-five teachers, four hundred students, and almost two thousand acres of farm and timberland. In 1928, the state purchased ten acres in the campus center where it erected the Taylor & Persley building. Buttrick Hall resembles the contemporaneous

Figure 8.5. Colored Masonic Temple, Birmingham.

Chambliss Children's House at Tuskegee [Catalog 24] but without the sophisticated entrance.[45]

THE COLLEGE QUADRANGLE

The last and largest of the Taylor & Persley Tuskegee works are Logan Hall gymnasium and auditorium and the flanking Hollis Burke Frissell Library and Samuel C. Armstrong Science Building for the nascent College Department [Catalog 25]. They were erected by T. C. Windham and Sons with steel and concrete framing and cladding of rough-textured, multi-toned bricks that look like Tuskegee's own that were no longer in production. The three buildings border a broad rectangle, the fourth side of which opens to the Montgomery Road. Phelps Hall still stood across the road and housed College Department administration. After Phelps was moved to the boys' quadrangle, the grass swath continued from the south side of the public road to the internal road ending in the Huntington Memorial Academic Building, which then served as the quadrangle's visual closure even if it did not stand on the centerline. Like the plan, the distinction between Tuskegee's secondary school and college courses was also fluid.

Defending the decision for a college department to a trustee who opposed this turn of events as not as Washington would have wanted, Moton pointed out that Tuskegee's high school students would be taking physical and social science courses in the college department's Science Building and that the larger library would serve the entire institution. Tuskegee was moving forward because the race was too, surely a Washingtonian precept.[46] College-level studies were in place by 1925 with four-year Bachelor of Science degrees in Agriculture or Education plus two-year diplomas in Home Economics and Trades. By 1931, students from Latin America, the Philip-pines, India, China, and Africa had joined black Americans in earning Bachelor of Science degrees in technical arts, agriculture, nurse training, home economics, business practice, music, and teacher training. This last was understood to be close to a liberal arts program even though it still retained industrial components from the Washington era. A boy from the Bahamas who came to learn the printer's trade took science courses in the College Department and prepared for dental school.[47] The Logan Hall auditorium-gymnasium housed inter-collegiate basketball, first-run movies on Saturday nights, dances, and concerts by traveling jazz and classical musicians, including a symphony orches-tra.[48]

The college quadrangle as built is a reduced ver-sion of a larger proposal. A 1930 Taylor & Persley blueprint shows that some college departments were to have their own new buildings in the old campus. In this scheme Armstrong Science and Frissell Library were to go between the Carnegie Library and the former Slater-Armstrong Agricultural Building, now Margaret Murray Washington Hall for home economics. The 1930 plan also showed a College of Technological Arts in front of the Emery dormitories, where Moton Hall now stands, and a college-level agricultural classroom building behind the five Willcox Trades buildings. There would also be another girls' dormitory north of Tantum Hall and a railroad station next to the visitors' private cars on the steep slope behind Sage and Olivia Davidson dormitories. Such large structures in the older campus probably would have disrupted the scale. In the 1930 plan the site of the Frissell (now Ford) Library was to have an even larger College Academic Building while that of the present Arm-strong Science would have gone to a boys' dormi-tory. Finally, a YMCA and YWCA structure was to fill the corner between the dormitory and Logan Hall. Logan would connect with the Alumni Bowl stadium behind it that was built 1924–1925 under David A. Williston's supervision. The quadrangle's shape and Logan Hall, which was under construction in late 1930, are the only survivors from this early plan. The grounds' previous uses stretched back to the beginning: the leased, unheated cabins on Varner land, the Pavilion, cadet training grounds, the Byington greenhouse [Catalog 21] and, in 1906, tennis courts. Their imprints do not remain.

RALPH ELLISON AND ALBERT MURRAY GO TO COLLEGE

Logan Gymnasium, Frissell Library, and Armstrong Science were built with the proceeds of a joint Hampton and Tuskegee development campaign that was stimulated by Washington's death and a large George Eastman donation that greatly expanded the endowment. It was, therefore, unusually free from individual donors' expectations. Collegiate learning signaled a post-Washington shift towards higher education, a change that would not be completed until after World War II. Expanding state support for African American county training schools and high schools was increasing the population of young people ready for more. And requirements for Alabama teaching credentials also meant moving up. The 1925–6 catalog listed four-year college-level programs in agriculture and education plus two-year diploma courses in home economics, education, and trades—a "junior college" in modern terms. By 1927 there was a College Department and by the mid-1930s Tuskegee could offer real opportunities for impecunious African Americans to advance intellectually, as Ralph Ellison and Albert Murray have proved. Ellison, who conjured a version of the institute in *Invisible Man*, is hard on his fictional

principal, a sanctimonious hypocrite rather than a believable Moton, as some have assumed he is meant to be, or Frederick D. Patterson, the actual principal when Ellison arrived. Ellison's hero rejected the "black rite of Horatio Alger performed to God's own acting script, with millionaires come down to portray themselves; not merely acting out the myth of their goodness, and wealth and success and power and benevolence and authority in cardboard masks, but themselves, these virtues concretely!"[49] The donors were being courted by the obsequious Bledsoe and a humbled student throng. Ellison biographer Arnold Rampersad believes Bledsoe is a composite of two particularly reviled teachers plus aspects of Ellison himself.[50] Bledsoe could also reflect the New York intellectuals' take on Booker T. Washington and the entire Tuskegee enterprise since Ellison lived there. Ellison surely owes his Chapel fantasy [Catalog 2] to distance and memory's enrichment as well as to sheer literary talent.

Still others who were Northern, older, bright and angry spared little love for the institute. Novelist-to-be Nella Larsen, a Chicago nurse who worked at the institute in 1916, evoked a lifeless, rigid showplace called "Naxos." But Larsen liked Moton, who had persuaded her to stay the two years that she did.[51] Another literary luminary, the Jamaican student and later poet Claude McKay remained only a short time in 1913 because of the school's "semi-military, machine-like existence."[52] There was always the stench of rigidity to repel those used to opportunity and personal freedom. But as Raymond Wolters has suggested, nonconformists usually left voluntarily and with little turmoil.[53]

Albert Murray, novelist and jazz critic, came to Tuskegee on a scholarship in the mid-1930s from the Mobile County Training School. A teacher had decided that his "Talented Tenth"—Murray's characterization—would attend Tuskegee rather than Fisk, Morehouse, or Talladega. Murray remembered the trumpet-playing Ellison, whom he overlapped by a year, and he wrote fondly of one John Gerald "Jug" Hamilton, an architecture student from Detroit who could quote Joyce, Proust, Woolf, and Stein and who challenged their coterie to read Faulkner as closely as they had been reading Hemingway. Murray was proud of his artistically ambitious friends and he wrote with real warmth about a teacher of English literature. Murray described precious hours of "after curfew darkness" in Sage Hall listening to jazz on the radio and he liked unimpeded time in the company of visiting musicians.[54] Murray's experience seems as good a send-off to a high literary career as any a school can offer. Ellison's Tuskegee years, not so fondly remembered, may have been a good start, too. Ellison discovered T. S. Eliot on his own while prowling the library stacks.

Sage Hall looms in Murray's account, as does Persley's Chambliss Hotel, otherwise "The Block," a hangout with shops on the ground floor and billiards tables above.[55] The Block was barely off-campus since it stood across the street from the Lincoln Gates. In Ellison's day, freshmen had to have written permission to go there. Well-lubricated on Cokes and milkshakes, Murray could "jive, wolf, and signify" with out-of-town sharpies, athletes, and big-league musicians. Murray was intrigued by Tuskegee's mythic aura. Distant legends of the heroic beginnings were so pervasive that Murray was surprised to learn that Portia Washington Pittman, then teaching music, could be Booker T. Washington's daughter, not his "great-great-great-granddaughter." Her very presence had compressed history into the present, as did the dormitories themselves with their "brick-red oldness."[56]

THE PLIGHT OF BLACK ARCHITECTS II

Taylor's buildings' "brick-red oldness" may have become ancient shards of heroism and hardship as well as triumphs in brickmaking and self-construction. But the new larger, and more modern Taylor & Persley buildings could have been pressed into service as emblems of racial progress and the long reach of black talent in design and building. This did not happen. The *Messenger's* 1933 account of the Armstrong Science Building and Frissell Library dedications fails to give design credit even though an exhibition of black artists was on display inside the library.[57] The *Messenger* had published a history quiz that sought names such as Alexander Dumas and Alexander Pushkin (both with African ancestry), Sojourner Truth, Harriet Tubman, Crispus Attucks, Frederick Douglass, Phillis Wheatly, Benjamin Banneker, Henry O. Tanner, Marian Anderson, and Alain Locke. Five answers were names of Tuskegeans: Booker T. Washington, George Washington Carver, Robert Russa Moton, Monroe Work, and Emmett J. Scott.[58] Taylor and Hazel were pioneers in African American architecture, Taylor as the first academically trained architect and Hazel as an early office-trained professional. Their buildings along with those by Pittman, Bailey, and Persley were all around them. But there seems to have been no awareness of this fact at this time or since, much less any celebration of its significance.

Perhaps Taylor himself had dropped the ball, or, in doing all that he did, had let this particular ball roll to the side. "He was more interested in helping humanity than he was in heaping up records about himself," according to a grandniece.[59] And he may have lost the occasional willingness to promote himself that he had when he was young. He might have found the effort immodest or an unnecessary drain on his energies since he had other responsibilities and income from other sources and, surely, a lifetime pride in other achievements. Or he may have thought that others were surpassing his place in the black design firmament. In 1924 *Opportunity* featured Paul R. Williams of Los Angeles as a design star.[60] Williams had built luxury mansions for whites as well as high-style buildings for black institutions. The month before the Williams article, *Opportunity* had published a photograph of Taylor & Persley's Colored Masonic Temple, but it did not name the architects because the building represented black economic success, not talent.[61]

Taylor was certainly aware of the problems that continued to beset black architects. Among his papers is an unsigned clipping from a 1931 *Chicago Defender*, a brief query entitled "Where are our architects?" "Dark men are entering schools of architecture yearly, while other dark men are being graduated from these schools each year." But what happens to them? Why are they maintaining secrecy about themselves? They must come out of their hiding places and get busy and, if they are already busy, they must tell the world.[62] Perhaps the exhibition of twelve black architects that year at Howard University, which now offered a professional architecture degree, had stimulated awareness of this under publicized profession. Taylor, one of the twelve, showed White Hall, Huntington Memorial Academic Building, Andrew Memorial Hospital, Tompkins Dining Hall, and the libraries at Wiley University and Livingstone College. Taylor & Persley, listed separately, showed the Academic Building at Selma University.[63]

Taylor's own papers reveal less concern about the designers' problems than about continuing racial limitations in the larger construction industry. His essay, "Shall the Negro Be Ousted from the Building Trades?" published in 1929 in the *Messenger*, voices ancient concerns about eroding opportunities.[64] Prescient Booker T. Washington, he wrote, had urged the very best in trades education to counteract racial exclusions. Taylor's own practice, "if this personal allusion to my own experience is pardoned," had shown him that the black builder was handicapped by undercapitalization. Clients do not want to deal with contractors who cannot finance a project because they do not want to be bothered by frequent requests for payment. Black-owned banks could help with loans if black people would only invest in them. But investment depends on personal savings. African Americans should spend less on clothes made by white men and put their money into the race's banks. Taylor understood that the entire race suffered from the segregation of capital, and his life experience confirmed what Washington had maintained all along: collective achievement and concomitant pride depend on wealth. In architecture this is especially true.

CHAPTER 9

LIBERIA

In spring 1929 Nellie C. and Robert R. Taylor traveled to Liberia, staying there for a little more than a month and building an adventure as well as a school. Taylor was representing the Advisory Committee on Education, a collection of seven missionary and philanthropic societies led by the Phelps-Stokes Fund (created in 1911 by legacy of Caroline Phelps Stokes, who died in 1909). The Committee was charged with founding the Booker Washington Agricultural and Industrial Institute and Taylor was to work with Liberian officials and an American educational advisor who was already in place. Taylor was to secure the institution, choose the site, and design the curriculum, campus, and first buildings. The Phelps-Stokes Fund had already sent the sociologist Thomas Jesse Jones, the Fund's education director and the principal author of *Negro Education*, to assess the country's education, which was primarily a matter of a handful of missionary schools. Jones concluded that the Hampton-Tuskegee model filled the greatest needs.

Tuskegee's own Liberian involvement dates at least from 1908, when Washington helped loan-seeking Liberian delegates meet with President Theodore Roosevelt. Liberians would have approached Washington because *Up From Slavery* had been translated into African languages and was widely known through the mission schools. The country needed money to repay loans from Great

Britain and France, both of which were threatening its borders from adjacent colonies. Roosevelt appointed a commission, with Emmett J. Scott to represent Washington, that traveled to West Africa in 1909 and recommended that the United States pay the debts and assume a protector role.[1]

Meanwhile, Tuskegee had its own Liberian involvement through the Phelps Stokes sisters, donors of Phelps Hall, the Chapel, Dorothy Hall, the Lincoln Gates and the boys' and girls' bathhouses. Olivia Egleston Phelps Stokes, whose ancestors had helped establish Liberia for freed American slaves, was sending African students to Tuskegee so they could build similar institutions upon returning. If Liberia fell to European domination, she reasoned, it would become a subject nation. But with Tuskegee-like education for its people, it could grow leaders, develop its economy, and preserve independence. Stokes wanted Tuskegee to take responsibility for an African school much as Yale University did for its China mission. She then assigned her Phelps Bible Training School of nearly two decades earlier the task of being the American anchor for her African educational and missionary goals.[2]

In 1910 Olivia Phelps Stokes authorized $50,000 for a "little Tuskegee" that a Methodist mission already in place would establish. Perhaps this was the occasion for the 1911 cornerstone ceremony for a "Tuskegee chapel" in Cape Palmas that the

Tuskegee Student mentioned.[3] Even though the Liberian government had committed land to the project, Booker T. Washington decided to delay it because of boundary disputes and the country's insolvency. Olivia Stokes agreed on revisiting her goal when times were better.[4] In addition, the Methodist administrators of Stokes' scheme thought startup costs too high because of Liberia's poor materials and shortage of builders. Some local woods resisted insects as American pitch pine did, but since there were no sawmills, everything would have to be imported.[5]

Another attempt at educational advancement cropped up in 1920. The New York State Colonization Society sent the black Morehouse College dean Benjamin Brawley to teach at the existing Liberia College and to act as point man for another try for an industrial institute. As Donald Spivey has told the story, Brawley was unprepared for the rough conditions and his students' poor academic preparation. Most were at the elementary level with a few with high school capabilities at the "college" where he had come to lecture. Brawley had not understood Liberia's lack of anything but a few mission schools when he solicited the assignment. He left within three months.[6]

The situation changed substantially in the mid-1920s with the arrival of two new players. Firestone Tire and Rubber Company was establishing plantations and needed help turning a subsistence-agriculturalist people into an organized work force. An optimistic article in a 1928 issue of *Opportunity* described Firestone's two-and-a-half year old success with Liberian development.[7] Harvey S. Firestone Jr. spoke warmly of the African carpenters, masons, mechanics, and auto drivers that the company had trained. Firestone was building villages of fifty houses each for workers who would arrive together from a single location. "It is our wish to interfere with their habits and customs as little as possible," Firestone wrote.[8] The company had an American doctor on staff and visiting experts in tropical medicine, forestry, and anthropology. It intended to do country-development right.

The second player was James Longstreet Sibley who arrived about 1925 under the auspices of the Rockefeller-funded General Education Board as educational adviser to Liberia's president.[9] As Alabama's state agent for black schools, Sibley had already worked with Washington, the Slater Fund, Julius Rosenwald, Taylor, and others on rural schools. Sibley first went to Liberia in 1925 and found himself inspired by Firestone's "missionary capitalism." He threw himself into the African task, organizing a 1927 conference on the subject at Hampton, helping revive Olivia Stokes' commitment, getting the land and, in late 1928, a legislative charter. Since Sibley and Taylor had collaborated on the *The Negro Rural School* and much else, he certainly would have known the architect-administrator's ripe skills.

Once in Liberia, Sibley and a German scholar embarked on a book, *Liberia, Old and New*, directed to government officials, missionaries, teachers, and investors.[10] Diedrich Westermann, his co-author, was trying to develop an African orthography in order to strengthen local cultures against the coming European onslaught. For example, he wanted Europeans to know enough of the indigenous languages to retain African place names when they mapped their acquisitions. *Liberia, Old and New* considered issues of clan society, law, education, folklore, music, crafts, and building in order to guide modernization by showing how to grow it "organically" out of indigenous life. On his own, Sibley published a series of elementary readers illustrated with Liberian children engaged in familiar activities. They should not have to deal with the incomprehensibility of foreign life as they learned to read.[11]

Liberia was a nation in the making. In 1929 there was no census, even for the capital Monrovia. There were no public educational, transportation, or health systems. Earlier attempts at modernization had failed, leaving discouraging artifacts knocking about the landscape. In 1935, when the novelist Graham Greene trekked from the Liberian back country to the "civilized" coast, he saw telephone poles that had lost their wires and the remains of a concrete bridge from which the approach roads had disappeared.[12] Greene characterized the house foundations that dotted the Monrovian hillsides as "follies." They had begun as investments—there being no other place to put money—but their owners lacked the means to finish them.[13] There were no banks after a British attempt failed in 1930 and no national currency. For the African American sociologist Charles S. Johnson, who was *Opportunity*'s editor at the time of the Firestone article, Monrovia was a festering morass of disease-breeding trash and mosquito-nurturing wells. Johnson spent seven months there.[14]

The nation was also politically complex since an elite settler class, descended from the freed African Americans the American Colonization Society had brought over, acted as the colonists, but without the resources that Europeans could bring to such an endeavor. Monrovia and the other coastal settlements had frame and corrugated iron buildings loosely modeled on the plantation houses the former slaves had fled.[15] The American Liberians were now facing governance problems of their own: tribal rebellions against intrusions into forest villages and allegations that descendants of slaves were themselves engaged in slave trading, a scandal from which the United States wanted to distance itself. In

1928 the respected scholar Raymond Buell charged Firestone with complicity with the Liberian government in using forced labor. Buell also thought that demographic conditions made such acts inevitable and that it would be naïve to expect otherwise. The U.S. State Department rejected Buell's claims and tried to discredit him.

This is the situation that Robert R. Taylor had entered.[16] While the slavery issue was not mentioned in Taylor's brief from the Phelps-Stokes Fund, everyone involved would have been keenly aware of it. The Phelps-Stokes Fund was in the anti-Buell camp, ignoring his charges. Anson Phelps Stokes Jr., chairman of the Fund's board, told Taylor that he would inform the State Department of the coming trip. Upon returning, the Department sent Taylor a mimeographed form letter inviting him to report any signs of forced labor. Otherwise, it was not part of his task.[17] But the following year a League of Nations commission that included Charles S. Johnson investigated the charges and decided that American Liberian district officers were indeed guilty of slavery.[18] They forced tribal chiefs to capture "boys" for road building, and they contracted these captives to French and Spanish colonies from which the boys often failed to return. Tribal chiefs who could or would not come up with their human quota might have to "pawn" their own children to make up the deficit. The report exonerated Firestone from direct involvement although there were lingering questions about how the government built the roads to the Firestone plantations. Graham Greene said he could not tell if labor was forced but thought Firestone probably guilty only of the lesser abuses of overcharging workers for food and repaying the republic for the privileges it had granted with a virtual loss of sovereignty.[19] Taylor, after a brief visit to the company's Du River plantation, wrote that

Firestone's achievement was "almost a miracle." He commented on "the favorable attitude of the native employees who were interviewed, as time permitted, without reservations."[20] But he would have had little interest in pursuing this matter since he was intent on the school. While he would not have wanted to divert that process or alienate anyone upon whom the school depended, he was probably speaking the truth as he saw it, as was his habit.

THE TAYLORS TRAVEL

Olivia Phelps Stokes died in late 1928, leaving another $25,000 to what was to be named the Booker Washington Institute. By early 1929 the Phelps-Stokes Fund invited Taylor to the task. Taylor actually received two sets of instructions, one from Thomas Jesse Jones and a longer one from Anson Phelps Stokes Jr., who, with Moton, had co-chaired the earlier initiative.[21] Jones charged Taylor with five tasks. The first was studying all geographical, educational, social, and governmental matters the school might address; the second, advising on location, plan, buildings, equipment, and whether initial construction should be for temporary or permanent buildings; the third, organizing a curriculum; the fourth, advising on staffing and leadership—for which Taylor's experience would be especially valuable, Stokes noted; and the fifth, forging links to government, mission, and colonizing agencies and to Firestone. Stokes also asked Taylor to gauge the school's support among the indigenous people and to develop a governance structure. He wanted Taylor to name a board that would balance all interests and be fiscally responsible because he and Moton would have to hand over his aunt's initial $50,000 as well as the $25,000 bequest. Taylor's mandate was for far more than educational programming, physical planning, and architectural design.

Taylor's Liberia trip made his reputation in African America and is the best-documented part of his life. It was widely reported in the national black press and earned the architect an honorary doctorate from Lincoln University, the elite school near Philadelphia that Taylor, as a boy, had hoped to attend.[22] Lincoln had always sought out Liberian students and considered itself in a special relationship. Upon his return Taylor wrote a report for the Phelps-Stokes Fund, an essential record of the experience. Nellie Taylor, who went too, left her own observations. And Taylor's expense account, detailing every item between Tuskegee and Monrovia, is extant.[23]

The first date in the expense account, February 28, 1929, records Taylor's telegram to Jones asking for drawing supplies. On March 17, after an institute sendoff with two hundred guests, Robert and Nellie Taylor took the train to New York.[24] They spent five days meeting with Phelps-Stokes personnel and purchasing books about tropical construction. They then sailed for Southampton and enjoyed four days of sightseeing in London and acquired the tropical supplies James Sibley had recommended before taking overnight passage to Rotterdam. The next day they toured that city in a hired car and, in the evening, boarded a German boat for the two-week voyage. The ship stopped at several ports on the West African coast, allowing still more sightseeing. Nellie found herself mesmerized by the beauty of the Liberian coast as the vessel finally lay moored off Monrovia. She had wanted to go to Africa as a child and, while away at school, had asked her parents for permission to train as a missionary. They refused, so this adventure was a particular fulfillment. Nellie was so moved by the green hills and white houses before her that she was startled when a man suddenly appeared at her side asking if she would be willing to greet an old friend. It was James Sibley, with whom the Taylors would live during their stay.

Nellie and Robert Taylor debarked into what they soon learned was a mild yellow fever epidemic. People they had expected to see were away in the country or at a Firestone plantation to avoid contagion. Taylor later said that if he had known about the epidemic he would have stayed with the ship, going on to South Africa and then back to Europe. The couple went to Sibley's house about a half mile from the beach and entered into—or at least Nellie did—a pleasant life of socializing with the foreign and American Liberian communities. Both groups, she observed, behaved like European colonials: elaborate social rituals and, always, formal dress for dinner. She described a wedding for which bride and her party were clothed by Parisian couturiers. The bride had acquired a sixteen-room house without electricity or plumbing, a situation that perplexed Nellie as to its worth.

Nellie wrote with pleasure of the profusion of hibiscus, frangipani, butterfly bush, spider lilies, and bougainvillea. But she missed fresh vegetables, milk, eggs, and poultry since most of what they ate was canned and imported. Upper-class Monrovians sometimes purchased fresh meat from passing ships, but the indigenous people subsisted on rice, dried fish, and vegetable roots. Nellie described the native adolescents' nudity. With time, she said, one ceased to notice that the lovely native women were clothed only from the waist down. She discussed the Liberian girls' lives—their secret training in the "bush" schools where they prepared for marriage, about divorce and polygamy, and even about how wives could help their husbands by staging a "planned infidelity." The other man, when caught, had to pay the husband a fine.

The Taylors traveled together to the Suehn mission run by African American Baptists and the Muhlenberg mission of German Lutherans. Taylor's report praised the fruits and vegetables grown at Suehn, noting that a Hampton graduate, Sarah E. Williamson, led this productive enterprise. His Tuskegee file includes snapshots of these places—some ramshackle and some well-tended buildings, including one with a metal water tower that rose from low underbrush.

Back in Monrovia the Taylors often heard "the heartbeat of Africa," the native drumming that could go on until dawn. Nellie Taylor confessed that when the rains came down "in curtains" cutting them off from civilization, and when the drumming never stopped, they dared not think about how far they were from home. One senses the challenge Liberia posed, but Nellie was also quick to say that her American Liberian friends did not envy her Alabama home even if it had electricity and plumbing. They could not understand how anyone could live with Jim Crow insults and they judged themselves the more fortunate.

KAKATA: THE BOOKER WASHINGTON INSTITUTE

Taylor did not arrive in time to choose the Booker Washington Institute site, as was intended, although he did examine and approve the decision. Arrangements had already been made to dedicate a thousand acres during a regional tribal council that President Charles D. B. King had scheduled. Shortly before Taylor arrived, the gathering of eight hundred chiefs took place at a village called Kakata about forty-five miles inland from Monrovia on a new road that also served a Firestone plantation. According to the press, two thousand people heard the United States minister to Liberia, the African

American William T. Francis, give the dedication address. The gathering had its inclusive charms. "Native chiefs resplendent in their holiday attire, Mandingo merchants in their long blue or white robes and crimson fezzes symbolizing their Islamic faith, European diplomats and merchants in spotless white, officers of the Liberian government and the Frontier Force dressed in fine western garb, educational missionaries—all were there at the founding of a school for all the tribes of Liberia."[25] A grandstand that had been erected on the "beautiful undulating plateau" was decorated in the flags of all countries with which Liberia had diplomatic relations. The school name was emblazoned on a white Altar of Industry—"intelligent" industry dedicated to Head, Hand, Heart, Home, and Health. Nearby stood ten columns, each bearing the name of a Liberian district. Tribal chiefs brought gifts: rice, palm kernels, coffee, a carpenter's hammer, cotton cloth, a needle and thread, a textbook on health measures.[26] The council was still in session a week later when Taylor arrived. He commented on the problems posed by the many languages. Speakers had to stop after every sentence so each group could hear its own translation, a process that took time and patience and reminded Taylor of American preachers lining out hymns in old-fashioned churches.

Nearby Kakata village gave Taylor a chance to examine native construction at close hand. Sibley and Westermann's *Liberia, Old and New* had described types of indigenous building.[27] Huts could be square, circular, oval, or rectangular in plan within the same community. Every village had at least one "palaver house" with hammocks and several fireplaces fitted with grilles for drying fish. Palaver houses served as men's centers, as did, more informally, smithies at the village's edge. House construction began with a clay base about eighteen inches high that formed a perimeter wall into which closely spaced upright poles were set. Women would then cover the poles with clay or mud, smoothing the walls and decorating them. If the base were wide enough it could serve as a bench outside the building and a bed within it. A pole roof structure supported palm thatch that was protected from insect damage by smoke from cooking fires below. Taylor commented that these techniques answered well to their purposes. His files include a photograph [Figure 9.1] of such a Kakata building. Kakata also had a guesthouse named "Dorothy Hall" after the Stokes sisters' Tuskegee structure. It had furniture that was made in the Firestone shops from native hardwoods. Kakata also had an upscale house for President King's temporary residence. Sociologist Charles S. Johnson termed it a "curious blend" of European and native construction—mud walls, thatch roof, and garage with chauffeur's quarters. Johnson also noted a new and seldom-used market and a military station.[28] The older indigenous huts were largely abandoned, he noted, because their occupants had fled deeper into the forest to escape the government's "civilizing" presence.

Taylor would also have seen tropical construction at the nearby Firestone plantation. The company was housing its American technicians in concrete-block bungalows, the blocks having been made and laid by Liberian workers. These bungalows had bathrooms, electric light, and refrigeration because Firestone had installed a power plant for the machine shop and radio connection to Akron.[29] Still another Liberian construction option that Taylor documented was a poured concrete building erected in Monrovia by an Irishman named Scanlan for the College of West Africa.[30] Monrovia's buildings were usually brick, stone, or concrete, the bricks having been imported or taken from abandoned

Figure 9.1. Photo by Robert R. Taylor of a building in Kakata, Liberia, 1929.

structures. Taylor thought that brickmaking might be an industry that the Booker Washington Institute could develop.[31]

The site that President King and the council had dedicated was chosen from nine that Advisory Committee on Education staff member Harold R. Bare had analyzed. Bare was an Iowa agriculture graduate. Taylor appended Bare's soils analyses to his report, approving the Kakata choice for soil quality as well as for the plentiful water supply from the nearby Du River.

During the month following the dedication, Taylor traveled, talked and listened, measured support, garnered more of it, and devised a curriculum. While dates and trips elude the record, we can read his conclusions in several places. He found Liberia to be "poor, woefully poor" but he was impressed by its possibilities. Most of its people lived in unmapped forests on a subsistence diet of rice and cassava, growing just enough to feed their own families.

Towns and the Firestone enclaves imported their food. Firestone actually purchased Chinese and Japanese rice that had come by way of Germany, the rice that Graham Greene thought was being sold at inflated prices. Yet Miss Williamson at the Suehn mission had served her guests familiar American vegetables that she had grown on land cleared only three months earlier, Taylor pointed out. Tropical fruits— banana, orange, pineapple, lime, mango, alligator pear, papaw, guava, and breadfruits—were abundant and this meant that small canneries could be scattered around the countryside to help feed the towns and provide an export commodity. Liberia needed salable products to earn capital for roads, schools, and, especially, a public health system. Infant mortality was as high as six out of seven babies. Most adults suffered from some disease.

Taylor made many suggestions for a diversified, sustainable economy that might yield exports beyond canned fruit. Forest products were plentiful, or could be—Firestone's rubber, of course, but also palm oil, cocoa, and woods such as black gum, mahogany, cherry, peach, and ironwood. Oil palms were already growing at the Kakata site and natives were harvesting them by a "tortuous" process. If the trees were planted systematically, simple machinery could extract oil that could compete with products from the Dutch East Indies. Coffee had once grown in Liberia, winning a prize at the Chicago Fair of 1893. Production had waned but could be revived to compete with Brazil, Taylor thought. He saw still other opportunities in breeding local poultry, swine and goats as well as in improved dairying techniques.[32] Finally, Liberia needed roads because the only ones outside Monrovia were those Firestone had built. Studying indigenous construction practices could yield an efficient road building system.[33] These tasks became Taylor's charges to BWI's agricultural division.

Turning next to the institute's department of mechanical industries, Taylor proposed that one of the school's first three staff members should be a builder since there was no one in the country capable of erecting the school. He suggested furniture manufacture as an early industry because of the fine local woods. This would earn money for the school and launch individual careers. He recommended that BWI build a sawmill and purchase simple woodworking machinery that could be hand-powered or run on gas or kerosene motors. The industrial department should teach concrete construction, plastering, and sheet metal for gutters, downspouts, and ornamental and practical cornices. There could also be painting instruction for decoration as well as for maintenance. Blacksmithing and tailoring were trades that could build on traditional village crafts. Since Liberian boys were as fascinated by cars and trucks as those elsewhere, automobile mechanics would be a good vocation even though there were then few cars on which to practice.

Taylor also spoke to other institutional needs. The school would need a doctor since the nearest one, at Firestone, was thirty miles away. Teachers from abroad would want an on-site physician and there was always the local population to treat. Taylor gave the Phelps-Stokes Fund's plan for religious schooling short shrift—only three sentences of a most general sort. BWI, like Tuskegee, should be generally Christian in tone but non-denominational, a point upon which President King had insisted. The president knew even if Olivia Egleston Phelps Stokes did not of his many Muslim tribes.

Taylor, Sibley, and the new school's board discussed Taylor's draft report on May 24. The board then sent its own report to New York, requesting that the first three BWI staff should be a builder, a doctor, and a principal and that the principal should be black. President King said that he did not expect a Booker T. Washington, a Major Moton, or a Professor Taylor, but he did hope for someone who would develop to their stellar leadership over time. The other faculty could be mixed, chosen for fitness rather than race. On Taylor and Sibley's recommendation, the board named a $3,000 salary for the principal and $2,400 for department heads with additional funds to be set aside for a vacation trip home at the end of the second year. The board reviewed physical plans "with a great deal of detail" that Taylor had made along with the campus layout.[34]

Taylor's own report listed the following as initial constructions: a large Academic Building and houses for the principal and the doctor as permanent buildings; teachers' and workers' houses; an agricultural building. The hospital, shops, and a boys' dormitory to come next could be in temporary construction. Some buildings on this list may be among the ten shown on a 1935 plan now in the Firestone company archives. It is not clear that Taylor's efforts were enacted by 1934 when the agriculturalist Harold R. Bare, now Acting Principal, mailed a description to Taylor. The school had almost finished the trades building. There was a large concrete structure with two classrooms and another room used as a chapel; a building with a shop, office, laboratory, library and, on the upper floor, an apartment; a concrete block principal's cottage; and a cow barn made of bricks that had been burnt on the grounds.[35] Brickmaking had started recently.[36] Three American teachers were

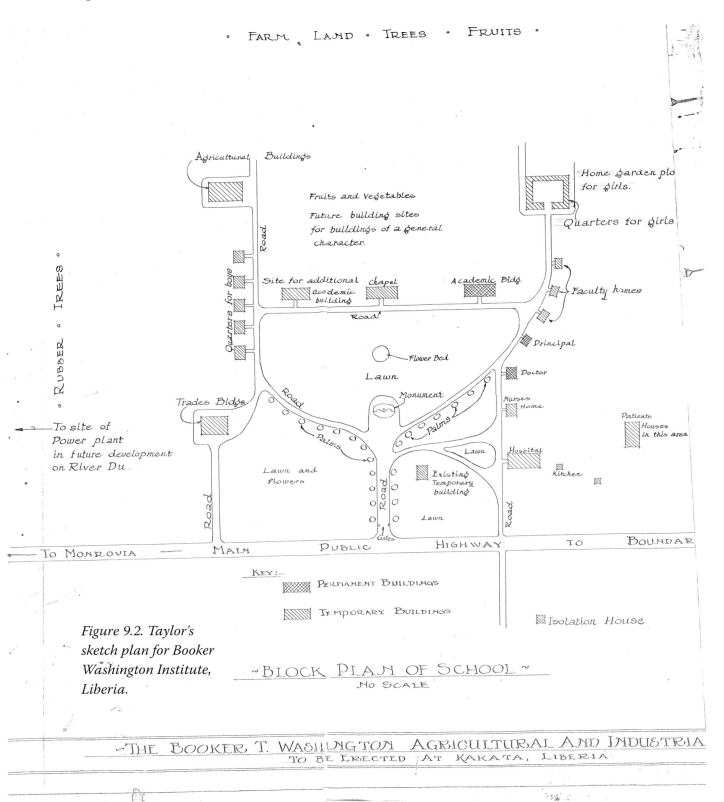

Figure 9.2. Taylor's sketch plan for Booker Washington Institute, Liberia.

there and fifty pupils in the fourth through eighth grades who, as at Tuskegee, spent alternate days in classes and in shops or the farm. Later that year, the Phelps-Stokes Fund asked Taylor, now retired from Tuskegee, to return to design. He wanted to accept but could not because of poor health.[37]

Taylor's report did insist that from the beginning there must be handsome permanent buildings to inspire confidence as well as temporary structures for immediate use. He described an Academic Building costing $27,000 as one of these. The ground level would have offices, five classrooms of which two in the center could become a single assembly room. A two-story porch on the south side would serve as roofed passages, there being no interior hallways. Two stairways would access four more classrooms, a museum, and the library on the second level. The building was to be concrete block with concrete flooring on the first level laid over three or four inches of pebbles. To keep insects from ascending inside the walls, Taylor prescribed bands of solid concrete block every five vertical feet on both exterior and interior walls. The ground floor would have steel doors and window frames. The upper story could be of wood dipped in creosote or "carbolineum," or it too could be steel and concrete. Ceilings were to be of painted "Celotex," the roof of 22-gauge galvanized iron, dipped and painted. Windows on the second level were to be inward-opening casements divided into four segments so that the upper half could be opened while the lower remained close. Windows would be screened in a fine copper mesh and have outward-opening blinds. Only Taylor's fine-tuned sense of proportion could have made this concoction visually palatable, never mind lending it the voice of institutional permanence. Taylor must have thought that the building had been finished by 1934 when he wrote to Bare asking for photographs.[38] Perhaps

this is the structure that Charles S. Johnson saw in 1930 when he said that the Booker Washington Institute had adapted the presidential villa's "synthetic architectural design."[39]

As for the report's other buildings, the principal's house was to have a living and dining room, several porches, a combination office, library and guest room, a pantry and kitchen, and, on the second story, three bedrooms, a bath, closets, and more porches. The house could be built and screened for less than $4,000. A similar house for the doctor would cost $500 less. Taylor does not describe his Trades Building, but a 1944 drawing in the Firestone archives that is signed by H. John Blann shows proposed changes to a standing structure that appears consistent with Taylor's designs. The Blann-drawn building has a footprint similar to the Trades Building on the 1935 campus plan. The porches or small rooms stepping out laterally from the central block and the crossed halls separating shops in that central volume seem familiar from a number of Tuskegee structures.

The report also listed four construction options for the most temporary buildings, two of which were based in traditional Liberian crafts. The first was the simplest: adaptations of native homes and palaver houses with ground-fixed poles to stiffen mud walls. These would have thatched roofs. Method two was the same but with galvanized iron roofing and a light coat of cement spread over exterior and interior surfaces. Method three used molded, sun-dried bricks. And method four, which Taylor recommended, was for walls made of mud rammed into metal or wooden forms until it dried. The formwork would then be removed and the mud walls coated with cement and sheltered by overhanging iron roofs. "Celotex" ceilings, window screening, and wood-framed blinds that were hinged at the top and had canvas or woven mat filling would complete the job. The floor would have woven mats laid on a cement coating on pounded earth. Such construction would be cool and comfortable, he suggested, and would last eight to ten years, maybe longer. French equatorial military barracks could have suggested this adaptation of traditional pisé walls since French colonies shared most of Liberia's border, but Taylor could also have read about pisé longevity in difficult climates in the tropical construction books he had purchased in New York.

After returning to Alabama, Taylor appended a campus sketch plan and drawings for several more buildings to his written report for the Phelps-Stokes Fund. The report describes the Kakata site as an irregularly shaped plateau rising some fifty feet above the Du River basin, a topography that reminded him of Tuskegee. The inked campus sketch plan, dated January 1930 and recently in the Tuskegee Facilities Department, is diagrammatic, lacking scale or topographic lines.[40] It shows a straight public highway about three-quarters of a mile long making an east-west cut across the lower third of the site between the north-south flowing Du River on the west and a parallel branch on the east. Taylor indicated rubber trees on the west, farmland with fruit trees on the north, and coffee trees on the east. It listed the buildings in between the rivers in groups: trades, agriculture, and boys' dormitories to the west; the academic building and chapel near the center; girls' dormitories and teachers' homes to the east; and a hospital in the south close to the road. BWI was not yet coeducational, but Taylor, knowing this to be a limitation, nevertheless designated a zone for girls and, in curriculum discussions, pointedly remarked that "homecrafts," along with industry and agriculture, were talismans of the good society. Booker T. Washington taught homemaking because wives who knew the charms that modernity could bring would motivate their husbands. But Tuskegee had also produced many women of exceptional achievement. In Liberia Taylor met Sarah E. Williamson, the Hampton graduate who led the Suehn mission. He certainly would have advocated the co-education that BWI eventually achieved.

WEST AFRICA AND THE GRAND TOUR

Nellie and Robert Taylor left Liberia on May 31, thirty-nine days after arriving and just in the nick of time. The yellow fever epidemic returned and intensified, killing many new friends. The scourge took Ambassador William T. Francis, whom Nellie had visited almost daily, but the Taylors' grief must have been greatest for his associate of decades, James L. Sibley, who died a scant four weeks after they left. Thomas Jesse Jones later commended Taylor's heroism in staying as long as he did. Jones asked Taylor to forward suggestions for Ambassador Francis's replacement to Moton or directly to the State Department.[41] Edward H. Berman has judged Sibley's death as Booker Washington Institute's tragedy because subsequent leaders caused friction with the indigenous population and became over-dependent on Firestone.[42] Sibley left the institute $5,000 and asked to be buried within it. The 1935 campus plan names the principal's house in his honor and locates a Sibley monument nearby.

The Taylors did not sail directly to Europe but rather east to Accra where they spent more than a week. They were traveling with Sarah Williamson and Rebecca Davis, a Jeanes teacher who was there for Sibley's main project, improving teaching capabilities through traveling supervisors. Taylor's instructions from the Phelps-Stokes Fund had suggested he visit Freetown in Sierra Leone and Accra in the Gold Coast to evaluate pre-collegiate institutions allied to British universities as rivals of BWI's industrial approach. The old dichotomy was playing itself out on distant shores. Taylor sensibly commented that Africans themselves would choose their educational systems once BWI was in place to offer an alternative. Robert and Nellie had stopped at Freetown on the voyage from Rotterdam, paying little attention to a town that Graham Greene would find seedy and decadent compared to Monrovia's "noble simplicity." A snapshot of an eclectic Islamic-style concrete building in Freetown remains among Taylor's papers, but neither he nor Nellie left other observations.

The Gold Coast was another matter. Coming after the Liberian sojourn, the Gold Coast—the future Ghana—stood out for its wealth and modernity. But this observation triggered Taylor's defense of "backward" Liberia. Like the English colonists in North America, Liberia's African American settlers were a heroic people. English and American settlers had both met danger on distant shores with the added problems of unfamiliar conditions, hostile natives, and debilitating climates. But the American-Liberians had it far worse because, as former slaves, they were inexperienced in business and government. Nor could they call for reinforcements from a home country that was invested in their future, unlike the English colonists of the North Atlantic America. The United States had started helping Liberia only recently. On the other hand, the British in Africa, as in Sierra Leone for example, had the advantage of their North American colonial experiences and could get better results. Taylor had a passion for fairness as well as loyalty to those who had been his hosts.

Robert and Nellie Taylor finally sailed for England in the middle of June, where they stayed for several weeks. They made a foray into Scotland and performed some service in London on Liberia's behalf. Taylor scrupulously charged that day's meals to his expense account. Robert and Nellie explored the city and enjoyed the fruits of a great civilization in Westminster Abbey, with its monuments to Tennyson and Shakespeare whom Taylor especially admired. Taylor also visited shipyards, factories, foundries, railroads, and banks—loci of the industrial power that underlay the intellectual and artistic achievements. "What ails Liberia?" he asked, thinking it over once again. "One of its greatest difficulties is the wrong attitude towards work . . . Any country, to develop and prosper and attain to power, must have an economic foundation, sure and strong, and that foundation comes through hard, unremitting, persistent, intelligent work."[43] In Liberia too much honor and recognition went to those in government, paper bureaucrats. "Work with the hands has got to be dignified and glorified. Industrial and agricultural laborers must have the same respect and honor shown them as officials of government and clerks."[44] His attitude to the American Liberians is close to the one Charles S. Johnson forged the following year. Unlike Graham Greene, who saw the governing class as still another victim of impossible isolation, climate, and history, Johnson would also fault a society that devalued manual labor and tolerated corruption. Taylor was kinder in his private musings than was Johnson in his public ones, but for him even this much was sharp criticism.

England was not the end of the adventure. Nellie and Robert Taylor left London on July 15 for a fifty-one-day Cooks' tour of Europe. They went to Brussels, Cologne, up the Rhine to Heidelberg, to four Swiss cities, the Italian lakes, Milan, Venice, Bologna, Florence, Rome, Naples, Capri, Pompeii, Genoa, Nice, and Paris. From there they took day trips to Tours, Fontainebleau, and Versailles. Surely this was a cap to an architectural career as well as a well-earned rest after weeks of tropical efforts and decades of devoted design and administration. Even though Taylor visited a few schools, the tour was a self-funded vacation that he did not discuss publicly. A few postcards remain among his papers along with the agency's typed itinerary that Taylor then annotated with minor changes in each day's arrangements. Robert and Nellie sailed from Le Havre on September 4 and were home fifteen days later. Three days after arriving he addressed a Sunday evening chapel service. Liberia was important to all friends of the race. "It is a test of the black man's capacity in government, and whatever the price may be in human lives, in money, in labor, in sacrifice, it will not be too great if Liberia is made into a great government."[45] He hoped that if any Tuskegee graduate were asked to render the country a service, he would take it as an opportunity rather than a sacrifice.

CHAPTER 10

WILMINGTON AGAIN

Taylor retired in August 1932 after suffering a heart attack earlier that summer. He was visiting his son in Chicago. Shortly thereafter his partner Louis H. Persley died while hospitalized with kidney disease. Taylor was still in Illinois in October when Robert R. Moton informed him that he would receive full salary for a year to help his recovery and, starting June 1933, he would receive a half-salary pension. Alabama had granted him architectural registration in 1931, the first year it was required, so he clearly had planned to continue his practice.[1] If he had not become ill, he would have had a full plate of work assuming that the board agreed to Moton's requested new buildings. Moton wanted to celebrate the institute's fiftieth anniversary with dormitories for nurses and single female teachers, more bathrooms in the girls' dormitories, another practice cottage, a YMCA and YWCA, and housing for 233 boys who were then living in the dilapidated Band Cottage (the former Forge), Phelps Hall (the former Bible School), Olivia Davidson Hall (the former Armstrong Hall), Cassedy Hall (the former Boys' Trades Building), and Thrasher Hall (the former Science Hall). Single male teachers and sometimes even married couples had to live in dormitory rooms, which Moton said increased faculty turnover. He needed teachers' cottages and a social hall for unmarried faculty. More guest rooms were also essential since both races

visited. And the Chapel needed new windows, a vestry, and seating.[2]

In a retrospective mood that August, Taylor noted that he owed his professional success to his early decision to take on any task, whether in his "line" or not. He would always do what was needed, thereby building a broad skill set. Praise began to flow in as the retirement was announced. Board chairman William Jay Schieffelin thanked him for designing and executing the "beautiful buildings and grounds which have commanded the admiration of those who walk there and also of those who visit the school." Tuskegee would be his enduring monument, Schieffelin said. Charles E. Mason, whose wife had given Andrew Hospital, offered simultaneous congratulations and condolences. George Foster Peabody, who heard about this turn of events somewhat later, told his longtime associate that he always thought of him whenever he saw the buildings or recalled their "splendid architectural features."[3] The board's own formal announcement praised Taylor's administrative and educational services, singling out his development of Washington's ideas in industrial education, the "high quality of his expert opinion," his administrator's grasp and insight, and "the fine integrity with which he performed his duties, and the tact and ease of all his contacts with officers, teachers, students, friends, and business associates."[4] This encomium did not mention architectural

Figures 10.1, 10.2. Photographs of Robert R. Taylor in his retirement years.

design or campus construction.

By the following January Taylor had moved back to Wilmington and was being honored as a returning citizen and famous architect and educator.[5] Taylor would later say that he left Tuskegee so his presence would not embarrass his successor, but he had always nurtured his North Carolina ties. He purchased a lot near the Gregory School in 1905 and, of course, later married a Wilmington teacher.[6] He visited his brother as long as the latter lived and continued a fatherly relation with John's progeny. A retirement "buddy" was a niece's husband, a doctor, with whom he spent leisurely

hours conversing on matters cultural, political, and architectural. A grandniece remembers "Uncle Rob" explaining that Booker T. Washington intended to elevate the entire race, not just the talented. Taylor visited Tuskegee often to be with his daughter Helen and her family. A granddaughter remembered the travels back and forth, Taylor to Tuskegee for Christmas and her Dibble family to Wilmington in summer, where the children had to practice quiet when their grandfather was resting.[7] Helen Taylor Dibble inherited her father's papers, lodging them in the Tuskegee archives where she worked during her later years. Among these documents are letters from 1934 to Harold R. Bare, the principal of the Booker Washington Institute in Liberia. Taylor had inquired about the school's progress but regretted that, even though he was reading about Africa, his health did not permit his returning to continue the work.[8]

Taylor's health did permit a decade of purposeful activity as well as meeting Moton's fishing challenges at his waterside retirement home in Virginia. Sometimes the challenge took place in Wilmington. Taylor's work was now advocacy rather than architecture. In 1934 he was promoting a federal Subsistence Homesteads project for African American farmers, working with the white Hugh MacRae, who may have been the boyhood friend who showed him a curved ball or a neighbor who told him about MIT. Taylor and MacRae traveled to Washington, D.C., in 1934, to plead the cause of the region's black farmers. Hugh MacRae is well known in North Carolina as a mining engineer, developer of the Grandfather Mountain and Wrightsville Beach resorts, a water and electric utilities magnate who built trolley lines, and an agriculturist whose own farm modeled crop diversification for the region. MacRae had built six small-farm communities for European immigrants—traveling abroad to select the families—and a depression-era agricultural resettlement enclave, Penderlea. But MacRae was also a leader of the 1898 coup that drove away so many black citizens. We cannot trace MacRae's intellectual journey from racist to apparent advocate although we do know that the latter dates at least to 1918, when Taylor asked Washington to invite him to a Tuskegee commencement. Although MacRae had previously been interested only in foreigners, Taylor wrote, he was "being won over to take an interest in Negro men, especially in farming operations." MacRae would provide the land, build model houses, and provide equipment on long-term low interest loans.[9] Taylor also asked George Foster Peabody to push the cause of black homestead developments in

an upcoming meeting with Subsistence Homestead officials. This would have been just when Hampton administrators were formulating support for Aberdeen Gardens homestead community, which was built. The Urban League's *Opportunity* urged African Americans to take advantage of this program. It was not meant to force people back to the isolated farms they had worked so hard to escape, *Opportunity* promised, but rather to provide gardens for partial self-support in "social experiment stations" that would be near towns with industrial jobs. Factory workers and part time farmers would have social and cultural amenities along with their own livestock and gardens to tide them through the industrial economy's inevitable downturns.[10]

Traces of Taylor's retirement life also crop up in newspapers. His letter in the *Wilmington Star* argued that the Works Progress Administration should fund recreational projects for the city's African American population. There could be no shortage of project ideas since the Colored Chamber of Commerce had already listed the city's needs: playgrounds, a swimming pool, and an ocean beach. Other wish-list essentials were schools, a hospital, a library, and paving and lighting in the black sections of town. Taylor explained that the moral tone that comes with recreation centers, schools, and libraries creates a law-abiding, self-respecting citizenry. He termed it a wonder that Wilmington's young did not misbehave more often than they did since the city granted them so few opportunities. Taylor had recently visited Atlanta, Montgomery, Nashville, and Louisville and saw far better facilities for black citizens in those progressive places. Furthermore, an improved, racially attractive Wilmington, which would have the unique advantage of the nearby Atlantic, would attract well-to-do African American visitors and they would bring money.[11] The Colored

Figure 10.3. A 1998 photo of Taylor's retirement home in Wilmington.

Chamber of Commerce, which had been founded in 1924 by John E. Taylor, among others, had committees that worked for law enforcement, sanitation, education, and health, promoting interracial understanding along the way. The Chamber also argued for agricultural agents for black farmers, a newspaper, a lyceum, and a YMCA and YWCA. Acting broadly, this Chamber engaged in community-building efforts that, as Raymond Gavins has observed, win autonomy and self-respect for its participants.[12] Gavins believes that black Wilmingtonians remembered the riots and reprisals all too well, but maintained silence because they did not want bad feelings to stunt their children's natural optimism.

These were the same people, he points out, who gave their own labor and money for black schools even though they had already paid taxes for the white ones. And they did so willingly because schools promote hopefulness.[13]

Taylor, too, worked to maintain hope until the end. In June 1939 he was elected vice-chairman of the Wilmington Inter-Racial Commission, which also addressed problems of inadequate schools, police brutality, unfair treatment in the courts, and a hostile economic and political environment.[14] As William M. Reaves has shown, Wilmington never lacked for courageous activists during the quiet decades after 1898. In 1941 Taylor wrote to U.S. Civil Service Commission director Arthur S. Fleming, whose radio address he had heard, to protest the discrimination embedded in the defense industry's demand for photographs on job applications.[15] The following year he joined the board of the black Fayetteville State Teachers College becoming, reportedly, the first African American board member of any state institution.[16] We do not know his role in Wilmington's federal housing project for African Americans, the New Brooklyn Homes, but in January 1943, shortly after his death, this low-rise complex was renamed the Robert R. Taylor Homes to mark the city's admiration and loss. The New Brooklyn neighborhood was the most deeply scourged in 1898. The housing project's white architect was Leslie N. Boney who had rebuilt the public Williston Industrial School for African

Americans and who would soon design and build two black churches.[17] The cadre of black architects and builders that Wilmington boasted before the Civil War seems to have been decimated—exactly what Taylor and the entire Tuskegee endeavor had tried to prevent.

Still other traces of Taylor's civic efforts and community stature slip into history through the white press. A letter he wrote to the *Wilmington Morning Star* praised its editor for endorsing financial support for education. Another discussed the city's water supply, perhaps in response to the Williston school's earlier destruction because the water pressure was too low to combat a fire. A short *Star* piece praised the "famous educator and architect" for his letter of thanks and check to the police pension fund because his house was not burgled while he was away.[18] The *Cape Fear Journal* published a Taylor article on a Negro Achievement Week proclamation by the mayor of Philadelphia and further notes on Taylor's Armistice Day address to a black church about Tuskegee's contribution to World War I. Many army technicians, he said, were trained in the institute's electrical, auto-mechanical, carpentry, and sheet metal divisions. On another occasion, the paper lingered on Robert and Nellie Taylor's twenty-fifth anniversary celebration. Souvenir views of European sights served as place cards and Nellie Taylor gave a talk. Tuskegee graduates often visited this eminent man, the article concluded.[19] On other occasions the paper congratulated him on his birthday or remembered his role in the Tuskegee Negro Farmers Conference, a program that had energized country life. "There are thousands of good rural homes because of the inherent qualities, training, and executive abilities of this noted architect."[20]

Sometimes the press exaggerated Taylor's Tuskegee role as when they credited him, with

Washington, with founding Negro Health Week. Sociologist Monroe Work and Emmett J. Scott were Washington's lieutenants on this effort, but it did lead him into medical advocacy.[21] In 1933 Taylor, represented his race when he joined the governor, the mayor, an Episcopal bishop, and the chairman of the county commission in awarding diplomas to four African American nurses. In 1939 he attended the opening of the black Community Hospital. A white Wilmingtonian, James B. Lynch, was the building's architect.[22] In 1939 the Southern Conference for Human Welfare invited him to the board but he declined because his health proscribed traveling to meetings in Chattanooga. Taylor was active in the Chestnut Street Presbyterian Church, asking daughter Helen to give because her grandfather had helped purchase the building. He also maintained a correspondence with George Washington Carver, exchanging admiration and plants.[23]

In 1937, on the occasion of Henry's college graduation, Taylor wrote to his five children, addressing them in descending birth order. He told them he was happy that all had earned college degrees and that he could pay the tuitions, but he was even happier that each had the requisite intelligence and character—the persistence, stamina, and ambition—to accomplish this goal and that none had misused their advantages to spoil the family name. Taylor understood that success could be elusive, even with advantages. He had known sadness, anxieties, and disappointments during his life, but on balance the pleasant outweighed the unpleasant leaving him with memories of interest and fulfillment. He was now looking forward to his life's last chapter and doing so without regret. He felt fine, he assured his family, but his circle of friends was narrowing and he was not going to make new ones. And he wanted to take this occasion to pass

Figure 10.3. Waterside pleasures.

along some guidance. " 'And these few precepts in thy memory keep,' " he urged his children, because they had helped him would help others. Keep your word. Be slow to make a promise but when you do, make sure that you fulfill it. Live simply and save for old age. Do not guarantee friends debts. "Neither a borrower or lender be for purposes of pleasure" although one might borrow or lend for a carefully considered business proposition. He quoted from memory but then changed it to suit his purposes a poem about taking advantage of Opportunity—the "he" of the following:

> "If sitting rise, if sleeping, wake, before he turns
>   away.
> It is the hour of fate, and those that follow him
> Reach every aim that man aspires to, and con-
>   quer every foe save death.
> But they who doubt or hesitate,
> Doomed to failure, misery and woe,
> Seek him in vain and uselessly implore."

Taylor had more to say. Courage is important since nothing is gained by cowardice, but courage must be tempered with prudence. One should be willing to sacrifice for worthy goals because this is how, over several million years, humanity has climbed to its "present imperfect state" with public education, democratic government, hospitals, comforts, conveniences, health, and culture. Sacrifice, self-denial, hardship and work have been behind all of the world's significant achievements. Despite Christianity's weaknesses and debatable assertions, religion should be respected for "the comfort and solace it brings to some and the check on evil inclinations to others." Taylor had distilled these lessons from experience. They had helped him and would help others, even in a changing world.[24] Taylor's son Rob, thanking him in a response, said he would always treasure the letter for the principles it espoused: "industry, honesty, courage, frugality, caution, vision, and Christianity."[25] A few years later Taylor would encourage Henry, when he was trying to start a Chicago haberdashery, with further advice. Building a business was a slow, painful process but it was the sustained effort that counted. Satisfaction comes from the prolongation of the achievement, not from the results alone. Taylor assured Henry that he had faith in him and suggested that he deal with gloomy periods by thinking of the warring history of Europe. Consider how courage and a stout heart were helping little Finland face its military threats.[26]

Taylor died of an abdominal aneurysm on December 13, 1942, in Tuskegee's Andrew Hospital after collapsing in the Chapel. The Dibble family remembered that his last words were that the Chapel was his masterpiece. Taylor was eulogized in Tuskegee and Wilmington for his principled character, his organizational abilities, his special tact on interracial matters, and his achievements as an educator and architect. Obituaries from Mobile, Pittsburgh, Norfolk, and Chicago remain among his papers along with the expected Tuskegee and Wilmington notices and one from MIT's *Technology Review*; Nellie Taylor had written the MIT president a week after his death.[27] A white Wilmington Chamber of Commerce official remarked on Taylor's "fine character, strict integrity, intelligent, progressive, if quiet and dignified mien." He had a "fine sense of civic obligation and responsibility," a typical summary that will stand in for others.[28] Years later, his daughter-in-law described him as "a lovely man to know," a thoughtful person who did not talk about himself. She never would have known that he had graduated from MIT had not others told her.[29] His son Edward described him as a "low keyed person," "very very kind, not greedy," and "eloquently intelligent," who had cared for his children himself after Beatrice died. It was his father's joy, Edward Taylor remembered, to describe the clear-span construction he had devised for the Tompkins Dining Hall, an account that must have merited repetition. Taylor made money, Edward Taylor remembered. He had investments including in the black-owned Oakley Chemical Company. When asked if his father was more the architect or the educator, Edward Taylor split the difference. He thought of himself as an educator—and here there was a deliberate pause in the telling—but he knew he was an architect.[30]

Granddaughter Helen Dibble Cannaday thought that had I talked longer with Edward Taylor, I might have learned about his professional disappointments or direct experiences of racism. But he would not have burdened his daughters and granddaughters with the bad memories. Harold Webb, who taught in Tuskegee's Department of Mechanical Industries under Taylor, noted his kindness. If he had to point out an error, he always suggested a sensible reason for the mistaken action so that face-saving could accompany the correction. He was, however, "a stickler for people working with the hands" and maintaining craft standards.[31] Granddaughter Ann Dibble Jordan remembered him as courtly and elegant, always formally dressed—except when under the grape arbor at his Wilmington home. Around the dining room table—he never sat in the breakfast room—he might add to a family discussion by advocating education and excellence. Excellence brought life's greatest satisfactions.[32] Robert R. Taylor lived quietly but, one is tempted to say, wisely within the social framework he was given while simultaneously trying to enlarge that frame's boundaries for all.

CATALOG OF TAYLOR'S TUSKEGEE BUILDINGS

Figure Cat. 1. Science (Thrasher) Hall.

1. SCIENCE (THRASHER) HALL

The first of Taylor's brick buildings emerged slowly and without fanfare, perhaps because there was no off-campus donor to please. Washington announced in a fall 1893 speech in Atlanta—a five-minute presentation the Principal traveled from Boston and back to make—that students were erecting a three-story brick building with laboratories, classrooms, and a boys' dormitory. The name was Science Hall, an echo of Hampton's Science Hall of 1890. Construction was slow. The second floor was finished November 1895 and the third started the following June. In 1897, the Drawing Division was still doing its work for the structure. Science Hall was published as Taylor's design in 1900 with masonry teacher James Matthew Greene from North Carolina credited as builder.[1] In 1903 Science Hall was renamed for journalist Max Bennett Thrasher, Washington's white New England-based publicist who had died unexpectedly while visiting Tuskegee. In 1904 Taylor showed the Executive Council drawings for turning the building into a boys dormitory. Thrasher Hall was still housing college freshmen in 1933, when Ralph Ellison arrived.[2] Since then it has been gutted and reconstructed as an academic facility.

Thrasher's design is far more than a colorless historical pastiche with its sophisticated tripartite rhythm of a two-story veranda that is embraced by solid corner pavilions on the first two levels, the academic ones. Students living in the third floor dormitory could access the upper veranda and the pavilion roofs as viewing terraces in shade and in sun. Taylor also linked this interwoven classical sophistication to the direct expression of John H. Washington's nearby Cassedy Hall. The dormitory's arched windows echo those on Cassedy's top floor, as Richard Dozier pointed out.[3] Even with the cupola and the veranda's third level missing, as they are now, Thrasher's astute proportions suggest Taylor's high-end training. Sharp-edged walls and assertive window hoods set off the bricks' rusticity, ennobling the handcrafted textures.

Figure Cat. 2a. The Chapel.

2. THE CHAPEL

Pleas for a chapel or auditorium had been traveling north with the *Southern Letter* since October 1893, almost two years before Olivia Egleston Phelps Stokes and her sister Caroline responded. The letter announcing their gift arrived two days after a distinguished Boston minister was soaked by rain while addressing a commencement in the leaky Pavilion. Washington thought the timing providential. Soon he was telling Olivia Stokes that Tuskegee had secured a "competent colored architect, Mr. R. R. Taylor," since her last visit. Columbia University professors William R. Ware and A. D .F. Hamlin, who had designed the Phelps Bible Training School, would not be needed. Ware did review Taylor's drawings.

Brickmaking had also improved since the Misses Stokes' last visit, Washington noted, so the chapel could be masonry rather than wood.[4] Three months later the sisters wrote that Taylor's drawings showed a building that was too elaborate for Tuskegee's treasured "simplicity." Four corner finials on the large tower and some smaller towers should be removed. The entrance could be smaller, they thought, and seating reduced from 2,000 to 1,500.[5] Taylor did new drawings while supervising Tuskegee's exhibit in the fair at Atlanta that autumn. In November he responded to the sisters' criticism of the wall buttresses. They too lacked simplicity and added expense. Taylor told Washington, to whom all correspondence went, that they must remain "on scientific principles." Taylor's margin sketches showed how the disputed buttresses strengthened the walls where the roof beams touched down, taking on additional weight while saving bricks on the wall segments between them.[6] The buttresses stayed, but the tower finials did not. The sisters were also concerned about heating the building, saying that portable stoves in the auditorium would be sufficient winter warmth since African Americans were attuned to outdoor living. But they graciously acceded to Washington's views and funded a basement furnace.[7]

Olivia and Caroline Phelps Stokes were also involved in the chapel's siting, therefore in campus planning. They proposed three different locations near Phelps Hall but eventually agreed with "those on the ground" that it could go on the undeveloped lower plateau to the west, near the institute cemetery [1897 Campus Plan]. The spot was visible from the central campus as well as from parts of the public road. It would have been hard to fit even the smaller chapel that the sisters proposed, much less the larger one that was built, into the old campus core since too much land was already taken. Washington would not have wanted a church close to the public road and larger than everything around it because it would suggest a denominational foundation. He really did not need a bible school either, or so he said afterwards, but the sisters wanted to give one and he judged them good for more.[8] A sketch plan in Olivia's letter showed the distant site terminating a visual axis from Phelps Hall moving west along the campus road and shooting over the valley to the chapel tower. The chapel would therefore be "in line" with her mother's memorial. A Frances Benjamin Johnston photograph records the sight line from Phelps to the chapel. [Figure 6.1] The sisters knew that the place Washington's preferred was "a nice quiet pleasant location" to boot, accessible to the public even if it was removed from the students' daily life.[9] Students would echo this observation when they termed their walk from the dining hall to evening services as "going into the country."

The chapel's final location then set the sisters

Figure Cat. 2b. East side of the Chapel, with girls drying laundry.

to thinking about connecting to the main campus. They urged a "pleasing curve" to the internal road as it extended along the natural terrace that was the valley's southern edge, and they wanted to line it with evenly spaced cedars and benches. A solemn mood already had been set by the cemetery cedars, "sentinel-like, guarding the resting place of our dead."[10]

Chapel construction began with a March 1896 groundbreaking, the school's camera recording the scene. The foundry had made new iron molds

to speed brick production. Forty students would eventually produce 1,200,000 bricks, according to dedication day statistics. By October 1897 a published photograph showed walls about five feet high along with the framing for the sloping floor.[11] (Construction history for this building as well as Thrasher Hall must await finding a run of the *Tuskegee Student* for the 1890s.) It was dedicated in March 1898, two years after groundbreaking, when the donors named it simply "the Chapel."

Black and white preachers spoke at the dedication, a veritable feast of interracial harmony according to the influential black editor of the *New York Age*. It was a "cathedral in the Black Belt" and the only church of any size or magnificence in which blacks and whites stood equal before God. All black Southerners must travel to this "mecca," T. Thomas Fortune thought. One local white minister thanked Northern wealth for providing the funding, insisting that Southerners would have helped too if they only had the means.[12] Other dedication accounts praised Taylor's design and John H. Washington's supervision. The latter was sweeping debris out the back door as the celebrants came in the front.

Black builders constructed the Chapel. William Watkins, a Montgomery contractor, was assisted by such "competent colored mechanics" as the Tuskegee-trained Augustus Perdue and the Hampton-trained Charles T. Russell.[13] Harry E. Thomas, who had studied engineering at MIT, provided steam heating with the help of the students of the foundry and plumbing division. Faculty member James M. Greene directed the brickmasonry and plastering while John C. Greene led the painting crew. Arthur Ulysses Craig, the electrical engineer from Kansas, installed the dynamo and wired what was Macon County's first electrically lit building. Two students designed the pews and cornice. This was the first Tuskegee building that could benefit from student skills, one observer noted, there now being enough advanced pupils. The class that would celebrate the first commencement within it took as its motto, "We Rise Upon the Structure We Ourselves Have Builded."[14]

The Chapel was splendid. Stone imposts, buttress caps, lintels, and sills made staccato-like exterior emphases reminiscent of MIT's Architectural Building [Figure Cat. 2b]. Three lancet windows marked the east-west axis from the entrances to the podium while four lancets lit the north-south transepts. The plan was a Greek cross but the building read asymmetrically from the exterior because

the 105-foot tower in the southeast corner, the one nearest the road and the old campus, ascended with such force. The girls' entrance was in its base. The boys entered in a low, forward-projecting vestibule in the northeast corner, facing the barns. The two projections together, the lower vestibule thrusting forward and the high tower pushing upwards, send what might seem a static main volume into a spiraling motion. Uniformed boys who marched in through the vestibule sat to the left of the "pulpit platform," or stage, while uniformed girls who marched in through the tower base sat to the platform's right—that is, the speaker's right. All eighty-eight teachers could sit on the platform and face their charges. A second level ascended in steps behind it for a choir of a hundred and fifty. Taylor enlarged the platform in 1902 and again in 1906 when he added balconies to the transepts so that 3,000 could attend the twenty-fifth anniversary celebrations. (There was already a balcony over the entrance side, bringing the earlier seat count to 2,400.) In 1905, J. G. Phelps Stokes gave a pipe organ in full confidence that the efficient architects who had designed the building would harmonize the case. Washington asked the sisters if they would mind if someone added an organ as if they did not know that the donor was their brother.

The Chapel must have been a challenge as well as an achievement for a young architect with only small buildings behind him. The interior walls were twenty-four-and-a-half feet high but the roof ridge above the trusses was twice that. Hammerbeam trusses spanned the sixty-three feet between the nave or transept walls while the "angle" trusses crossing the central square where the nave and transepts intersected on the square's diagonals had to bridge eighty-seven feet. By day the Chapel was lit by a warmly suffused glow from the tinted windows. "Imagine a lofty, spacious church, beautifully finished in native woods and brilliantly lighted with electric lights," T. Thomas Fortune commands us. "A thousand young colored men and women sit facing the platform."[15] This would have been an extraordinary experience for tenant farmers and sharecroppers attending a Negro Conference. Washington was always clear that the Chapel belonged to them, to the race. A student from the 1930s knew it as one of the New South's celebrated buildings and was proud to have met a mason who worked on it. "I spent many an hour day-dreaming, gazing up into the ceiling of this building and wondering how the men who did it ever conceived of it, much less how they constructed it. Many a man can dream, but to place foundations under their dreams is the test of reality."[16] All the music was not good and all the speeches were not spellbinding, but gazing up to wonder on the hammerbeams was better than sleeping through the dull parts, he said.

The Chapel appears in Ralph Ellison's *Invisible Man* as the site of the nameless protagonist's decision to leave this "Eden": "And I remember the chapel with its sweeping eaves, long and low, as though risen bloody from the earth like the rising moon; vine-covered and earth-colored as though more earth-sprung than man-sprung . . . I remember the evenings spent before the sweeping platform in awe and in pleasure, and in the pleasure of awe." Ellison's protagonist had debated on its stage, "directing my voice at the highest beams and farthest rafters, ringing them, the accents staccato on the ridgepole . . . a play upon the resonance of buildings." One of Taylor's hammerbeams became for him "that seasoned crossarm or tortuous timber mellowed in the kiln of a thousand voices."[17]

The Chapel served for concerts, commencements, conferences, and evening meetings of Washington and his students until 1910. It burned from the roof during an electrical storm in January 1957.[18] In 1969 Tuskegee replaced the irreplaceable with a dramatic brick and tile-faced structure designed by Paul Rudolph in concert with Tuskegee architects Louis Fry Jr. and John Welch. Rudolph, a New York architect who had graduated from nearby Alabama Polytechnic Institute (now Auburn University), was dean of the Yale School of Architecture when planning of the new chapel began.

3. THE OAKS

The Oaks, a Queen Anne-style brick house, was built in 1899 on Washington's privately owned lot across the public road from his 1890 frame house on the campus. Taylor billed Washington directly for the plans.[19] The house is of pressed brick with "shingling" stamped into sheet metal, and an oval window placed horizontally on the third level to mark the entrance at the joint where a chimney fictively pins folded volumes into the ground. "Two Brooklyn friends" funded it to free Washington from worrying about his family's future should something happen to him. Trustee William H. Baldwin, president of the Long Island Railroad and Washington's principal advisor, justified the fourteen-room five-bath house by citing Margaret Murray and Booker Washington's exhaustion, their need for off-campus privacy, and space to entertain visitors. John D. Rockefeller Jr. slept in The Oaks' ground-floor guest room. Margaret Murray Washington occupied the house from her husband's death in 1915 until her own ten years later, when the institute purchased it. The U.S. National Parks Service acquired The Oaks in 1974 and maintains it as a house museum.

The first floor has a parlor, Mrs. Washington's

Figure Cat. 3a. The Oaks.

Figure Cat. 3b. The Oaks from campus.

study, and a dining room, breakfast room, and kitchen along with the guest room and bath. The latter is near the entrance but isolated from both service and family rooms by hallways. The second floor has three interconnecting bedrooms for Booker, Margaret, and Portia, Washington's daughter by his marriage to Fanny Norton Smith (d. 1884). A fourth bedroom, above the guest suite and similarly isolated by hallways, was shared by the sons of Olivia Davidson Washington (d. 1889), Booker T. Jr. (or "Baker"), and Ernest Davidson. One hall led to Washington's study, added in 1902, with its fireplace, balcony, and views in three directions over his gardens and livestock. Students who served the house lived on the third floor and took meals with the family. [20]

4. Slater-Armstrong Memorial Trades Building

Within a year of the Chapel groundbreaking, its walls barely started, Washington told Caroline and Olivia Egleston Phelps Stokes that the coming "workshops" for boys would preserve the Chapel's sanctity even though it was close to it. The new Boys' Trades Building would gather the industries then housed in Cassedy, the forge and blacksmith shop, and several frame structures in the crowded east, and move them to the broad western plateau. Twenty thousand dollars for this came from the Randalls Charities Fund of Boston, the rest from the philanthropist and Tuskegee trustee George Foster Peabody. The site was not fixed until December 1898, but construction then proceeded quickly. John H. Washington, the job's "presiding genius," topped it with a flag in mid-July 1899 even as Taylor, now in Cleveland, was sending down the drawings. It was dedicated January 10, 1900, the Tuskegee press crediting the architect by name rather than "our campus architect" or "the drawing instructor." Washington used the building to dramatize trades education in *Working with the Hands* (1904). Electrical engineering students wired it. Steam engineering students installed and operated the 125-horsepower engine and 75-horsepower boiler. Students made 800,000 bricks that were laid by student masons. Plastering, carpentry, painting, and tinroofing students brought the number to 196 artisans trained on the job.[21]

Described by Washington as a "double Greek cross," with shops and ancillary spaces for fifteen trades, Slater-Armstrong had an extended plan—280 by 300 feet at the longest dimensions—that provided many shops with daylight on three sides. The plan was actually four Greek crosses connected so that two arms of each defined an inner courtyard.

The front segments were two stories high, the back ones a single story with monitor roofs. Vehicles could access the central court on the north side. The dynamo was in a rear wing.

Wide arched openings through some interior brick walls [Figure Cat. 4b] connected building sections and adjacent shops as did a narrower arched opening in the interior brick wall of an architectural drawing room at MIT, another motif that went from Boston to Tuskegee. Trades depending on heavy machinery shared the ground floor with storage, a reading room, and another for exhibitions. The ground floor trades were wheelwrighting, blacksmithing, tinsmithing, brickmaking, plastering, carpentry, machinery repair, woodworking, and ironworking, printing, and the foundry. Carriage trimming, harness making, upholstering, painting,

tailoring, an electrical laboratory, and architectural and mechanical drawing rooms were on the second floor. The drawing room was in the forward-stretching wing on the north side—the right side in the photograph. Interior views show brick walls, heavy timber roof framing, and a network of exposed electrical wiring for suspended lamps, a language not unlike that of MIT's Architectural Building of a few years before.

The Boys' Trades Building was a finely tuned triumph on the exterior with paneled chimneys, varied window shapes, and a two-story recessed arch with flanking roundels—an Italian Renaissance motif—on the two front wings' facades. Projecting brick courses at several levels emphasized the

Figure Cat. 4a. Slater-Armstrong Trades Building.

Figure Cat. 4b. Slater-Armstrong Trades Building, carpentry shop with arch.

building's horizontal character that complemented the verticals of the nearby Chapel. The entry has a two-story pedimented portico and a cupola that lends a domestic flavor as if it were a dormitory, an orphanage, or a retirement home for genteel widows rather than tough-minded industrial structure like Cassedy Hall, MIT's Architectural Building, or its own interior. Although one description alludes to it as a "temple of industry," Taylor probably decided to accommodate the nearby Chapel and its donors with learning and careful modulations while reinforcing the campus's bucolic tone. It might help the Phelps Stokes sisters' idea that their Chapel's neighbors were "workshops," the cozy Arts and Crafts tone intended. As it turned out, the sisters still had four more buildings to give.

The Boys' Trades Building burned in October 1918 to be replaced by five separate New Trades Buildings on approximately the same site that were later renamed Willcox Trades Buildings. Taylor did not design them. The new structures met advancing industrial standards with high, wide, and light spaces spanned by metal trusses. Four are clad in purchased buff brick, with the one in the southwest corner built with the last of Tuskegee's own product. The front building has a vaguely castellated style. The complex was dedicated in May 1921 and cost $300,000.

Wallace A. Rayfield, the former Tuskegee teacher who was now in Birmingham, drew the first plans for the five separate New Trades Buildings that were meant to cost $200,000, but the built design was by William A. Hazel, soon to leave Tuskegee to develop an architecture degree at Howard University, and his partner Albert I. Cassell, a Cornell-trained Howard architect. Hazel's sketch for Building B, made several months after the Rayfield announcement, lists in the entablature famous historic printers to indicate that the printing shop was within. Another drawing shows buff bricks with red brick trim. The Architectural Drawing Division made the construction drawings and specifications. Windham Brothers, the black Birmingham contractors who built it, employed some student masons, painters, and carpenters. The complex was renamed in 1931 to a honor recently deceased board chairman, William G. Willcox, and it stands today, modified only slightly.[22]

5. Huntington Hall

Collis P. Huntington was the first of several railroad barons who gave buildings or, in the case of the all-important William Henry Baldwin Jr., financial expertise and donor contacts. Huntington had been sending money to Tuskegee since the mid 1880s although not as much as he had been giving Hampton. In 1889 Washington sent Huntington a lithograph of Armstrong Hall, perhaps to assert Tuskegee and Hampton's close ties using the name of Hampton's founder and Washington's mentor. Or perhaps it suggested that dormitories were always welcome. Huntington would later provide $50,000

Figure Cat. 5. Huntington Hall.

for the endowment fund and a boiler and engine to the Boys' Trades Building. His widow, Arabella, would honor him with the Huntington Memorial Academic Building.

In 1898, after studying Washington's annual report, Huntington wrote that he might provide a girls' dormitory. Eleven days later, Taylor sent drawings to New York where Seth Low, then president of Columbia University, reviewed them. Huntington requested specifications and announced that Mrs. Huntington would give $10,000. Arabella Huntington had grown up in straitened circumstances near Tuskegee, meeting the unhappily married millionaire in her mother's boarding house—or so the story goes. She mailed a check in early 1899 and received a photograph of students at work.

The building's marble cornerstone is inscribed May 25, 1899. The dormitory was roofed a year later and dedicated on November 12, 1900. After Collis Huntington's death, Arabella married his nephew, Henry E. Huntington, with whom she developed the eponymous museum, library, and gardens in San Marino, California.

Huntington Hall was sited above a steep ravine but at the lower part of the slope that would later become the girls' quadrangle. The *Southern Letter* for March 1900 noted that the "colored architect" Robert R. Taylor designed it but did not mention that he was then living in Cleveland. In January 1901 the *Southern Letter* published the partially completed building. The unusual arches of the Huntington veranda may have been inspired by a grander version on a Wilmington hotel built when Taylor was leaving for Boston.

The completed Huntington Hall garnered rare aesthetic observations in the *Tuskegee Student*, which usually focused on, say, the blacksmithing students' fire escapes. William Sidney Pittman, Taylor's on-campus assistant, wrote the article. The building was an "outgrowth of the colonial type" with Indian red bricks and red mortar. The exterior walls projected forward at the ends to make the whole appear more massive and to frame the veranda while its "Tuscan design" exemplified the "architectural simplicity and neatness" to which the school had always aspired. "Somber red" corrugated iron roofing looked like terra cotta and the cement capitals of the brick pilasters appeared to be marble. Such imitations gained strength from the building's "plain and unpretentious" material, the author argued.

Inside were twenty-two bedrooms with two beds each, a sitting room with a fireplace, and laundry and bathroom facilities in the half-basement. Handrails were stained mahogany but the other yellow pine woodwork harmonized with the white plastered walls. Pittman also described Huntington's services: the dimensions of the steam lines from the nearby power plant, cast-iron radiators with bronze finishing in rooms and hallways, and the switch on the ground floor that, at "taps," turned off the hanging electric lamps in the bedrooms. Each hall had a piped "water supply closet" with a sink and concrete floor. Pittman's account ends on the qualitative. From the two-story rear porches (now missing) girls could enjoy the "sweet scented and healthful grove of evergreens" behind the building and an "endless view of green hills and forestry." Tuskegee completion accounts are usually hard-edged narratives of cost savings plus the number of students who learned trades. Pittman's material specificity and the dollops of aesthetic consideration are rare.

Huntington Hall was emptied for guests for the 1901 commencement and, in 1906, the twenty-fifth anniversary celebration. Washington assigned visitors to student quarters to teach them, too, through direct experience that donations did double duty in education and buildings. Every part of the room—the woodwork, wiring, heating, plumbing, and furniture—was student-made, Washington would say, just as everything they ate was a triumph in farming, cooking, and serving. Brick and concrete replaced Huntington's wooden veranda in the 1930s. The galleries on the rear were removed in 1971 and the building's interior was gutted and rebuilt in 2005.[23]

6. DOROTHY HALL, GIRLS' INDUSTRIAL BUILDING

The boys' and girls' industrial buildings were conceived together, or so it appears from Taylor and Washington's December 1898 site meeting. But the funded boys' building was quickly underway while the *Southern Letter* was still asking for a donor for the other. A bird's-eye lithograph of an idealized campus published mid-1899 locates a girls' trades building set further east of where it would eventually go. This version was a two-story block with an arched wall panel around the central entrance and two roundels flanking the arch, the same Renaissance motif that is on the forward wings of Boys' Trades. The bird's-eye also suggests other campus improvements that donors might like to undertake such as an administration building with a clock tower, the Pavilion rebuilt on its site but in brick and with a monitor roof, and an enlarged and reconfigured Alabama Hall, also on its existing site.[24]

That May (1899) Washington announced that a New York lady (Caroline Phelps Stokes) would fund the girls' industrial building. Soon there was a shipboard letter from Washington directing his brother to work with Taylor and business manager Warren Logan to design a building that would be "cheap and plain, but good and substantial" with plenty of room.[25] Washington had met with Olivia Egleston Phelps Stokes and her sister Caroline in New York before he sailed for Europe. John H. was to make the bricks that summer, compensating for bad weather by using two work crews. Washington wanted to be sure that delays did not cause the donors to lose interest. The building was to be no more than two stories high and must allow for expansion. For a solution, Taylor flanked a two-story central block with three one-story pavilions connected at the corners, the pavilions being built to support a second story for the expansion. Taylor sited it on a steep slope so that the lowest or basement level had light in the rear for a laundry. Washington thought this part could be only half the size of the 1890 Steam Laundry because modern machinery was more compact. Like the Boys' Trades Building, the girls' is horizontally massed and at a domestic scale in deference to the vertical swing of the nearby Chapel.

Washington's directives also detailed the program. Caroline Phelps Stokes, Margaret Murray Washington, and the head of the girls' trades divisions—not named in the correspondence but in fact Jane E. Clark, an Oberlin College graduate—had been involved. Caroline Phelps Stokes was the sisters' lead correspondent for this structure. There must be two of each: "model" kitchens, sitting rooms, dining rooms, and bedrooms as well as large rooms for dressmaking, millinery, and plain sewing. There must also be classrooms, offices, and a reception room. Unaware that Taylor had bolted to Cleveland, Washington expected to find the drawings in New York when he returned the first week of August. Taylor wrote to Washington late that month saying that he would be glad to accept the assignment. He also said why he decamped: he wanted to learn new construction methods. On September 9, Taylor billed Tuskegee at his institute rate for three weeks of work. He was turning the Cassedy industrial building into a boys' dormitory, doing more on the Boys' Trades Building, and designing the girls'. Three weeks later Washington replied that the board's finance committee had accepted his proposals. Changes in his preliminary drawings were under way at Tuskegee. John H. Washington would send Taylor the penciled notations so that he could make the final drawings.[26]

Figures Cat. 6a, 6b. Top, Dorothy Hall's earlier exterior. Bottom, post-1908 exterior in a recent view.

Drawings for the girls' trades building had also gone to New York even though the site was still unsettled as far as Caroline Phelps Stokes was concerned. On September 11, 1899, she wrote that she would defer to Washington's judgment but cautioned that if the Chapel area were chosen, landfill would be needed to get enough high ground, or so her memory suggested. Caroline had an excellent memory for topography. Both she and her sister wanted bricks of the same color and shingles of

Figure Cat. 6c. Dorothy Hall Stair Tower. The three-brick-wide keystone above the lower window reaches nine rows up toward the sign.

the same material as the Chapel. But Caroline was still promoting sites in the eastern campus near Phelps Hall, her mother's memorial. She liked two or three spots near Alabama and Porter halls and, further west, the spot where the New Laundry (now Carver Museum) would go. Caroline then rejected the eastern industrial zone because the neighboring boys' dormitories would be noisy.[27] She agreed with interior changes on Taylor's drawings but questioned the shape of the central stair tower's roof. "No doubt your architect will wish to consult Mr. Ware, who has before kindly given his opinion, as to some of these general details, and that can be done, I should think, when more finished sketches are prepared."[28] Columbia professor William R. Ware, who had designed Phelps Hall with Olivia, consulted in turn with New York engineer William Barclay Parsons, perhaps because the site was steep.[29] From the Girls' Industrial Building on, Taylor would follow the lead of Porter and Armstrong halls in placing buildings at a plateau's edge so they could be entered from the level hilltop but have a basement story with windows on the sides and rear. This kept the scale comfortable and maximized the limited flat land.

Caroline Phelps Stokes also studied heating details, ventilation, and facilities for the building she led. She suggested a "model dressing room" without running water but also a real bathroom to teach hair care to nurses and maids. She clearly thought that Tuskegee was training household servants rather than teachers and independent homemakers even though Washington said repeatedly that Tuskegee women graduates commanded higher salaries as educators. Tuskegee never intended to train maids and there is little evidence that it did.[30] Washington forwarded Caroline's letter to Taylor who replied that her suggestions could be accommodated except that for the high-pitched roof and tower since "there is no interior construction necessitating this."[31] Caroline may have wanted a taller tower as spiritual indicator of the "earnest Christ like character" that the girls would absorb from their studies within.[32] The sisters were religious and hoped that those they served might grow in that dimension too. Perhaps Taylor was responding to the sisters' feelings by ennobling the girls' literal ascent up the tower's stairs. Or perhaps, as an architect, he was simply using light from the landing window and the girls' movement as succoring aesthetic events. Surely the witty decorative brickwork binding its exterior and exalting the large window, plus the subtle gesture of the lower arch's keystone extending up towards the "Dorothy Hall" sign, shows a devoted attention to the form and its material. [Figure Cat. 6c]

Olivia Stokes, who always shared in the Girls' Industrial Building discussions, contributed too, sending photographs to the Tuskegee architecture office for inspiration, assuming, it seems, that Taylor was there. One was of a schoolhouse near her family's ancestral home in Connecticut. The other was of Butterfield Hall, a Dartmouth College building with a high-style Italian Renaissance façade.[33] Two weeks later, Taylor asked Washington to stop John H. from digging foundations from the small sketch Taylor had sent.[34] Larger drawings would come soon. By now, the end of October, even Caroline had conceded that the Chapel area was best for "accessibility, light, and a dignified appearance," but she also cautioned that the building should be at least a hundred feet from the Boys' Trades Building and set "more diagonally" to distance it from the road.[35] As built, the wings of the boys' and girls' buildings that were nearest each other were a hundred feet apart. The sibling structures were on parallel axes even

though they were not directly opposite, an alignment that was lost in 1920 when the Boys' Trades Building was rebuilt on a different axis.

The Girls' Industrial Building would have been well under way by the beginning of the following year, January 1900, when Isaac Newton Phelps Stokes got into the act. The sisters' nephew had returned from the Ecole des Beaux-Arts in Paris and stood ready to help his aunts in their many philanthropic endeavors.[36] Stokes penciled ideas "that the architect might like to consider," perhaps Caroline's tower again, onto Taylor's drawing of the projecting staircase. Taylor dealt with this one by suggesting that Mr. Stokes would surely agree that his design meant larger windows that would cost more than his aunt's gift had provided. "Remember, we make bricks and buy windows." That October, 1900, Taylor told Washington that he would decide soon about returning. He was glad to hear that the girls' building and Huntington Hall promised to be satisfactory.[37]

Despite the problems of shifting sites and changing towers, the building was ready for dedication in April 1901. Frank Doubleday, who had just published *Up From Slavery*, and John D. Rockefeller Jr. were among the trainload of distinguished visitors come to do honor. Caroline Stokes named her building Dorothy Hall for an ancestor. Reverend E. Winchester Donald of Boston's Trinity Church, the rained-upon commencement speaker from Pavilion days, returned to announce that the building was "the expression of the knowledge and artistic training of a member of the faculty, Mr. Robert R. Taylor."[38] Paul Laurence Dunbar read a poem that asked God to bless the donors "who come with open hearts to help and speed the striving women of a struggling race."[39] Black women should be their people's pride and this building showed the dignity of their toil. Soon Washington would cast his programs for girls as comparable to those for the "best class" of white girls at an expensive and exclusive seminary in Massachusetts where young women combined intellectual work with practical training in the art of home management.[40] The press, as usual, took the building's objective aspects, the H plan with the entrance between the western arms. The northern side, devoted to laundry, had below-grade drying rooms that Caroline Stokes made sure were well ventilated by light wells on the high-ground front as well as full windows on the downhill rear. The southern side held dressmaking and millinery on the ground floor with classes in food preparation and serving on the second.

After the dedication, Caroline Stokes returned to New York with her enthusiasm intact. Dorothy Hall did not detract from the dignity of the Chapel, as she had feared, and she liked the bricks' color even though it was not the same as the Chapel's. Washington forwarded the compliments to Taylor. Caroline then asked if Tuskegee needed student bathing facilities and a student-made wrought iron gate at a new entrance that would serve the Chapel and industrial zone.[41] Frances Benjamin Johnston would align her photograph of the resulting Lincoln Gate's main piers so they framed Dorothy Hall and the Chapel [see Catalog 13]. Caroline now had her cluster of family donations even though it was only in sight of Phelps Hall, not adjacent to it. Caroline then settled into another project: printing postcards that showed Dorothy Hall and the Chapel nestled together, the horizontally massed Dorothy complementing the vertical thrusts of the Chapel. She gave the cards to the institute to sell.

Changes to Dorothy Hall began soon enough—in 1903—with the addition of guestrooms and baths. The expansion was needed by 1907. Taylor toured Northern girls' industrial schools at Caroline's expense, and Washington sent her Taylor's plans for the $16,938.47 renovation.[42] Since the sisters thought this too high, Washington then proposed a more modest effort. The sisters waffled and decided that long-term needs trumped economy, choosing the more expensive scheme and agreeing to pay for furniture since they were assured that Taylor and Margaret Murray Washington had kept costs down. The expansions, which consisted of second stories on the one-story pavilions, housed upholstery, mattress making, basketry, childcare, and model rooms for teaching housekeeping. As with Phelps Hall, the sisters also responded to hints that their benefaction needed still more for maintenance, repair, or, in the case of Phelps, conference, consultant, and teacher subsidies. When Washington pointed out that Tuskegee hosted twenty or so guests a day and that renovations to Dorothy Hall would make their visits more comfortable, he was gently prodding a well-exercised generosity.[43]

In 1915, when a still newer laundry was underway, the vacated spaces were remodeled for guests. The second floor southeast corner would later hold the Peabody Room for trustees' meetings.[44] Henry Ford installed an elevator in 1937 for the aging George Washington Carver, now a resident. And scientist L. Albert Scipio and his family would live in Dorothy Hall as did other new faculty after World War II. Dorothy Hall is now gutted of historic fabric, but much of the shell remains as part of a conference center and hotel.

7. The Carnegie Library

In early 1900 Washington's white publicist Max Bennett Thrasher published a wish list that included a combination administration building and library. It would cost $15,000, a figure that grew to $20,000 in Washington's annual report. This may be the never-built, clock-towered administration building shown in the 1899 bird's-eye lithograph that stands where Huntington Memorial Academic Building would go.[45] The proposed structure would not interfere with Phelps Hall, as Olivia Stokes noted approvingly as she and her sister considered funding it.[46] By December, Washington and Andrew Carnegie were discussing a library to "elevate the whole race."[47] Tuskegee could build one for less than $20,000 since students would do the work. Five days later Carnegie's secretary relayed his employer's agreement for the third Carnegie school library, as opposed to one for a town. It was the first in either category for African Americans.

On January 1, 1901 the Executive Council decided on the site near Washington's 1890 frame house, then serving as the library, that faced north over the campus road and down toward Alabama Hall. Its projecting Ionic portico would be seen

Figure Cat. 7a. Carnegie Library.

Figure Cat. 7b. Carnegie Library entrance.

cal pilaster-like panels.[48] Booker T. Washington, at home in The Oaks across the public road, could also enjoy the architectural consideration. The portico itself faced north or downhill towards Alabama Hall during its first nine years, but it would eventually command an elongated quadrangle after Alabama was razed, as Chapter 6 detailed. Perhaps Taylor anticipated the clearing, placing the library so it could dominate a mall that would take a decade to emerge.

Library excavations were underway in March 1901 when the Chicago Unitarian minister Jenkin Lloyd Jones stopped by. Jones, who was well known in liberal religious circles, was a Tuskegee donor as early as 1887 and would lead Chicago's memorial service for Washington when the latter died.[49] Construction proceeded quickly. That April, Washington sent plans to Olivia Stokes, presumably for a courtesy review by a valued donor. She hoped it would be as light inside as Dorothy Hall was and she approved of summertime ventilation through chimneys.[50] That June, Washington sent a photograph of working students to Carnegie in Scotland. In September, with the roof framing underway, Taylor wrote a description for a gentleman in Boston, wording it as if he was in Tuskegee rather than Cleveland, a subterfuge requested by Washington. The library was finished in January 1902, a year after siting, and dedicated in April. The *Tuskegee Student* noted that it was to have steam heat, electricity, and speaking tubes.[51] Stacks, reading rooms, and a librarian's office were on the ground floor, with an assembly room holding 225, two study rooms, two magazine rooms, and a museum on the second.

Eighty distinguished Northerners arrived for the dedication on a Robert C. Ogden train of supporters and patrons for needy Southern schools,

from the eastern campus. [Figure 6.1] From the west, the side of the building and the portico in the opposite profile crowns a hill above the second industrial zone and the Chapel. The act of leaving the Chapel and climbing the hill to the old campus would make the library's eastern side with its profiled portico a goal. Taylor also acknowledged the view from the public road on the south, the library's back, by striping the back wall with verti-

black and white. There were newspaper editors, college presidents and professors, and potential donors who had come to see the fruits of Booker T. Washington's theories. They admired the open reading room and learned that the building would have cost $50,000 without student workers. Andrew Carnegie did not attend although Carnegie-inspired homilies peppered the day. One must continue to get "motive power" from within even though there is now a fine library, or one needs good bricks to make good buildings. Carnegie and Washington were both born in dire circumstances, the audience heard, raising themselves through disciplined effort. The following year Carnegie pledged $600,000 to the Tuskegee endowment after a fundraiser in Carnegie Hall. He later agreed to give the white town a library and he eventually accepted Washington's recommendations for twenty-two libraries at other black schools. Richard Dozier, who has considered Washington's advocacy for other African American institutions, credits the Principal for black Carnegie libraries in New Orleans and Houston. Tuskegee's was the second Carnegie in the South, following Atlanta's white one.[52]

Tuskegee's library stands today as the best remaining of Taylor's early work even with its eradicated interior. The facade differs slightly from a rendering by William S. Pittman that Washington published at least twice. Pittman had "finished the Perspective Water Color sketch for Carnegie Library and had it photographed." Taylor often assigned presentation perspectives to a student.[53] One publication has "Taylor & Pittman, Architects" inscribed within the image. The Pittman drawing also has balustrades on the roof's center, a device that Olivia Stokes thought confused the building's clear and simple lines. And Pittman's drawing has white-painted wood pilasters at the corners of the main block. But the library as built is better for the material continuity of brick panels instead of white pilasters. This final detailing strengthens the portico in a satisfying fashion and the varying window shapes and rhythms show Taylor's eye and hand on the job. The *Tuskegee Student* reported a "notable classical appearance" and praised the allusion to "the stately colonial buildings of the South."[54]

By 1917 there were sixteen Carnegie libraries at African American schools, seven of which had been published in the *National Negro School News* of 1912.[55] All have some type of classical embellishment, usually large columns, to make a civic presence. A 1904 library at Alabama Agriculture and Mining College (now Alabama A & M University) in Normal and a 1905 one at Florida Agriculture & Mining College (now Florida A & M University) in Tallahassee are like Tuskegee's in that a columnar portico projects from the main block, but they lack Taylor's proportional sensitivity, his design sophistication. Taylor's 1906 Carnegie Library for Wiley University in Marshall, Texas, was also included in the article but not his 1905 building for Livingstone College in Salisbury, North Carolina. Taylor's Tuskegee library joined others by major firms of the period—McKim, Mead and White, Carrere and Hastings, York and Sawyer, and Julia Morgan—in a 1907 publication and it is also among fifteen small illustrations in a 1909 article in *Colliers*.[56] The library was remodeled for the music department in 1931, when Hollis B. Frissell Library opened in the college quadrangle. In 1973 the Carnegie building was gutted and rebuilt within, the two stories becoming four.

8. THE BOYS' AND GIRLS' BATHHOUSES

Caroline Stokes soon found another Tuskegee project, bath facilities with swimming pools. Knowing about New York's tenement house reforms if only through her nephew, an author of the state's recent reformed tenement law, she brought an urban edge to the Tuskegee task by investigating the city's public baths. In October 1901, she reviewed Taylor's drawings for a co-ed bathhouse, the sexes split by times of access. This project then changed to separate gendered units, both with pools, eliciting another New York-Tuskegee-Cleveland correspondence.[57] Washington and Taylor also looked at public baths in Northern cities and Caroline once again advised Taylor to consult experienced architects. In one letter, she asked for recessed round-arched entrances that would eliminate the verandas Taylor had proposed, expressing herself in a vigorous thumbnail sketch in the margin.[58] Here Taylor went with the patron's idea. But he also adjusted other elements

Figure Cat. 8. Girls' bathhouse.

to Caroline's arch "for appearances' sake," changing his hipped roof to a frontal gable to accommodate the arch's visual thrust. Taylor estimated it would cost $400 more to expand both units because they would need longer trusses, more bricks, nine hundred extra square feet of concreting, and deeper footings to contend with their hillside sites. He numbered each point in his usual systematic fashion and clarified with sketches the foundation footings on sloping sites. He also appended "Architect" to his signature, the seldom-used handle asserting his professionalism, perhaps, in the face of Caroline's designing self.[59] Taylor then estimated the smaller girls' building at $5,200, the boys' at $6,400. Girls could do without a locker room because their facility was near their dormitories. The girls' facade was aligned with that of Hamilton Cottage and Douglass Hall on the western edge of what would later develop into the quadrangle. Even though the larger boys' bathhouse would be near Olivia Davidson (formerly Armstrong) Hall, Thrasher, Cassedy, and Rockefeller boys' dormitories—the latter begun after the bathhouse was underway—boys living in distant barracks or off-campus cabins

needed lockers.[60]

By December 1901, Taylor had mailed from Cleveland two sets of plans and a two-page description of materials and the mechanical systems. The brick structures would have tinted mortar, a tin roof, a ceiled hall, a room for the attendant, a waiting room, four showers with hot and cold water, two water closets, four-foot-square dressing rooms, and a pool. The girls' pool was to be 20 by 35 feet, the boys' 30 by 55 feet. Final drawings for the girls' unit were mailed with those for the Office Building, the boys' bathhouse arriving later. Taylor had also started a dormitory and was waiting for the go-ahead on preliminary designs for the Huntington Memorial Academic Building. By July 1902, the boys' bathhouse walls were almost finished. The structure was complete in June 1903, coming in at $1,200 below the 1901 estimate.[61] The smaller unit for girls was piped that July and was ready for inspection the following February.[62] This one cost $1,180 more than the estimate because of site problems. The girls' bathhouse was taken down by 1940 but the boys' unit lived on as the Reserve Officer Training Corps armory until it was razed in 2002.

9. ROCKEFELLER HALL BOYS' DORMITORY

In March 1901 Washington wrote to Frederick T. Gates, John D. Rockefeller's assistant for philanthropy, to ask for $34,250 for a dormitory for 150 young men who were then sleeping in shanties and overcrowded rooms. "We do not want luxury for our students, but desire to make them comfortable to the end that they can do their best work." Gates told Rockefeller that he thought this "a good and needed investment that has many unusually attractive features."[63] Soon his heir would join the Robert C. Ogden party of philanthropists and educators on the train to Dorothy Hall's dedication. Rockefeller Jr. stayed in The Oaks, leaving behind a razor strap that Washington hastened to return.[64] In December 1901, a few days after Booker T. Washington's infamous dinner at the White House, "Junior" would invite the Principal to address his New York bible class and then to tea and dinner at his parents' home. Promise of a donation followed.[65]

Taylor sent the drawings for Rockefeller Hall to Tuskegee early the following May, 1902. By June, the philanthropist had pledged $34,000 for building and furnishings on the condition that money not spent would not be charged. He would return the drawings with comments soon. Gates then

Figure Cat. 9a. Rockefeller Hall, 1906.

sent Taylor's drawings to A. D. Houghton, a white architect under Rockefeller contract for the family's principal African American philanthropy, Spelman College in Atlanta. Houghton praised Taylor's plans as "economical and convenient," but had his own concerns. He wanted to limit the veranda to the first floor because the upper level would not be used. He suggested double rather than single bedroom windows for ventilation, plus strengthening the structure and simplifying the woodwork. Houghton would make additional drawings that would be sent to Tuskegee with the returned originals.[66] Taylor, for his part, wanted Rockefeller and Houghton

to understand that educational needs meant that students must draw fully lap joints, anchors, bolts and other elements that would be taken for granted in normal architectural practices.[67] In September, Rockefeller, home from his wedding trip, wrote that a one-story veranda might not be best for the structure's appearance but that Tuskegee should decide—as long as the solution remained within budget. Rockefeller Hall has Houghton's single-story veranda and double windows.

Rockefeller Jr. brought his bride to Tuskegee for the May 1902 Carnegie Library dedication while construction on his father's donation was underway but before the veranda appeared. That September John H. Washington directed Taylor, momentarily

Figure Cat. 9b. Rockefeller Hall, 2001.

in Alabama, to take workers from the Office Building and Dorothy Hall in order to push the dormitory. It was closed in and glazed when Frances Benjamin Johnston photographed it in November 1902. By spring 1903, guest rooms and two bathrooms were being slipped into building, the expense coming out of the $1,000 that Taylor and Washington had hoped to return to the donor.[68] In the end they managed to return $249 that Rockefeller then sent back as a gift. Tuskegee accounting broke the building cost into nearly equal amounts for the masonry (including plastering) and carpentry divisions. Lesser sums went to painting, tinning, heating, plumbing, lighting, furniture and landscaping. Architectural fees were not listed, probably because Rockefeller had earlier questioned this expense, then listed at $1,390, because he assumed Taylor was on salary and that he and John H. Washington would superintend construction as part of their normal duties. Once again, Washington hid Taylor's Ohio residency from the donors. When Gates visited Rockefeller Hall in early 1904, he said that the cost—$200 per student—was remarkably low since other institutions spent $600 to $1,000.[69] Gates later

wrote to Taylor to ask for the address of the African American architect William Augustus Hazel, which Taylor supplied.

Rockefeller Jr. and Washington remained in constructive contact after completion, the philanthropist promoting Tuskegee to his friends and considering sewering the school. A 1908 note from Washington thanking Rockefeller for an evening in his New York home mentioned the profits from a Bar Harbor visit. The letter earned a reply praising Washington's "great simplicity." "It seems to me that therein to no little extent lies your power for good among your people and ours."[70] In a Sunday night Chapel talk Washington admired the philanthropist's eloquence. There was "no tom-foolery to Rockefeller. . . no Latin or Greek quotes. He speaks and writes in a plain manner, with one syllable not two, or two, not three. His is the power of simplicity, without showing off, and he may be the richest man in the world."[71] Perhaps the modest elegance and "imposing yet simple appearance" of Taylor's dormitory records a shared ideal of right action and its inevitable eloquence as well as the agreement to keep it cheap.[72]

10. THE OFFICE BUILDING

A rare Taylor-Washington planning discussion survives about Washington's own office in the Office Building. Taylor told Washington that his ground floor room would face the campus rather than the public road so he could oversee his domain. The memo, we read, accompanied blueprints with arrows to show the views to Alabama Hall and beyond it to the farms; to Parker Cottage and Huntington Hall more directly opposite; to Porter Hall with the unfinished Rockefeller Hall in the distance; and, further east, Olivia Davidson Hall and, perhaps, the former industrial quarters. Following Washington's instructions, Taylor had made the windowsills high so that passersby would not see seated occupants. But this could be changed easily with a raised platform if the Principal wanted to watch the campus from his desk.[73] A decade later, Washington would fix the office as campus center by posting below his window a six-panel bulletin board listing daily events throughout the institution. The system was modeled on one he had noticed in the Boys' Trades Building.[74] Everyone must know what others were up to.

The *Tuskegee Student* announced an anonymous gift of $15,000 for the administration building in November 1901 following a June *Southern Letter* request for the same. Modern scholarship has revealed the donor to be Standard Oil's Henry Huddleston Rogers.[75] Washington knew Rogers, Famous then as now for ruthlessness, as a man whose "large business affairs had given him a broad vision and a practical grasp of public and social questions."[76] Rogers put a special train on his Virginia railway so that Washington could address black communities during a swing through the state and the two would soon partner on Tuskegee's rural schools project.

Tuskegee's Office Building stands between the campus and public roads with doors facing both directions. The 1890 frame Principal's house and Carnegie Library were to the west and Phelps Hall

Figure Cat. 10a. Office Building, 1902.

Figure Cat. 10b. Office Building, 2001.

to the east. Design was underway in February 1902, the foundations being laid in March. That April, Taylor mailed plans from Cleveland to Emmett J. Scott with instructions to pass them on to John H. and Booker T. Washington.

By July 1902, John H. was complaining about construction errors. Walls built without belt courses had to be taken down and windowsills were too low so that even more walls had to be redone. The carpentry shop's template was badly sized and all this was costing money. He was implying either that Taylor should be there to supervise if he was in Cleveland or, if in Tuskegee, he should be doing a better job. Two months later John H. was at it again, this time about construction debris near Rockefeller Hall. The phrasing here suggests that

Taylor was now on the scene.[77] When Frances Benjamin Johnston photographed the Office Building in early November, the roof was planked but lacked its metal finish and the windows were framed but without sash. A memo from Taylor to Scott charged the Opelika Lumber Company with such poor sash that the school must demand a refund.[78] The Opelika firm furnished window sash for Tantum Hall several years later, the problems presumably having been resolved.

The Office Building was finished in late 1903, the *Tuskegee Student* characterizing its style as "Mormon," presumably a misprint for "Norman."[79] It had four fireproof bank vaults and identical entrances at the same off-center end from the campus and public roads. In the early 1920s the building acquired a federal post office, "Tuskegee Institute." Washington's successor Robert Russa Moton renovated the principal's office with more glamorous wood paneling than the original matchboard wainscoting with plaster and a picture rail above. Booker T. Washington's office shared this standard finish with all academic interiors. The building has particularly inventive brick trim around the entrances, bands of headers spaced at their own width to make a checkerboard [Figure 3.10]. Taylor usually varied trim from building to building, the patterns at openings, eaves, and water tables showing students that limited means can still yield visual wealth. The Office Building's center as seen from the public road has a sly piece of Taylorean wit. The easternmost of two otherwise identical windows has a wooden panel crossing it to mark the stair landing behind it. The other window is uninterrupted because it lights a room, not a staircase.

11. HUNTINGTON MEMORIAL ACADEMIC BUILDING

William Sidney Pittman was involved in this important structure, or at least in his own estimation since he claimed it as his own design. An article about Pittman in the *New York Age* that was reprinted in the *Tuskegee Student* gave it to Pittman as did accounts by Emmett J. Scott and Lyman Beecher Stowe. But Tuskegee business agent Warren Logan said that Taylor designed all Tuskegee buildings with Pittman's assistance and Washington congratulated Taylor for the large but inexpensive structure as if he too were weighing in on a controversy. [80]

Authorship is clear. The "preliminary" drawings (so inscribed) were made in Cleveland, sent down for execution and remain in the files. The completed building is too close to those designs and to Taylor's handwritten directions for changes. Design character—the triadic massing, the finely tuned proportions, the relation of window voids to weighted walls, and the syncopated rhythms of varied window shapes and sizes—is Taylor's rather than Pittman's personal aesthetic, as we can see from the younger man's later buildings.

The 53,441 square foot structure was shown in four inked plans of 24 by 30 inches for "The

Figure Cat. 11a. Huntington Memorial Academic Building, 1906.

Huntington Memorial Building." Taylor sent them from Cleveland on April 10, 1902, along with those for the boys' bathhouse and sketches for another dormitory, probably Douglass Hall. These plans may be Taylor's only significant surviving drawings other than his MIT thesis, and they correspond closely to an undated, two-page, typed description of an "Academic Building to cost $58,892" that was amended in his hand. The drawings also correspond to an elevation published in the *Tuskegee*

Catalogue of 1903–1904 that differs in small ways from the executed structure. This elevation shows a one-story, arcaded entry porch rather than the one-story paired columnar one that was built. It also has pediments over the two large windows that extend from the third to fourth level that are not on the finished structure. In the drawing, the window groups on the second or middle level of the end bays form classical *serliana*—or "Palladian" or "Venetian" window, as the form is more widely known. It is well known to the classically educated architect such as Taylor who used it for the Chambliss Children's House entrance [Catalog

Figure Cat. 11b. Huntington Memorial Academic Building, 1989.

24], where columns separate a central arch from two lower, flat-topped openings. As built on Huntington Academic, however, the side openings are arched too, a pragmatic modification for construction in brick because stone, the preferred material for this high-end motif, was lacking.[81]

The month before the drawings left Cleveland, Arabella Huntington pledged $50,000 for a memorial to the recently deceased Collis P. Huntington. That April, Taylor wrote that since suggestions had arrived from the future Academic Department head, Roscoe Conkling Bruce, still a Harvard student, he assumed that Washington wanted him to design it. Two months later and still in Cleveland, Taylor wrote that Pittman was wrong about drawings that were described in a telegram. In July, Taylor mentioned that Pittman was finishing drawings with some changes and asked Warren Logan to tell him to show them to the Executive Council. But in September Taylor, now in Tuskegee, telegraphed Washington to ask for another month to complete the work because he had returned to Cleveland. Taylor and Washington discussed the building in October, Taylor dealing with the pilasters that Archer Huntington, Arabella's son, wanted. Huntington would have them on the base, but Taylor said that since they would be "purely ornamental" they would look better on an upper level so the ground floor could be "plain, simple looking, and strong." Fortunately, Taylor managed to keep pilasters off the base's rustication, a ridiculous notion to the visually literate. That November, Frances Benjamin Johnston photographed a display of "Columns Turned by Students for the Academic Building." These were the paired porch columns that replaced the arcades in the catalog drawing and the plans. [82]

Roofing of Huntington Academic began in December but construction proceeded fitfully through 1903, often halting because materials were not in hand. By September, John H. was telling Taylor to hire outside masons to finish the walls so the roof could go on before winter and the interior ready for an April 1904 dedication. That December, Washington asked for a picture to circulate among donors and the press. In February 1904, Taylor told Washington that the building would not be ready in April. The cost of materials had risen and there were too many other buildings underway—Douglass Hall, an Emery dormitory, the Office Building, and the doctor's cottage. Tuskegee had outstripped its student workers and would have to hire outsiders, and this would cost too much.[83]

Faced now with cost overruns, Taylor listed thirteen design changes that would save $9,000. These included omitting eaves brackets and two gables on the elevation (the pediments of the *Tuskegee Catalogue* drawing), replacing the arcaded masonry porch with flat wooden lintels (the columned veranda), simplifying door and window casings, and omitting wainscoting, an arch over the central hall, and the impressive central stairs. The stairs were to be a wide run that divided into reverse flights after a broad landing. Instead, there would be only the straight runs at the side entrances, which were on the Cleveland drawings. The "stately" structure was almost finished in June. The interior was plastered, the flooring laid, doors hung, and blackboards in place in July and Washington could safely invite Mrs. Huntington and Archer to an October or November dedication, an invitation that, in the end, they were unable to accept. Archer Huntington sent a check for $8,892, the balance of his mother's pledge against Taylor's 1901 estimate. Soon Taylor was summarizing Huntington's pedagogical triumphs for public dissemination. "We have made fifteen plasterers from our student body," etc. Washington singled out a particular student foreman for his "simple honesty, an unobtrusive confidence and self-reliance that abundantly testify to his manliness." The boy had developed his character by meeting his responsibilities.[84]

In the end, the resulting "high school," as it was termed, was remarkably close to Taylor's initial documents: the inked plans and the typescript description from Cleveland. The basement contained a sixty by seventy-one foot girls' gymnasium plus lockers, toilets, and cloakrooms on the west side, near the girls' dormitories. As Bettina Berch has pointed out, physical education for girls was a progressive hallmark, even in African America.[85] The boys' east side, near their dormitories, had a weight room. Nine classrooms ranged along the corridor between the boys and girls side entrances on the first floor. A wing projecting to the rear on the east side was a large drawing room with windows on three sides, an emblem of progressivism as were two science laboratories, also with windows on three sides, occupying the same square footage on the two floors above. An exhibit room and a museum flanked the entrance. The building had brought together disparate subject areas from four other buildings just when, according to Washington's crit-ics, he and Roscoe Conkling Bruce were reducing academic and "literary" learning to favor industrial training in a narrow sense.

Taylor's Cleveland plan also showed a sample twenty-five by thirty foot classroom with blackboards on three walls, a teacher's desk and locker, and thirty-five student desks. The interior brick walls were a foot thick. The second floor had a physics laboratory above the drawing room, more classrooms, a lecture room with seats on risers, a library, offices, two rest rooms for women and girls on the west side and two for men and boys on the east. The third floor had the chemistry laboratory above the physics laboratory below, seven classrooms, and an 885-seat auditorium with a gallery that was supported on cast-iron posts around three sides. Special windows on the upper façade loosely signaled this special gathering place. The *Tuskegee Student* pronounced the building "imposing in design" while Emmett J. Scott said the facility, though "sensible and unostentatious," was one that would "awaken a sense of pride in every pupil who enters its portals."[86] Huntington Memorial was renovated in 1965 but burned in 1991 during another renovation, an architectural tragedy on the scale of the Chapel fire forty years before.

12. DOUGLASS HALL GIRLS' DORMITORY

Douglass Hall slipped into the campus with little fanfare, presumably because the Colorado-based donor did not need the attention. Taylor wrote from Cleveland on his fortieth birthday, June 8, 1902, that the girls' dormitory plans were almost complete. The *Tuskegee Student* announced the $25,000 project the following month. Brick walls were nearly finished by early November, when Frances Benjamin Johnston showed the masons at work. By September the following year John H. Washington was complaining that workers needed better supervision, their idleness being obvious to passersby.[87]

The "Colorado man" who gave the dormitory had asked Washington to choose a name in honor of a "noted Negro." Washington named Frederick Douglass, who had addressed Tuskegee's 1892 commencement and whose death three years later left the leadership void that Washington's Atlanta address was intended to fill. Douglass's son read a Paul Laurence Dunbar poem honoring his father at the dedication.

Following the donor's request, Douglass was built for steam heat and electricity. The *Tuskegee Student* reported that the "Indian red" bricks from the efficient new machines were harder and more attractive than those of the Cassedy era. Douglass Hall was 23,860 square feet and housed 103 girls, a number that became 130 in 1904 when the basement was remodeled. Taylor prescribed white or silver-gray walls for the below-grade bedrooms. An arched doorway at Douglass's lower end led to

Figure Cat. 12. Douglass Hall.

a 450-seat lecture hall that took advantage of the site's double slope. Taylor had become expert at setting buildings on hillsides, but this is the first time he slipped an auditorium under the building, probably without the donor's knowledge. The Dean of Women instructed girls on health, morals, and manners in this room, but it also housed Negro Conference events, Sunday concerts and, in 1912, the International Conference of the Negro. Douglass was remodeled after a fire in 1934 and the interior reworked again in 1964.[88]

The mysterious Colorado donor of Douglass Hall turned out to be William Jackson Palmer, a Quaker-born railroad baron who had become interested in freedmen during the Civil War. Palmer pioneered railroad services across the west and into Mexico, founded Colorado College and Colorado Springs, and gave buildings to Hampton. [89]

13. THE LINCOLN GATES

The Stokes sisters' Lincoln Gates began with Caroline's undated proposal that New York ironworkers should forge its ornamental ironwork. In May 1901, however, she postponed the project until Tuskegee could develop its own competence in wrought iron. Discussions were restarted the following year and then lagged again. Four Taylor designs went North and the sisters combined two of them to invent a fifth. The first Taylor scheme was too massive, they wrote, the second inappropriately castelled, the third "graceful and well thought out" but with an overhead closure that would interfere with high vehicles. They liked a fourth scheme but wanted the stone finials on the third design's piers.

Caroline Stokes then took up her pen, as she had for the bathhouses, redrawing the upper ironwork curves to make them steeper, more emphatic. Taylor kept this modification. The sisters then suggested the name "Lincoln" because he had opened opportunities for the race, but if this conflicted with another usage or was provocative in the region, "Armstrong" would do as well. [90] The sisters' may have become more attuned to Southern sensitivities after their insistence on a tall flagpole and army-post sized U.S. flag for President McKinley's visit.[91] (Washington had actually hoisted the first Macon County stars and stripes after the war.)

In November 1902 Frances Benjamin Johnston photographed students building a road from the western campus up the hill towards the Practice Cottage and the public road. Late the next month, Taylor asked Washington to decide where this road should meet the public one so they could begin building the gates. Soon, Taylor was worrying about funding the stone finials. Construction records fade again until spring 1904, when the *Tuskegee Student* published a completion photograph with the materials listed: Flemish bond brick, limestone caps, a Georgia marble tablet, and the hand-forged ironwork. The gates were forty-four and a half feet wide with the central opening sixteen feet between sixteen-foot-high posts, a "simple design with a substantial and handsome effect," the writer opined. Side gates for pedestrians were eight feet wide. Students did the drawing, brickwork, and ironwork and they helped cut the limestone finials.[92] In 1906 Frances Benjamin Johnston photographed the gates from an angle so that the central piers framed Dorothy Hall's rear and the Chapel, nesting at least these three Stokes donations. The pedestrian gate on the right reveals distant white barns. The gates were still in place in 1919 when William A. Hazel drew a plan of the area, but they were soon moved and then moved again, as L. Albert Scipio has shown, to accommodate a more level and more direct entrance into the new campus zone.[93] The piers have been adapted for recent fencing surrounding the campus.

Figure Cat. 13. Lincoln Gates.

14. THE EMERY DORMITORIES

The four boys' dormitories given by E. Julia Emery and placed near the Boys' Trades Buildings were constructed sequentially between the summer of 1903 and 1909. An American living in London, she was moved to give by *Up From Slavery*. Miss Emery was a Cincinnati real estate heiress and sister-in-law of Mary M. Emery who commissioned the spectacular garden suburb Mariemont that was designed by the planner John Nolen. Thomas J. Emery, acting as his sister's agent, required plain buildings and strict accounting, each dormitory depending upon his approval of the last.

Concerned about fire, Thomas Emery decided that the buildings would be only two stories high and at least 80 feet apart. (They are about 130 feet apart.) Since Southern land was "worth nothing," Emery reasoned, using more of it would not drive up costs. Emery's own architect made a sketch for Taylor's guidance. Emery also responded to Washington's suggestion for "a dining hall with a kitchen underneath" by replying that the Principal was trying to interest the family in what would be built anyway without its aid.[94] The Thomas Emery correspondence suggests an unusual imperviousness to Washington's charms. Emery's fire concerns amount to planning since they dictated a new boys' residential zone in the western campus. The boys' area in the east, with the purpose-built bathhouse and dormitories as well as the buildings adapted from older industrial structures, was hilly and

Figure Cat. 14a. Emery Dormitories.

crowded [1903 and 1911 Campus Plans].

Taylor must have diverted from the Cincinnati architect's sketch since Thomas Emery was dismayed when he met with Washington in New York in late 1903. He had seen the uncompleted Emery I during an inspection trip. Emery faulted the projecting center gable in the roof, the dormers, and the two-story veranda. The tin flashing where the gable folds into the roof would rust and leak and the dormer windows were unnecessary because the windows in the end gables would ventilate the attic. Finally, the two-story veranda was wasteful. Taylor, whose nature was generous, wanted the boys on the second floor to enjoy a warm evening's release on the veranda's upper level. Emery did not.

Taylor responded to Emery's criticism by telling Washington that he would not insist on a center gable for the second Emery even though it would improve its appearance. The savings would be $173 of a total $12,416 in cuts that Thomas Emery had proposed. The three last dormitories, therefore, are even sparer than the first. Emery I finally opened in late December 1903 after a construction push with hired workers. Washington then wrote to Miss Emery in London to thank her on behalf of the boys who had until then been living in unheated cabins.[95]

For Emery II, Washington again hired expensive outside workmen in May 1904 because "the donors are still in the frame of mind" to give more. Taylor's description of Emery II lingers on the crossed interior hallways. The long dimension is 110 feet and the short one 41. The stairs in the short hall just beyond the crossing have a large window at the landing that reads as a feature from the rear, as does the small window underneath it. Emery II had a sitting room and 38 double bedrooms, each with a curtained closet. The veranda columns were among the largest the shops had ever turned.

Emery III opened September 1905, its plans listed among the Drawing Division's output for the year. The *Tuskegee Student* characterized it as "purely colonial." The school announced Emery IV in June 1906, but it was not finished until 1909. All were renovated 1929–1932 and again in 1957. All are stubbornly elegant on the exterior despite Thomas Emery's strictures. Textured bricks, sensitive proportions, and astute detailing can go far to compensate a

Figure Cat. 14b. Bricks mimicking an Ionic entablature.

deprived budget. The classical Ionic entablatures rendered in brick at eaves level are particularly fine, descending, as they do from dentil cornices through a plain frieze and then an architrave with three fascia. They could be a MIT blackboard drawing and they would have been close to cost-free. The rear windows have another telling touch that is reminiscent of Dorothy Hall's stair tower. Rows of relentlessly identical bedroom windows are relieved by a large one in the middle that lights the stair landing. It floats above a tiny, three-paned opening that is capped by a full-sized segmental brick arch and still another extended keystone that pierces the wall above. Wit joined grace where Emery might not have bothered to look.[96]

15. TANTUM HALL

James B. Tantum, a Trenton, New Jersey, widower and physician who had prospered in real estate, heard Washington speak during one of his tours. On his deathbed, he asked his daughter to give Tuskegee a building from his estate. In January 1905 Margaret Tantum, now an orphan in her late teens, wrote to Washington to ask for a catalog and a list of the school's needs. She then proposed a building costing $20,000 or less. She particularly wanted to help student "bible workers" but understood that this might not be what was needed. In mid-July Washington sent preliminary drawings that, Taylor said, were made by student Albert G. Brown with only a little help.[97] Taylor wrote a description of the 37-room dormitory to cost $25,000 with large columns to "put it in the style of Colonial architecture."[98] He noted that "many of the residences in this part of the country are built in this style of architecture, and the building will thus be in harmony with the architecture of the surrounding country."[99] Margaret Tantum replied that her father liked Colonial best.[100] Taylor's regional associations allude to a style that was popular across the country and that, like the Carnegie Library, surprises a century later for the

Figure Cat. 15a. Tantum Hall, west side.

possible racial implications. A dormitory for black girls with a monumental projecting portico standing a half-mile from a colonnaded antebellum mansion and another half-mile from cotton merchants' columnar houses could be interpreted as a racial challenge rather than historicizing neighborliness, as discussed in chapters 5 and 6.

The Tantum donation revived an earlier dormitory project that had languished for lack of funding. That one was to be near Huntington Hall and Parker Cottage. But by July 1905 someone, presumably Washington, had decided to change the location of what by then had become the Tantum project to the valley's western edge, removing it from the existing girls' zone. Tantum was then sited in the turkey yard, near the Chapel, Dorothy Hall, and the barns [1911 Campus Plan]. That set and the plans received, Margaret Tantum mailed a $5,000 down payment.[101] As built, Tantum Hall is too large for the Huntington area unless Parker Cottage were demolished. It is not clear from Taylor's memos if large columns were to be on the first, unfunded project but, while the Huntington Hall area was still involved, he planned the "porch" that became, at the turkey yard site, "very large Ionic columns" on both front and rear or, as another memo put it, "a porch on the back of the building similar to the one on the front, thus making it appear about the same on the two sides."[102] The final decision for the two colonnades would be made "as we work up the drawings."[103]

Abandoning large columns on the entrance side would save money, of course, but as Richard Dozier has pointed out, a western entrance elevation with a

Figure Cat. 15b. Tantum Hall, entrance.

continuous horizontal flow rather than tall columns' upward thrust would better complement the nearby Chapel's verticality. Taylor's ability to weave buildings together was essential to Tuskegee's campus tapestry. Margaret Tantum did not involve herself in these discussions even though Washington extended the invitation by sending drawings.

By the end of July Tuskegee had received the down payment and the donor a promise of blueprints as soon as the plans were completed. That December Miss Tantum agreed to adding a YWCA office on the second floor if it did not increase costs. In April 1906, Tantum Hall, now underway, served as the demonstration building for the twenty-fifth anniversary celebrations. Guests could see its window and door frames in the Boys' Trades Building

Figure Cat. 15c. Tantum Hall, east side.

and they could watch students dig clay, mold and burn bricks, and lay them in walls. [104] Washington invited his youngest donor to the great occasion, but she declined. Her celebration would be a year later when she, her aunt, and her pastor attended the dedication. The service was planned for the rear portico, which kept its six great columns even if the front lost them. The audience was to sit on the lawn below, but the weather did not cooperate so the Chapel had to suffice. Department head Jane E. Clark, honored the 245 students who had learned by building. The pastor, remembering James Tantum's wishes, averred that carefully planned structures that are made of the best materials modeled the well-designed life. Margaret Tantum consented to

stand for a moment so that the girls could see her face. [105]

Tantum Hall had thirty-seven rooms, a tin roof, and tin and wood cornices. The twenty-two and a half foot columns came from the American Column Company in Battle Creek, Michigan. Final accounts show a cost overrun of $159.20, $18.70 more than the expenses accrued by the architectural drawing division. The financial breakdown among the trades was similar to that for Rockefeller Hall but this time architectural drawing was included.

Tantum Hall now assumed Huntington Hall's task of sheltering trustees and their families for the February meetings. It later housed single women teachers and nursing students. An interior renovation in 1965 wisely preserved the two-story stair-hall with its engaging handrails, the most inventive of Tuskegee's remaining staircases. The upper part of the hallway stands behind a curious façade. The row of arched windows marching the length of the building facade is inexplicably interrupted by a segment of blank wall near the center. The effect is reminiscent of Cassedy Hall, where an irregular scansion suggests mysterious programming and lively accidents of occupation within. The Tantum façade's southern end has an answering syncopation on the first floor. The asymmetry of these interruptions is barely noticeable but still engages the eye and relieves the relentless march of identical windows down a long facade. It is a pleasurable if subliminal tease.

16. TOMPKINS DINING HALL

Tompkins Dining Hall looms from its surroundings for its size, large orders on three sides, and dome that, capitol-like, rises above the tree line. The main entrance is a slightly projecting frontispiece with pediment on four very large columns. This is on the west-facing long side that edges the quadrangle, but there are also two impressive entrances on the short ends. Tompkins is of such substance that it has lasted a century with few modifications in either form or usage.

A white architect, James W. Golucke of Atlanta, designed Tompkins. Perhaps Taylor passed the job to an experienced builder in concrete and steel. Golucke had around thirty courthouses to his credit, including Macon County's in the center of Tuskegee. Taylor guided programming and planning, made structural changes, and did the interior fittings. He argued the building to the Tuskegee board and was supervising architect well before October 1907, when Golucke died. Board chairman Seth Low gave Taylor full credit at dedication.

Golucke's authorship is known because one of Taylor's MIT classmates had written to solicit the job. "Ordinarily, the work of designing the buildings at Tuskegee is done on the school grounds," Taylor replied, "but in the case of one or two buildings here recently, it has been done by outside architects. The building that you doubtless refer to is the dining room, but the drawings for this have already been made by an Atlanta architect." He then recalled merry evenings in his schoolmate's Cambridge home, regretted his friend had not written sooner, and promised consideration for future work. The name Golucke is in an internal Taylor memo.[106] James Wingfield Golucke was a self-trained carpenter-architect who was building

the Romanesque Revival Macon County courthouse about when Tompkins started. But Golucke was jailed in Georgia for malfeasance on another project and died while incarcerated.[107]

Tuskegee's project was initiated in May 1903 with a $20,000 legacy from the estate of Mrs. Cornelia C. Tompkins of New York City who had given fifty dollars in 1893. Charles Tompkins of Southport, Connecticut—whose middle initial varies in the telling—was named as the donor in all Tuskegee accounts, but the gift from his widow could have originated in her mother's inheritance from the Wakefield shipping fortune.[108]

Taylor's continuing importance to Tompkins is clear. In June 1903, as institute architect, he told Washington that the drawings could not be finished until the Principal decided how he wanted to subdivide the basement. Taylor thought it could hold a large assembly room and a commissary where visitors could purchase meals. Preliminary drawings were ready by the middle of that month, but it would be more than a year later, August 1904, before the drawings were finalized. Trustee George Foster Peabody had wanted to change both site and size, the first because the building would block views from the public road, he thought, the second because it was too expensive. Estimates had now mounted to $60,000 and the trustees' policy was to approve buildings only after they were fully pledged. In November 1904, Washington, then in Boston, told Taylor to begin construction although he still wanted to check the exact location. The following January, Taylor addressed the trustees in New York because, as Emmett J. Scott put it, "You can argue it best." Taylor, presumably with Golucke, had sited the dining hall on a steep slope so they could insert an auditorium underneath it, a proposal that made Washington nervous. The donor was not in a posi-

Figure Cat. 16a. Tompkins Dining Hall, archival photograph.

tion to object.[109]

The *Tuskegee Student* formally announced the coming dining hall in February 1905, noting that $39,000 of the required $65,000 was in hand. That March, Taylor sent Washington three proposals for the main building and an attached kitchen block so he could study tradeoffs in convenience, privacy, and cost. The first proposal partitioned the 78-foot by 185-foot dining hall—the main mass—into four areas for faculty and students. Washington disliked it because the room would not be fully visible from every seat. He wanted students to feel their unity. The second option, which Taylor preferred, included a sectional drawing to show that the assembly hall was carved into the slope of the hill. It was not only under the dining hall but seems to have extended to an even lower level under the kitchen block. "The teachers' dining room is placed above the floor of the assembly room but below the kitchen," implying a three-story annex with the auditorium stage as the bottom level, the teachers' dining room above it, the kitchen on top at the level of the students' dining room. As built, the annex was separate from the main block except for where the kitchen is continuous with the dining hall, bridging a gap

that has now been filled in. In the built version, the full auditorium, including the stage, remained in the main block, under the dining hall. In 1925 students traced the original drawings onto linen, as they did for many other fragile blueprints that were then discarded. Six 1925 Tompkins sheets remain in the Physical Facilities Department, but the originals are gone, as are those for most early Tuskegee structures.[110]

Taylor's third option for Washington's consideration was almost the same as number two but with the teachers' dining room at the same level as that of the students. But this would mean, Taylor said, that the teachers must climb many more stairs to reach their separate outside entrance. This scheme wasted space and cost more money, he explained. Washington had wanted the teachers and students at the same level with a glass partition between them.[111] The teachers' dining room ended up in the annex below the kitchen but above a basement and graced with a high ceiling. The ceilings of the students' dining hall, the kitchen and the teacher's dining room were about thirty feet in the drawings but probably closer to twenty-eight as built. Tall windows brought far more light to the essential ritual of dining together than its dim, low-ceilinged predecessor in Alabama Hall. On the exterior, the lower part of the main block has channeled horizontal brick bands to simulate stone rustication, a firm visual base for the large orders above. The annex, which is now connected on every level, is still a differentiated service structure on the exterior without columns or a rusticated base.

Taylor's structural contributions were also important. He first thought an uninterrupted dining hall impossible because intermediary supports must help the seventy-eight foot width, but he then devised a system of cantilevered wooden beams that made the leap and even supported the dome above. Taylor argued his structure on wood's centuries-old track record in great churches and public buildings. Wood was proven, steel not.[112] His son Edward remembered his father's delight in describing his solution. Harold Webb, a Tuskegee graduate who taught plumbing and heating late in Taylor's career, recalled that visiting engineers worried that the dome, which could not be seen from within, rested on a clear span [see Figure 6.2]. Taylor's structure has since been replaced by metal framing and the clear span was lost when posts were inserted in the late 1940s. The posts are slender, however, and do not seriously compromise the room's impressiveness.

Not all details were settled by the summer of 1905. Taylor told Washington that he did not have "the completed plans as made out by the architects" and therefore could not answer a question. Washington, meanwhile, was soliciting funds more aggressively than he liked to meet the $65,000 estimate. The following March 1906 Solon Jacobs and Company in Birmingham wrote business agent Lloyd G. Wheeler that they were shipping girders that were almost 43 feet long. One weighed six tons. In April, the dining hall drawings were listed as part of the Architectural and Mechanical Drawing Division's work for the previous year. Walls were going up that summer, but in November the brickmasons were transferred to an Emery dormitory while the blacksmiths were riveting and bolting. Perhaps they were putting in the iron beams that held the dining room floor above the auditorium or installing the Roebling Construction Company's kitchen undercroft of terra cotta arches on iron beams. Taylor said the structure would prevent the kitchen noise from disturbing the teachers below. H. E. Thomas of the Machine Shop directed the ironwork, the school's largest job to date. Thomas had trained in

engineering at MIT, perhaps when Taylor was there, but he did not earn a degree. In March 1907, Taylor traveled to Hampton, Washington, Annapolis, New York, and Boston to study institutional kitchens. Almost a year later brickmasons were laying the second story and carpenters inserting window frames some of which had been displayed at the anniversary celebration almost two years before. But work kept stopping because funding had dried up or because the Emerys, White Hall and the Dorothy Hall additions, all with hovering donors, needed attention. Some Tompkins walls had to be rebuilt after winter damage. The 1908 commencement included student Joseph North of Charleston, South Carolina, talking about "Designing and Framing the Roof of the Dining Hall." [113]

Concern over the behemoth's progress remained even though construction was advancing by mid 1908 when Seth Low asked the New York engineer William Barclay Parsons to review the drawings. Parsons approved them after suggesting further bracing of the four Howe trusses on which the dome rested because he was concerned about wind loads.[114] A year later Washington still wanted students to be able to see the dome's interior from their dining room, but Taylor said that would cost too much. Taylor then deemed the joists under Alabama Hall, which would soon be razed, in good condition and usable under the auditorium floor.[115] Taylor billed the institute $125 for architectural services. That December Walter T. Bailey and William A. Hazel were drawing furniture, Hazel having already advised on interior colors.[116] But soon Washington would host 300 guests in the teachers' dining room. A few weeks later a visitor, having dined to the music of a string band, wrote that he had fallen into a fountain of youth where old men were made young and tired men rested. Tompkins must have been finished since it was working that old Tuskegee magic. Or maybe the fountain was real. A fountain in the vestibule lounge was removed in 1937.[117]

Tompkins Dining Hall was dedicated during the 1910 February trustees' meeting. Board chair Seth Low said that square meals were now coming out of a round kitchen, alluding to its curved eastern wall. He tied the witticism to the race's increasing capabilities, Washington's persistent point as he constantly flagged black achievement. Washington

Figure Cat. 16b. Tompkins Dining Hall, recent view.

defended the auditorium on the grounds that even though the Stokes sisters had generously allowed the Chapel to be used for secular events, they really wanted its sanctity preserved. For their part, students were glad that they could move from evening meals to vespers below without trekking through the night. At the dedication, Low urged Taylor to the platform, saying that, like Christopher Wren in St. Pauls, his monument was all around him. The *Tuskegee Student* claimed that 180 teachers enjoyed their private dining hall, 2,000 students theirs, and that 2,500 could find a seat in the auditorium. The final cost was $175,000, far more than the $65,000

estimate and Cornelia Tompkins' $20,000 legacy but no account has emerged about where the difference came from.[118]

Washington remained typically involved with his building, trying even a year later to persuade Taylor to change the entrances, which the architect declined to do, and requesting black walnut tables for the students. Where could Tuskegee get the wood and how much would it cost?[119] A cold-storage area was inserted into the kitchen wing in 1929, after Washington's death. A plan inscribed "for Mr. Taylor's Office" and signed by the Cincinnati mechanical engineers Fosdick and Hilmer recorded this area two years later. Rooms had been assigned for bread storage, a steward's office, meat refrigeration, vegetable refrigeration, dishwashing, pastry making, a bakery, and ice cream production, these specialized units flanking the main kitchen that had the curving eastern wall. The auditorium was used until it was supplanted in the early 1930s by the combination auditorium-gymnasium in Logan Hall. Tompkins' steeply sloped auditorium floor was leveled in 1965 and is now a student center. The faculty dining room served the Tuskegee Airmen of World War II and held United Service Organization entertainments for them and the army units there for technical training. It is now a game room of remarkable proportions. A 1965 drawing by Booker Conley modifies the rooms flanking the central entrance to the main hall to accompany an enlarged balcony overlooking the student's space.

THE RESTAURANT PROJECT

With the dining hall advancing during the spring of 1908 and the final decision to take down Alabama Hall, Washington asked Taylor for a sketch and estimates for a house or restaurant where students could purchase extra meals and teachers, visitors, and guests could eat in three separate dining rooms. There could also be a private dining room for special occasions with white people "if necessary"—the modifier left unexplained—plus six to eight bedrooms with baths. Taylor made preliminary drawings but the project did not come to fruition.[120]

The restaurant project raises the issue of on-campus interracial life without settling it, perhaps because as the larger culture shifted towards fiercer segregation, Tuskegee's did too—but without any pride in the fact to report. During the 1890s Washington told prospective visitors that the town was at ease with on-campus hospitality and interracial events. But as Jim Crow deepened, co-racial dining must have become increasingly problematic. The white civil rights activist Mary White Ovington tells us that in 1904 at Atlanta University the white teachers of black students were shunned outside the school because they ate with their charges. But these meals meant much to the students because they could converse with white people as equals, she remarked. Early Tuskegee's visitors ate at separate tables in the Alabama Hall teachers' dining room. Visitors often asked in advance if they could join faculty or students at meals. After home economics moved into Margaret Murray Washington Hall (the former Slater-Armstrong Agricultural Building), Dorothy Hall increased its guesthouse capability, one with its own dining room. During later decades, white visitors regularly joined faculty in the Tompkins Dining Hall while visiting academics, black and white, might eat and sleep in the homes of faculty colleagues.[121] Tuskegee appears to have had a flexible set of options during those sensitive times.

17. THE NEGRO BUILDING, MONTGOMERY

The exhibition building for Alabama's black people at the Alabama Agricultural Association fair in Montgomery, October 1906, was one of the projects Taylor had in hand when Beatrice died. Early in the planning stage he wrote that this was to be "a distinctly Negro Building in every particular," meaning that everything was made by black men. "We do it all, put up buildings, following any style of architecture, and pay for it."[122] Exhibits were to include ten framed drawings from the school's Architectural Drawing Division and photographs of Alabama buildings owned by black craft unions or secret societies.[123] Landscape and horticulture teacher David A. Williston and the gardening class laid out the grounds.[124] Washington was granted a Negro Day at the fair with no whites on the grounds in return for the promise that he would not bring in Northern black speakers. Northerners did not understand Southern ways, the officials made clear.[125]

Montgomery historian Mary Ann Neeley has attributed the building to Walter T. Bailey, then head of the Architectural Drawing Division. A photograph shows a classical exterior that is different from Taylor's usual and, perhaps, lacking his typical elegance. Taylor's role was the planning and production, the structure being prefabricated at Tuskegee and assembled in Montgomery by ten students under the direction of Mitchell D. Garner, a Carpentry Division instructor. It was an L in plan, 77 by 90 feet with a 20-foot high exhibit room, a large dining room, and a kitchen. Dining and resting facilities would have been otherwise unavailable to the fair's black visitors.[126]

18. WHITE HALL GIRLS' DORMITORY

The Brooklyn housing philanthropist Alfred T. White and his sisters were longtime Tuskegee "friends." Responding to the Whites' inquiry in late 1906, Washington suggested $20,000 in tools and machinery rather than a building would be most welcome. Replacing Alabama Hall was not a priority because Tantum Hall was underway. But the White siblings wanted a permanent memorial to their merchant father. A girls' dormitory was announced in June 1907 as a $50,000 gift from "a generous Brooklyn family" that did not want its name known.[127] Washington sent a preliminary sketch that included a "clock steeple" that could be changed to a smaller cupola without the timepiece if the donors preferred.[128] That August, Taylor met with Seth Low at his city home to discuss the design and strategize Taylor's presentation to the White family. Low praised Taylor's idea of "moving" Alabama Hall by placing the new building on the western edge of the level area. A devoted trustee and experienced architectural client, Low devoted a paragraph to the problems that came with the proposed site's steep fall while simultaneously expressing confidence in Taylor's ability to solve them.[129] Taylor soon announced drawing division head Walter T. Bailey would begin the working drawings.[130] White and his sisters must have been pleased with the results because the following year they gave an additional $25,000 to help defray an institutional deficit, again requesting anonymity.[131]

The *Tuskegee Catalogue, 1909–1910* announced the building as ready for occupancy in September 1909, a quick construction for a large building. It was dedicated at the February 1910 trustees meeting in a separate ceremony from that for the Tompkins

Dining Hall and Milbank Agricultural Building. With its 20,000 square feet, freight elevator, 60 bedrooms, a dean's suite, reception rooms, and guestrooms and baths, it was the largest dormitory to date. The White siblings visited a year later and were feted in the "beautiful" building that grateful occupants praised for being free of Alabama Hall's kitchen smells. The girls spoke of lessons learned in gratitude, correct living, skilled work, service to others, and love of the beautiful, climaxing their speeches with a cheer:

> Whom are we glad to see?
>   *The Whites!*
> What do they bring?
>   *Light!*
> What must we do?
>   *Right!*
> Rah!

Figure Cat. 18. White Hall.

The Whites in turn praised the courtesy, enthusiasm, discipline, and responsiveness of everyone they met. "I trust we drank in enough of the Tuskegee spirit to enable us to pass along to others something of the inspiration which we received ourselves," A. T. White wrote Washington after it was over.[132]

The donors nevertheless remained unsatisfied with their deed. White wanted to remove the cupola, which he thought "squatty" (Figures 8.1 and 8.2) in favor of a taller clock tower. Taylor met with White in New York and agreed to another design. Three weeks later Washington sent two sketches to which White replied that Taylor should calculate the cost of the simpler one. If Taylor or Washington preferred the other, he could calculate that, too. An awkward design by William A. Hazel dated 1911 is probably one of these and a drawing signed by W. T. Bailey of the whole building with the clock tower as it was built must be the other.[133] The decision was problematic because steel would have to be inserted into the existing building to take the additional weight.[134] But discussions dragged on while still other ideas were fielded and rejected. White suggested an independent clock tower, like Hampton's. Washington wanted a clock added to the Chapel tower but White vetoed changing a building given by others. In September, White was reviewing Tuskegee's blueprints with New York architect W. B. Tubby. Drawings traveled back and forth all fall, sometimes crossing paths. Finally, on April 6, 1912, Tubby instructed White that the most recent design would be erected—starting that day. Tubby had already designed the steel supports because the school lacked expertise.[135] The results cost another $10,095.

White must have enjoyed the process, even after further complications arrived with the clockworks that are beyond detailing here. That September he and his sisters gave $25,000 towards the new power plant, rewarding Tuskegee for its patience through what must have been a frustrating episode. Taylor and Washington then discussed tower access so girls could see the clockworks in action. In April 1913, Washington sent White a photograph, a bill, and a request to relay his gratitude to Mr. Tubby.[136]

White Hall's exterior may well be a collaboration between Taylor and Bailey. The triadic massing and the rhythmic pilaster strips on the rear suggest Taylor's ingrained classicism. But the narrow windows seem crowded between the pilasters and the window disposition, with arched heads on a lower floor rather than the upper, is unusual. The curving upper edges of the parapets border the steps also register a different voice. White Hall was gutted and the interior rebuilt in 2004.

19. JOHN A. ANDREW MEMORIAL HOSPITAL

A 1920 study by a committee of the American Medical Association named Tuskegee's John A. Andrew Memorial Hospital as one of the four good facilities for the nation's African Americans and the only one south of Washington, D.C. More recently, a medical editor has termed it one of the four first-rate Southern hospitals for African Americans before 1940, the others being in New Orleans, Durham, and Norfolk. Even in 1968, when there were black-run hospitals in almost every Southern state, Tuskegee's was a leader.[137]

Washington took public health seriously. Peter A. Coclanis has suggested that we underestimate the disease rate and its effects on the malnourished poor of the post-bellum South, a situation he likens to conditions today in some developing countries. Washington's compulsion to cleanliness and order makes considerable sense in this context instead of being a neurosis or culturally driven obsession, as other critics have had it.[138] Washington inaugurated National Negro Health Week in 1915, shortly before his death, but this act culminated decades of continuing efforts for the school and the region.

Richard Dozier has outlined the institute's medical history. Its second doctor was the first black woman physician, Dr. Hallie Tanner Dillon, the artist Henry O. Tanner's sister.[139] In 1892, when Alabama had no facility to train African Americans for this essential profession, Tuskegee established a three-year nurse-training program. In 1910 Washington outlined his goal for a regional hospital that would expand nursing opportunities and offer medical internships to black doctors trained elsewhere. By then there were several black medical schools but few hospitals where graduates could practice.[140]

Figure Cat. 19a. Andrew Hospital.

Tuskegee had built a "hospital" in residential Greenwood in 1892 that was probably a dispensary. After a smallpox epidemic played itself out using Parker Cottage as the infirmary, Taylor built the frame Pinehurst Hospital at the northern end of the deep valley that separated the older and newer campus. This site, chosen in January 1901, established a future medical zone. The following December, the *Tuskegee Student* published the hospital elevation and the next month, a year after the site had been chosen, announced an anonymous gift of $4,000 to build it. (The donor was Mrs. Thomas G. Bennett of New Haven.) Tuskegee's physician and surgeon was now John Andrew Kenney who arrived in 1902 after training at Shaw University in

Raleigh and interning at the Freedman's Hospital in Washington, D.C. Kenney was soon detailing the campus's dangerous sanitary conditions. Kenney stayed until 1923, defying the Ku Klux Klan during the Veteran's Hospital crisis of 1923 but then fleeing further threats for New Jersey, where he established a private hospital.[141]

Pinehurst Hospital was a two-story, triple-gabled wooden structure that is consistent with Taylor's style. It had a plaster-surfaced operating room heated by a coal and wood stove and twenty-five beds in two wards. In 1904 Tuskegee built a nearby house for Kenney that survived until 2001. When Andrew Hospital opened in 1912, Pinehurst was remodeled into faculty apartments that were razed in 1982.[142]

Not content with Pinehurst, Kenney was soon

Figure Cat. 19b. Pinehurst Hospital.

lobbying for a larger hospital to serve the region. Tuskegee was financially and medically prepared, he said, since Pinehurst had seen a hundred successful operations over two years. Prosperous patients were coming from as far as South Carolina and Georgia and leaving profits to support clinics for the poor. As president of the black National Medical Association, Kenney decreed a Tuskegee conference where his guests could donate their services. This became an annual April event to which black physicians from throughout the South brought their toughest cases for consultation.[143]

Design for a larger hospital was underway by June 1911. Taylor and Kenney had sited it north of the mule barn because the ground was high, far from the main road, and sheltered by trees [1911 Campus Plan]. Simultaneous planning for a new agricultural campus, destined by 1908 for further west, would open the area for other purposes. Washington needed distance between the farm detritus—flies and smells—and the hospital's plant.

Fundraising soon began for a brick building with tile floors and wainscoting in the operating rooms. The first week in July, Taylor and Kenney were in Boston conducting the final negotiations with the donors and reporting their success to Washington, who was in New York. Then came the usual complications. Taylor told Washington he could not draw the elevation for publicity purposes until the plans were fixed. Nor could he estimate costs without the finished drawings. Kenney accepted a size reduction that Taylor thought necessary, a situation that then led to John H. Washington's complaints about the four weeks it would take Walter T. Bailey, in

Tuskegee, to redraw it. At one point Taylor asked Washington to thank the Tuskegee and Cornell-trained architect Vertner Tandy and his partner George W. Foster for lending space in their New York office and an afternoon of Foster's talent.[144] Taylor may have drawn up the changes himself.

In the fourth week of August Taylor sent eight blueprints to Washington's summer home on Long Island with lists of major materials and interior features. He promised detailed drawings and specifications would follow. The *Manufacturer's Record* for August 10, 1911, had just announced that Tuskegee would build to Taylor's plans the "semi-fireproof" elevator building costing $50,000. It was to have a slate roof and "artificial stone" or "cement" trim produced at the school. At the August 11 groundbreaking, Washington announced that it would be named for John A. Andrew, the wartime governor of Massachusetts who founded a black Union regiment, and it would cost $58,000. A year later, with the brickwork almost finished, two thousand guests, five hundred of whom were black Alabama Freemasons, watched the cornerstone being laid to Masonic rites. Taylor was a Scottish Rite Freemason.[145]

Construction proceeded through the fall of 1912. Design was arduous because of the unfamiliar machinery manufactured elsewhere for which the locations had to be exactly dimensioned. The construction sequence was tightly timed, each fixture or steam line readied for insertion at the right time. In the end, the pressure on the architect was too much and Taylor's doctor ordered him to leave. Washington agreed to a change of scene, a "genuine rest" of a few days and a place on a Pullman car headed to Washington, D.C. Taylor's Washington doctor released him a month later in time for the Masonic ceremony.

Mrs. Charles E. Mason of Boston, Governor Andrew's granddaughter, finally acknowledged that the hospital was her gift. This took place at the February 1913 dedication, when White Hall was also celebrated. Two trains came from the North. Julius Rosenwald brought the president of the University of Chicago, the city's superintendent of schools, and a dean of Northwestern University in one of them. The train rolled onto campus to student applause. A few hours later Seth Low's train arrived from New York. The resulting assemblage was "as large and as important a body of men and women of wealth and standing" as ever gathered in the South. [146]

Taylor gave Low the keys to the latest "colonial style" building at the dedication ceremony. The exterior motif of single-story colonnaded veranda with three columns gathered at the corner that ran "behind" a double-height columnar portico, has a history dating at least to the School of Surgery in Paris of 1775. One can assume that there were photos of this building at MIT and at the University of Illinois as well, where Bailey trained. But the motif is also familiar from Thomas Jefferson's University of Virginia and, almost contemporarily with Andrew Hospital, at All Saints College in Vicksburg, Mississippi. A photograph was in *Architectural Record* the month Tuskegee's hospital was designed.[147] The colonnade has a roof terrace for patients staying on the second floor. The building's overall disposition seems Taylorean in its proportions and massing, but the evenly disposed, somewhat oddly shaped windows are not to his usual beat. Perhaps, as at White Hall, they may record Bailey's hand.

In 1930, shortly before Taylor retired, Andrew Hospital was expanded westward in a wing for a clinic. Ten years later the hospital expanded eastward with a similar wing for an infantile paralysis center. Andrew Hospital was destroyed in 1969, but the second wing remains.

20. THE NEW LAUNDRY

Plans for an expanded and independent laundry, which would relieve space in Dorothy Hall, were underway in November 1913. Seth Low told Washington that the trustees' New York-based Investment Committee would review the site and drawings as well as the Tuskegee-based Committee on Buildings and Grounds. An unsigned, undated blueprint of the area among Low's papers shows the laundry surrounded by the older buildings, the original Boys' Trades Building, the Lincoln Gates, and the Practice Cottage, all now gone [1932 Campus Plan].

Taylor had already staked the site that the Investment Committee would see when it arrived the following February. But the Investment Committee, with Low as chairman, wanted the laundry to go in the northeast ravine near the power plant rather than up front and adjacent to Dorothy Hall, in order to save on steam piping and avoid another steep site. Correspondence between Low and Washington mentions a "colored sketch" of an arcaded walkway or hyphen connecting it to Dorothy Hall.[148] A month before the meeting, Washington persuaded Low to the Dorothy Hall location because it would keep the girls away from the boys working at the power plant. Washington may have meant this or he might have wanted to keep the girls and their fine building out front, ennobling their industry with an airy, light-filled, classical monument. Laundry work could be expressed as morally uplifting at elite white schools too, as an elegant one at the Abbot Female Academy in Andover, Massachusetts, suggests. A prestigious Boston firm designed it slightly before Tuskegee's.[149]

Figure Cat. 20a. New Laundry.

Construction began immediately because Washington wanted to impress certain visitors. In July, the institute put automatic sprinklers out to bid for the new building and for the Boys' Trades Building. Construction slowed in September because, Taylor said, students "piddle away too much time." "Practice work" is slow, he reminded Washington. It speeded up in October and by mid-December the door and window frames were finished. Washington congratulated Taylor on hiring only a few outside workers.[150] Construction continued on the entry after dedication. The projecting temple front with its pediment and arcades is missing from a photograph of the building's early completion, leaving a grim face.[151] The final design was shown under construction in the March 1917 *Southern Letter*. There are twelve uniformed cadets and a teacher, "a class in practical geometry" according to the caption, arranged on a scaffold to measure the building's upper parts. Photographs that demonstrate Washington's pedagogy would taper off as the Moton era continued.

The New Laundry is a minor gem of architectural classicism. Its temple-like façade with a pediment over the arcades and ennobling pilaster strips on four sides granted forever the prestige Washington wanted for the less prestigious tasks. Even the water table at the base of the walls is special, increasing

Figure Cat. 20b. New Laundry entrance, bearing signage of current use.

in depth and complexity as the hillside falls away by using projecting strips of parallel or diagonally laid bricks, headers and stretchers. Such details engage questing eyes, especially those of young bricklayers learning their craft's enrichments. In 1938 Tuskegee's laundry was remodeled as an office, laboratory, and museum for George Washington Carver. The U.S. National Parks Service has owned and operated it since 1974 as the Carver Museum and National Historic Site visitors center.

21. THE AGRICULTURAL CAMPUS

The Agricultural Department's building history is vaguer than that for academic and industrial buildings despite the fact that farming was central to Tuskegee's mission. Washington wanted his students to understand that modern, scientific farming could be less arduous and more profitable than the hopeless drudgery most of them had fled. Farms, with animals and broad landscapes, must distance themselves from the academic, residential, administrative and even the industrial core that absorbed the casual visitor's attention.

In 1883, the Slater Fund awarded the fledgling institution a farm manager's salary and soon there was a stable (1884) and the barn with a cupola (1889).[152] This last stood on the western rim of the valley that would separate the later Chapel and second industrial zone from the girls' dormitories. Eventually, this site would head the 835-acre Home Farm, 135 acres of which were in truck gardens. By 1900 Tuskegee also owned the 800-acre Marshall Farm four miles away. Three hundred and fifty acres there were in corn, sugar cane, potatoes, grain, and hay while four hundred were in pasture for dry cows, beef cattle, and sheep, hogs, mules, and horses. The farm had two teachers to handle a night school for the thirty to forty-five boys who lived and worked there until they had saved enough for day school on the main campus.[153]

THE WOODEN BARNS

The Home Farm's 1889 barn burned in 1895, taking with it the institute's dairy herd. This was the rare Tuskegee fire that some thought might be arson. Dogs had barked at one in the morning as if strangers were about.[154] With money from "Brooklyn friends" and insurance in hand, Washington directed Taylor to design a barn that was not built immediately. Underused structures behind the Boys' Trades Building served for several years. Tuskegee did erect a brick creamery in 1899. Then came a poultry house and eventually the dairy barns, which Washington authorized his brother to build in early 1900 after he had settled details with Taylor and George Washington Carver. Board chairman William H. Baldwin was pleased with Taylor's plans[155] [1903 Campus Plan]. The luminous complex of white timber structures, their crisp planes accentuated by dark trim, spread out from the burnt barn's site, which was visible from the public road, and would have sent a triumphant message if any arsonists passed by. Washington wanted his visitors to see the farm buildings too, specifying that a piggery be arranged so that infant animals as well as adults could be viewed from a carriage.

Taylor's drawings for the horse or mule barn, set north of the cow barn, came with an explanation of why it would cost more than the other, larger one. The horse stalls were to be made of thicker lumber because its denizens would kick them, and there was a seventy-seat lecture hall. Taylor adjusted to these extra expenses by putting the horse barn along a contour in the topography to lower excavation costs. This left it at an odd angle to the cow barn. The horse barn was two hundred feet long and, like the cow barn's eastern front, had a cupola to lend presence from across the valley.[156] The cow barn was an "E" in plan with the three parallel bars that housed the stalls connected by a 175-foot stem on the building's east side, facing the campus. The outer prongs were a hundred twenty feet long, the inner one shorter.

The agricultural complex continued to grow after the two barns were finished. In late 1903 Washington told his architect to make a "permanent and substantial plan" because "we are doing things too carelessly." He was to hire an outside architect if he could not attend to it himself.[157] Eight months later Taylor reported that a storage shed had been contracted, foundations laid for two silos, and drawings made for the cow barn's expansion; he included blueprints for the Principal's approval. The central prong of the "E" now extended some twenty-five feet beyond the others. By 1905 there would be a frame hennery, tool house, piggery, slaughterhouse, and carriage house and, by 1906, three octagonal silos would rise to a height that could be seen from the far western fields. The brick creamery remained long after the farm center moved to its final location. It served as boys' housing, an alumni center, and a theater until 1998, when it was taken down. A parking lot marks where the wood barns and the silos once stood.

THE SLATER-ARMSTRONG MEMORIAL AGRICULTURAL BUILDING

In early 1896, the *Southern Letter* announced an Agricultural Building. It was built as a research center and sited near the main road in the lower Chapel area. A year later Alabama's governor and the U.S. Secretary of Agriculture dedicated it as a federal experiment station. George E. Wood, a white New Yorker who had designed the Armstrong-Slater Memorial Trades School at Hampton, was the architect and a Tuskegee graduate in brick masonry the contractor.[158] Mary Stearns of Belmont, Massachusetts, a friend of the recently deceased Olivia Davidson Washington and the widow of the radical abolitionist George L. Stearns, gave half the money. The building was initially named for the Stearns couple, but this was soon changed to honor John F. Slater and Samuel Chapman Armstrong, perhaps, as Richard Dozier has suggested, because Tuskegee was courting Slater funding. Or perhaps "Stearns" was too radical a handle for sustained Southern exposure. The Stearns estate was a stop on the underground railway, and George L. Stearns shipped arms to Kansas to aid John Brown's insurgency. Funding also came from New York banker Morris K. Jesup, the Slater Fund's treasurer. In 1904, Jesup

Figure Cat. 21a. Slater-Armstrong Agricultural Building, George E. Wood with Taylor additions.

Figure Cat. 21b. West side, Dairy Barn and Silos.

would give the first in a series of eponymous wagons and trucks that brought instruction in scientific farming into the distant countryside.

The *Southern Letter* article included a sketch of the coming building and a plan that showed a one-story veterinary wing that was never built. The brick, hip-roofed structure on a stone base was dedicated in January 1898 in a grand spectacle. Eight hundred students waved blazing pine knots when Secretary James Wilson arrived and "sky rockets" exploded into the night air. "The whole campus was as light as day." Students had shaped farm products into arches spanning the campus road and bunting and flags were draped on buildings with lamps blazing from windows. An audience said to number 5,000, including white people, heard the secretary, the governor, and Slater Fund officers evoke a bright future through scientific agriculture. The Tuskegee choir sang "My Old Kentucky Home" and the eminent dined in the Science Building.[159]

In 1901 Taylor, then in Cleveland, expanded the Agriculture Building's wings by bringing them forward. After completion of the Milbank Agricultural Building in 1910, The Wood and Taylor structure became a general storehouse and commissary that supplied the institute and outside community with produce, hardware, animal feed, fuel, and building materials. In 1930, it was renamed for Margaret Murray Washington, assigned to home economics, and survived until recently. But first it helped lure Secretary Wilson's protégé, George Washington Carver, to Tuskegee.

In the initial discussions, the Slater Fund agreed to support an agricultural experiment station but cautioned that it would have to be directed by a white man since Slater officers knew of no qualified black agricultural scientist. So Washington had to acquire the credentialed Carver. Carver's tenure was brief as department head since his administrative weaknesses undermined his creativity and charisma. By 1904, when the newly arrived George Bridgeforth was directing the farm expansion, Carver was given an independent laboratory and classes so he could do research, teach as he wanted, write, and serve as ambassador to the outer world. Carver's effect on students was legendary and his bonds with white admirers invaluable. In the 1920s, with Washington gone, Carver was said to be America's most famous black man.[160]

THE GIRLS' AGRICULTURAL PROGRAM

At the turn of the century, Margaret Murray Washington was developing an agriculture program for young women. Publicists photographed girls tending gardens and beehives within easy view of the public road, the Agricultural Building serving as backdrop. Pictures of young ladies engaged in horticulture, beekeeping, and loading milk cans on a dairy cart appeared in Washington's *The Story of My Life and Work* in 1901. In 1904 Washington detailed his wife's two-year curriculum. Girls could learn poultry, market gardening, livestock care, floriculture, and landscape gardening. He said that the program was similar to what the Washingtons had seen at a British agricultural college for well-born women and to that of the Minnesota College of Agriculture, where fifty girls studied similar subjects. Typically, Washington associated Tuskegee with progressive educational ventures elsewhere in order to assert a modern context along with the idea that healthful outdoor work was not for one race alone, nor one gender. In Minnesota, he said, both boys and girls learned to "plan farm buildings and to lay out the grounds artistically."[161] Photographs of boys and girls in Tuskegee forestry and chemistry classes appeared in the mainstream magazine *Cosmopolitan* in 1902.[162] And Max Bennett Thrasher listed still other coeducational opportunities. Women studied in the Phelps Bible Training School; girls and boys learned typesetting together; and ten girls had joined thirty boys in the tailoring shops. In 1921 Taylor would report that girls had qualified in tailoring, shoemaking, accounting, linotype, carpentry, and harness making, all in the Boys' Trades Department.[163]

Two Greenhouses

Tuskegee built two greenhouses during the first decade of the new century. The first (1904) stood between the Slater-Armstrong Agricultural Building and the Boys' Trades Building and was given by Mrs. C. L. Byington of Stockbridge, Massachusetts. It had a frame headhouse with a double-glazed growing shed. The second was built in 1908 from the legacy of Miss Alice Byington, also of Stockbridge. Seth Low announced the donation. "The Byington" as the second greenhouse was

known, had a twenty-two foot wide brick head house with raised parapets and wall buttresses at the gable ends. Its glazed shed had three-foot high brick foundations that continued the headhouse's width for a total length of 75 feet. A separate boiler provided steam heat. The Byington stood about 200 feet south of the public road in the eastern campus, near the entrance from town. Washington asked that the greenhouse be in a conspicuous spot so that people on the public road could see flowers year round.[164]

Milbank Agricultural Building

Washington's 1907–08 report to the Slater Fund considered changes in the Home Farm and a plan to acquire contiguous farmland to compensate for that lost to expanding industrial and academic departments.[165] He fixed the agricultural expansion

Figure Cat. 21c. Milbank Agricultural Building by William S. Pittman.

Figure Cat. 21d. Dairy Barn, recent view.

in summer 1909 with the Milbank Agricultural Building set along a new road some two thousand feet west of the Chapel.[166] Milbank was completed in 1910 to designs by William Sidney Pittman. Taylor did minor interior changes and oversaw construction. In March 1909 Taylor had written that "If the plans prepared by Mr. Pittman are substantially correct," they should be turned into blueprints and sent to the Principal who would forward them to the donor. Pittman, by then Washington's son-in-law, was practicing in Washington, D.C.[167] Joseph Citro, who interviewed Portia Washington Pittman in 1971, credits him with Milbank as well as one or possibly two buildings of 1909 at the Kentucky Normal and Industrial School for Colored Persons, now Kentucky State University in Frankfort. Visual analysis supports this. The massing of Kentucky's remaining Hume Hall and that of Milbank is unitary and blocky rather than triadic and diffused. The walls are visually thin with shallow reveals at the

windows. And the square-headed window openings lack the variations in shape, size, and rhythm with which Taylor typically enlivened walls. The Elizabethan or Jacobean gables and the protruding porch that evoke sixteenth-century predecessors in England and British America are also similar to a probable Pittman building, Blanton Hall (1916), at Voorhees College in Denmark, South Carolina. Milbank's curving gables established a fresh motif for the coming brick farm group. Taylor modified the idiom in his 1914–15 Veterinary Hospital, discussed below, and he or other Tuskegee architects would modify it again for the 1918 Dairy Barn and 1919 Horse Barn.[168]

Washington remembered that he had been exhausted and "on the border of discouragement" at the end of a long day of fundraising when he called on Mrs. Elizabeth Milbank Anderson at her New York home and found a warm welcome. Mrs. Anderson promised $20,000 for a building named for her father, Jeremiah Milbank, a founder of the Borden Milk Company. The first scheme was for a "separate

Figure Cat. 21e. Horse Barn, recent view.

building to cost $25,000 to $27,000, known as The Jeremiah Milbank Mechanical Building," to house industries: brickmasonry, plastering, tile setting, plumbing, mechanical drawing, electrical work, machine work, and a foundry. They then settled on an agricultural building with laboratories, offices, and classrooms. Mrs. Anderson's husband, the artist Abraham Archbold Anderson, reviewed the drawings, suggesting that the third floor auditorium be rearranged so that the audience did not face the windows. He also wanted a speaker's entrance to the stage and, on the ground floor, more separation of the creamery and soil room. In May 1909, Washington urged Taylor to meet with Anderson when next in New York. Both Andersons were significant philanthropists of their era, giving facilities for the poor and buildings to Barnard College. The Milbank Memorial Fund continues to support medical and educational research. [169]

Milbank's construction was soon underway. In

May, Tuskegee ordered roofing slate, a rare Tuskegee material. That June, the Committee on Buildings and Grounds—Washington, Warren Logan, and trustee W. W. Campbell—officially approved it along with poultry colony houses, brooder and incubator structures, and goose and duck houses. All were placed far west of the Boys' Trades Building. Milbank was on the last high ground before the terrain sank into a bog [1932 Campus Plan]. That October Taylor billed the school for architectural services on Milbank, the Dining Hall, and White Hall. [170]

PLANNING THE AGRICULTURAL CAMPUS

The Agricultural Department had long been losing money, the reason for George R. Bridgeforth's promotion that relieved Carver of its administration. Washington's report to the trustees for 1907–08 proposed the new road west and developments that would be carried out in several three-year stages to address this issue. Tuskegee would sell some land, purchase nearer tracts, and move the farm center to gain efficiency. Dairy products and vegetables sold to the public were already bringing in profits, Washington reminded everyone, as he defended the department that was at the core of his vision but now under trustee scrutiny.

Seth Low, himself a gentleman farmer, took Tuskegee's agricultural problems as his special mission. He twice sent his farm manager, G. D. Brill, to assess the situation. Brill offered a host of recommendations including soil reconstruction and reducing the dairy herd to a few productive cows. Brill wanted to limit butter production to the amount for the teachers' tables, which was what the dairy classes had to produce in order to teach the craft. Butter from Australia was cheaper than the homemade, as Brill had learned on Low's farm. Students could then have whole milk instead of skimmed and, more importantly, they could learn that farming made money.

The decision for a new farm center away from the one that was glowingly visible from the Lincoln Gates and Washington's office became a process that was true planning because it prescribed actions to be implemented at a later date. Discussions centered on the cost of moving crops from fields to barns and then manure from the barns to fields. Since the calculations suggested putting the barns nearer the fields, the proposal cleared the first barn area for Andrew Hospital. Washington did protest sacrificing to construction land that he had enriched over the decades, arguing that the soil had finally become profitable.[171]

In early 1910 Seth Low asked Washington to prepare a plan for all farm buildings. He also advised plowing legumes into the soil and he devised a way to credit students for farm work.[172] Taylor sent preliminary sketches for two barns for the hill east of Milbank to Washington in May 1911. He made cost estimates for frame buildings but noted

that lower-maintenance brick would be only 25 percent more. An addendum outlined widening the road from Boys' Trades to Milbank and extending it some 2,600 feet further through the farmland to join the public road to the Chehaw station.[173] Brill and Low wanted the barns to go even further west, beyond Milbank, but Low then softened his opinion, remembering that the road extension would cost still more, thereby courteously giving Washington reason to override his ideas. Like the Stokes sisters a decade before, Low was eager to participate at every level but deferred to Washington in the end.

Aside from access, there were more problems with Low's vision. Engineer Walter Franz's 1911 topographic map stops before the area west of Milbank so does not show that the land beyond was swampy. Planning was also complicated by the question of whether the coming cold storage plant would go near the new barns in a new farm center or near the power plant and dining hall. Low responded by sending another expert, a refrigeration engineer with whom he had worked at Columbia. Low told the visitor that Tuskegee had "a very capable architect and plenty of construction ability." Discussions were ongoing in July 1914 when a fire destroyed the wooden horse barn, killing 34 mules.[174]

By October 1914, in a directive for a Veterinary Hospital, we learn that the new barns had been sited where they would later be built, along the hill's crest between Milbank and the old campus. Cow and horse barns would flank the Veterinary Hospital between them, the dairy barns to the viewer's left (west), the horse and mule barn to the right (east), but this was delayed because, as Low explained, the Red Cross's war needs trumped Tuskegee's. Barn drawings would have been finished in 1914 or 1916 under the direction of Walter T. Bailey, head of the Architectural Drawing Division. An April

1917 blueprint shows the area as it would emerge around 1921. The agricultural buildings stretched along the road from a slaughterhouse to the west on the road's north side and the poultry area with the division's classrooms and offices south of the road.[175] Milbank came next on the northern side, then the Dairy Barn, the Veterinary Hospital, and the Horse Barn. On lower land further east, where most of the vegetables were grown, one found the piggery and the truck garden "house" with its bathrooms for girls. A new cannery, also finished in 1917, was on the south side of the road, across from the truck garden building.

THE CANNERY

The board's executive and investment committees decided that would not accept the gift of a new cannery unless they could be certain it would cover all costs. Low, who had asked for this assurance, knew the donor, one Miss Blanchard from Northeast Harbor, Maine. (The earlier cannery was in the lower end of the valley, near the 1890s practice school and behind the New Laundry.) Taylor proposed the location for several reasons. It was near the Boys' Trades Building boiler house, lessening the cost of steam lines. It was on the new farm road and near the truck gardens. And it was across from the truck garden "house" with its girls' toilets. The cannery plan showed a preparation room with a concrete floor and an annex processing room with the steam kettles. Boys' and girls' cloakrooms separated a wood-floored storage room from the two workrooms. Walls were to be of vertical boards dressed on both sides with wood strips covering the joints. The cannery would cost $2,000, a sum that Miss Blanchard's gift must have covered since construction started the following month.[176]

THE VETERINARY HOSPITAL

In December 1913, Washington asked Taylor what a veterinary hospital would cost. The following October, Washington told Seth Low that the camera manufacturer George Eastman would fund one and that plans and location should be decided by the Committee on Buildings and Grounds. Low thought the drawings should go to the trustees at their February meeting and that it should be located "near the barns," meaning the future ones near Milbank. Meanwhile, Taylor asked Washington for permission to travel since it was customary for architects to study the most advanced examples of any specialized type. Taylor visited the University of Pennsylvania's veterinary hospital while in Philadelphia on other business. Preliminary drawings went to the trustees and, a few weeks later, Taylor was meeting with the architects of Harvard University's veterinary hospital, the example he thought best. He met its architects, Frederick Ward Putnam and William Cox, through Charles E. Mason, husband of Andrew Hospital's donor. Construction proceeded slowly. In November 1915, Taylor ended more than two decades of correspondence with Booker T. Washington by promising to send to *American Carpenter and Builder* a photograph of students building the roof trusses. Two days later Washington was dead.[177]

The Veterinary Hospital contained operating, storage, serum, drug, and waiting rooms, offices, classrooms, a laboratory, and, in the low rear wing with the roof monitor, eight large-animal stalls and a soaking pit. It served its intended purpose through the late 1940s and stood unused until spring 2008, when it was destroyed. The building was a minor masterpiece of visual persuasion. The nesting-box continuity between small elements such as the

Figure Cat. 21f. Veterinary Hospital.

stone caps on the wall buttresses, the medium-sized elements such as windows, and larger volumetric elements is progressive, rhythmic and satisfying. There is a subtle relationship between the operating room's large window with its segmental arch, the textured wall above it, and the overarching, stepped gable with its minor curves outlined against the sky. Using a simplification of Pittman's Milbank curved gable as an agriculture signifier, Taylor had broken what might have been a blocky hunk into a lyrical triadic mass. It was a small building of large distinction.

THE BRICK BARNS

Washington's death in November 1915 led to an outpouring of attention from the many who admired him. Camera manufacturer George Eastman was among the most generous. His gifts had started in 1902 when, after reading *Up From Slavery*, he donated $5,000 that he then doubled to an annual $10,000. Eastman memorialized Washington's death with a $250,000 matching grant to be applied to projects the Principal had wanted. Washington's last report asked for two new dormitories (eventually given by others) and for moving the farm center. An undated note among the Low papers also mentions a matching gift scheme directed to small donors in order to purchase Washington's birth cabin.

A photo that Washington had published in 1900 identified the squared log hut along with two later boyhood homes.[178] Eastman would also fund the photography division that Washington had long wanted. In 1924, Eastman awarded $30 million to be divided among MIT, the University of Rochester, Hampton, and Tuskegee. The latter's share would help build the College Department.[179] But even with the outpouring, construction of the brick barns was delayed until 1917–18 for the Dairy Barn and 1917-1921 for the Horse Barn. Both barns had steel windows, therefore, flat lintels without Taylor's typical rhythmic variations. Their visual appeal depends on the curving gables, assemblages of stone-capped wall buttresses, and the overall proportions, the last being Taylor's strongest design tool. Drawings and blueprints for the Horse Barn, dated January and March 1917, are initialed by drawing room instructor Louis Persley, as supervisor. The drawings themselves would be by students. That for the long west elevation shows three different gables marking the building's three parts: a straight-edged gable for the long north wing that housed vehicles, a curving central gable for the central animal stalls, and a simpler curved gable for the southern wing with its office, classroom, and feed, harness and other storage spaces. Soldiers stationed at Tuskegee for war-time technical training did some of the Dairy Barn construction. The Horse Barn was recently demolished in part for the construction of a multistory building, but the outer skin was left intact as the ground floor of the new building's enclosure. The Dairy Barn was taken down some years after a fire.

22. ELLEN CURTISS JAMES HALL

The Taylor & Persley buildings more than those of the Washington era slipped into the scene with little fanfare because Principal Robert R. Moton did not focus on them as engines of racial advancement that proved an idea. For Moton, construction and race theory took a back seat to other institutional efforts.

Arthur Curtiss James gave the first Moton era dormitory, naming it to honor his mother, who had given Hampton a boys' dormitory. James was an heir of the Phelps Dodge mining fortune and, as well, the family's abolitionist background and philanthropic reach. He inherited $26 million in 1916. Tuskegee dedicated the dormitory in May 1921, concurrent with the Horse Barn and the five new trades buildings that replaced Taylor's complex.[180] Set near the hospital—it would shelter nursing students among others—at the north end of the long valley, James Hall had a rear veranda to take advantage of the valley views, as did Tantum.

Unlike Taylor's earlier dormitories, James Hall had dormer-lit bedrooms in the attic and an Arts and Crafts styling with exposed rafter ends and paired brackets under the horizontal beam on which the rafters rested. The four levels of bedrooms lend it a more institutional flavor than the two-story buildings of the Washington era. James housed 135 girls in 50 bedrooms and had three sitting rooms and three baths. It has been gutted and rebuilt within.

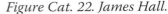

Figure Cat. 22. James Hall.

23. SAGE HALL

Blueprints dated 1922 that remain in the Physical Facilities Department show a rich array of community rooms for this boys' dormitory. There were laundry and storage facilities in the basement, boys' and teachers' reception rooms on the main floor along with guest rooms with private baths, and a recreation room and YMCA office on the third. Like James Hall, there are dormer-lit attic bedrooms on the fourth level and, again like James, the exterior is styled in an Arts and Crafts vein with exposed rafters resting on horizontal beams that are visually supported by paired brackets. The *Manufacturer's Record* for July 26, 1924, announced a four-story boys' dormitory costing $85,000 using student builders. Students in brickmasonry and geometry were working on it in January 1925 and it was "almost completed" that August.[181] Dedication was February 1926.

In 1907, shortly after her husband's death, Margaret Olivia Slocum Sage created the Russell Sage Foundation for social science research. She was seventy-eight when she inherited her husband's railroad and banking fortune and she applied it to philanthropy as fast as she could. By 1915, when she died, she had dispensed an estimated $23 million on a variety of enterprises including Forest Hills Gardens, New York, which was meant to show developers that neighborhoods designed to the British garden suburb model could yield profits. Sage Hall has been gutted and rebuilt inside and now houses girls.

Below, Figure Cat. 23a. Sage Hall. Right, Figure Cat. 23b. Sage Hall Entrance.

24. CHAMBLISS CHILDREN'S HOUSE

As a "normal school" from its inception, Tuskegee always had a "model," "practice," or "training" school so that students could teach under supervision and faculty children could have the best in primary education. In 1881, soon after arriving, Washington arranged for Hampton graduates to staff the town's black public school and for this or perhaps another to follow the institute to the Bowen farm, landing in a former stable. It reputedly held 250 children, many of whom may have registered but been unable to attend on a regular basis.[182] Sometime in the 1890s, the institute's own practice school was relocated to a purpose-built, L-plan building with a gable roof and a cupola. Photographed by Frances Benjamin Johnston in 1902 [Figure 4.8], it stood in the southern end of the valley that separated the newer western campus from the old center.

Figure Cat. 24a. Children's House.

Looking like a normative country school but better maintained, the dark trim that contrasts with the white surfaces is how Taylor achieved crispness in wood buildings rather than brick. There is no hint of the coming horizontal massing, the banks of double-hung windows, and the low, often hipped roofs that would characterize Tuskegee's later rural school projects, including those funded by Julius Rosenwald that chapter 7 discussed.[183]

Washington's school-building ambitions expanded in size, programming, and image as did the institute itself. By June 1900, the *Southern Letter* was calling for a new building for 174 students. The following year Taylor told Washington that he had started construction at a site chosen by John H. Washington and himself without the Executive Council's approval, perhaps because it was not on campus. Washington must be sure to see it. Two days later construction was halted for shortages of materials because of ongoing demands for the Carnegie Library, Pinehurst Hospital, and Slater-

Armstrong Agricultural Building extensions.[184] The new practice school eventually arrived as the picturesque Children's House with its three acres of gardens cresting a hill in the residential area. It was south by southwest of the fourth Emery dormitory. The sprawling one-story H-plan structure, partially funded by a gift of $2,000 from Mrs. Quincy Shaw of Boston, was dedicated in November 1901. It flew a U.S. flag that had been sent from New Bedford, Massachusetts, a city with abolitionist credentials.[185] This is where Julius Rosenwald spent time when he visited in 1911 before deciding to help build rural schools himself.[186]

The Children's House had classrooms, of course, but also three "model" rooms for teaching housekeeping. There were also rooms for manual training and drawing, not unlike the contemporaneous facilities at the Hillside Home School in Spring Green, Wisconsin, that Frank Lloyd Wright designed for the offspring of prosperous mid-westerners. At Hillside, both boys and girls learned housekeeping and gardening. The Children's House's kindergarten was founded slightly after Hampton's Whittier kindergarten and also after Alabama's first two white kindergartens. Tuskegee kindergarteners celebrated the movement's founder Friedrich Froebel's birthday and, simultaneously, it honored carpenters and

Figure Cat. 24b. Chambliss Children's House.

their role in protecting the family. Carpenters build "houses of different dimensions. . . with Building Gifts, which develop the ideas of high and low, large and small, wide and narrow." Froebel's "Gifts" were blocks or other materials in primary colors and geometries. They are widely known today because Frank Lloyd Wright celebrated their powers. Taylor was traveling to and from Cleveland when the Children's House was built, and while he designed most Tuskegee buildings of the era, clear documentation on this one has not yet surfaced.

Tuskegee's final primary school, the Chambliss Children's House of 1929-1930, later the Business House, is a 16,584 square-foot brick building set within the campus. The campus location put it closer to the Veterans Hospital, a vast institution next to the institute that had multiplied the area's black professionals who would want the best for their young. The name honored William V. Chambliss, a Tuskegee graduate who has been described as one of the wealthiest Negroes in east central Alabama. Chambliss earned a Tuskegee diploma in 1890, taught in public schools elsewhere, and then took charge of the institute dairy herd. He became an independent farmer and then stockholder in and

Figure Cat. 24c. Chambliss Children's House Entrance.

superintendent of the Hampton-based Southern Improvement Company. Financed by Robert C. Ogden and William H. Baldwin Jr., the developers helped sharecroppers buy small farms. The Chambliss-led Alabama unit purchased 4,000 acres next to an adjunct Tuskegee farm, dividing it into forty- to eighty-acre parcels and selling them on long-term, low-interest loans. It built about seventy cottages as part of the process. Washington once said that Chambliss could produce "fifty times as much cotton with a pen as with a hoe," his point being that the world did not care about how cotton is produced—or wealth is made—as long as it comes. The business entrepreneur, therefore, was as worthy as the farmer.[187] Chambliss died in 1928, leaving Tuskegee his Chambliss Block hotel and shops across from the Lincoln Gates and the rest of his estate.[188]

There are several sets of drawings for the Chambliss Children's House signed by Taylor & Persley, Architects and dated February or April 1929. The second version of the April set has the stucco-filled roundels flanking the entry rather than the inscribed square panels on the first April set. Both April versions have "Miller Wardrobes," as they are inscribed, that are shallow stage-like recesses in a classroom wall with hooks for students' wraps. They are framed to suggest a proscenium stage or, taking in the cabinetry built into the walls, a colonial fireplace wall. The building uses modern materials such as hollow tile partitions and banked groups of steel-framed windows that face either east or west. The teachers' desks would be on the south or north so that the windows stay on the student's left side—writing right arms should not shadow the paper, as Chapter 7 discusses.

Taylor & Persley's classicizing entrance had a visual strength that compensates for the repetitious window shapes and the machine made, evenly colored and smoothly textured bricks. The windows were grouped in twos on each side of the entrance, then fours, then sixes, and then fours again to light classrooms on each side of the double-loaded corridor. These vary the rhythm in a way that compensates for the uniform shape. The portico is a *serliana*, also termed a "Venetian" or "Palladian" opening, a form that bears a high classical sophistication. A central arch rests on Tuscan columns that are flanked by openings with flat lintels or architraves that are also the base of the arch. It is far more ambitious an entrance than others among the Rosenwald schools. The Chambliss Children's House follows Rosenwald schools precisely in the classroom orientation to the cardinal directions. It also gains from Taylor's Palladio-honed five-part composition. The ends step forward, each under their own gable, to embrace the spreading wings that, in turn, embrace the *serliana* centerpiece. A school bell is above it all, silhouetted against the sky.

Miraculously, it seems, the Chambliss Children's House interior has survived intact until, as of this writing, 2011. It is the best preserved of any pre-World War II Tuskegee structure and the best preserved Taylor interior other than The Oaks. There were seven graded classrooms, two extra or "practice" classrooms, and a double-sized kindergarten room with its own fireplace and bathrooms. The classrooms, with their Miller Wardrobes, still had stretches of original blackboards and cork display panels. The stucco wall surfaces remained unimpaired, their particular roughness so engaging that the same substance in the entrance roundels seems to announce a theme. The basic classroom bar building is 250 feet long with the entrance lobby breaking through the long corridor to where the participant could step down, ceremonially, into the auditorium on the entrance's axis. This last, the stem of an upside-down "T," was a 600-seat hall with a stage, a splendidly proportioned explosion of high, light-drenched space. Banks of variously sized windows on the north and south dissolve the walls. The rough-cast surfaces around them reach above the exposed steel trusses that support a gabled roof. One saw spatial grandeur rather than a dropped ceiling that would hide the engaging structural works.

Charles H. Gibson Jr., Taylor's assistant director of Mechanical Industries and the building's construction supervisor, attended elementary school in the predecessor Children's House.[189] Gibson and William V. Chambliss proved between them that Tuskegee could truly build on its success, its own graduates.

25. THE COLLEGE CAMPUS: LOGAN HALL, FRISSELL LIBRARY, AND ARMSTRONG SCIENCE HALL

The *Manufacturer's Record* for March 6, 1930, announced that Taylor & Persley would design a $500,000 auditorium and gymnasium—the future Logan Hall—along with a library and a science building at $250,000 each. Principal Robert Russa Moton contracted in October with the architects and with the black-owned T. C. Windham Construction Company of Birmingham.[190] Taylor was invested in this firm and may have been an officer. The March announcement suggests that the Taylor & Persley college plan discussed in Chapter 8, which showed the auditorium/gymnasium on its eventual site but not the library or science building on theirs, had changed. The buildings were to be of steel frame or reinforced concrete construction. Of the four subcontractors, two were black-owned firms. Thirty-one Tuskegee masons, carpenters and electricians contributed their skills. The rough-textured bricks with their varied coloring looked like Tuskegee's self-made ones but were not.[191] The Tuskegee brickyard had closed around 1920 when William Gregory retired. Logan Auditorium partially opened January 9, 1931 and was finished the following summer. The name honored the forty-two-year service of Hampton-educated Warren Logan, treasurer and acting principal to Washington and Moton. Logan retired in 1924 but remained on the board until his death in 1942, another of Tuskegee's unsung talents.[192]

Logan Hall is a complex structure that successfully merged athletic and entertainment facilities. The clear-span main space of 76 by 109 feet was a maple-floored gym ringed by two levels of balconies. The two upper levels of small windows in

Figure Cat. 25a. Logan Hall.

the building's facade and sides open above them. The small windows punctuating massive fields of brick with widely-spaced wall buttresses have a vaguely military air, like an armory. Inside, there was a raised stage with a corresponding step-down space beneath for storing auditorium chairs. In its auditorium mode, the floor and the balconies could seat 3,514. Logan was a center of Tuskegee social life for decades with its first-run movies, famous musicians, and intercollegiate basketball games. The ground floor, which was below grade at the entrance but emerging at the sides and rear, had showers and lockers for boys and girls, classrooms, fencing and boxing rooms, a broadcasting studio, and, under the stage and chair-room, a thirty by sixty foot swimming pool. This level connected at the rear to the Alumni Bowl, built from August 1924 to October 1925 under landscape architect David A. Williston's supervision.

The "Washington Gymnasium and Auditorium" plaque shown in drawings for what was later named for Warren Logan honored not Booker T. but rather James B. Washington, his adoptive younger brother, who systematized athletics in the 1890s and organized a football match between Tuskegee and Atlanta University in 1894. In 1926 Taylor, then Vice Principal, and his youngest son Henry were among the hundred fifty Tuskegeans on a special train to Philadelphia to join 35,000 others to watch Tuskegee trounce Lincoln University at the University of Pennsylvania's Franklin Field. The train had three Pullman cars, two coaches, and dining and baggage cars for the teams, band, and supporters. It stopped at stations along the way to greet alumni who had gathered.[193] Surely this was institutional triumph, a high-end, on-the-road celebration.

Logan Hall serves as the base of a U-shaped plan that opens onto the public road and the early campus across it. The Frissell (now Ford) Library stands on the west side of the quadrangle and the Armstrong Science Hall on the east side to form a courtyard that, in its generalized breadth and lack of arboreal articulation, is a weaker form than the girls quadrangle that had emerged some two decades before. The east and west structures are three stories high and 50,000 to 60,000 square feet in size. Brief dedication accounts in the Tuskegee press no longer linger on construction history or student and donor involvement as did such reports in the Washington era, but they do introduce the two Hampton principals for whom the buildings were named. Hollis Burke Frissell, a former chaplain, was Hampton's second principal, succeeding Samuel Chapman Armstrong, as Moton succeeded Washington. A dedication address suggests a parallel between Armstrong and Washington as their schools' "founders" with Frissell and Moton as their "builders." Both institutions were moving on.

Armstrong Hall, which had an auditorium, laboratories and classrooms for English, history, and other college-level subjects, had a more ar-

Figure Cat. 25b. Armstrong Science Building.

ticulated classical façade, with a stepped brick pediment behind a stone triangular one, and major orders—engaged columns or single and double pilasters—binding the upper floors. In late 1931 the Cincinnati consulting engineers Fosdick and Hilmer contracted 200 tons of structural steel from the Southern Steel Works of San Antonio for this building. Frissell Library, with pilasters on the two upper floors but not the hint of triadic massing and central emphasis of the facing Armstrong, had modern library facilities, a gallery, museum, archives, a special collection of black history, and the invaluable lynching records that sociologist Monroe N. Work had amassed. Its April 1933 dedication included an exhibition of African American art but there was no mention of the black architects, contractors, and craftsmen who designed and built it.[194] In 2001 it was gutted, rebuilt within, and renamed the Ford Motor Company Library.

Notes

Notes to the Introduction

1 Short biographies of 168 black architects are in Dreck Spurlock Wilson, ed., *African-American Architects, A Biographical Dictionary, 1865–1945* (New York and London, 2004). See also Karen E. Hudson, *Paul R. Williams, Architect, a Legacy of Style* (New York, 1993); David Vassar Taylor with Paul Clifford Larson, *Cap Wigington, An Architectural Legacy in Ice and Stone* (St. Paul, 2002); and Allen R. Durough, *The Architectural Legacy of Wallace A. Rayfield, Pioneer Black Architect of Birmingham, Alabama* (Tuscaloosa, 2010).

2 Mentor A. Howe, "Come to the Fair!" *Phylon, the Atlanta University Review of Race and Culture* 1, no. 4 (1940): 314–22. Paul Williams, "I Am a Negro," *American Magazine* 124, no. 1 (July 1937): 59, 161–63. Karen E. Hudson, *The Will and the Way, Paul R. Williams, Architect* (New York, 1994), 32.

Notes to Chapter 1

1 David Bryant Fulton [pseud. Jack Thorne], *Hanover, or the Persecution of the Lowly* (M.C.L. Hill, 1900), 133.

2 Booker T. Washington, *The Story of the Negro* (New York, 1909), 2: 81.

3 Robert R. Taylor to Charles Taylor, 28 September 1929, Taylor files, Tuskegee Archives.

4 I am grateful to Henry Louis Gates Jr., genealogist Johni Cerny, and Kathy Reed for census and other data on Henry Taylor's and Emily Still's records and to Dr. Louise King Sindos, Sarah Louise's granddaughter, for family history. For the Taylor family in Wilmington see also Gina White, "Historic Family to Reunite," *Wilmington Morning Star*, June 18, 1986; "A Descendant of Henry Taylor in First Family Reunion July 4 Weekend," *Wilmington Journal*, July 3, 1986; and William M. Reaves, "Strength through Struggle," *The Chronological and Historical Record of the African-American Community in Wilmington, North Carolina, 1865–1950* (Wilmington, NC, 1998), 471–72. A studio photograph of Henry Taylor is in Catherine W. Bisher, Charlotte V. Brown, Carl R. Lounsbury, Ernest H. Wood III, *Architects and Builders in North Carolina: A History of the Practice of Building* (Chapel Hill, 1990), 266.

5 Both parents are listed as mulatto in the 1880 census. Taylor does not refer to his mother in his personal papers. Her Fayetteville birthplace is on son John E. Taylor's death certificate, a copy of which is in the Bill Reaves Collection, Hanover County Public Library. In the 1850 census, the Fayetteville household of Richard Still (34) and Maria (36) included Edward Still (8) and Emily Artis (16). Next door resided Prisa Artis (58) and a boy, J. H. Artis (12). Prisa is listed as black but the others as mulatto.

6 Three-page, third-person typescript biography of c.1924, annotated in Taylor's hand. Taylor files, Tuskegee Archives.

7 Robert C. Kenzer, *Enterprising Southerners: Black Economic Success in North Carolina, 1865–1915* (Charlottesville, VA, 1997), 118.

8 Photo in Tony P. Wrenn, *Wilmington, North Carolina, An Architectural and Historical Portrait* (Charlottesville, VA, 1984), 214.

9 There is extensive work on African American builders in Wrenn, *Wilmington*. See also, Catherine W. Bisher, Charlotte V. Brown, Carl R. Lounsbury, Ernest H. Wood III, *Architects and Builders in North Carolina: A History of the Practice of Building* (Chapel Hill, 1990); Catherine W. Bisher, "Black Builders in Antebellum North Carolina," *The North Carolina Historical Review* LXI (October 1984), reprinted in Catherine W. Bishir, *Southern Built: American Architecture, Regional Practice* (Charlottesville, 2006), chapter 3. See also Catherine W. Bishir, *The Bellamy Mansion, Wilmington, North Carolina* (Raleigh, 2004); Reaves, "Strength through Struggle"; and Nancy N. Beeler, "Solomon Nash," *Lower Cape Fear Historical Society Bulletin* 38, no. 1 (May 1994). See also Edward F. Turberg's research in Clifton Daniel, "Made by Black Hands," *Wilmington Sunday News Star*, February 20, 1994.

10 Frederick Law Olmsted, *A Journey in the Back Country* (New York, 1860), 180–81.

11 Fulton, *Hanover*, 7.

12 Taylor to Washington, 4 August 1902, reel 207. For the Wilmington insurrection see David S. Cecelski and Timothy B. Tyson, eds., *Democracy Betrayed: The Wilmington Race Riot of 1898 and Its Legacy* (Chapel Hill, 1998); H. Leon Prather, *We Have Taken a City: Wilmington Racial Massacre and Coup of 1898* (Cranbury, NJ, 1984); and the 1898 Wilmington Race Riot Commission, "Final Report, May 31, 2006" (PDF) http://www.ah.dcr.state.nc.us/1898-wrrc/report/report.htm.

13 Author interview, Taylor grandniece Josephine Cooper, 18 September 2006. For the letter from John E. Taylor, see Robert Taylor to Washington, 4 August 1902, reel 207, Washington Papers, Manuscript Division, Library of Congress (hereafter, LC). Unattributed reels and boxes throughout the Notes are from this source. Because my reading of the Booker T. Washington Papers straddled microfilming, some references are to boxes and some are to reels.

14 The siblings living at home in 1880 were John Edward, twenty-three and a railroad agent; his wife, Lida, twenty-two; Anna Maria or Mariah, a twenty-year-old teacher; Sarah Louise, fifteen; and Robert Robinson, thirteen. Anna Maria as well as John E. had studied at Howard University, according to family tradition. She would marry the Howard-educated physician James F. Shober, who established a Wilmington practice. Sarah Louise would marry lumber merchant John Whiteman. See also "The Henry Taylor Family History," *Wilmington Journal*, July 3, 1986; Gina White, "Historic Family to Reunite," *Wilmington Morning Star*; and Reaves, "*Strength through Struggle*," 465–66, 472.

15 Josephine Cooper shared an early twentieth-century photograph of the house. Standing in front are John E. and Lida Taylor, their grown daughters, and Robert R. Taylor and his two eldest children, Robert Rochon (b. 1899) and Helen.

16 114 North Eighth Street. See Lene Watson, "The House that Henry Built," *Wilmington Coast* (Spring 1993): 49–55. This is a two-story frame structure with eave brackets, a type that Tony P. Wrenn has dubbed the "Wilmington Plain Style." Wrenn, *Wilmington*, 111, 507.

17 H. Leon Prather Sr., "We Have Taken a City: A Centennial Essay," in Cecelski and Tyson, eds., *Democracy Betrayed*, 17.

18 Wrenn, *Wilmington*, 193–94, and Reaves, "*Strength through Struggle*," 22–23.

19 Wrenn, *Wilmington*, 90, 179.

20 Bishir, *The Bellamy Mansion*, 28.

21 Joe M. Richardson, *Christian Reconstruction: The American Missionary Association and Southern Blacks, 1861–1890* (Athens, Ga., 1986), 65.

22 Fulton, *Hanover*, 92.

23 George A. Woodward, Gregory Normal Institute (New York, c. 1902) See also Wrenn, *Wilmington*, 264–65, and Reaves "*Strength through Struggle*," 164–66.

24 Robert R. Taylor to William H. Johnson, president of Lincoln University, 12 September 1929, Taylor files, Tuskegee Archives. For Lincoln University see Raymond Wolters, *The New Negro on Campus, Black College Rebellions in the 1920s* (Princeton, 1975), 178–80.

25 Reaves, "*Strength through Struggle*," 465–66, 473. Shober was descended from educated, Moravian-owned slaves.

26 Taylor to Johnson, 12 September 1929, Taylor files, Tuskegee Archives.

27 Three-page typescript biography, c.1924, in Taylor files, Tuskegee Archives.

28 Diane Cobb Cashman, personal communication, 17 February 1994; see also Diane Cobb Cashman, *Headstrong, the Biography of Amy Morris Bradley, 1823–1904: A Life of Noblest Usefulness* (Wilmington, NC, 1990), 225–26.

29 J. B. MacRae, a black Wilmingtonian, wrote a eulogy for Taylor that remains in his files in the Tuskegee Archives.

30 For Hugh MacRae (1865–1951), see William S. Powell, ed., *Dictionary of North Carolina Biography* (Chapel Hill, 1979–1996); R. H. Fisher, *Biographical Sketches of Wilmington Citizens* (Wilmington, NC, 1929), 64–66; and Emma Woodward MacMillan, *Wilmington's Vanished Homes and Buildings* (Raleigh, 1966), 63–64.

NOTES TO CHAPTER 2

1 Taylor to E. J. Scott, 7 April 1911, box 601.

2 *Technique 1890* (Boston, 1889), 58.

3 Taylor's granddaughter Ann Dibble Cook to Dreck S. Wilson, (c. 1980).

4 Kimberly Alexander, personal communication, 25 October 1994.

5 See Clarence G. Williams, "From 'Tech' to Tuskegee: The Life of Robert Robinson Taylor, 1868–1942," <http://libraries.mit.edu/archives/mithistory/blacks-at-mit/taylor.html>.

6 For Ware and architectural education at MIT see Caroline Shillaber, *Massachusetts Institute of Technology School of Architecture and Planning, 1861–1961: A Hundred Year Chronicle* (Cambridge, MA, 1963), 24–31; Mary N. Woods, *From Craft to Profession, The Practice of Architecture in*

Nineteenth-Century America (Berkeley, 1999), 68–70; and J. A. Chewning, "William Robert Ware at MIT and Columbia," *Journal of Architectural Education* 33, no. 2 (November 1979), 25–29. The curriculum was detailed in "Architectural Education in the United States I: The Massachusetts Institute of Technology," *American Architect and Building News* 24, no. 658 (4 August 1888): 47–49.

7   Clarence G. Williams, "From 'Tech' to Tuskegee," 2.

8   Samuel C. Prescott, *When M.I.T. Was "Boston Tech" 1861–1916* (Cambridge, 1954), 98.

9   Nellie C. Taylor to Dr. Karl Compton, President of MIT, 21 December 1942, Taylor file, MIT Museum.

10   *Technique 1890*, 152. Yearbooks were published a year after the class's graduation, so this would honor an earlier class.

11   Ibid.

12   From a Course IV description regularly printed in *Technology Architectural Review*, a MIT publication.

13   *The American Architect and Building News* 24, no. 658 (4 August 1888): 46.

14   *Technology Architectural Review* 1 (15 June 1888) reported that "the architecture library would be on the third floor of the new building now under construction on Copley Square." The New Building replaced the Annex that was razed in 1886.

15   Photograph 4036, MIT Museum.

16   A textbook notice for the Garnier Freres, Paris, edition, of "Vignola," with 72 plates and priced at $3, appeared in the *Technology Architecture Review* (31 May 1890). The Cori drawings were by Emmanuel Brune. Two students edited the journal from 1887 to 1890, when they graduated. They then inaugurated *The Architectural Review*, a professional journal. For Ware's drawing collection and pedagogy, see pamphlet by Kimberly Alexander Shilland, "Drawings at Work" (MIT Museum, n.d.). For the Boston campus, see Samuel C. Prescott, *When M.I.T Was 'Boston Tech,' 1861–1916* (Cambridge, MA, 1954).

17   For the history of this development, see Prescott, *When MIT was 'Boston Tech,'* 135–39, and Mark Jarzombek, *Designing MIT: Bosworth's New Tech* (Boston, 2004), 9.

18   MIT Museum photo AR 231.

19   MIT Museum photo 2212.

20   Labeled plans of the Architectural Building are in a scrapbook at MIT Museum.

21   Henry Lewis Johnson, *Photogravure Views of the Mass. Institute of Technology* (Boston, 1889).

22   E. J. Scott, "Training Head and Hand," *Tuskegee Student* 20 (April 1901).

23   Dreck S. Wilson interviewed Taylor descendants around 1980.

24   Richard O. Card, personal communication, 16 December 1994.

25   Robert R. Taylor, "The Scientific Development of the Negro," in *Technology and Industrial Efficiency* (New York, 1911), 169.

26   F. D.Patterson to Nellie Taylor, December 1942 or January 1943, Taylor files, Tuskegee Archives; Dorothy Taylor, personal communication, 1 November 1993. Other sources allude to a Cleveland episode after MIT but before Tuskegee: *National Cyclopedia of the Colored Race, 1919*, 494. (A typescript draft is in Taylor's files, Tuskegee Archives); obituary in the *Wilmington Star News*, December 20, 1942, clipping in Taylor files, Tuskegee Archives. A posthumous narrative claims that Taylor had been invited to join a schoolmate in a firm that his friend's father would set up in the state of Washington. ("National Negro Health Week" radio script, 3 April 1946, Taylor files, Tuskegee Archives.)

27   Clarence Williams,"From 'Tech' to Tuskegee," 4.

28   The typescript press release, probably from the mid-1920s, is in the Taylor files in the Tuskegee Archives. It is inscribed for a publisher at the top of the page in Taylor's hand. Drafts of several third person press releases that are corrected in Taylor's hand are in Taylor's files, Tuskegee Archives.

29   Taylor to Washington, 20 June and 2 August 1892, reel 111.

Notes to Chapter 3

1   Booker T. Washington, *Up From Slavery* (New York, 1901), 108.

2   See Samuel R. Spencer Jr., *Booker T. Washington and the Negro's Place in American Life* (Boston, 1955), 118, and Louis R. Harlan, *Booker T. Washington: The Making of a Black Leader, 1856–1901* (New York, 1972), 111. Harlan's *Booker T. Washington: The Wizard of Tuskegee, 1901–1915* (New York, 1983), and Harlan et. al, eds., *The Booker T. Washington Papers*, 14 volumes (Urbana, IL, 1972–1984), hereafter Harlan, ed., *BTWP*, are also essential.

3   "Booker T. Washington to Friends, 4 July 1881" as reprinted in "Tuskegee Institute Centennial Celebration and Sixty-fourth Anniversary Founder's Day Observance, 1981" (pamphlet). See also *Southern Workman* 10, no. 9 (September 1881), and Anson Phelps Stokes, *Tuskegee Institute, the First Fifty Years* (Tuskegee, 1931), 60–61.

4   William Archer, *Through Afro-America* (New York, 1910), 404.

5 Barbara Burlison Mooney, "The Comfortable Tasty Framed Cottage: An African-American Architectural Iconography," *Journal of the Society of Architectural Historians* 61, no. 1 (March 2002): 49.

6 For early Hampton see Helen W. Ludlow, "The Hampton Normal and Agricultural Institute," *Harper's New Monthly Magazine* 47 (October 1873): 672–85; Francis Greenwood Peabody, *Education for Life, The Story of Hampton Institute* (New York, 1919): 109, 128, 134–35; and Robert Francis Engs, *Educating the Disfranchised and Disinherited: Samuel Chapman Armstrong and Hampton Institute, 1839–1893* (Knoxville: 1999). For buildings and planning see Paul R. Baker, *Richard Morris Hunt* (Cambridge, 1980); Charles E. Brownell, Calder Loth, William Rasmussen, and Richard Guy Wilson, *The Making of Virginia Architecture* (Richmond, 1992) 308–9; John Taylor Boyd, Jr., "The Hampton Normal and Agricultural Institute, Hampton, Va.," *Architectural Record* 46 (August 1919): 123–32; and John H. Spencer, "Hampton Institute, Department of Architecture (1871)" in Dreck S. Wilson, ed., *African American Architects, A Biographical Dictionary 1865–1945* (New York, 2004), 183–86.

7 Paul R. Baker, *Richard Morris Hunt* (Cambridge, 1980), 192.

8 Washington, *Up From Slavery*, 51.

9 Robert Francis Engs, *Freedom's First Generation, Black Hampton, Virginia, 1861–1898* (Philadelphia, 1979), 244.

10 Baker, *Richard Morris Hunt*, 193.

11 Richard K. Dozier, "Black Architects and Craftsmen," *Black World* 26 (May 1974): 9–11, and "Tuskegee: Booker T. Washington's Contribution to the Education of Black Architects," (Arch. D. diss., University of Michigan, 1990), 41. See also E. J. Scott, "Training Head and Hand," *Tuskegee Student* (20 April 1901), which is also published as "The New South Again," *The Colored American* 9, no. 51 (Washington, D.C., 6 April 1901).

12 The new name was the institute's third: Tuskegee State Normal School (1881–87), Tuskegee Normal School (1887–92), Tuskegee Normal and Industrial Institute (1892–1937), Tuskegee Institute (1937–85), and Tuskegee University (1985–). The earliest campus description is in Helen Ludlow, ed., *Tuskegee Normal and Industrial School . . . Its Story and Its Songs* (Hampton, VA, 1884), 9–40. See also Washington, *Up From Slavery*; Max Bennett Thrasher, *Tuskegee, Its Story and Its Work* (Boston, 1900), chapter 4; and William Gregory, "A Student's Account of the School's Opening," in Anson Phelps Stokes, *Tuskegee Institute: The First Fifty Years* (Tuskegee, 1931). The definitive modern account remains Harlan, *The Making of a Black Leader*. See also Dozier, "Tuskegee;" and L. Albert Scipio II, *Pre-War Days at Tuskegee: Historical Essay on Tuskegee Institute, 1881–1943* (Silver Spring, MD, 1987).

13 Booker T. Washington, "The Educational Outlook in the South" (1884), in E. Davidson Washington, ed., *Selected Speeches of Booker T. Washington* (Garden City, NY, 1932), 2.

14 Booker T. Washington as quoted by Robert J. Norrell, *Up From History, The Life of Booker T. Washington* (Cambridge, MA, 2009), 62–63.

15 For Porter see Washington, *Up From Slavery*, 139–45, 159; *New York Evening Post*, 9 June 1885, reprinted in Harlan, ed., *BTWP* 2, 277–79; *Southern Workman* 11, no. 5 (May 1882); Warren Logan, "Resources and Material Equipment," in Washington, ed., *Tuskegee and Its People* (New York, 1905), 40; Harlan, *The Making of a Black Leader*, 137; Thrasher, *Tuskegee*, 42.

16 "Boys" and "girls" is Tuskegee usage even though photographs show students who look adult. The average age in the 1890s was eighteen and a half.

17 *Tuskegee Student*, 15 March 1906.

18 *Southern Letter*, October 1884.

19 *Southern Letter*, June and October 1884; Ludlow, ed., *Tuskegee*, 12–14, 37; Scipio, *Pre-War Days*, 35.

20 *Southern Letter*, June and July 1888; Booker T. Washington, *The Story of My Life and Work* (Toronto, 1901), 124–25; Scipio, *Pre-War Days*, 35.

21 *Southern Letter*, June 1888; repeated in Washington, *The Story of My Life*, 124–25; Logan, "Resources and Material Equipment," in Washington, ed., *Tuskegee and its People*, 40.

22 Ludlow, ed., *Tuskegee*, 13; Thrasher, *Tuskegee*, 30–31.

23 M. B. Thrasher, "Tuskegee Institute and Its President," *Appleton's Popular Science Monthly* LV (September 1899): 603.

24 Booker T. Washington, "Our New Citizen," in E. Davidson Washington, ed., *Selected Speeches*, 48.

25 Booker T. Washington, "The Educational Outlook in the South" (1884), in E. Davidson Washington, ed., *Selected Speeches*, 4.

26 Booker T. Washington, *The Story of the Negro: the Rise of the Race from Slavery* (New York, 1909), 64.

27 W. E. Burghardt. Du Bois, ed., *The Negro Artisan* (Atlanta, 1902), 13–21. See also Ira Berlin, *Slaves Without Masters, the Free Negro in the Antebellum South* (New York, 1974).

28 For brickmaking see Washington, *Up From Slavery*, 150–53; William Gregory, "A Student's Account of the

School's Opening" and J.F.B. Marshall, "Extract of Letter from General Marshall," both in Stokes, *Tuskegee Institute*, 62–68; and Donald E. Armstrong, Jr., "Brick Making and the Production of Place at the Tuskegee Institute," *Arris, The Journal of the Southeast Chapter of the Society of Architectural Historians* 15 (2005): 28–36. See also Harlan, *The Making of a Black Leader* 142–45; Dozier, "Tuskegee," 95–99; and Thrasher, *Tuskegee,* 79.

29 William Gregory, "A Student's Account," in Stokes, *Tuskegee Institute.*

30 Max Bennett Thrasher, *Tuskegee* (Boston, 1900), 143.

31 Booker T. Washington, "Mind and Matter," in James T. Haley, ed., *Afro-American Encyclopedia* (Nashville, 1896), 99.

32 Quoted by Ray Stannard Baker, *Following the Color Line; An Account of Negro Citizenship in the American Democracy* (New York, 1908), 221.

33 From E. Davidson Washington, ed., *Selected Speeches,* 43.

34 Washington, "Mind and Matter," 98.

35 Booker T. Washington, "The Virtue of Simplicity," in *Character Building* (New York, 1902), 35.

36 Washington, *Up From Slavery,*150.

37 Robert R. Taylor, "Brickyard," undated typescript (c. 1904), box 529. The brickyard and clay pits occupied 15 acres. The division was using two number 8 Brenner machines and two 20 by 75-foot drying sheds while producing two million bricks a year valued at around $15,000.

38 J.R.E. Lee in "Souvenir Program for the Exercise of Founders Days and the Fiftieth Anniversary of the Tuskegee Normal and Industrial Institute," April 12–14, 1931, Alabama Department of Archives and History, Simpson Records, LPR 76, box 2, folder 7; http://www.archives.state.al.us/timeline/1861/tuskegee.html.

39 *New York Evening Post*, June 9, 1885, in Harlan ed. *BTWP* 2, 278–79.

40 L.W.B. "Is He a New Negro," *Chicago Inter Ocean*, October 2, 1895, in Harlan, ed., *BTWP* 4, 35.

41 Elbert Hubbard, *A Little Journey to Tuskegee* (Tuskegee, nd.), 10, pamphlet reprinted from *The Philistine* (July 1904).

42 *Outlook* 100 (30 March 1912): 708.

43 Archer, *Through Afro-America*, 107–8, 110–11.

44 "Tuskegee's 25th Anniversary," *Voice of the Negro* 3, no. 5 (May 1906): 316.

45 Harlan, *The Wizard of Tuskegee*, 104–6.

46 Julia Ward Howe, "Atlanta University & Tuskegee, Largely Reminiscent," handwritten paper, November 1898, Julia Ward Howe Papers, container 2, Manuscript Division, Library of Congress.

47 William H. Holtzclaw, "A School Principal's Story," in Washington, ed., *Tuskegee and Its People*, 121.

48 Quoted by Joseph Citro, "Booker T. Washington's Tuskegee Institute: Black School-Community, 1900–1915," (D. Ed. diss. Univ. of Rochester, 1972): 408.

49 John W. Robinson, "Cotton-Growing in Africa," in Washington, ed., *Tuskegee and its People*, 190.

50 V. S. Naipaul, "Reflections: How the Land Lay," *The New Yorker*, 6 June 1988, 96.

51 Lewis A. Smith, "A Dairyman's Story," in Washington, ed., *Tuskegee and Its People*, 257–58.

52 Rash Behari Day, *My Days with Uncle Sam* (Dacca, 1919), 208.

53 Cleveland W. Eneas, *Tuskegee Ra! Ra! An Autobiography of My Youth* (Nassau, 1986,), vi, vii, viii, 12.

54 Russell C. Atkins, "Tuskegee's Vocational Program for Men," *Journal of Educational Sociology* VII, no. 3 (November 1933), 177.

55 Robert R. Moton, "Special Report of the Principal to the Board of Trustees, April 1930," p. 21, in Julius Rosenwald Fund Collection, Amistad Research Center, Tulane University.

56 Naipaul, "Reflections: How the Land Lay," 95.

57 Gregory, "A Student's Account," in Stokes, *Tuskegee Institute*, 65.

58 *Southern Letter*, June 1884.

59 *Southern Letter*, August 1886.

60 *Southern Letter*, January 1888.

61 John H. Washington to Booker T. Washington, 9 March 1890, in Harlan, ed., *BTWP* 3, 35.

62 Moses Pierce to Washington, 1 Nov. 1889, quoted in Harlan, *The Making of a Black Leader,* 145. Pierce, a friend of John Fox Slater, gave $200 for the initial land purchase plus money for tools, seeds and equipment.

63 *Southern Letter* and the *Tuskegee Student* for December 1889.

64 White-uniformed students are shown at work in Washington, ed., *Tuskegee and its People* (1905), opp. p. 254. After the opening of Milbank Agricultural Building in 1910, the brick creamery became a boys' dormitory, then the "alumni hut," and finally a theater until it was taken down in 1998 to expand a parking lot.

65 For the barracks see Harlan, ed., *BTWP* 2, 234, and *Taylor to Washington*, 31 December 1898, reel 144.

66 Booker T. Washington, *Working with the Hands*, 100–1.

67 *Southern Letter*, December 1886.

68 Washington, *Up From Slavery*, 55–56, and Harlan, ed., *BTWP* 3, 303.

69 Harlan, ed., *BTWP* 4, 521, and Washington, *Up From Slavery*, 306–10.

70 Harlan, ed., *BTWP* 8, 422. A list of 34 floats plus other photographs ready for purchase from Herbert P. Tresslar of Montgomery is in reel 262.

71 Robert G. Sherer, *Subordination or Liberation? The Development and Conflicting Theories of Black Education in Nineteenth Century Alabama* (University, AL, 1977), 145, and Emmett J. Scott and Lyman Beecher Stowe, *Booker T. Washington, Builder of a Civilization* (New York 1916), 158.

72 Max Bennett Thrasher, "The Tuskegee Negro Conference," *The Outlook* (March 1901): 483–87. For the conference see Allen W. Jones, "Improving Rural Life for Blacks: The Tuskegee Negro Farmers Conference," *Agricultural History* 65 (Spring 1991).

73 Scott and Stowe, *Booker T. Washington*, 144–45.

74 For John H. Washington see Booker T. Washington essay in *Tuskegee Student*, 17 January 1903. John H. drew as well as constructed Willow Cottage, the boy's hospital, Cassedy Hall, and the Steam Laundry. The Cassedy Hall cornerstone was laid on 28 May 1891 (*Southern Letter*, June 1891). The laundry was finished in October 1892, while the brick dairy was underway.

75 Booker T. Washington, "Extract from Address Delivered at Fisk University, Nashville, Tennessee, 1895," in E. Davidson Washington, ed., *Selected Speeches*, 38–39.

76 John H. Washington to Taylor, 30 December 1905, reel 530.

77 Rockham Holt, *George Washington Carver, An American Biography* (New York, 1943), 144. For John H. Washington (1852–1924) see *Tuskegee Student*, 17 January 1903; *Southern Letter* 24 (February 1924); and "Biographical Sketches of Persons Interred in the Tuskegee Institute Cemetery," 1983 typescript, Tuskegee Archives.

78 Alice J Kaine to Washington, 30 November 1895, in Harlan, ed., *BTWP* 4, 87. John H. suffered a nervous breakdown in 1915 when his brother died and retired on full salary. He died in 1924. See *Tuskegee Student* (March 1924).

79 See Jacqueline James, "Uncle Tom? Not Booker T," *American Heritage* XIV, no. 5 (August 1968): 51–100, which is based on Marquis James's unfinished biography.

80 See Lewis Flint Anderson, *History of Manual and Industrial School Education* (New York, 1926); Charles Alpheus Bennett, *History of Manual and Industrial Education, 1870–1917* (Peoria, 1937); and C.M. Woodward, *The Manual Training School* (Boston, 1906). For African Americans and industrial education see Berenice M. Fisher, *Industrial Education: American Ideals and Institutions* (Madison, 1967), 155–65; August Meier, "The Beginning of Industrial Education in Negro Schools," *Midwest Journal 7* (Spring 1955): 21–44, and *Negro Thought in America, 1880–1915: Racist Ideologies in the Age of Booker T. Washington* (Ann Arbor, 1963), 88–99; Donald Spivey, *Schooling for the New Slavery, Black Industrial Education 1868–1915* (Westport, CT, 1978); and Raymond Wolters, *The New Negro on Campus, Black College Rebellions of the 1920s* (Princeton,1975), 3–28.

81 Personal communication, Margaret Jinks Hall, 23 December 1993.

82 Robert Samuel Fletcher, *A History of Oberlin College from its Foundation Through the Civil War* (Oberlin, OH, 1943), 634, 635, 646.

83 "Integrated Education," *The American Monthly Review of Reviews* 23 (June 1901): 651.

84 Scott and Stowe, *Booker T. Washington*, 62–63.

85 Donald Generals, "Booker T. Washington and Progressive Education: An Experimentalist approach to curriculum development and reform" [sic], *Journal of Negro Education* 69, no. 3 (Summer 2000) 215–34; Bettina Berch, *The Woman Behind the Lens, the Life and Work of Frances Benjamin Johnston, 1864–1952* (Charlottesville, 2000), 46–56; Museum of Modern Art, The Hampton Album (New York, 1966).

86 Warren Logan, "Life in and Around the School From a Teacher's Standpoint," in Ludlow, ed., *Tuskegee Normal and Industrial School*, 20.

87 Booker T. Washington, "Unimproved Opportunities," 10 February 1895, in Harlan, ed., *BTWP* 3, 509.

88 Spivey, *Schooling for the New Slavery*, 54–59.

89 Wolters, *The New Negro on Campus*, 10–11.

90 Meier, "The Beginning of Industrial Education in Negro Schools," 21–44.

91 Augustus Field Beard, *A Crusade of Brotherhood: A History of the American Missionary Association* (Boston, 1909), 3–4.

92 *Proceedings of the Trustees of the John F. Slater Fund for the Education of Freedmen, 1893* (Baltimore, 1893), 13.

93 Three critics of industrial education for African Americans are Spivey, *Schooling for the New Slavery*; Sherer, *Subordination or Liberation?* 45–58, and James D. Anderson, *The Education of Blacks in the South, 1860–1935* (Chapel Hill, 1988).

94 Wolters, *The New Negro on Campus*, 7.

95 Harlan, ed., *BTWP* 3, 187.

96 C. M. Woodward to Washington, 2 June 1892, reel 111.

97 C. M. Woodward, "The Teacher of Tool Work," (undated National Education Association offprint) reel 112.

98 *Southern Letter*, October 1884.

99 *Southern Letter*, March 1888.

100 *Southern Letter,* May 1891.

101 Sign in 1906 Frances Benjamin Johnston photograph J694-417, Prints and Photographs Division, Library of Congress.

102 Gregory, "A Student's Account," in Stokes, *Tuskegee Institute*, 67.

103 Typed report, *Industrial Department, 1896–1897*, page 18, reel 206.

104 Dozier, "Tuskegee," 50.

105 James D. Anderson, *The Education of Blacks in the South, 1860–1935* (Chapel Hill, 1988), 156.

106 Booker T. Washington, "Mind and Matter," in *Afro American Encyclopedia* (1895), 96

107 *Southern Letter*, January 1887.

108 *Southern Letter,* May 1892.

109 Thrasher, *Tuskegee*, 143.

110 Harlan, ed., *BTWP* 3, 17; *Southern Letter*, September 1890.

111 Booker T. Washington, "Address Delivered at the Forty-third Annual Meeting of the National Education Association, 1904," in *Selected Speeches,* ed. E. Davidson Washington, 143.

112 *Southern Letter*, July 1900.

113 *Southern Letter*, January 1887, May 1892, January 1895, and December 1901.

114 Thrasher, *Tuskegee,* 131.

115 *Southern Letter*, April 1890; Thrasher, *Tuskegee,* 150; Monroe Work, *Industrial Work of Tuskegee Graduates and Former Students During the Year 1910* (Tuskegee, 1911), 24.

116 Washington, *Working with the Hands*, 225.

117 Gabriel B. Miller, "The Story of a Carpenter", in Washington, ed., *Tuskegee and Its People*, 178–79; *Southern Letter,* January 1902.

118 *Southern Letter,* February 1900; Citro, 486.

119 Donald P. Stone, *Fallen Prince: William James Edwards, Black Education, and the Quest for Afro-American Nationality* (Snow Hill, AL, 1989), 173. For a photograph, see Thomas Jesse Jones, ed., *Negro Education, A Study of the Private and Higher Schools for Colored People in the United States, vol. 1* (U.S. Department of Interior, Bureau of Education Bulletin 38-39, Washington D.C. 1916-1917) plate 33 B.

120 *Tuskegee Student*, 17 December 1921 and 1 November 1922. *Southern Letter*, November 1908.

121 Thrasher, *Tuskegee,* 140. Scott and Stowe, *Booker T. Washington*, 244–45; Work, *Industrial Work of Tuskegee Graduates* 33 and folio. The house built for John H. Washington next to Booker T.'s is similar to Jailous Perdue's Montgomery house but different from the Architectural Drawing Division's typical work. See Harlan, ed., *BTWP* 8, folio.

NOTES TO CHAPTER 4

1 *Southern Letter*, November 1892.

2 *Tuskegee Student*, April 20, 1901.

3 *Catalogue of the Tuskegee Normal and Industrial Institute,* 1894-5, 42; John Gilmer Speed, "The Tuskegee Plan," *Harpers Weekly* 39 (September 14, 1895), 876-879.

4 *Tuskegee Catalogue, 1901-1902.*

5 *Tuskegee Student,* April 20, 1901. This was also published on the front page of *The Colored American* (Washington, D.C.) 9, 51 (April 6, 1901) and probably elsewhere.

6 Robert R. Taylor, "The Scientific Development of the Negro," in *Technological and Industrial Efficiency* (New York, 1911), 169.

7 Speed, "The Tuskegee Plan," 876-879.

8 *Catalogue of the Tuskegee Normal and Industrial Institute,1894-1895*, 42-44.

9 *Southern Letter*, February 1894.

10 *Catalogue of the Tuskegee Normal and Industrial Institute, 1894-1895*, 90, and *Catalogue. . . 1896-1897*, 89-91.

11 Russell T. Atkins, "Tuskegee's Vocational Program for Men," *Journal of Educational Sociology* 7, no. 3, November 1933, 179.

12 W. E. Burghardt Du Bois, ed. *The Negro Artisan* (Atlanta, 1902), 7.

13 E. Davidson Washington, ed., *Selected Speeches of Booker T. Washington* (Garden City, NY, 1932), 67.

14 Du Bois, ed. *The Negro Artisan*, 104.

15 W. E. Burghardt Du Bois, and Augustus Granville Dill, eds., *The Negro American Artisan* (Atlanta, 1912).

16 Zach Watson Rice, "Claflin University: Educating African-Americans for Architecture and Building," paper delivered to the Society of Architectural Historians, 1994. R. Charles Bates, *The Elementary Principles of Architecture and Building* (Boston, 1892) is in Henry-Russell Hitchcock, *American Architectural Books, A List of Books, Portfolios and Pam-*

phlets on Architecture and Related Subjects Published in America Before 1895 (Minneapolis, 1962). See also Giles B. Jackson and D. Webster Davis, *The Industrial History of the Negro Race of the United States* (Richmond, 1908 and Freeport, N.Y., 1971), 120, and Ellen Weiss, *An Annotated Bibliography on African-American Architects and Builders* (Philadelphia, 1993), 12. See also Dreck Spurlock Wilson, "Robert Charles Bates (c1872-unknown)" and "Claflin University, Manual Training Department (1872)" in Wilson, ed. *African American Architects*, 28-29.

17 Rice, "Claflin University" 12.

18 Rice, "Claflin University," and Barbara Cook Williams, "William Wilson Cooke (1871-1949)" in Wilson, ed., *African American Architects*, 108-111.

19 *Proceedings of the John F. Slater Fund for the Education of Freedmen, 1895-1896*, 33, 34.

20 John H. Spencer, "Hampton Institute, Department of Architecture, in Wilson, ed., *African American Architects*, 184.

21 William Gregory, "A Student's Account," 67.

22 *Southern Letter*, August 1897. Portia Washington Pittman told Joseph Citro that her former husband helped lead a student revolt in 1897 but that Margaret Murray Washington saved him from expulsion. Joseph Citro, "Booker T. Washington's Tuskegee Institute: Black School-Community, 1900-1915," [D. Ed. Diss., Univ. Rochester 1973] 395. See also Susan G. Pearl "William Sidney Pittman (1875-1948)," in Wilson, ed., *African American Architects*, 319-321.) In November 1897 Pittman wrote to Washington on Drexel stationery to report his grades and ask for money for a coat. Reel 3.

23 Emmett J. Scott, "The New South Again," *The Colored American* 9:51 (April 6, 1901).

24 Washington, *Working with the Hands*, 76-77.

25 "Architectural Drawing at the Tuskegee Normal and Industrial Institute," *Architects and Builder's Magazine* 5 (May 1904) 377-378.

26 Dozier, "Tuskegee," 72; Monroe N. Work's record of five architects along with 33 blacksmiths, 56 brick masons, and 42 carpenters among the 347 industrial graduates, is in W. E. Burghardt DuBois and Augustus Granville Dill, eds. *The Negro American Artisan*, 123.

27 *Who's Who in Colored America, 1930-1932* (New York, 1933), 408-409; Monroe Work, *Industrial Work of Tuskegee Graduates and Former Students During the Year 1910* (Tuskegee, 1911) 29; "Vertner W. Tandy," (obituary) *New York Times*, November 8, 1949, 31. See also Carson A. Anderson, "Vertner Woodson Tandy (1889-1949)," in Wilson, ed., *African American Architects* 389-392, and

28 Dozier, "Tuskegee" 73.

28 Dozier, "Tuskegee"74, and Robert T. Coles, "John Edmonson Brent (1889-1962)" in Wilson, ed. *African American Architects*, 61-63.

29 Dozier, "Tuskegee," 74; Work, *Industrial Work of Tuskegee*, 29; Kerry Downs and Elizabeth Rosin, "Charles Sumner Bowman (c1873-unknown)," in Wilson, ed., *African American Architects*, 49-51.

30 J.A. Chewning, "William Robert Ware at MIT and Columbia," *Journal of Architectural Education* 33, 2 (November 1979) 29; and Mary N. Woods, *From Craft to Profession, the Practice of Architecture in Nineteenth Century America* (Berkeley 1999) 199.

31 See Betty Bird, "Thematic Study of African American Architects and Builders in Washington, D.C., Phase II," draft 1994; and Paul Kelsey Williams, "John Anderson Lankford (1874-1946)," in Wilson, ed. *African American Architects*, 253-256. See also *Who's Who of the Colored Race* (1915) and *Who's Who in Colored America* (1933). Dozier, "Tuskegee," 176-179, and Harrison Moseley Ethridge, *The Black Architects of Washington, D.C.: 1900 to Present* (D. Arts diss., The Catholic University, 1979), 15. Lankford published his work in *Report of Lankford's Artistic Church and Other Designs* (Atlanta, 1916 and Washington, D.C., 1924).

32 Members of the class of 1915 are available at http://www.afrigeneas.com/library/schoolrosters/Tuskegee/html.

33 See Thomas Tyler Potterfield, Jr. "Charles Thaddeus Russell (1875-1952)," in Wilson, ed. *African American Architects*, 364-365.

34 Dozier, "Tuskegee," 74, 77.

35 Wesley Howard Henderson, "Tuskegee Normal and Industrial Institute, Mechanical Industries department," in Wilson, ed., *African American Architects*.

36 *Southern Letter*, October 1914 and January 1915. I am grateful to Enrique Vivioni for the Puerto Rican registration information.

37 U.S.Census, 1900.

38 "Prize List for Senior Class," reel 581; *Southern Letter* November 1908.

39 The disassembled album, "Architectural and Mechanical Drawing, Tuskegee Normal and Industrial Institute" is in the Prints and Photographs Division of the Library of Congress.

40 Harlan, ed. *BTWP*, 4, 161.

41 Drexel Institute saved two Pittman drawings intended for the Paris exposition. One is a "large scale plan" of the institute library for which Pittman was paid. The other was a watercolor shown at the previous commencement

and purchased for permanent exhibition. (Pittman to Washington, November, 30 1899, reel 3.)

42 Arthur Ulysses Craig (1871-1959) must have added zest during his brief Tuskegee tenure. During one summer he studied the Sloyd woodworking for children at Naas, Sweden, and industrial education in London, Stockholm, and Goteberg. After leaving Tuskegee in 1901, he reportedly operated a poultry farm and dairy in Washington, D.C., served as principal of the Armstrong Manual Training Night School, began public playgrounds in D.C., advised on manual training in several cities, helped design an automobile, founded and designed a settlement house, and initiated turning Frederick Douglass's home into a museum "on the Mount Vernon model." Craig later moved to New York where he was a mechanic, draftsman, heating engineer, teacher, and editor of a Harlem newspaper. In 1932 Craig married Taylor's sister-in-law. See *Who's Who of the Colored Race,* 1915, 79-80, and Harlan, ed., *BTWP* 5, 431.

43 Dozier, "Tuskegee," 47-59.

44 John H. Washington report for 1896-1897 is in reel 206.

45 *Southern Letter,* March 1897.

46 See Charles L. Marshall, "The Evolution of a Shoemaker," in Washington, ed. *Tuskegee and Its People,* 347-354; and J. F. Banks, "Historical Summary of Christiansburg Institute," in Charles W. Crush, ed., *The Montgomery County Story, 1776-1957* (Jamestown, Va.), 1957), 135; and www.christiansburginstitute.org/btw. The second contract is in the *Tuskegee Student,* April 16, 1910.

47 John H. Washington to Booker T. Washington, 23 August 1895, reel 120.

48 *Proceedings of the Trustees of the John F. Slater Fund for the Education of Freedmen, 1896* (Baltimore, 1896), 22.

49 Taylor to Washington, 1897-1898 annual report, reel 144.

50 *Southern Letter* April 1898; Taylor to Warren Logan, 22 November 1898, reel 144.

51 *Southern Letter,* January and March 1897. For Mt. Meigs see Cornelia Bowen, "A Woman's Work," in Washington, ed., *Tuskegee and Its People* (New York, 1905), 22 and *Outlook* 58, 11 (March 12, 1898), 674-75.

52 *Southern Letter,* May and June 1894.

53 *Southern Letter* June 1893.

54 *Southern Letter,* February 1893. See also Thomas J. Calloway, "Booker Washington and the Tuskegee Institute," *New England Magazine,* XVII, 2 (October 1897) 144, and Allen W. Jones, "Improving Rural Life for Blacks: the Tuskegee Negro Farmers Conference," *Agricultural History* 65 (Spring 1991), 85-104.

55 *Southern Letter,* June 1893. Albert Shaw, "Negro Progress on the Tuskegee Plan," *Review of Reviews* (April 1894), 440; *Southern Letter,* November 1900.

56 Harlan, *The Wizard,* 213.

57 According to the *Proceedings of the John F. Slater Fund for the Education of Freedmen* (Baltimore, 1893), 33, Taylor was one of five industrial teachers earning $300 per year. Two other male faculty made $200 and the lone woman $100.

58 *Southern Letter,* August 1894.

59 Washington to William Eugene Hutt, 3 February 1894, in Harlan, ed., *BTWP* 3, 390-391; Hutt to Washington, 3 May 1893, reel 112.

60 *New York World* quoted in Washington, *Up From Slavery* (New York, 1901), 239.

61 *Tuskegee Student,* May 23, 1908, as quoted in Joseph Citro, "Booker T. Washington's Tuskegee Institute" 134.

62 Robert J. Norrell, "Understanding the Wizard: Another Look at the Age of Booker T. Washington," in W. Fitzhugh Brundage, ed., *Booker T. Washington and Black Progress: "Up From Slavery" 100 Years Later* (Gainesville, 2004), 58-80. See also Norrell, "*The House I Live In," Race in the American Century* (Chapel Hill, NC, 2005), chapter 2.

63 Speech to Harvard alumni, 1896, in E. Davidson Washington, ed., *Selected Speeches of Booker T. Washington* (N.Y., 1932), 53.

64 Elliott M. Rudwick and August Meier, "Black Man in the 'White City': Negroes and the Columbian Exposition, 1893," *Phylon,* 26 (1965), 354-361; Ida B. Wells et.al., "The Reason Why The Colored American Is Not In The World's Columbian Exposition" (Chicago, 1893), includes cuts of Tuskegee's Porter and Phelps on pages 48 and 52.

65 For the fair see Robert W. Rydell, *All the World's a Fair: Visions of Empire at American International Expositions, 1876-1916* (Chicago, 1984); Sharon M. Mullis, "Extravaganza of the New South: The Cotton States and International Exposition, 1895," in *The Atlanta Historical Bulletin* 20, 2 (Fall 1976), 17-36; Bruce Harvey and Lynn Watson-Powers, "'The Eyes of the World Are Upon Us': A Look at the Cotton States and International Exposition of 1895," *Atlanta History* 39, 3/4 (Fall/Winter 1995), 5-11; "The Negro at the Atlanta Exposition", *Literary Digest* 12, 1 (November 1895), 6; Walter G. Cooper, *The Cotton States and International Exposition and South, Illustrated* (Atlanta, 1896); Alice M. Bacon, *The Negro and the Atlanta Exposition,* Trustees of the John F. Slater Fund, Occasional Papers No.7 (Baltimore, 1896); and L.W.B. "Is He a New Negro?" *Inter Ocean* (Chicago) reprinted in Harlan, ed. *BTWP* 4, 34-42.

66 L.W.B. "Is He a New Negro?" 42.

67 Quoted in Bacon, *The Negro and the Atlanta Exposition*, 23.

68 *Literary Digest* 12 November 1895, 6.

69 Bacon, *The Negro and the Atlanta Exposition*, 24, 25. The Negro Building is in Rydell, *All the World's a Fair*, 86; *Afro-American Encyclopedia, or Thoughts, Doings and Sayings of the Race*, Nashville, 1896; and Cooper, *The Cotton States and International Exposition*, 30 and 57-63.

70 Washington, *Up From Slavery*, 209, and Micki Waldrop, "Cotton States and International Exposition Negro Building, Atlanta, Georgia (1895)," in Wilson, ed., *African American Architects*" 112-114. Bradford Lee Gilbert of New York was the architect.

71 L. W. B. "Is He a New Negro?" 38-39; Cooper, *The Cotton States and International Exposition*, 61; *Southern Letter* August and September 1895; Chicago *Inter Ocean*, 2 October 1895, in Harlan, ed. *BTWP* 4, 3.

72 Taylor to Washington 25 November 1895, reel 120.

73 Bacon, *The Negro and the Atlanta Exposition*, 25.

74 Taylor to Washington, October 14 and 28, reel 120; and Harlan, ed., *BTWP* 4: 83. Taylor was living at 193 Houston Street in Atlanta.

75 Other women building donors in approximate chronological order are: Mrs. Collis P. (Arabella) Huntington (Huntington Hall and Huntington Memorial Academic Building); Mrs. Thomas G. Bennett (Pinehurst Hospital); Mrs. Quincy Shaw (Children's House); E. Julia Emery (four Emery dormitories); Mrs. C. L. Byington and Alice Byington (two greenhouses); Cornelia C. Tompkins (Tompkins Dining Hall); Margaret Tantum by her father's legacy (Tantum Hall); Mrs. Charles E. Mason (Andrew Hospital); Elizabeth Milbank Anderson (Milbank Hall); Miss Blanchard (the second canning factory); and Mrs. Russell Sage (Sage Dormitory). The Stokes sisters, Mrs. Anderson, and Mrs. Sage were among the nation's early significant women philanthropists.

76 Rash Behari Day, *My Days with Uncle Sam* (Dacca, 1919), 219-220.

77 Max Bennett Thrasher, *Tuskegee, Its Story and Its Work*, Boston 1900, 84. See also M.B.T., "Tuskegee Institute and its President," *Appleton's Popular Science Monthly* LV (September 1899), 592–610.

78 Mary White Ovington, *The Walls Came Tumbling Down* (New York, 1970), ix, 74.

79 Thrasher, *Tuskegee*, 84-85.

80 M.B.T., "Tuskegee Institute and Its President," 609.

81 *The Independent*, 1910, 1452-1453. See also Emmett J. Scott and Lyman Beecher Stowe, *Booker T. Washington, Builder of a Civilization* (Garden City, 1916), 57-58; "Integrated Education," *American Monthly Review of Reviews*, 23 (June 1901) 650.

82 See Washington-Parker correspondence in Harlan, ed. *BTWP*, 3, 498- 501; May 1894 report to the trustees published in *Afro-American Encyclopedia*, 1896; and *Southern Letter* November 1894, March 1895, and March 1896. The *Southern Letter* attributed the drawings to M.D. Garner, a student from Montgomery. Construction was underway by March 1895 and the girls were in by the 1896 commencement. For the Practice Cottage see Booker T. Washington, *Working with the Hands* (New York, 1904), 100-102.

83 *Southern Letter* January 1898.

84 Harry H. Johnston, *The Negro in the New World* (London, 1910), 405, 408, and Harlan, *Wizard of Tuskegee*, 288.

85 Taylor to Washington, 4 May 1900, reel 169.

86 Photographs of farmer Washington are in Booker T. Washington, *Working with the Hands* (New York, 1904), and in Emmett J. Scott and Lyman Beecher Stowe, *Booker T. Washington, Builder of a Civilization* (Garden City, 1916), 307.

87 The first may have been built in 1883, the second in 1898 using War Department plans that Taylor had purchased. (Taylor to Washington, 31 December 1898, reel 144.)

NOTES TO CHAPTER 5

1 Helen Dibble Cannady held her grandfather's marriage certificate. Robert Rochon Taylor's widow supplied the 10 April 1899 birth date. (Dorothy Taylor interview with Dreck S. Wilson, 1980). For Robert Rochon Taylor, see Chyla Dibble Evans, "Robert Rochon Taylor (1899–1957)," in Dreck Spurlock Wilson, ed., *African American Architects, A Biographical Dictionary (1865–1945)* (New York, 2004), 397–399.

2 Taylor to Washington 10 April 1899, reel 154.

3 Taylor to Washington, 24 August 1899, reel 154.

4 *Tuskegee Student*, June 30, 1900.

5 Taylor to Washington, 10 June 1902, reel 207.

6 Taylor to Washington, 13 June 1901, reel 188.

7 Roy Lubove, "I.N. Phelps Stokes: Tenement Architect, Economist, Planner," *Journal of the Society of Architectural Historians* 23, no. 2, 75–87; Deborah S. Gardner, "Practical Philanthropy: The Phelps-Stokes Fund and Housing," *Prospects* 15 (1990), 359–411.

8 In his 1934 application for Illinois architectural registration Taylor said he had been a draftsman for Hopkinson and then worked in other offices. (Taylor files, Tuskegee

Archives.) The 1899–1900 MIT alumni register has him drafting for Hopkinson; the 1900–1902 register reports draftsman at Myrtle Court. Taylor to Washington, 7 November 1899 is on Hopkinson stationery. For Hopkinson, see *Cleveland Plain Dealer*, May 15, 1950.

9 Russell H. Davis, *Black Americans in Cleveland* (Cleveland, 1972), 154. I am grateful to Barbara Hall and Linda Herman, for valued information.

10 Taylor to Washington, 10 July 1900 (filed under 1902), reel 207.

11 Taylor to Washington, 27 October 1900, reel 169.

12 Carver to Washington, 4 October 1901, box 4.

13 Washington to John H. Washington, 27 March 1900, box 4, Washington Collection, Tuskegee Archives.

14 Taylor to Scott, 12 April 1901, reel 187.

15 Taylor to Washington, 13 July 1901, reel 188.

16 Taylor to Washington, 14 October 1901, reel 188.

17 *Tuskegee Student*, December 21, 1901.

18 Taylor to Washington, 19 and 20 February and 10 April 1902, reel 207.

19 John H. Washington to Taylor, 18 June 1902, reel 207.

20 Taylor to E. J. Scott, 20 June 1902, reel 207.

21 Rash Behari Day, *My Days with Uncle Sam* (Dacca, 1919), 210.

22 Taylor to Washington 22 July 1902, reel 207.

23 Taylor to Washington, September 2 and 3, 1902, reel 207

24 Max Bennett Thrasher, *Tuskegee* (Boston, 1900), 210, 214. In November 1902 Frances Benjamin Johnston photographed Rayfield and an unidentified assistant with seventeen members of a "Class in Mechanical Drawing." See Booker T. Washington, *Working with the Hands* (New York, 1904), opposite p. 78.

25 Taylor (in Cleveland) to Washington, 8 June and 14 and 22 July 1902, reel 207.

26 Pittman to Washington, 17 October 1900, reel 3.

27 *Tuskegee Student* November 21, 1902; A Voorhees officer attributed plans for the Central Building and a girls' dormitory to a Tuskegee graduate. (Martin A. Menafee, "A School Treasurer's Story," in Booker T. Washington, ed., *Tuskegee and Its People* [New York, 1905] 159.) Washington wrote that several buildings were designed and built by Tuskegee students. (Booker T. Washington, "Twenty-five Years of Tuskegee," *The World's Work* March 11, 1906, 7450.) The 1980 National Register of Historic Places nomination form attributes a 1905 building to William Wilson Cooke, a distinguished black practitioner then teaching at Claflin College. Pittman's characteristic curving gables and projecting

entrance porches appear on two later Voorhees buildings, the Bedford Dining Hall (1912) and Blanton Administration Building (1914). The latter is similar to his 1909 Milbank Agricultural Building at Tuskegee (Catalog 21) and his 1909 Hume Hall in Frankfort, KY. For Voorhees and female leadership, see Angel David Nieves, "Voorhees: Elizabeth Evelyn Wright's 'Small Tuskegee' and Black Education in the Post-Reconstruction South," *Arris, Journal of the Southeast Chapter of the Society of Architectural Historians*, 13, 2002, 25–37. For arson attacks see Laura R. Dawson, *A Vision for Victory, A Pictorial History of Voorhees College, 1897–1997* (Virginia Beach, VA, 1997).

28 Pittman to Washington, 12 November 1901 and 10 February 1903, reel 3.

29 Allen R. Durough, *The Architectural Legacy of Wallace A. Rayfield: Pioneer Black Architect of Birmingham, Alabama* (Tuscaloosa, 2010). See also Elizabeth Meredith Dowling, "William Augustus Rayfield (1874–1941)," in Wilson, ed., *African American Architects* 338–340. According to John M. Schnorrenberg, Rayfield earned a two-year certificate at Pratt Institute in 1899 but did not attend Columbia University, as most biographies claim. Dozier credits him with the 1899 three-story extension to Alabama Hall ("Tuskegee," 100) and has published a Rayfield watercolor rendering in *Spaces and Places* (Tuskegee, 1982). The *Tuskegee Student*, July 6, 1907, reported that Rayfield was designing Calhoun Hall in Eatonville, Florida, the Voorhees Institute seal, and a church and a school in Birmingham. See also Vinson E. McKenzie, "Booker T. Washington's Men of Architecture: Pioneering African-American Architects, Their Lives and Careers," typescript 1993, 24–26, Tuskegee Archives.

30 For Pittman, see Susan G. Pearl "William Sidney Pittman (1875–1948)," in Wilson, ed., *African American Architects*, 319–321; Mary Barrineau, "The Pride of Sydney Pittman," *Dallas Times Herald*, December 7, 1986; and William Hayes Ward, "A Race Exhibit" in *The Colored American* 13, no. 6 (December 1907), 447.

31 Karen E. Hudson, *The Will and Way, Paul R. Williams, Architect* (New York, 1994), 11.

32 W. Eugene Thomas at Lincoln Institute in Kentucky to Washington, 31 March 1910, reel 322.

33 Booker T. Washington, *Up From Slavery* (New York, 1901), 80, 81, 88, 122, and 155; and Washington, *My Larger Education* (New York, 1911) 263–275.

34 W.E. B. DuBois, "Of Mr. Booker T. Washington and Others," *The Souls of Black Folk* (Chicago, 1903).

35 Washington, *Up From Slavery*, 281.

36 Booker T. Washington, *Character Building* (New York, 1902), 40–41.

37 Harlan, *The Wizard of Tuskegee*, 129.

38 Sheldon Hackney, *Populism to Progressivism in Alabama* (Princeton, 1969), 180–181.

39 Harlan, *The Making of a Black Leader*, 317; Citro, "Booker T. Washington's Tuskegee Institute," 145.

40 Catherine W. Bishir, "Landmarks of Power: Building a Southern Past, 1885–1915," *Southern Cultures* (Inaugural Issue, 1993), 5–45; reprinted in Catherine W. Bishir, *Southern Built: American Architecture, Regional Practice* (Charlottesville, 2006), chapter 10; Wilson, *The Colonial Revival House*, 50–60.

41 Stanton Becker Von Grabill (pseud. Rubert Fehnstroke) *Letters from Tuskegee, Being the Confessions of a Yankee* (Birmingham, Alabama, 1905).

42 Emmett J. Scott, "Present Achievements and Governing Ideals," in Washington, ed. *Tuskegee and Its People*, 23–26. Rickard K. Dozier quoted Scott to make this point (Dozier, "Tuskegee," 41).

43 Augustus Field Beard, *A Crusade of Brotherhood: A History of the American Missionary Association* (Boston, 1909), 176.

44 Maxine D. Jones and Joe M. Richardson, *Talladega College, The First Century* (Tuscaloosa, Alabama, 1990), 13–14.

45 Washington to Taylor, 24 December 1910, box 89 .

46 Washington to Taylor, 14 January 1901, reel 188.

47 Michael Scott Bieze, "Ruskin in the Black Belt: Booker T. Washington, Arts and Crafts, and the New Negro," *Source, Notes in the History of Art*, XXIV, 4, Summer 2005, 24–34 and "Booker T. Washington and the Art of Self-Representation," (D. Ed. diss. Georgia State University, 2003).

48 Harlan, ed., *BTWP*, 11, 247. See also Booker T. Washington, *My Larger Education* (New York, 1911), 272, 284, 285.

49 Scott and Stowe, *Booker T. Washington*, 228 .

50 William J. Edwards, *Twenty-five Years in the Black Belt*. (Tuscaloosa, 1993).

51 Library Bureau to Washington, 14 December 1901, reel 188.

52 Washington to L.G. Wheeler, 3 October 1906, box 31, folder 226, Washington Collection, Tuskegee Archives.

53 Scott and Stowe, *Booker T. Washington*, 145–146.

54 Washington, *Working with the Hands,* 123.

55 Washington to Alexander Robert Stewart, 27 June 1914, in Harlan, ed., BTWP 13, 72–73.

56 Booker T. Washington, "Negro Homes," *Century Magazine* LXXVI (May to October 1908) 71–79.

NOTES TO CHAPTER 6

1 *Tuskegee Student*, November 16, 1910, June 17, 1911, and March 11, 1912. Seth Low correspondence confirms Bailey as the cold storage plant's architect.

2 The jobs were a façade for an 1874 building and a brick Beaux-Arts style wrapping for an 1835 frame structure. For the competition win see *Tuskegee Student*, November 16, 1910. For the Old Ship AME Zion Church see *Tuskegee Student*, March 11, 1912. The Chicago building was demolished in 2001. Linda O. McMurry, *George Washington Carver, Scientist and Symbol* (New York, 1981), 65.

3 J.A. Lankford, "The Negro as an Architect and Builder," *Proceedings of the National Negro Business League Sixth Annual Convention, 1905*, 163.

4 Booker T. Washington, *Working with the Hands* (New York, 1904), 72–78.

5 Washington, *Working with the Hands*, 73.

6 *Tuskegee Student* April 9, 1910.

7 Washington, *Working with the Hands*, 78.

8 Op.cit., 70.

9 Joseph F. Citro, "Booker T. Washington's Tuskegee Institute: Black School-Community, 1900–1915," (Ed.D. diss. University of Rochester: 1973) 346–359.

10 Bruce report to Washington, 1903, in Citro, 354.

11 Citro, op. cit. 353–354.

12 Citro, op. cit. 354–55.

13 Citro, op.cit. 443, note 116.

14 Citro, op. cit. 359.

15 Citro, op.cit. 351.

16 Citro, op. cit 357.

17 Ibid.

18 Citro, op. cit. 360–361.

19 Citro, op.cit. 352.

20 Citro, op.cit. 362.

21 Citro, op. cit. 369–372.

22 Linda O. McMurry, *George Washington Carver: Scientist and Symbol* (New York, 1981) and *Recorder of the Black Experience, A Biography of Monroe Nathan Work* (Baton Rouge, 1985).

23 Washington to Taylor, February 13 and 26, 1903 and Taylor to Washington, February 27 and 28, 1903, reel 228.

24 Williston to Washington 31 March 1902 (requesting employment); Taylor to Scott, 6 March 1903 and Washington to Taylor, 7 March 1903, reel 228. Williston to Washington 1 May 1906, box 548 (resigning); Taylor to Washington, August 6 and 10, 1908, box 567 (planning greenhouses); *Tuskegee Student* July 4, 1908. In 1909 Taylor sent Wash-

ington an outline of Williston's responsibilities as head of a new department. (Taylor to Washington, 29 September 1909, box 577.) At age 91 Williston served on the committee that recommended Paul Rudolph's chapel. For David Augustus Williston (1868–1962) see also Douglas A. Williams "David Augustus Williston," in Dreck Spurlock Wilson, ed. *African American Architects, a Biographical Dictionary, 1865–1945* (New York, 2004), 453–455. Kirk Muckle and Dreck Wilson, "David Augustus Williston, Pioneering Black Professional," *Landscape Architecture* 72,1 (January 1982), 82–85; and Cari Goetcheus, "Booker T. Washington, the Man and His Landscape," *CRM: Cultural Resources Management 8* (1999), 31–33.

25 Beatrice Taylor to Washington, 24 March 1903, reel 228.

26 For Greenwood, see *Southern Letter* June 1893; *Tuskegee Student*, April 28, 1906; Louis R. Harlan, *Booker T. Washington, The Wizard of Tuskegee, 1901–1915* (New York, 1983), 169–170; Richard K. Dozier, "Tuskegee, Booker T. Washington's Contribution to the Education of Black Architects." (Arch. D. diss., University of Michigan) 132–137; and Emmett J. Scott and Lyman Beecher Stowe, *Booker T. Washington, Builder of a Civilization*, 158. The 1904 plan is in Dozier, "Tuskegee," 133 and L. Albert Scipio II, *Pre-War Days at Tuskegee: Historical Essay on Tuskegee Institute, 1881–1943* (Silver Spring, MD., 1987), 66.

27 Scott to Taylor, 24 March 1904, and the report are in box 529.

28 Warren Logan to Washington, 26 November 1895, in Harlan, ed., *BTWP* 4, 83–84.

29 Booker Conley remembers the night and Johanna Hays' interviews of others agree on the fire's cause.

30 *Southern Letter*, June 1896. D. I. Carson of New York gave the telephone system.

31 Thomas Monroe Campbell, *The Moveable School Goes to the Negro Farmer* (Tuskegee, 1936), 45, 50.

32 Alice J. Kaine to Booker T. Washington, 30 November 1895, in Harlan, ed., *BTWP* 4, 87–88. Kaine, from the Wisconsin Industrial School for Girls, was hired with Slater money to improve the girl's residences, kitchens, and laundry. MIT's first woman graduate, Ellen Swallow Richards, whose degree was in sanitary chemistry and who headed the MIT household department, had recommended her. (Harlan, ed., *BTWP* 3, 469.).

33 Washington to Taylor, 31 May 1904, box 530.

34 Typescript two-page autobiography, c. 1925, Taylor files, Tuskegee Archives.

35 John A. Kenney to Executive Council, 26 May 1903, in Harlan, ed., *BTWP* 7, 159–164.

36 John H. Washington to Taylor, 12 November 1903, reel 229.

37 Citro, 282–288.

38 *Tuskegee Messenger* December 27, 1930.

39 Taylor to W. J. Schieffelin, 18 May 1939, Taylor files, Tuskegee Archives.

40 Taylor to Frank E. Perkins, 30 October 1905, box 5, and Taylor to L.G. Wheeler, 21 February 1906, box 19, Washington Collection, Tuskegee Archives.

41 Carla Willard, "Timing Impossible Subjects: the Marketing Style of Booker T. Washington," *American Quarterly* 53, 4 (December 2001), 624–669.

42 Robert J. Norrell, "Understanding the Wizard: Another Look at the Age of Booker T. Washington," in W. Fitzhugh Brundage, ed, *Booker T. Washington and Black Progress: "Up From Slavery" 100 Years Later* (Gainesville, 2004), 58–80. Harlan, *The Wizard* 28–29.

43 Harlan, *The Wizard*, 166–169.

44 Thomas Dixon, Jr., "Booker T. Washington and the Negro: Some Dangerous Aspects of the Work of Tuskegee," *Saturday Evening Post* 178, August 19, 1905.

45 Louis R. Harlan, *Booker T. Washington, The Making of a Black Leader, 1856–1901* (New York, 1972), 317; Citro, 145.

46 Washington and Francis Jackson Garrison, October 5 and 12, 1905, *BTWP* 8, 396 and 402.

47 For the Atlanta riot see Leon F. Litwack, *Trouble in Mind: Black Southerners in the Age of Jim Crow* (New York, 1998), 315–319; Philip Dray, *At the Hands of Persons Unknown, the Lynching of Black America* (New York, 2002), 162–167; and David Levering Lewis, *W. E. B. Du Bois, Biography of a Race, 1868–1919* (New York, 1993).

48 Rosa Parks, *Rosa Parks: My Story* (New York, 1992), 6.

49 Robert J. Norrell, *Reaping the Whirlwind, The Civil Rights Movement in Tuskegee* (New York, 1985), chapters 1 and 2.

50 Louis R. Harlan, "The Secret Life of Booker T. Washington," in Raymond W. Smock, ed., *Booker T. Washington in Perspective* (Jackson, Miss., 1983).

51 Norrell, "Understanding the Wizard," in Brundage, ed., *Booker T. Washington and Black Progress*, 58–80.

52 Michael Scott Bieze, "Ruskin in the Black Belt: Booker T. Washington, Arts and Crafts, and the New Negro," Source, *Notes in the History of Art*, XXIV, 4 (Summer 2005), 24–34.

53 Jacqueline James, widow of Marquis James, adapted a part of the manuscript in "Uncle Tom? Not Booker T." *American Heritage* XIX, 5 (August 1968), 51–100.

54 *Tuskegee Student*, April 14, 1906.

55 The hen house history is on a sign in a Johnston photo-

graph. (Photo J694–417, Prints and Photographs Division, Library of Congress).

56 Sven Becker, "From Tuskegee to Togo: The Problem of Freedom in the Empire of Cotton," *Journal of American History* 92, no. 2 (September 2005).

57 *Tuskegee Student*, May 5, 1906.

58 The topographic map is in the Physical Facilities Department and is reproduced in *Scipio, Pre-War Days*, 76–77.

59 Harlan, *BTWP* 3, 469–70.

60 Kirk Muckle and Dreck Wilson, "David Augustus Williston," *Landscape Architecture*, 72, no. 1 (Jan 1982) 82–85.

61 Kenrick Ian Grandison, "Negotiated Space: The Black College Campus as a Cultural Record of Postbellum America," *American Quarterly* 51, no. 3 (September 1999): 530–532.

62 Personal communication, 15 October 2001.

63 Interview Ann Dibble Jordan, August 2004, and Edward Pryce, October 2006. Pryce came as a student in 1934 and returned to teach in 1948.

64 Kenneth Severens, *Southern Architecture: 350 Years of Distinctive American Building* (New York, 1981), 156.

65 Taylor to Washington, 25 October 1905, reel 530. Interview Booker Conley, 28 September 2006.

66 *Tuskegee Student*, March 15, 1902. The plan is at the Loeb Library at Harvard University.

67 *Tuskegee Student* , June 4, 1904.

68 The plan is filed at January 10, box 559.

69 Low to Washington 3 August 1907, reel 54; Taylor to Washington, 22 July 1907, box 559; Scipio, *Pre-War Days at Tuskegee*, 409.

70 Washington to Taylor, January 9, and Taylor to Washington, 24 January 1905, box 538.

71 Washington to Taylor, 18 April 1905, box 538. The house stood at the corner of the main public road and the road west of the Chambliss commercial block.

72 Edward Taylor, interview 17 May 1989.

73 Washington to Robert C. Ogden, 28 May 1906, in Harlan, ed., *BTWP* 9, 13–14; Taylor to Washington, 1 August 1906, box 548; undated typed draft annotated in Taylor's hand, Tuskegee Archives.

74 Washington to Taylor, 27 August 1906, box 548, LC; John H. Washington to Taylor, 9 August 1906, box 27, Washington Collection, Tuskegee Archives.

75 Taylor to Washington, 26 November 1909, box 577, LC.

76 Taylor to Washington, 13 March, 6 May, 9 July 1907, box 559. For the Baldwin monument see *Tuskegee Student* January 19, 1907, Dozier, "Tuskegee," 129–130; *Scipio, Pre-War Days*, 96. For Bosworth, see Mark Jarzombek, *Designing MIT: Bosworth's New Tech* (Boston, 2004), 56–62.

77 Taylor to Washington, 13 March 1907, box 559.

78 Washington to Caroline Phelps Stokes, 24 June 1907, reel 79.

79 Taylor to Washington, 3 August 1907, box 559, and Low to Washington, 3 August 1907, reel 54.

80 Andrew S. Dolkart, *Morningside Heights, A History of its Architecture and Development* (New York, 1998), 108.

81 *Tuskegee Student*, August 26 and September 29, 1905.

82 *Tuskegee Student*, August 11 and September 8, 1906. Interview, Helen Dibble Cannaday, 27 December 1993.

83 Edward Taylor, personal communication, 17 May 1989.

84 Taylor to Washington, 7 September 1906, box 547

85 Boxes 25 through 29, Washington Collection, Tuskegee Archives; Washington to Taylor, July 12, and Taylor to Washington 19 July, 1906, box 548; for Bailey attribution, see Mary Ann Neely, "Alabama State Fair Negro Building, Montgomery (1906)," Wilson, ed., *African American Architects*, 5–6.

86 Taylor wrote to Jackson on August 22, the same day that he asked Scott for help. Scott replied August 25 that he would mention Taylor's interests when he and Jackson met, reel 27.

87 *Tuskegee Student*, October 27, 1906. A *New York Age* piece on Pittman was reprinted in the *Tuskegee Student*, November 3, 1906. See also Susan G. Pearl, "Jamestown Ter-Centennial Exposition Negro Building, Virginia (1907)," in Wilson, ed., *African American Architects* 228–230.

88 Taylor to Washington 1 September 1904, box 530; Washington to Taylor, 26 August 1904, reel 3.

89 Taylor to Washington, 15 September 1904, box 530.

90 Taylor to Washington, 30 March 1905, reel 262. He asked reappointment of David A. Williston and Charles T. Russell.

91 Bailey to Washington, 15 April 1904 and 3 June 1905, box 890. See also Tim Samuelson, "Walter Thomas Bailey (1882–1941)," in Wilson, ed., *African American Architects*, 15–17.

92 *Tuskegee Student* June 17, 1911 and W. T. Bailey, "Report of Architectural Drawing Division for Year 1910–1911," typescript, box 602.

93 Washington to Taylor, 25 May 1906, box 548.

94 *Tuskegee Student*, November 16, 1910, June 17, 1911, and March 11, 1912. Seth Low correspondence confirms Bailey as the cold storage plant's architect. The jobs were a façade for an 1874 building and a brick Beaux-Arts style wrapping

for an 1835 frame structure. For the competition win see *Tuskegee Student*, November 16, 1910. For the Old Ship AME Zion Church see *Tuskegee Student*, March 11, 1912. The Chicago building was demolished in 2001.

95 Melby's job application, 12 August 1906, box 890. For the raise, Taylor to Washington, 29 May 1907, box 559. "Junior architect" is from "The Negro Nevertheless a Factor in Architecture," *Negro History Bulletin* 3, 7 (April 1940), 102. See also Dreck Spurlock Wilson, "John Alexander Melby (1880–1943)," in Wilson, ed., *African American Architects*, 277–279.

96 Taylor and Washington memos, 25 May and 22 July 1909; 26 May and 23 December 1910; 6 June 1911; 19 February 1912; 8 and 28 December 1914; *Tuskegee Student* September 1915; and Louise Daniel Hutchinson, "William Augustus Hazel (1854–1929)," in Wilson, ed. *African American Architects*, 195–197.

97 Taylor to Washington, 21 July 1909, box 576; Washington to Taylor 26 December 1909, box 577; Hutchinson, "William Augustus Hazel (1854-1029)." A photograph of a 1913–1914 Hazel-signed drawing of Tuskegee buildings with smokestacks and a dome is framed by Paul Dunbar's poem, "The Tuskegee Song," that praised industry and culture. (Photo 9050, Prints and Photographs Division, Library of Congress.)

98 For Hazel and Howard, see Harrison Mosley Ethridge, "The Black Architects of Washington, D.C., 1900–Present," (D. Arts diss. The Catholic University of America, 1979) 42.

NOTES TO CHAPTER 7

1 *Tuskegee Student*, November 16, 1910, June 17, 1911, and March 11, 1912. Seth Low correspondence confirms Bailey as the cold storage plant's architect.

2 Harry E. Thomas, head of the Steam Engineering Division, studied at MIT but did not graduate. He came to Tuskegee in 1894. Thomas was born in Ohio in 1866 and was retired by 1930 and living in Cleveland. (*Tuskegee Messenger* April 26, 1930).

3 *Tuskegee Student*, April 9, 1910.

4 Harlan, *The Wizard*, 243 and 495, n. 15.

5 November 21 to December 1, 1914 is in box 649.

6 Thomas J. Calloway, "The American Negro Artisan," *Cassier's Magazine* 25 (November–April 1903/4), 445.

7 *Tuskegee Student* May 18, 1907.

8 Devereaux Bemis generously supplied the planning discussions but found no evidence of execution.

9 Louis R. Harlan, "Booker T. Washington and the Politics of Accommodation," in Raymond W. Smock, ed., *Booker T.*

Washington in Perspective (Jackson, MS, 1988), 167. Taylor exhibited both libraries at Howard University in 1931. Photos of both remain in his Tuskegee files. For Salisbury, see Scott to Taylor, 15 June 1907, box 559. For Wiley see *Tuskegee Student*, May 18, 1907 and signed Taylor drawing in Dozier, "Tuskegee," 187. See also *National Negro School News*, III, no. 1 (January 1912) 8.

10 Taylor to Scott, 10 August 1908, box 567.

11 Martin to Wright, 14 October 1910, from MS 22.8, Papers of Darwin D. Martin and Frank Lloyd Wright, courtesy of the University Archives, State University of New York at Buffalo. I am grateful to Jack Quinan for bringing this material to my attention.

12 Scott to Taylor, 25 August 1909, box 577. The J. H. Palmer cottage was built 1908–1909 for the institute registrar. ("Report of Committee on Buildings and Grounds to Trustees, 26 June 1909," box 131, Low Papers, Columbia University.).

13 Jenkin Lloyd Jones, "'The Race Problem," *Proceedings of the National Negro Conference, 1909* (New York, 1909), 131–135. See also Washington to Jones, 23 April 1887, Jenkin Lloyd Jones Papers, box III, folder 33, Meadville/Lombard Theological School. Jones organized a Chicago memorial service for Washington.

14 For a thorough historical and formal analysis of Wright's Rosenwald school, see Jack Quinan , "Frank Lloyd Wright, Darwin D. Martin, and the Whittier-Rosenwald School for Hampton Institute," *Arris* 21 (2010), 20-37. See also, Richard Joncas, "Buildings for Learning" in David G. De Long, ed., *Frank Lloyd Wright and the Living City* (Weil am Rhein, Germany, 1998), 118, and Mary S. Hoffschwelle, *The Rosenwald Schools of the American South* (Gainesville, Florida, 2006), 142–144.

15 The 1911 map is in Scipio, *Pre-War Days at Tuskegee*, 76–77.

16 H.E. Thomas to Taylor, 29 April 1915, and an undated letter filed in the 1904–1905 correspondence. Lord Construction Company in Philadelphia built the power plant to Franz's design. F. W. Thirkield of Rochester, N.Y. installed six miles of underground steam lines. (Taylor to Washington, box 663).

17 Taylor to Washington 1 April 1915, box 663.

18 Low to Washington, 18 April 1911, box 137, Low Papers, Columbia University.

19 Low to Washington, 3 March 1911, box 133, Low Papers, Columbia University.

20 Taylor to Washington, 1 May 1911, box 602.

21 Taylor to Washington 1 June 1911, box 602.

22 Taylor to Washington, 6 June 1911, box 602.

23 Washington to Taylor, 15 July 1911, and Taylor to Washington, 27 July 1911, box 602.

24 *Tuskegee Student*, July 17, 1911.

25 Reel 55. The undated document is filed among the 1911 papers. Taylor and Lee earned $1800 a year, Washington's secretary Emmett J. Scott $1900, and Business Manager Warren Logan, who came in 1883, $2100.

26 Washington to Taylor, 12 July 1911, box 602.

27 "So much discussion" is in William M. Reaves, *"Strength through Struggle," the Chronological and Historical Record of the African-American Community in Wilmington, North Carolina, 1865–1950* (Wilmington, N.C., 1998), 48. See also Harlan, *The Wizard*, 264; Harlan, ed. *BTWP*, 10, 499–462; *Tuskegee Student*, October 22 and November 5, 1910.

28 *Tuskegee Student*, November 4, 1911. Nellie Chestnut's surname is spelled variously with one to three t's. All versions were common in Fayetteville, N.C., where she was born. She may have been related to novelist Charles W. Chesnutt from Fayetteville before he moved to Cleveland.

29 *Tuskegee Student*, November 11 and 25 and December 9, 1911.

30 Robert R. Taylor, "The Scientific Development of the Negro," in *Technology and Industrial Efficiency* (New York, 1911), 167–170.

31 W.E. Burghardt Du Bois, ed., *The Negro Artisan* (Atlanta, 1902), 13–23. For a recent discussion see Ira Berlin, *Slaves Without Masters, The Free Negro in the Antebellum South* (New York, 1974).

32 Taylor, "Scientific Development," 168.

33 *Ibid*. 170.

34 Taylor to J. E. Moorland, 18 September 1915, Taylor files, Tuskegee Archives.

35 James D. Anderson, *The Education of Blacks in the South, 1860–1935* (Chapel Hill, N.C., 1988), 156–157.

36 *Tuskegee Catalogue 1912–1913*, 105–106; *National Negro School News* 3, January 1, 1912, 7–8.

37 Horace Mann Bond, *Negro Education in Alabama: A Study in Cotton and Steel* (Washington, D.C., 1939), 275, and Charles Wesley Archbold to Henry Huddleston Rogers, April 1908, in Harlan, ed., *BTWP* 9, 491–492.

38 Washington to Clinton J. Calloway, 8 November 1909, Harlan, ed., *BTWP* 10, 193.

39 Washington to Taylor, 18 July 1907, box 559.

40 Washington to Taylor, 8 August 1911, box 602.

41 Taylor to Washington, 18 August 1911, box 602.

42 For Rising Star see Booker T. Washington, *My Larger Education* (New York, 1911), 148–149; Scott and Stowe, *Booker T. Washington, Builder of a Civilization*, 44–45; and Booker T. Washington, "New Type of Rural School," *Survey* 19 (March 1913), 837–838.

43 Washington to Taylor, 20 September 1912, box 618.

44 Taylor to Washington, 19 October 1912, box 618.

45 Taylor to Washington, 12 December 1912, box 618.

46 Mary S. Hoffschwelle, *The Rosenwald Schools of the American South* (Gainesville, Florida, 2006).

47 *Tuskegee Student* July 10, 1915.

48 Roi Ottley, "Many Negroes Owe Happy Homes to R. R. Taylor," *Chicago Daily Tribune*, May 21, 1955.

49 Jeff Mansell and Trina Binkley, "The Rosenwald School Building Fund and Associated Buildings (1913-1937)", National Register of Historic Places Multiple Property Documentation Form, U.S. Department of the Interior (Washington D.C., 1997) 20. Hoffschwelle, *Rosenwald Schools*, 39. A different list of the six is on the National Trust for Historic Preservation website, http://www.rosenwaldschoolscom./history.html. They are Loachapoaka and Chewacla in Lee County, Notasulga and Brownsville in Macon County, and Big Zion and Madison Park in Montgomery County.

50 Both are shown in the *Southern Letter*, July 1915.

51 Hoffschwelle, *Rosenwald Schools*, 39.

52 Hoffschwelle, *Rosenwald Schools*, 39; Upper right on the frontispiece of *The Negro Rural School and its Relationship to the Community* (Tuskegee, 1915), and photo page 42; Thomas Jesse Jones, ed., *Negro Education, A Study of the Private and Higher Schools for Colored People in the United States*, U.S. Department of Interior: Bureau of Education Bulletin 38–39, 1916–1917, vol. 1 (Washington D.C., 1917), plate 3. Plans of Madison Park have yet to be found.

53 *Southern Workman* XLIX, 5 (May 1920), 220.

54 Hoffschwelle, *Rosenwald Schools*, 77–78.

55 Samuel L. Smith, *Builders of Goodwill, the Story of the State Agents of Negro Education in the South, 1910–1950*, Nashville, 1950, 15–16. For James L. Sibley see Chapter 9. Edward E. Redcay, *County Training Schools and Public Secondary Education for Negroes in the South* (Washington D.C., 1935), and Horace Mann Bond, *Negro Education in Alabama: A Study in Cotton and Steel* (Washington, D.C., 1939), 264–266.

56 Hoffschwelle, *Rosenwald Schools*, 51.

57 Sibley to Taylor 16 November 1914, SG 15442 folder 1 "T 1913–1914," Alabama Department of Archives and History. Mary S. Hoffschwelle graciously shared her research with me.

58 Thomas Jesse Jones, ed., *Negro Education, A Study of the*

Private and Higher Schools for Colored People in the United States, Department of Interior, Bureau of Education Bulletin (Washington D. C., 1917), vol. 1, plate 13.

59 http//mcgregor.lib.virginia.edu/davis/FMPro.

60 The photograph and the school's history is in Jackson Davis, "Building a Rural Civilization," *The Southern Workman* XLIX, 11 (Nov. 1920) 502.

61 Plans are in *The Negro Rural School,* 87 and 88.

62 Anna S. L. Brown, "Down Mobile Way," *Opportunity* 2, 17 (May 1924), 151–154.

63 Redcay, *County Training Schools,* 40.

64 *Community School Plans,* Nashville 1921.

65 Hoffschwelle, *Rosenwald Schools,* chapter 3.

66 Jones, ed., *Negro Education,* vol. 1. This volume focuses on buildings and grounds.

67 Jones, ed, *Negro Education,* 215, 220. The report did fault some Tuskegee construction. The ends of floor joists fit too tightly into the brick walls of one building, not leaving enough air to prevent decay (page 226).

68 See William B. Rhoads, *The Colonial Revival* (New York: 1977), 157, 461–474; Richard Guy Wilson "What is the Colonial Revival?" in Wilson, ed., *Re-creating the American Past: Essays on the Colonial Revival,* Charlottesville, 2006; and Richard Guy Wilson, *The Colonial Revival House,* New York, 2004.

69 Paul Venable Turner, *Campus, an American Planning Tradition* (New York, 1984), 204–212.

70 Jones, ed., *Negro Education,* vol. 1, 207 and vol. 2, 66.

71 James D. Anderson, *The Education of Backs in the South 1868–1935* (Chapel Hill 1988).

72 Eric Anderson and Alfred A. Moss, Jr., *Dangerous Donations: Northern Philanthropy and Southern Black Education, 1902–1930* (Columbia, Missouri, 1999), 202–210. For Du Bois's view of *Negro Education,* see David Levering Lewis, *W.E.B. Du Bois, Biography of a Race, 1868–1919* (New York, 1993), 546–551.

73 Harlan, ed. *BTWP* 3: 469–470. Jabez L. M. Curry to Washington, quoted in Harlan, ed, *BTWP* 3, 475.

74 Nolen's four-page report, dated 15 April 1911, is in box 70, Low Papers, Columbia University. Washington to Low, May 1911, reel 55, promoted a topographical map for a comprehensive development.

75 David A. Williston (1868–1962) arrived in 1902, stayed for some years, and then served Tuskegee from Washington D.C. until his death.

NOTES TO CHAPTER 8

1 In 2006, a medical conference studied Washington's records and diagnosed a stroke, ruling out the popular but mistaken assumption of syphilis. *New York Times,* May 7, 2006, 20. This issue and his other medical problems are in Louis R. Harlan, *The Wizard of Tuskegee* (New York, 1983), Chapter 18.

2 See Emmett J. Scott and Lyman Beecher Stowe, *Booker T. Washington: Builder of a Civilization* (New York, 1916), opp. 58 and 290. Both photographs were taken between 1910 and 1912 when White Hall had a cupola rather than the present clock tower.

3 Taylor to Moton, 9 July 1919, box 21, Moton Local Correspondence, Tuskegee Archives.

4 Taylor to Moton, 27 November 1920, Taylor files, Tuskegee Archives.

5 *Tuskegee Student* November 1, 1922.

6 Taylor to Moton, 27 November 1920, Taylor files, Tuskegee Archives.

7 Robert J. Norrell, *Reaping the Whirlwind; The Civil Rights Movement in Tuskegee* (New York, 1985), 21.

8 Taylor to Moton, 28 August 1922, box 29, Moton Papers, Tuskegee Archives.

9 Robert J. Norrell, "Understanding the Wizard: Another Look at the Age of Booker T. Washington," in W. Fitzhugh Brundage, ed, *Booker T. Washington and Black Progress: "Up From Slavery" 100 Years Later* (Gainesville, FL, 2004), 58–80, and Harlan, *The Wizard* (New York, 1983).

10 Raymond Wolters, *The New Negro on Campus: Black College Rebellions of the 1920s* (Princeton, 1975), 148–150.

11 Taylor to Charles A. Wickersham, president of the Western Railroad of Alabama, 15 December 1921, Taylor files, Tuskegee Archives.

12 See Wolters, *New Negro on Campus,* 137–191; Pete Daniel, "Black Power in the 1920s: The Case of the Tuskegee Veterans Hospital," *Journal of Southern History* 37, 3 (August 1970), 368–388; Norrell, *Reaping the Whirlwind,* 27–30; see also Adam Fairclough, "Tuskegee's Robert R. Moton and the Travails of the Early Black College President," *The Journal of Blacks in Higher Education* 31 (Spring 2001), 94–10; Albon L. Holsey, "A Man of Courage," in Williams Hardin Hughes and Frederick D. Patterson, eds. *Robert Russa Moton of Hampton and Tuskegee* (Chapel Hill, 1956), 127–143; and *Opportunity* 1, 9 (September 1923), 287.

13 For the cross burning, see W. Montague Cobb, "John Andrew Kenney, MD, 1874–1950" in *Journal of the National Medical Association,* 42, 3 (May 1950), 176. Cobb describes a different resolution: Kenney and a fellow officer of the black National Medical Association met with President

Harding.

14 For the oral tradition see Daniel, "Black Power," 378 and Wolters, *The New Negro on Campus* 174–75.

15 Taylor to the editor of the *Mobile Register*, July 7, 1923, Moton Papers, box 33, and typescript in Taylor's files, Tuskegee Archives.

16 *Tuskegee Messenger* January 1926.

17 R. R. Taylor, "Tuskegee's Mechanical Department," *The Southern Workman* 50, 10 (October 1921) 457–468.

18 "Tuskegee Institute After Forty-Two Years," *Opportunity* I, no. 4, April 1923, 18.

19 *Ibid.* 464.

20 Harold Webb interview, 21 August 1986.

21 Edward Taylor interview 17 May 1989.

22 Dorothy Taylor interview with Dreck S. Wilson, 13 October 1980. Chyla Dibble Evans, "Robert Rochon Taylor (1899–1957)," in Wilson, ed, *African American Architects* 397–399. Robert Rochon operated the sawmill.

23 Dorothy Taylor interview, 13 October 1980.

24 Edward Taylor interview 17 May 1989.

25 *Tuskegee Messenger* January 9, 1926.

26 As "Robert R. Taylor," Robert Rochon wrote "A Demonstration in Modern Housing," *Opportunity* (March 1931), 82–85 and "Low Cost Housing in America," *Crisis* 40 (November 1933) 257. See also Roi Ottley, "Many Negroes Owe Happy Home to R. R. Taylor," *Chicago Daily Tribune*, May 21, 1955; Nicolas Lemann, *The Promised Land* (New York, 1991), 72–75; and Arnold R. Hirsch, *Making the Second Ghetto, Race and Housing in Chicago, 1940–1960* (Cambridge, England, 1983), 176 and 223. There is a sketch of this "soft-spoken, gentle sort of person with a nice sense of humor, quiet humor" in Donald A. Krueckeberg, ed., *The American Planner, Biographies and Recollections* (New York, 1983), 333–334. The Tuskegee City License of 1922 for "Robert R. Taylor and Sons, Contractors" is in the elder Taylor's files.

27 *Tuskegee Student*, October 1923; *Tuskegee Messenger* August 1926.

28 Three page typescript amended in Taylor's hand, Taylor files, Tuskegee Archives.

29 *St. Luke Herald* (Richmond) March 14, 1925, clipping in Taylor files.

30 *Tuskegee Messenger,* January 15, February 12 and 26, 1927; *Southern Letter* February 27, 1927.

31 *Tuskegee Messenger,* July 16, 1930.

32 John M. Barry, *Rising Tide, the Great Mississippi Flood of 1927 and How it Changed America* (New York, 1997), 392–394.

33 David Burner, *Herbert Hoover, a Public Life* (New York, 1979), 193–197.

34 Albon Holsey, "Relief and Reconstruction in the Mississippi Flood Areas," *Tuskegee Messenger*, July 16–30, 1927.

35 Jesse O. Thomas, "In the Path of the Flood" and editorial, *Opportunity* V, no. 8 (August, 1927) 222.

36 "Wilmington Negro Who Aided Hoover Now Back in City," *Wilmington Morning Star*, 1927. (Clipping, labeled "Wednesday the 17th", no month, in Taylor's Tuskegee file).

37 See also Pete Daniel, *Deep'n as it Come, the 1927 Mississippi River Flood* (New York, 1977); American Red Cross, *Final Report of the Colored Advisory Commission, Mississippi Valley Flood Disaster, 1927*, Washington D.C., 1927; Glenn R. Conrad and Carl A. Brasseaux, *Crevasse! The 1927 Flood in Arcadiana*, Lafayette, LA, 1994.

38 Robert R. Moton to Herbert Hoover, 13 June 1927, Herbert Hoover Presidential Library, National Archives and Records Service, *http://www/pbs.org/wgbh/amex/flood/ps_moton1.html.*

39 1980 National Register of Historic Places nomination for the First African American Methodist Church in Athens.

40 Taylor to Persley, 21 July 1920, box 16, Moton Local Correspondence, Tuskegee Archives.

41 "Tuskegee Architect L. H. Persley Dead," *New York Age*, July 23, 1932; interviews, adoptive daughter Gwendolyn Persley Henderson, 2001, 2005; See also Kara Michele Alston, "Louis Hudson Persley (1890–1932)," in Wilson, ed., *African American Architects*, 317–318.

42 The *Manufacturer's Record*, May 4, 1922 and October 4, 1928 and interview, Muriel Jackson, Macon Public Library, 2001.

43 The building is listed as "Taylor and Persley" in the 1931 exhibition at Howard University and a photo is in Taylor's files. For Selma University see Robert G. Sherer, *Subordination or Liberation: The Development and Conflicting Theories of Black Education in Nineteenth Century Alabama* (University: Alabama, 1977), 111–113.

44 Two-page typescript in Taylor's Tuskegee files. For the Colored Masonic Lodge see *Manufacturer's Record* April 28, 1924 and *Opportunity* 2, no. 23, November 1924. Both articles have photos showing the present eight stories. These and a photo in Taylor's file dispute recent interpretations that the building was erected in three stages, of four then two and two stories. See also Alice Meriwether Bowsher, *Community in Alabama, Architecture for Living Together,* Montgomery 2007, 26–27. The white Masonic temple is in *Views of Birmingham, Alabama* (New York,

1908).

45 For attribution and the brick and steel construction, see *Manufacturer's Record*, March 6, 1930. A photo is at *www.wilcoxareachamber.org*. See also 1994 National Register of Historic Places nomination by W. Edward Hooker III.

46 R. R. Moton to Edgar B. Stern, 3 December 1929, Julius Rosenwald Fund Collection, Amistad Research Center, Tulane University. Stern, a New Orleans businessman and philanthropist who built Dillard University, was Julius Rosenwald's son-in-law.

47 Cleveland W. Eneas, *Tuskegee Ra! Ra! An Autobiography of My Youth* (Nassau, 1986).

48 Booker Conley interview, 7 April 2006.

49 Ralph Ellison, *Invisible Man* (New York, 1952), 87.

50 Arnold Rampersad, *Ralph Ellison, A Biography* (New York, 2007), 228–229.

51 The story "Quicksand" is in Charles R. Larson ed., *An Intimation of Things Distant: The Collected Fiction of Nella Larsen* (New York, 1991).

52 Quoted in Wolters, *The New Negro on Campus*, 143.

53 Wolters, op.cit. 145.

54 Albert Murray, *South to a Very Old Place* (New York, 1971), 109, 124.

55 The *Manufacturer's Record*, May 4, 1922, reports that L. H. Persley, Architect, had designed the Chambliss Hotel "The Block" for $30,000–$40,000. William V. Chambliss, the Tuskegee graduate who built it, gave the building to the institute in 1928, when he died. Seven drawings are in the Tuskegee Facilities Department. The shops, reading left to right, were a store, a café operated initially by Margaret Murray Washington, a drug store, haberdashery, barbershop, and, around the corner, a photography studio and the entrance to the hotel above with its billiards table and facilities for ladies. For William V. Chambliss, see Catalog 25, the Chambliss Children's House.

56 Ellison, *Invisible Man*; Murray, *South to a Very Old Place*, 125, 121, 109.

57 *Tuskegee Messenger*, April 1933.

58 *Tuskegee Messenger*, March 1933.

59 Mrs. Gladys Baskervill, Taylor's grandniece, to author, 5 August 1986.

60 *Opportunity* 2, December 1924, 380–81.

61 *Opportunity* 2, November 1924, 350.

62 "Where Are Our Architects?" *Chicago Defender* February 14, 1931 (clipping, Taylor files, Tuskegee Archives).

63 "Exhibition of the work of Negro-Architects Presented by the Department of Architecture, Howard University," (three-page pamphlet, Moorland-Spingarn Research Cen-

ter, Howard University). The exhibition ran from May 12 to 28, 1931. Other exhibitors were Walter T. Bailey, John E. Brent, R. Lester Buffins, Albert I. Cassell, Curtis Elliott, John A. Lankford, Howard H. Mackey, McKissack and McKissack, Edward R. Williams, Paul R. Williams, David A. Williston, Howard students J. Alonzo Plater, Clarence B. Wheat, William F. Winder, and Illinois student Ralph A. Vaughn.

64 R. R. Taylor, "Shall the Negro Be Ousted from the Building Trades?" *Tuskegee Messenger*, February 23, 1929.

NOTES TO CHAPTER 9

1 For Liberia, see Edward H. Berman, "American Influences on African Education: the Role of the Phelps-Stokes Fund's Education Commissions," in *Comparative Education Review* l5:2 (1971) 132–145; Edward H. Berman, "Tuskegee-in-Africa," in *Journal of Negro Education* 41 (Spring 1972), 99–112; Manning Marable, "Ambiguous Legacy: Tuskegee's 'Missionary' Impulse and Africa During the Moton Administration, 1915–1935," in *Black Americans and the Missionary Movement in Africa*, ed. Sylvia M. Jacobs (Westport, 1982), 77–93; Donald Spivey, *The Politics of Miseducation: The Booker Washington Institute of Liberia, 1929–1984* (Lexington, Kentucky, 1986); Harlan, *The Wizard of Tuskegee*, 271–73; and Harlan, ed., *BTWP* 10, 104–5, 190 and *BTWP* 11, 297.

2 Olivia Phelps Stokes to Washington, 19 August 1909 and 9 March 1910, reel 80.

3 *Tuskegee Student* June 17, 1911.

4 Washington to Olivia Stokes, 25 November 1910, and Olivia Stokes to Washington, 7 February 1911, reel 80.

5 I.B. Scott to Washington, 2 August 1912, *BTWP* 11, 297. Scott was the Methodist Bishop for Africa.

6 Spivey, *The Politics of Miseducation*, 21–27.

7 James C. Young, "Liberia and its Future," *Opportunity* 6, 11 (November 1928), 327–331.

8 *Ibid.*, 328.

9 James Longstreet Sibley (1883–1929) and his work in Alabama and Africa are most fully portrayed in Charles William Dabney, *Universal Education in the South*, 2 (Chapel Hill: 1936), 521–526, and Samuel L. Smith, *Builders of Goodwill, the Story of the State Agents of Negro Education in the South, 1910–1950* (Nashville, 1950), 15–16.

10 James L. Sibley and D. Westermann, *Liberia, Old and New, a Study of its Social and Economic Background with Possibilities of Development* (Garden City, NY, 1928). For Westermann, see "Liberia's Distinguished Visitors," *The Liberia Educational Outlook*, May 1929. Sibley was the

journal's managing editor.

11 The primer and three readers published by Ginn & Co. were described in a clipping attached to a letter from Anson Phelps Stokes, Jr., to Taylor, 21 March 1929. The clipping (Lester A. Walton, "Liberia to Have a Tuskegee of its Own," *The World*, Sunday, March 17, 1929) is in the Phelps-Stokes Fund Records, box 3, folder 10, Schomberg Center for Research in Black Culture, New York Public Library.

12 Graham Greene, *Journey Without Maps* (London, 1950), 275, 286.

13 *Ibid.*, 286–287.

14 Charles S. Johnson, *Bitter Canaan: The Story of the Negro Republic* (New Brunswisk, NJ, 1987), 152–53.

15 For photographs of Liberian houses and similar southern American ones see Max Belcher, Svend E. Holsoe, and Bernard L. Herman, *A Land And A Life Remembered: Americo-Liberian Folk Architecture* (Athens, GA, 1988).

16 John Stanfield describes Buell-report politics in the introduction to Johnson, *Bitter Canaan*. See also Elizabeth L. Normandy, "African-Americans and U.S. Policy Towards Liberia, 1929–1935," *Liberian Studies Journal* 18, no. 2 (1993), 203–230; J. Gus Liebenow, *Liberia, The Evolution of Privilege* (Ithaca, 1969), 66–69; and the 1931 novel by George S. Schuyler, *Slaves Today, A Story of Liberia* (College Park, Maryland, 1969).

17 William R. Castle, Assistant Secretary of State, to Taylor, 6 December 1929, Taylor files, Tuskegee Archives.

18 Liebenow, *Liberia*, 68.

19 Arthur J. Knoll, "Firestone's Labor Policy, 1924–1939," in *Liberian Studies Journal* 16, 2 (1991), 67.

20 Quoted in Marable, "Ambiguous Legacy," 88.

21 Thomas Jesse Jones to Taylor, 21 March 1929, copy courtesy of Dreck S. Wilson; Anson Phelps Stokes to Taylor, 21 March 1929, box 3, folder 10, Phelps-Stokes Fund Records, Schomberg Center.

22 The honor was announced in the *Tuskegee Messenger*, June 29, 1929, while Taylor was still abroad.

23 Taylor's accounts are in the printed "Report of R.R. Taylor upon the Booker Washington Agricultural and Industrial Institute at Kakata, Republic of Liberia, October 1929"; the fifteen page typescript, "Liberia, Some Observations"; "The Outlook in Liberia," as described in the *Tuskegee Messenger*, October 12, 1929; and the clipping "New Day Dawns for Liberia with Opening of Agricultural and Industrial School, Says Dr. Taylor," in *New York Age*, 28 September, 1929. These, his expense account, photographs, and Nellie Taylor's handwritten memoir, are in his Tuskegee files.

24 *Tuskegee Messenger*, March 23, 1929.

25 *Tuskegee Messenger*, May 25, 1929.

26 The description comes from "Tuskegee Grounds Dedicated at Kakatown," *Liberia Educational Outlook* 2, no. 1, January 1929.

27 Sibley and Westermann, *Liberia*, 171–173.

28 Johnson, *Bitter Canaan*, 200.

29 Young, "Liberia and Its Future," 329.

30 A photo remains in Taylor's files.

31 A two-page typescript, "Extract from Dr. Falkner's article," is with 1912 Olivia Phelps Stokes material in reel 80.

32 Spivey misreads Taylor's report to say that Taylor named only rubber as a useful forest product. The error supports the position that the school's true aim was a Firestone-controlled mono-economy. Spivey, *The Politics of Miseducation*, 34–35.

33 In 1953, when John Gunther passed through, there were ten miles of paved roads in a country he described as the size of Tennessee or Ohio. John Gunther, *Inside Africa* (New York, 1953), 844.

34 Sibley to Jones, 25 May 1929, James L. Sibley Correspondence for January–June 1929, Phelps-Stokes Fund Archives, Schomburg Center for Research on Black Culture.

35 Bare to Taylor, 30 July 1934, Taylor files, Tuskegee Archives.

36 Berman, "Tuskegee-in-Africa," 109.

37 Taylor to Bare, 29 June 1934, Taylor files, Tuskegee Archives.

38 *Ibid.*

39 Johnson, *Bitter Canaan*, 200.

40 The "Block Plan of School," sheet number 1, is 24" x 35" including an inked border.

41 Thomas Jesse Jones to Taylor, 31 July 1929, Taylor files, Tuskegee Archives.

42 Berman, "Tuskegee-in-Africa" 108.

43 Robert R. Taylor, "The Outlook in Liberia," *Tuskegee Messenger*, October 12, 1929.

44 Taylor, "Liberia, Some Observations," 11.

45 Taylor, "The Outlook in Liberia."

NOTES TO CHAPTER 10

1 Taylor's Alabama license was number 43 according to Vinson E. McKenzie's unpublished manuscript.

2 "Fiftieth Anniversary Report, 1931," 15–18, Julius Rosenwald Fund Collection, Amistad Research Center, Tulane University.

3 Moton to Taylor, 9 and 19 July and 12 October 1932; Taylor

to Moton, 13 August 1932; Schieffelin to Taylor, 5 August 1932; Mason to Taylor, 5 August 1932; Peabody to Taylor, 2 August 1934. Taylor files, Tuskegee Archives.

4 Typescript, 28 October 1932, Taylor files, Tuskegee Archives.

5 Moton to Taylor, 4 and 11 January, 1933.

6 Taylor to W. J. Shieffelin, 18 May 1939, Taylor files, Tuskegee Archives. The lot was on South Seventh Street. Clippings January 24 and 25, 1905, Bill Reaves Collection, New Hanover County Public Library.

7 Helen Dibble Cannaday interview, December 1993.

8 Taylor to Bare, 29 June and 24 November 1934, Taylor files, Tuskegee Archives.

9 Taylor to Moton, 6 May 1918, box 13, Moton Local Correspondence, Tuskegee Archives.

10 MacRae and Alvin S. Johnson correspondence 1935, Taylor to George Foster Peabody, 14 July 1934 and 17 August 1935, Taylor files, Tuskegee Archives. See also John P. Murchison, "Subsistence Homesteads Experiment and the Negro," *Opportunity*, 12, 8 (August 1934) 244. For MacRae, see William S. Powell, ed., *Dictionary of North Carolina Biography*, 4 (Chapel Hill, 1979–1996), 191–192 and R. H. Fisher, *Biographical Sketches of Wilmington Citizens* (Wilmington, 1929), 65–66.

11 The *Cape Fear Journal*, March 21, 1936, reprinted the article from the March 12, 1936 *Wilmington Star*. Clipping, Taylor files, Tuskegee Archives. A similar letter, 21 August 1935, is in the Bill Reaves Collection, New Hanover County Public Library and in William M. Reaves, *"Strength Through Struggle," The Chronological and Historical Record of the African-American Community in Wilmington, North Carolina, 1865–1950* (Wilmington, NC, 1998), 318–321.

12 Raymond Gavins, "Fear, Hope and Struggle," in David S. Cecelski and Timothy B. Tyson, eds. *Democracy Betrayed: The Wilmington Race Riot of 1898 and Its Legacy* (Chapel Hill, 1998), 194–195. For the Colored Chamber of Commerce see Reaves, 318–319.

13 Gavins, "Fear, Hope and Struggle," 196.

14 Reaves, *"Strength Through Struggle,"* 203.

15 Taylor to Arthur S. Fleming, 21 October 1941, Taylor files, Tuskegee Archives.

16 Certificate, Taylor files, Tuskegee Archives. The "only Negro" on a state board is in a radio biography of 3 April 1946. "National Negro Health Week Radio Program," typescript, Taylor files, Tuskegee Archives.

17 The New Brooklyn Homes project was announced in 1938 and dedicated in 1940. Reaves, *"Strength Through Struggle,"* 205–207. Other Boney buildings for the black community are in Reaves 100, 116, and 159. In 1953 Robert Rochon

Taylor presented a picture in his father's memory. (Memorial program, "Dr. Robert R. Taylor, 1869–1942," 17 March 1953) Taylor files, Tuskegee Archives.

18 *Wilmington Morning Star,* April 1, 1937, February 29 and October 7, 1940.

19 *Cape Fear Journal,* March 28, 1936; November 13, 1937; October 31, 1936. Clippings, Taylor files, Tuskegee Archives.

20 *Cape Fear Journal,* October 31, 1936. Clipping, Taylor files, Tuskegee Archives.

21 Louis R. Harlan, *Booker T. Washington, The Wizard of Tuskegee, 1901–1915* (New York, 1983), 233–236.

22 Reaves, "Strength Through Struggle," 224–226.

23 Taylor to the Board of the Southern Conference for Human Welfare, 20 March 1940; Taylor to Helen Dibble, 1 November 1940, Taylor files, Tuskegee Archives.

24 Taylor to Robbie, Helen, Ed, Bea and Henry, 26 June 1937, Taylor files, Tuskegee Archives.

25 Robert Rochon Taylor to Taylor, 6 July 1937, Taylor files, Tuskegee Archives.

26 Taylor to Henry Taylor, 3 February 1940, Taylor files, Tuskegee Archives.

27 Nellie C. Taylor to Dr. Karl Compton, 21 December 1942, Taylor files, MIT.

28 Louis T. Moore in *Cape Fear Journal,* December 19, 1942. Taylor files, Tuskegee Archives.

29 Dorothy Taylor interviews 1 November and 5 December 1993. Dorothy Taylor to Dreck S. Wilson, c. 1980. Dorothy Taylor told Wilson that her father-in-law was six feet, three inches tall and weighed 190 pounds. Louise King Sindos described "mesmerizing, hypnotic" blue eyes (Interview, 4 May 2011). Ann Dibble Jordan noted green-blue eyes, physical impressiveness, and the "shocking patch of white hair on the side of his head." (Ann Dibble Cook to Dreck S. Wilson, n,d., Wilson files, Washington, D.C.).

30 Interview, Edward Taylor, 17 May 1989.

31 Interview, Harold Webb, 21 August 1986.

32 Interview, Ann Dibble Jordan, 8 August 2003.

NOTES TO CATALOG

1 Louis R. Harlan, ed., *Booker T. Washington Papers* [hereafter *BTWP]* 3, 372, 521; John H. Washington 1896-1897 report, reel 206. Max Bennett Thrasher *Tuskegee, Its Story and its Work* (Boston, 1900), 41, 49.

2 Louis R. Harlan, *Booker T. Washington, the Making of a Black Leader* (New York, 1972), 246; Washington to Taylor, 2 November 1904, box 530. See also *Southern Letter* June

1894. Later plans as a dormitory are in L. Albert Scipio, *Pre-War Days at Tuskegee* (Silver Spring, Maryland, 1987), 160.

3   Richard K. Dozier, "Tuskegee: Booker T. Washington's Contribution to the Education of Black Architects" (D. Arch. diss., Univ. Michigan: 1990) 110.

4   Washington to Olivia Stokes, 31 May 1895, quoted in Dozier, "Tuskegee," 112.

5   Olivia Stokes to Washington, 27 August, 1895, reel 79.

6   *Ibid.*; Taylor to Washington, 7 November 1895, reel 120.

7   Olivia Stokes to Washington, 9 May, 6 June, and 29 October, 1896, reel 79.

8   Washington to Harvard University President Eliot, 20 October 1906, in Harlan, ed., *BTWP* 9, 96-98.

9   Olivia Stokes to Washington, 11 February 1896, reel 79.

10   *Southern Letter* , April 1896.

11   Thomas J. Calloway, "Booker T. Washington and the Tuskegee Institute," *New England Magazine* (October 1897), 137.

12   T. Thomas Fortune, "A Cathedral in the Black Belt," *New York Sun*, April 3, 1898.

13   H. E. Thomas to Taylor, undated letter [c. 1913-14], box 529.

14   Sources are *Southern Letter* June 1896 and April 1898; John W. Whittaker, "The Institute Chapel," *Tuskegee Messenger* (October 1929); M.B.T., "Tuskegee Institute and Its President," *Appleton's Popular Science Monthly* LV (September 1899), 602; and Booker T. Washington, *The Story of My Life and Work* (Toronto, 1901), 421. See also Dozier, "Tuskegee" 42, 45, 110-113; Scipio (*Pre-War Days*, 105-106) publishes architectural drawings that were traced from the originals in 1923.

15   Fortune, "A Cathedral in the Black Belt."

16   Cleveland W. Eneas, *Tuskegee, Ra! Ra! An Autobiography of My Youth* (Nassau, 1986), 39–41.

17   Ralph Ellison, *Invisible Man* (New York, 1952), 85-88.

18   Johanna Hays generously shared her research, and Booker Conley remembered the night.

19   Taylor to Washington, 4 May 1900, reel 169. See also Taylor to Washington, 3 May 1899, 4 May 1900, and 20 January 1903, reels 154, 169, 228.

20   John Whitfield of the National Park Service is writing a history of the house. See also Manning Marable, "Tuskegee National Historic Site: The Oaks," National Park Service report, 1980; 12 measured drawings in the Historic American Buildings Survey, Library of Congress; Dozier "Tuskegee," 123-125; Harlan, *The Making of a Black Leader*, 302; and Scipio, *Pre-War Days*, 98-99. For the grounds see

Cari Groetcheus, "Booker T. Washington, the Man and His Landscape," *Cultural Resources Management (CRM)* 8 (1999) 31-33.

21   For the Boys' Trades Building see Washington, *The Story of My Life and Work*, 409-411; Booker T. Washington, *Working with the Hands* (New York, 1904), 56-57; Booker T. Washington, ed., *Tuskegee and Its People* (New York, 1905), 46-7; Site selection is in Olivia Stokes to Washington, 26 July 1897, reel 79 and Taylor to Washington, 31 December 1898, reel 144. See also *Tuskegee Student*, January 13 and July 13, 1899 plus January 19, 1901 for the perspective drawing signed by Taylor. Plans are in the Sanborn Map Co. insurance map for 1903.

22   For the fire, see *Southern Letter*, October 1918. For the new trades buildings see *Manufacturer's Record*, February 6, 1919 and *Tuskegee Messenger* May 9, 1921.

23   Sources for Huntington Hall are Booker Conley, "Historic Buildings, Tuskegee Institute, a Report of Conditions, 1980, 31, typescript, Tuskegee Archives; Dozier, "Tuskegee" 140; Scipio, *Pre-War Days*, 149; Harlan, ed. *BTWP* 2, 388, and 4, 553-554; *Tuskegee Student* November 23, 1899, November 19, 1900, and July 2, 1904; *Southern Letter* March 1900 and January 1901; Huntington to Washington, 14 November 1898, 5 and 19 December 1898, and 6 January 1899, box 144; Taylor to Scott, 12 April 1901, reel 187; Washington, *The Story of My Life and Work*, 376; and Washington, *Working with the Hands*, 79-80. Pittman's undated typed description is filed under October 1900 in reel 3. For the Orton Hotel veranda, built when Taylor left for Boston, see Beverly Tetterton, *Wilmington: Lost But Not Forgotten* (Wilmington, NC, 2005), 117.

24   The birds-eye is reproduced in color in Scipio, *Pre-War Days*, 55. See also *Tuskegee Student*, 19 October, 1899.

25   Booker T. Washington to John H. Washington, 12 May 1899, quoted in Harlan, *BTWP* 5, 114.

26   Taylor and Washington, 9 and 30 September 1899, reel 155.

27   Undated, unsigned partial letter filed under Caroline Phelps Stokes, reel 79. The sisters dictated their letters to the same secretary, leaving unsigned fragments without attribution.

28   Caroline Phelps Stokes to Washington, 16 October n.d., reel 79.

29   Parsons to Washington, 29 June 1910, box 131, Seth Low Collection, Columbia University.

30   Booker T.Washington, "The Successful Training of the Negro," *World's Work*, VI, 4 (August 1903), 3750.

31   Taylor to Washington, 26 September 1899, reel 155.

32 Caroline Phelps Stokes to Washington, 29 October 1900, reel 79.

33 *General Catalogue of Dartmouth College for 1910-1911,* folio section.

34 Taylor to Washington, 30 October 1899, reel 155.

35 Caroline Phelps Stokes to Washington, 16 October 1899, reel 79.

36 For Isaac Newton Phelps Stokes, his aunts, and philanthropic housing see Deborah S. Gardner, "Practical Philanthropy: the Phelps-Stokes Fund and Housing," in *Prospects* 15, 1990, 359-411.

37 Caroline Phelps Stokes to Washington, 23 January, 1900, reel 79; Taylor to Washington, 16 February 1900, reel 168. Taylor to Washington, 27 October 1900, reel 169.

38 *Tuskegee Student,* April 27, 1901.

39 Paul Laurence Dunbar, "On the Dedication of Dorothy Hall," *The Complete Poems of Paul Laurence Dunbar* (New York, 1918), 214.

40 Washington, *Working with the Hands* 99-100.

41 Caroline Phelps Stokes to Washington, 8 May 1901, reel 79.

42 Washington to Caroline Phelps Stokes, 24 January 1907, reel 79.

43 Washington to the Misses Stokes 20 January 1908, reel 80; Olivia to Washington, 23 September 1908, reel 79; Washington to Taylor, 24 March 1908, box 506.

44 Jennie D. Moton, "Dorothy Hall," *Tuskegee Messenger,* October 1929.

45 The colored lithograph is in Scipio, *Pre-War Days*, 55. The Henderson Lithography Co., Cincinnati, published it. The *Tuskegee Student* for October 19, 1899 mentioned it.

46 Olivia Stokes to Washington, 27 January n.d., reel 79.

47 Thrasher, *Tuskegee,* 189; for the library see also Booker T. Washington, *Up From Slavery* (New York 1901), 191; Louis R. Harlan, *The Wizard of Tuskegee, 1901-1925* (New York 1983), 134, 139; Harlan, ed. *BTWP* 6, 158; Dozier, "Tuskegee" 181-185; Scipio, *Pre-War Days* 98-99; Booker Conley, "Historic Buildings, Tuskegee Institute, a Report of Conditions," 1980, Tuskegee Archives; *Tuskegee Student,* January 26, March 23, April 20, July 27, and September 7, 1901, and January 11, March 15, April 12, May 3, 1902; *Southern Letter,* December 1901; and correspondence among Washington, Carnegie, and his secretary James Bertram, for 15 and 20 December 1900, reel 34.

48 Kenrick Ian Grandison argues that the library and Science/Thrasher face the campus interior to protect themselves from hostile whites on the public road. See Grandison, "Negotiated Space: the Black College Campus as a Cultural Record of Postbellum America," *American Quarterly* 51, 3, September 1999, 529-579. A counter-argument is in Ellen Weiss "Tuskegee, Landscape in Black and White," *Winterthur Portfolio* 36 (Spring 2001), 19-37. Further evidence for my view is in the Emery dormitories' siting, Catalog 4. They were not sited to keep out intruders but because of the donor's concerns about fire.

49 *Tuskegee Student,* March 23, 1901.

50 Olivia Phelps Stokes to Washington, 15 April 1901, reel 79.

51 *Tuskegee Student,* May 3, 1902.

52 For the town library see Washington to E. P. George, 16 January 1904, reel 561. For others see Dozier, "Tuskegee," 181-187.

53 Pittman to Washington, 16 March 1901, reel 3; Washington published it in *The Story of My Life and Work,* opp. 362, and in *Southern Letter,* December 1901.

54 *Tuskegee Student* May 14, 1904.

55 *National Negro School News* 3,1 (January 1912).

56 Theodore Wesley Koch, *A Portfolio of Carnegie Libraries* (Ann Arbor, 1907), and Andrew Carnegie, "Fifty Million Dollars: The Library Gift Business," *Collier's* (5 June 1909), 14-15.

57 Caroline Phelps Stokes to Washington, 8 May, 5 September, and 1 October 1901, reel 79.

58 Caroline Stokes to Washington, 18 November (n.d., c.1901) reel 79.

59 Taylor to Washington 28 November, 1901, reel 188.

60 Taylor to Washington, 18 December 1901, reel 188.

61 Taylor to Washington, 10 April 22 and July 1902, reel 207, and 1 June 1903, reel 229.

62 John H. Washington to Taylor, 10 July 1902, reel 207; Taylor to Washington, 28 February 1903, reel 228 and 1 June 1903, reel 229.

63 Washington to F.T. Gates, and Gates to Rockefeller Jr., 12 March 1901, Rockefeller Family Archives Record group 2, box 38, folder 259, Rockefeller Archives Center, Tarrytown, N.Y. Rockefeller correspondence is also in reel 68 of the Washington papers. The *Tuskegee Student* reported construction from June 15, 1901 (announcement of the gift), September 7 (foundations excavated), and December 7 (walls going up) in reels 188, 207, and 228.

64 Washington to Rockefeller, Jr., 27 April 1901, reel 68.

65 Rockefeller, Jr. to Washington, 21 December 1901, Harlan, ed. *BTWP* 6, page 357.

66 Gates to Washington, 7 June 1901, Rockefeller Archive Center.

67 Taylor to E.J. Scott, 17 June 1901, reel 188.

68 Taylor to Washington, 19 May 1903, reel 229.

69 Washington to William Henry Baldwin, 23 April 1904; Harlan, ed., *BTWP* 7, 488.

70 John D. Rockefeller, Jr. to Washington, 24 August 1908, reel 6.

71 Booker T. Washington, *Character Building* (New York, 1902).

72 *Tuskegee Student*, June 15, 1901.

73 Taylor to Washington, August 1902 (date illegible), reel 207.

74 J. L. Whiting, *Shop and Class at Tuskegee* (Boston, 1940), 10.

75 Charles Wesley Archbold to Henry Huddleston Rogers, (n.d.) April 1908, in Harlan, ed., *BTWP* 9, 491-492.

76 Booker T. Washington, *My Larger Education* (New York, 1911), 73.

77 John H. Washington to Taylor, 10 July and 12 September 1902, reel 207.

78 Taylor to Scott, (fall) 1904, reel 251.

79 See Warren Logan, "Resources and Material Equipment," in Washington, ed., *Tuskegee and its People*, 50; *Tuskegee Student* November 9, 1901, February 15, 1902, and July 2, 1904; See also Dozier 139-140 and Scipio 100-101.

80 *Tuskegee Student* November 3, 1906; Scott and Stowe, *Booker T. Washington*, 241. Logan, "Resources and Material Equipment" in Washington, ed., *Tuskegee and Its People*, 51; *Tuskegee Student* October 1, 1904.

81 Taylor to Washington 10 April 1902, reel 207; Taylor paper, December 1901, reel 188.

82 Arabella Huntington to Washington, 14 March 1902, reel 557; Taylor to Washington 10 April, 8 June, 14 and 22 July, 3 September 1902, reel 207; 8 October 1902, box 521. *Tuskegee Student*, December 12, 1902; Library of Congress Prints and Photographs J 694-470.

83 John H. Washington to Taylor, box 523; Booker T. Washington to Scott, 26 December 1903, box 5.

84 Taylor to Washington, 17 February 1904, box 529, and 20 July and 8 August 1904, box 530; *Tuskegee Student* June 4, 1904; Washington to Archer Huntington, 18 and 26 July 1904; secretary to Washington, 26 July 1904, reel 561; Washington, *Working with the Hands*, 82.

85 Bettina Berch, *The Woman Behind the Lens, the Life and Work of Frances Benjamin Johnston, 1864-1952* (Charlottesville, 2000).

86 *Tuskegee Catalogue 1896-1897*; Washington, ed., *Tuskegee and Its People*, 51; See also *Tuskegee Student* December 12, 1902; Emmett J. Scott, "Present Achievements," in Washington, ed. *Tuskegee and Its People*, 24-25.

87 *Tuskegee Student*, July 5, 1902. John H. Washington to Taylor, 30 September 1903, reel 229.

88 *Tuskegee Student* December 12, 1902; Harlan, ed. *BTWP* 3, 230-231; Taylor to Executive Council, 9 December 1904, box 530; Conley 33; Dozier, "Tuskegee" 140; Scipio, *Pre-War Days* 149, 156.

89 John S. Fisher, *A Builder of the West: the Life of General William Jackson Palmer* (Caldwell, Idaho, 1939), 76, 306-307.

90 Caroline Phelps Stokes to Washington, 8 May 1901, 14 March, 15 and 30 May 1902, reel 79.

91 Caroline Phelps Stokes to Washington, 14 March and 15 and 30 May 1902, reel 79.

92 *Tuskegee Student*, May 21, 1904.

93 Taylor to Washington, 23 December 02, reel 207; Taylor to Scott, 22 and 23 January 1903, reel 228; Scipio, *Pre-War Days*, 69.

94 Harlan, *The Wizard of Tuskegee*, 130-131; Thomas Emery to Washington, 28 May 1903, reel 559; Washington to Taylor, 2 November 1904, box 530.

95 Washington to Taylor, 12 November and 11 December 1903 box 5, Washington Collection, Tuskegee Archives; Thomas Emery to Washington, 2 January 1904, reel 559; Taylor to Washington, 16 January 1904, box 529; Washington to Thomas Emery, 19 January 1904, reel 559; *Tuskegee Student* December 26, 1903 and July 2, 1904; Washington to E. J. Emery, 19 January 1904, reel 561.

96 Washington to Taylor, 30 May 1904, box 530; *Tuskegee Student* June 4, 1904; Taylor draft, 28 January 1904, box 530; Taylor's report, April 1906, box 569; Taylor to Washington, 27 April 1907, box 559.

97 Taylor to Washington, July 11 1905, box 538.

98 Two-page typescript, July 11, 1905, "Description of Tantum Memorial Hall," reel 568.

99 Ibid.

100 Trentoniana Collection, Trenton Public Library; Margaret W. Tantum and Washington, reels 262 and 577.

101 Taylor to Washington, 11 Sept 1903, reel 229; 7 July 1905, box 538; "turkey yard" is in *Tuskegee Student*, September 16, 1911; Margaret W. Tantum to Washington, 7 July 1905, reel 262.

102 Taylor to Washington, 11 July 1905, box 538.

103 Taylor to Washington, 7 and 11 July 1905, box 538; Taylor to Scott 16 March 1906, quoted by Dozier, "Tuskegee," 150.

104 *Tuskegee Student* April 14, 1906.

105 *Tuskegee Student*, April 20, 1907; Conley, 1980.

106 Taylor to Frank E. Perkins, 30 October 1905, box 5,

Washington Collection, Tuskegee Archives; Taylor to Lloyd G. Wheeler, 21 February 1906, box 19, Washington Collection, Tuskegee Archives.

107 For the Macon County court house see Richard K. Dozier and Major Holland, "Guide to Tuskegee's Historic Resources" (Tuskegee, 1983); for James W. Golucke (1857-1907) see *Dictionary of Georgia Biography*, I, 1983.

108 Jesup MacKennan, Executor, to Washington, 4 May 1903, reel 229; *Tuskegee Student* February 26, 1910; *Tuskegee Catalogue 1909-1910*; Cornelia C. Tompkins to Washington 18 April 1893, reel 113. Barbara Hall traced Cornelia Tompkins to the Wakefield shipping fortune.

109 Taylor to Washington, 10 June 1903, reel 229 and 1 August 1904, box 530. Washington, *The Story of My Life and Work*, 372-373; Scott to Taylor, 8 December, 1904; Washington to Taylor, 15 and 16 December 1904, box 530.

110 *Tuskegee Student*, February 11, 1905; Taylor to Washington, 14 March 1905, box 538.

111 Washington to Taylor, 23 November 1904, box 530 and 14 March 1905, box 538; Booker Conley interviews 12 December 2005 and 7 April 2006; Edward Taylor interview, 17 May 1989; Harold Webb interview, 1988. For a fascinating social analysis see Carla Willard, "Timing Impossible Subjects: the Marketing Style of Booker T. Washington," *American Quarterly* 53, 4 (December 2001), 624-669.

112 Taylor to Washington in New York City, 21 April 1909, box 576.

113 Taylor and Washington, 14 March and 7 July 1905, box 538; 10 November 1906, box 547; 5 May, 5 June, and 9 July 1908, box 566; Washington to Margaret W. Thacher, 18 April 1905, reel 568 and 5 August 1908, box 567; *Tuskegee Student*, June 30, April 14, 1906, March 30, 1907, January 14, 1908, and January 29, 1910; Roebling Construction Company to Lloyd G. Wheeler, 8 March 1906, Tuskegee Archives; *Southern Letter*, June 1908.

114 William Barclay Parsons to Seth Low, 5 August 1908, reel 54.

115 Taylor to Washington, 29 September 1909, box 577.

116 Taylor to Washington, 21 April 1909, box 576 and 22 July, 29 September, 26 October, and 26 December, 1909, box 577; *Tuskegee Student*, January 8, 1910.

117 Department of Architectural and Mechanical Drawing plan, 1937, Physical Facilities Department, Tuskegee.

118 *Tuskegee Student* February 12 and 26 and July 30, 1910.

119 Washington to Taylor, 22 February 1911, box 538 and 28 March 1912, box 617.

120 Washington to Taylor, May 1908, and Taylor to Washington, 6 August 1908, box 566.

121 Mary White Ovington, *The Walls Came Tumbling Down* (New York, 1997), 54. Henry S. Enck, "Tuskegee Institute and Northern White Philanthropy: a Case Study in Fund Raising, 1900-1915," *Journal of Negro History*, 65, 1980, 343; Booker Conley and Clarice Dibble Walker interviews, October 2006 and October 2007.

122 Taylor report, 12 May 1906, box 548.

123 Washington Memo, 21 September, 1906, box 548; Taylor to Lloyd G. Wheeler, 23 August 1906, box 28, Washington Collection, Tuskegee Archives.

124 William F. Black to Washington, 18 July 1906 and Taylor to Scott, 21 July 1906, box 26, Washington Collection, Tuskegee Archives.

125 Alabama Agricultural Association to Washington, 27 July 1906, box 26, Washington Collection, Tuskegee Archives.

126 Mary Ann Neely, "Alabama State Fair Negro Building" in Dreck Spurlock Wilson, ed., *African American Architects, a Biographical Dictionary, 1865-1945* (New York, 2004), 5-6. Lloyd G. Wheeler to Taylor, 1 August 1906 and Taylor to Wheeler, 23 August 1906, boxes 27 and 28, Washington Collection, Tuskegee; *Tuskegee Student*, October 6 and 20, 1906.

127 Washington to A.T. White, 1903, reel 88; *Southern Letter* February-March 1921; Washington to White, 22 December, 1906, reel 573; *Tuskegee Student* June 8, 1907.

128 White to Washington, 10 June 1907, reel 88; Washington to Low, 10 July 1907, reel 54; Washington to Taylor, 11 July 1907, box 559.

129 Low to Washington 3 August 1907, reel 54.

130 Taylor to Logan, 21 August 1907, box 559.

131 Washington and White correspondence 17 March through 12 May, 1908, reel 88; and 21 May 1908, reel 573.

132 *Tuskegee Student* February 12, 1910 and March 24, 1911; White to Washington, 26 February 1911, reel 88.

133 Both drawings are in the Physical Facilities Department.

134 Taylor to Washington, 1 May and 19 August 1911, box 602; Washington and White, 23 May and 14 July 1911, reel 88.

135 Taylor to Washington, 24 January 1912, box 617.

136 17 February 1913, box 632; Washington to A.T. White, April 1913, reel 88.

137 *Tuskegee Student*, December 1920-January 1921; Edward H. Beardsley, *A History of Neglect, Health Care for Blacks and Mill Workers in the Twentieth-Century South* (Knoxville, 1987), 37; Montague Cobb, *Journal of the National*

Medical Association (Colored), 54 (1947), 204; Herbert M. Morais, *The History of the Negro in Medicine* (New York, 1968), 82.

138 Peter A. Coclanis, "What Made Booker Wash(ington)?, The Wizard of Tuskegee in Economic Context," in W. Fitzhugh Brundage, ed., *Booker T. Washington and Black Progress: Up From Slavery a Hundred Years Later"* (Gainesville, FL 2003), 81-101.

139 Dozier, "Tuskegee" 156; Harlan, *The Making of a Black Leader,* 185.

140 Harlan, *The Wizard of Tuskegee,* 233-236; Booker T. Washington, article in *American Journal of Nursing* (November 1910); Dozier Tuskegee 157, 167.

141 Scott and Stowe, 1916, 159; *Tuskegee Student* January 18, 1902 and September 16, 1911; Scipio, *Pre-war Days,* 53; Kenney to Washington, 27 November 1903, *BTWP* 7, 353-355; W. Montague Cobb, "John Andrew Kenney, M.D., 1874-1950," *Journal of the National Medical Association* 42 (May 1950), 175-177; Thomas J. Ward, Jr., *Black Physicians in the Jim Crow South* (Fayetteville, Arkansas: 2003), 249-251.

142 *Tuskegee Student,* January 26 and December 7, 1901, January 18, 1902, and September 16, 1911; Eliot and Washington, 7 September and 20 October, 1906, *BTWP* 10, 71-72 and 96-98.

143 *BTWP* 10, 338-339.

144 Taylor to Kenney, 2 June 1911, box 602; Taylor to Washington, 14 August 1911, box 602. Correspondence among Booker T. Washington, John H. Washington, Kenney, and Taylor is in boxes 602 and 618.

145 Taylor, John H. Washington, and Booker T. Washington correspondence, 14 August 1911, box 602; 6 July, 10 and 14 August 1912, box 618.

146 *Tuskegee Student,* March 13, 1913.

147 Russell F. Whitehead, "The Old and the New South," *Architectural Record* 30, July 1911, 84.

148 Low and Washington, 25 November, 4, 15, 17 and 29 December 1913; 5 and 13 January 1914, reel 55.

149 Susan J. Montgomery and Roger G. Reed, *Phillips Academy, Andover: An Architectural Tour* (New York, 2000), 108.

150 Washington and Taylor, 14 and 24 January, 22 September, 2 and 15 October, and 15 December, 1914, box 649.

151 Photo, Library of Congress USZ62-132953. The Library also holds the Historic American Buildings Survey drawings of 1978-1979.

152 Helen Ludlow, ed., *Tuskegee Normal and Industrial School . . . Its Story and Its Songs* (Hampton, VA, 1884), 12-13;

Southern Letter December 1889 and *Tuskegee Student,* December 1889.

153 Washington, *The Story of My Life and Work,* 408-409.

154 *BTWP* 4, 83-84.

155 Washington to John H. Washington, 27 March 1900, box 4, Washington Collection, Tuskegee Archives; Thrasher, *Tuskegee,* 49-50.

156 Taylor and Washington, 23 March 1902 [filed 1901] reel 187, and 20 July and 23 September 1904, box 530; Warren Logan, "Resources and Material Equipment," in Washington, ed. *Tuskegee and Its People,* 48.

157 Washington to Taylor, 2 November 1903, reel 229.

158 Harlan, ed., *BTWP* 4, 143, 162.

159 R. C. Bedford report in the *Montgomery Advertiser* as reprinted in the *Southern Letter,* January 1898.

160 For Carver and a close examination of Tuskegee's institutional workings, see Linda O. McMurry, *George Washington Carver, Scientist and Symbol* (New York: 1981); see also Dozier, "Tuskegee," 113-116.

161 Washington, *Working with the Hands,* 118.

162 "Problems in Education," *Cosmopolitan,* September 1902.

163 *The Southern Workman* 50, l0 (October 1921) 457-468.

164 First greenhouse: *Tuskegee Student* January 28, 1905 and 1909 Sanborn Co. insurance map. Second greenhouse: Scipio, *Pre-War Days,* 145; Low to Washington, 18 February 1908, reel 54; Taylor to Williston, 6 and 8 August 1908, box 567; Committee on Buildings and Grounds report June 1909, box 131, Seth Low Papers, Columbia University; 1920 Sanborn Co. insurance map.

165 *Proceedings of the Trustees of the John F. Slater Fund for the Education of Freedmen* (Baltimore 1907), 18.

166 "Report of Committee on Buildings and Grounds to the Trustees," 26 June 1909, box 131, Seth Low Papers, Columbia University.

167 Taylor to Lloyd G. Wheeler, 11 March 1909, box 576.

168 Joseph F. Citro, *Booker T. Washington's Tuskegee Institute: Black School-Community,* 1900-1915 (D. Ed. diss. University of Rochester, 1972), 487; *Southern Letter ,* September 1918).

169 Washington to Elizabeth Anderson, 4 November 1909, and other undated missives, reel 582; Washington, in New York, to Taylor, 6 May 1909, box 576.

170 Report, 26 June 1909, box 131, Seth Low Papers, Columbia University. Taylor to Washington, 26 October 1909, box 577; Elisabeth M. Anderson to Washington, 31 October, n. d.; and Washington, "Memo for Mrs. Anderson," n.d., reel 582.

171 Washington, "Annual Report, 1907-1908."

172 Citro, op. cit. 138.

173 Taylor, Williston, and Bridgeforth as committee reporting on Taylor letterhead to Washington, 20 May 1911, box 69, Seth Low Collection, Columbia University; Taylor to Washington, 2 May 1911, box 602; Bailey's barn preliminaries: Taylor to Washington, 2 May 1911, box 602.

174 Washington to Taylor, 12 Oct 1912, box 618. Brill, Low, Madison Cooper, Bridgeforth, Taylor, John H. and Booker T. Washington correspondence, spring 1911, box 133, Low Papers, Columbia University. *Tuskegee Student* July 4, 1914.

175 "Report of the Committee on Buildings and Grounds, June 26, 1909, to Trustees, New York City," Low Collection, Columbia University, box 131.

176 Washington to Taylor, 4 December 1913 and 31 December 1915, box 633; Low to Washington, 25 November 1913, reel 55.

177 Washington and Low, 13 and 19 October 1914 reel 56; Taylor and Washington, 19 and 28 October and 1 December 1914, box 649; 2 March and 10 November 1915, box 663.

178 In Washington, *The Story of My Life and Work*, opp. 13.

179 Low to William M. Scott, 26 November 1915, box 64, Low Papers, Columbia University; Cynthia Beavers Wilson, "Chronicling Tuskegee in Photographs: a Simple Version," in Richard J. Powell and Jock Reynolds, *American Art from Historically Black Colleges and Universities* (Cambridge: 1999), 164-165; *Tuskegee Student* May 9, 1921.

180 *Southern Letter*, May 1921; *Tuskegee Student* May 9, 1921; *New York Times*, October 1, 1916 and June 5, 1923.

181 *Tuskegee Messenger*, January 17 and August 15, 1925.

182 Harlan, *Making of a Black Leader*, 125-126; Washington *The Story of My Life and Work*, 102.

183 The valley school is undocumented because the 1890s are illegible in the microfilm edition of the *Tuskegee Student*.

184 "Delays in work," 24 June 1901, reel 188.

185 Warren Logan, "Resources and Material Equipment," in Washington ed., *Tuskegee and Its People*, 49; *Tuskegee Student* November 1901; Stokes to Washington 29 October 1900, reel 79.

186 M. R. Werner, *Julius Rosenwald: the Life of a Practical Humanitarian* (New York: Harper, 1939), 122.

187 Washington, *Working with the Hands*, 220.

188 For Chambliss and the Southern Improvement company see Harlan, ed. *BTWP* 2, 373 and 10, 606; *Tuskegee Student*, May 11, 1901; *Southern Letter*, June 28, 1928. See also Monroe Work, *Industrial Work of Tuskegee Graduates and Former Students During the Year 1910* (Tuskegee: 1911), 20-21.

189 *Tuskegee Messenger*, April 26, 1930; *Southern Letter* (July 1930).

190 *Manufacturer's Record*, March 6 and October 16, 1930.

191 Booker Conley remembered that the Jenkins Brick Company in Montgomery later made rustic bricks for Tuskegee purchase. (Interview, 13 December 2006).

192 *Tuskegee Messenger*, March 14-28, 1931.

193 *Tuskegee Messenger*, November 13, 1926.

194 Scipio, *Pre-War Days*, 137-138; *Manufacturer's Record*, December 17, 1931; *Tuskegee Messenger*, April 1933.

INDEX